The story of Burnt

From the Icela

Sir George Webbe Dasent

Alpha Editions

This edition published in 2024

ISBN : 9789362924988

Design and Setting By
Alpha Editions
www.alphaedis.com
Email - info@alphaedis.com

As per information held with us this book is in Public Domain.
This book is a reproduction of an important historical work. Alpha Editions uses the best technology to reproduce historical work in the same manner it was first published to preserve its original nature. Any marks or number seen are left intentionally to preserve its true form.

Contents

SIR GEORGE DASENT'S PREFACE ....- 1 -

SIR GEORGE DASENT'S INTRODUCTION. ....- 5 -

ICELANDIC CHRONOLOGY. ....- 20 -

CHAPTER I. ....- 26 -

    OF FIDDLE MORD. ....- 26 -

CHAPTER II. ....- 27 -

    HRUT WOOS UNNA. ....- 27 -

CHAPTER III. ....- 30 -

    HRUT AND GUNNHILLDA, KINGS MOTHER ....- 30 -

CHAPTER IV. ....- 33 -

    OF HRUT'S CRUISE. ....- 33 -

CHAPTER V. ....- 34 -

    ATLI ARNVID SON'S SLAYING. ....- 34 -

CHAPTER VI. ....- 36 -

    HRUT SAILS OUT TO ICELAND. ....- 36 -

CHAPTER VII. ....- 39 -

    UNNA SEPARATES FROM HRUT. ....- 39 -

CHAPTER VIII. ....- 41 -

    MORD CLAIMS HIS GOODS FROM HRUT. ....- 41 -

CHAPTER IX. ....- 43 -

    THORWALD GETS HALLGERDA TO WIFE. ....- 43 -

CHAPTER X. ....- 45 -

    HALLGERDA'S WEDDING. ....- 45 -

CHAPTER XI. ....- 47 -

    THORWALD'S SLAYING. ....- 47 -

CHAPTER XII. ....- 49 -

    THIOSTOLF'S FLIGHT. ....- 49 -

CHAPTER XIII. ....- 53 -

    GLUM'S WOOING. ....- 53 -

CHAPTER XIV. ....- 56 -

    GLUM'S WEDDING. ....- 56 -

CHAPTER XV ....- 58 -

    THIOSTOLF GOES TO GLUM'S HOUSE. ....- 58 -

CHAPTER XVI. ....- 59 -

    GLUM'S SHEEP HUNT. ....- 59 -

CHAPTER XVII. ....- 60 -

    GLUM'S SLAYING. ....- 60 -

CHAPTER XVIII. ....- 63 -

    FIDDLE MORD'S DEATH. ....- 63 -

CHAPTER XIX. ....- 64 -

    GUNNAR COMES INTO THE STORY. ....- 64 -

CHAPTER XX. ....- 65 -

    OF NJAL AND HIS CHILDREN. ....- 65 -

CHAPTER XXI. ....- 66 -

    UNNA GOES TO SEE GUNNAR. ....- 66 -

CHAPTER XXII. ....- 68 -

    NJAL'S ADVICE. ....- 68 -

CHAPTER XXIII. ....- 71 -

    HUCKSTER HEDINN. ....- 71 -

CHAPTER XXIV. ....- 74 -

    GUNNAR AND HRUT STRIVE AT THE THING. ....- 74 -

CHAPTER XXV.	- 77 -
UNNA'S SECOND WEDDING.	- 77 -
CHAPTER XXVI.	- 78 -
OF ASGRIM AND HIS CHILDREN.	- 78 -
CHAPTER XXVII.	- 79 -
HELGI NJAL'S SON'S WOOING.	- 79 -
CHAPTER XXVIII.	- 80 -
HALLVARD COMES OUT TO ICELAND.	- 80 -
CHAPTER XXIX.	- 81 -
GUNNAR GOES ABROAD.	- 81 -
CHAPTER XXX.	- 83 -
GUNNAR GOES A-SEA-ROVING.	- 83 -
CHAPTER XXXI.	- 87 -
GUNNAR GOES TO KING HAROLD GORM'S SON AND EARL HACON.	- 87 -
CHAPTER XXXII.	- 89 -
GUNNAR COMES OUT TO ICELAND.	- 89 -
CHAPTER XXXIII.	- 91 -
GUNNAR'S WOOING.	- 91 -

CHAPTER XXXIV. ....- 94 -

   OF THRAIN SIGFUS' SON. ....- 94 -

CHAPTER XXXV. ....- 97 -

   THE VISIT TO
   BERGTHORSKNOLL. ....- 97 -

CHAPTER XXXVI. ....- 98 -

   KOL SLEW SWART. ....- 98 -

CHAPTER XXXVII. ....- 102 -

   THE SLAYING OF KOL, WHOM
   ATLI SLEW ....- 102 -

CHAPTER XXXVIII. ....- 105 -

   THE KILLING OF ATLI THE
   THRALL. ....- 105 -

CHAPTER XXXIX. ....- 108 -

   THE SLAYING OF BRYNJOLF THE
   UNRULY. ....- 108 -

CHAPTER XL. ....- 110 -

   GUNNAR AND NJAL MAKE PEACE
   ABOUT BRYNJOLF'S SLAYING. ....- 110 -

CHAPTER XLI. ....- 111 -

   SIGMUND COMES OUT TO
   ICELAND. ....- 111 -

CHAPTER XLII. ....- 114 -

   THE SLAYING OF THORD
   FREEDSMANSON. ....- 114 -

CHAPTER XLIII. ....- 116 -

   NJAL AND GUNNAR MAKE PEACE
   FOR THE SLAYING OF THORD.................................- 116 -

CHAPTER XLIV. ....- 118 -

   SIGMUND MOCKS NJAL AND HIS
   SONS. ....- 118 -

CHAPTER XLV. ....- 122 -

   THE SLAYING OF SIGMUND AND
   SKIOLLD. ....- 122 -

CHAPTER XLVI. ....- 125 -

   OF GIZUR THE WHITE AND GEIR
   THE PRIEST. ....- 125 -

CHAPTER XLVII. ....- 126 -

   OF OTKELL IN KIRKBY. ....- 126 -

CHAPTER XLVIII. ....- 128 -

   HOW HALLGERDA MAKES
   MALCOLM STEAL FROM KIRKBY. ....- 128 -

CHAPTER XLIX. ....- 130 -

   OF SKAMKELL'S EVIL COUNSEL. ....- 130 -

CHAPTER L. ....- 134 -

    OF SKAMKELL'S LYING. ....- 134 -

CHAPTER LI. ....- 136 -

    OF GUNNAR. ....- 136 -

CHAPTER LII. ....- 139 -

    OF RUNOLF, THE SON OF WOLF
    AURPRIEST. ....- 139 -

CHAPTER LIII. ....- 140 -

    HOW OTKELL RODE OVER
    GUNNAR. ....- 140 -

CHAPTER LIV. ....- 142 -

    THE FIGHT AT RANGRIVER. ....- 142 -

CHAPTER LV. ....- 145 -

    NJAL'S ADVICE TO GUNNAR. ....- 145 -

CHAPTER LVI. ....- 147 -

    GUNNAR AND GEIR THE PRIEST
    STRIVE AT THE THING. ....- 147 -

CHAPTER LVII. ....- 150 -

    OF STARKAD AND HIS SONS. ....- 150 -

CHAPTER LVIII. ....- 153 -

    HOW GUNNAR'S HORSE FOUGHT. ....- 153 -

CHAPTER LIX..- 155 -

    OF ASGRIM AND WOLF UGGIS' SON...- 155 -

CHAPTER LX. ....- 156 -

    AN ATTACK AGAINST GUNNAR AGREED ON..- 156 -

CHAPTER LXI..- 158 -

    GUNNAR'S DREAM. ....- 158 -

CHAPTER LXII. ....- 160 -

    THE SLAYING OF HJORT AND FOURTEEN MEN..- 160 -

CHAPTER LXIII..- 163 -

    NJAL'S COUNSEL TO GUNNAR. ....- 163 -

CHAPTER LXIV..- 165 -

    OF VALGARD AND MORD. ....- 165 -

CHAPTER LXV. ....- 167 -

    OF FINES AND ATONEMENTS......................................- 167 -

CHAPTER LXVI..- 169 -

    OF THORGEIR OTKELL'S SON.....................................- 169 -

CHAPTER LXVII. ....- 170 -

    OF THORGEIR STARKAD'S SON. ....- 170 -

CHAPTER LXVIII.	- 172 -
OF NJAL AND THOSE NAMESAKES.	- 172 -
CHAPTER LXIX.	- 174 -
OLAF THE PEACOCK'S GIFTS TO GUNNAR.	- 174 -
CHAPTER LXX.	- 176 -
MORD'S COUNSEL.	- 176 -
CHAPTER LXXI.	- 177 -
THE SLAYING OF THORGEIR OTKELL'S SON.	- 177 -
CHAPTER LXXII.	- 180 -
OF THE SUITS FOR MANSLAUGHTER AT THE THING.	- 180 -
CHAPTER LXXIII.	- 182 -
OF THE ATONEMENT.	- 182 -
CHAPTER LXXIV.	- 184 -
KOLSKEGG GOES ABROAD.	- 184 -
CHAPTER LXXV.	- 187 -
THE RIDING TO LITHEND.	- 187 -
CHAPTER LXXVI.	- 188 -

GUNNAR'S SLAYING. ....- 188 -

CHAPTER LXXVII. ....- 193 -

GUNNAR SINGS A SONG DEAD. ....- 193 -

CHAPTER LXXVIII. ....- 195 -

GUNNAR OF LITHEND AVENGED. ....- 195 -

CHAPTER LXXIX. ....- 197 -

HOGNI TAKES AN ATONEMENT
FOR GUNNAR'S DEATH. ....- 197 -

CHAPTER LXXX. ....- 198 -

OF KOLSKEGG: HOW HE WAS
BAPTISED. ....- 198 -

CHAPTER LXXXI. ....- 199 -

OF THRAIN: HOW HE SLEW KOL. ....- 199 -

CHAPTER LXXXII. ....- 202 -

NJAL'S SONS SAIL ABROAD. ....- 202 -

CHAPTER LXXXIII. ....- 204 -

OF KARI SOLMUND'S SON. ....- 204 -

CHAPTER LXXXIV. ....- 206 -

OF EARL SIGURD. ....- 206 -

CHAPTER LXXXV. ....- 208 -

THE BATTLE WITH THE EARLS.................................- 208 -

CHAPTER LXXXVI. ....- 209 -

   HRAPP'S VOYAGE FROM
   ICELAND. ....- 209 -

CHAPTER LXXXVII. ....- 214 -

   THRAIN TOOK TO HRAPP. ....- 214 -

CHAPTER LXXXVIII. ....- 220 -

   EARL HACON FIGHTS WITH
   NJAL'S SONS..- 220 -

CHAPTER LXXXIX. ....- 224 -

   NJAL'S SONS AND KARI COME
   OUT TO ICELAND. ....- 224 -

CHAPTER XC. ....- 225 -

   THE QUARREL OF NJAL'S SONS
   WITH THRAIN SIGFUS' SON. ....- 225 -

CHAPTER XCI. ....- 229 -

   THRAIN SIGFUS' SON'S SLAYING. ....- 229 -

CHAPTER XCII. ....- 234 -

   KETTLE TAKES HAUSKULD AS
   HIS FOSTER-SON. ....- 234 -

CHAPTER XCIII. ....- 235 -

NJAL TAKES HAUSKULD TO FOSTER...- 235 -

CHAPTER XCIV..- 236 -

   OF FLOSI THORD'S SON..- 236 -

CHAPTER XCV...- 237 -

   OF HALL OF THE SIDE. ....- 237 -

CHAPTER XCVI..- 238 -

   OF THE CHANGE OF FAITH. ....- 238 -

CHAPTER XCVII. ....- 240 -

   OF THANGBRAND'S JOURNEYS. ....- 240 -

CHAPTER XCVIII. ....- 241 -

   OF THANGBRAND AND GUDLEIF............................- 241 -

CHAPTER XCIX..- 244 -

   OF GEST ODDLEIF'S SON. ....- 244 -

CHAPTER C. ....- 246 -

   OF GIZUR THE WHITE AND HJALLTI..- 246 -

CHAPTER CI. ....- 247 -

   OF THORGEIR OF LIGHTWATER.............................- 247 -

CHAPTER CII. ....- 249 -

THE WEDDING OF HAUSKULD,
THE PRIEST OF WHITENESS......................- 249 -

CHAPTER CIII..- 253 -

THE SLAYING OF HAUSKULD
NJAL'S SON...- 253 -

CHAPTER CIV. ....- 257 -

THE SLAYING OF LYTING'S
BROTHERS..- 257 -

CHAPTER CV..- 260 -

OF AMUND THE BLIND. ....- 260 -

CHAPTER CVI. ....- 262 -

OF VALGARD THE GUILEFUL..................- 262 -

CHAPTER CVII. ....- 264 -

OF MORD AND NJAL'S SONS....................- 264 -

CHAPTER CVIII...- 265 -

OF THE SLANDER OF MORD
VALGARD'S SON. ....- 265 -

CHAPTER CIX. ....- 268 -

OF MORD AND NJAL'S SONS....................- 268 -

CHAPTER CX. ....- 269 -

THE SLAYING OF HAUSKULD,
THE PRIEST OF WHITENESS......................- 269 -

CHAPTER CXI. .... - 271 -

    OF HILDIGUNNA AND MORD VALGARD'S SON. .... - 271 -

CHAPTER CXII. .... - 273 -

    THE PEDIGREE OF GUDMUND THE POWERFUL. .... - 273 -

CHAPTER CXIII. .... - 274 -

    OF SNORRI THE PRIEST, AND HIS STOCK. .... - 274 -

CHAPTER CXIV .... - 275 -

    OF FLOSI THORD'S SON. .... - 275 -

CHAPTER CXV. .... - 277 -

    OF FLOSI AND HILDIGUNNA. .... - 277 -

CHAPTER CXVI. .... - 280 -

    OF FLOSI AND MORD AND THE SONS OF SIGFUS. .... - 280 -

CHAPTER CXVII. .... - 282 -

    NJAL AND SKARPHEDINN TALK TOGETHER. .... - 282 -

CHAPTER CXVIII. .... - 284 -

    ASGRIM AND NJAL'S SONS PRAY MEN FOR HELP. .... - 284 -

CHAPTER CXIX.	- 289 -
OF SKARPHEDINN AND THORKEL FOULMOUTH.	- 289 -
CHAPTER CXX.	- 292 -
OF THE PLEADING OF THE SUIT.	- 292 -
CHAPTER CXXI.	- 294 -
OF THE AWARD OF ATONEMENT BETWEEN FLOSI AND NJAL.	- 294 -
CHAPTER CXXII.	- 296 -
OF THE JUDGES.	- 296 -
CHAPTER CXXIII.	- 300 -
AN ATTACK PLANNED ON NJAL AND HIS SONS.	- 300 -
CHAPTER CXXIV.	- 304 -
OF PORTENTS.	- 304 -
CHAPTER CXXV.	- 305 -
FLOSI'S JOURNEY FROM HOME.	- 305 -
CHAPTER CXXVI.	- 306 -
OF PORTENTS AT BERGTHORSKNOLL.	- 306 -
CHAPTER CXXVII.	- 308 -

THE ONSLAUGHT ON BERGTHORSKNOLL. ....- 308 -

CHAPTER CXXVIII. ....- 311 -

NJAL'S BURNING...- 311 -

CHAPTER CXXIX. ....- 316 -

SKARPHEDINN'S DEATH. ....- 316 -

CHAPTER CXXX. ....- 321 -

OF KARI SOLMUND'S SON. ....- 321 -

CHAPTER CXXXI. ....- 324 -

NJAL'S AND BERGTHORA'S BONES FOUND...- 324 -

CHAPTER CXXXII. ....- 327 -

FLOSI'S DREAM. ....- 327 -

CHAPTER CXXXIII. ....- 329 -

OF FLOSI'S JOURNEY AND HIS ASKING FOR HELP..- 329 -

CHAPTER CXXXIV. ....- 332 -

OF THORHALL AND KARI. ....- 332 -

CHAPTER CXXXV. ....- 336 -

OF FLOSI AND THE BURNERS. ....- 336 -

CHAPTER CXXXVI. ....- 338 -

OF THORGEIR CRAGGEIR.	- 338 -
CHAPTER CXXXVII.	- 339 -
OF EYJOLF BOLVERK'S SON.	- 339 -
CHAPTER CXXXVIII.	- 343 -
OF ASGRIM, AND GIZUR, AND KARI.	- 343 -
CHAPTER CXXXIX.	- 347 -
OF ASGRIM AND GUDMUND.	- 347 -
CHAPTER CXL.	- 348 -
OF THE DECLARATIONS OF THE SUITS.	- 348 -
CHAPTER CXLI.	- 351 -
NOW MEN GO TO THE COURTS.	- 351 -
CHAPTER CXLII.	- 362 -
OF EYJOLF BOLVERK'S SON.	- 362 -
CHAPTER CXLIII.	- 364 -
THE COUNSEL OF THORHALL ASGRIM'S SON.	- 364 -
CHAPTER CXLIV.	- 369 -
BATTLE AT THE ALTHING.	- 369 -
CHAPTER CXLV.	- 378 -

OF KARI AND THORGEIR..- 378 -

CHAPTER CXLVI. ....- 382 -

THE AWARD OF ATONEMENT
WITH THORGEIR CRAGGEIR. ....- 382 -

CHAPTER CXLVII. ....- 385 -

KARI COMES TO BJORN'S HOUSE
IN THE MARK...- 385 -

CHAPTER CXLVIII. ....- 387 -

OF FLOSI AND THE BURNERS. ....- 387 -

CHAPTER CXLIX. ....- 390 -

OF KARI AND BJORN. ....- 390 -

CHAPTER CL. ....- 393 -

MORE OF KARI AND BJORN. ....- 393 -

CHAPTER CLI. ....- 396 -

OF KARI AND BJORN AND
THORGEIR. ....- 396 -

CHAPTER CLII. ....- 398 -

FLOSI GOES ABROAD. ....- 398 -

CHAPTER CLIII. ....- 400 -

KARI GOES ABROAD. ....- 400 -

CHAPTER CLIV. ....- 402 -

GUNNAR LAMBI'S SON'S SLAYING.	- 402 -
CHAPTER CLV.	- 405 -
OF SIGNS AND WONDERS.	- 405 -
CHAPTER CLVI.	- 407 -
BRIAN'S BATTLE.	- 407 -
CHAPTER CLVII.	- 414 -
THE SLAYING OF KOL THORSTEIN'S SON.	- 414 -
CHAPTER CLVIII.	- 416 -
OF FLOSI AND KARI.	- 416 -
FOOTNOTES:	- 418 -

SIR GEORGE DASENT'S PREFACE

(ABRIDGED.)

What is a Saga? A Saga is a story, or telling in prose, sometimes mixed with verse. There are many kinds of Sagas, of all degrees of truth. There are the mythical Sagas, in which the wondrous deeds of heroes of old time, half gods and half men, as Sigurd and Ragnar, are told as they were handed down from father to son in the traditions of the Northern race. Then there are Sagas recounting the history of the kings of Norway and other countries, of the great line of Orkney Jarls, and of the chiefs who ruled in Faroe. These are all more or less trustworthy, and, in general, far worthier of belief than much that passes for the early history of other races. Again, there are Sagas relating to Iceland, narrating the lives, and feuds, and ends of mighty chiefs, the heads of the great families which dwelt in this or that district of the island. These were told by men who lived on the very spot, and told with a minuteness and exactness, as to time and place, that will bear the strictest examination. Such a Saga is that of Njal, which we now lay before our readers in an English garb. Of all the Sagas relating to Iceland, this tragic story bears away the palm for truthfulness and beauty. To use the words of one well qualified to judge, it is, as compared with all similar compositions, as gold to brass.[1] Like all the Sagas which relate to the same period of Icelandic story, Njala[2] was not written down till about 100 years after the events which are described in it had happened. In the meantime, it was handed down by word of mouth, told from Althing to Althing, at Spring Thing, and Autumn Leet, at all great gatherings of the people, and over many a fireside, on sea strand or river bank, or up among the dales and hills, by men who had learnt the sad story of Njal's fate, and who could tell of Gunnar's peerlessness and Hallgerda's infamy, of Bergthora's helpfulness, of Skarphedinn's hastiness, of Flosi's foul deed, and Kurt's stern revenge. We may be sure that as soon as each event recorded in the Saga occurred, it was told and talked about as matter of history, and when at last the whole story was unfolded and took shape, and centred round Njal, that it was handed down from father to son, as truthfully and faithfully as could ever be the case with any public or notorious matter in local history. But it is not on Njala alone that we have to rely for our evidence of its genuineness. There are many other Sagas relating to the same period, and handed down in like manner, in which the actors in our Saga are incidentally mentioned by name, and in which the deeds recorded of them are corroborated. They are mentioned also in songs and Annals, the latter being the earliest written records which belong to the history of the island, while the former were more easily remembered, from the construction of the verse. Much passes for history in other lands on far slighter grounds, and many a story in Thucydides or Tacitus, or even in Clarendon or Hume, is believed on evidence not one-tenth part so trustworthy as that which supports the narratives of these Icelandic story-tellers of the eleventh century. That with occurrences of undoubted truth, and minute particularity as to time and place, as to dates and distance, are intermingled wild superstitions on several occasions, will startle no reader of the smallest judgment. All ages, our own not excepted, have their superstitions, and to suppose that a story told in the eleventh century,—when phantoms, and ghosts, and wraiths, were implicitly believed in, and when dreams, and warnings, and tokens, were part of every man's creed—should be wanting in these marks of genuineness, is simply to require that one great proof of its truthfulness should be wanting, and that, in order to suit the spirit of our age, it should lack something which was part and parcel of popular belief in the age to which it belonged. To a thoughtful mind, therefore, such stories as that of Swan's witchcraft, Gunnar's song in his cairn, the Wolf's ride before the Burning, Flosi's dream, the signs and tokens before Brian's battle, and even Njal's weird foresight, on which the whole story hangs, will be regarded as proofs rather for than against its genuineness.[3]

But it is an old saying, that a story never loses in telling, and so we may expect it must have been with this story. For the facts which the Saga-teller related he was bound to follow the narrations of those who had gone before him, and if he swerved to or fro in this respect, public opinion and notorious fame was there to check and contradict him.[4] But the way in which he told the facts was his own, and thus it comes that some Sagas are better told than others, as the feeling and power of the narrator were above those of others. To tell a story truthfully was what was looked for from all men in those days; but to tell it properly and gracefully, and so to clothe the facts in fitting diction, was given to few, and of those few the Saga teller who first threw Njala into its present shape, was one of the first and foremost.

With the change of faith and conversion of the Icelanders to Christianity, writing, and the materials for writing, first came into the land, about the year 1000. There is no proof that the earlier or Runic alphabet, which existed in heathen times, was ever used for any other purposes than those of simple monumental inscriptions, or of short legends on weapons or sacrificial vessels, or horns and drinking cups. But with the Roman alphabet came not only a readier means of expressing thought, but also a class of men who were wont thus to express themselves.... Saga after Saga was reduced to writing, and before the year 1200 it is reckoned that all the pieces of that kind of composition which relate to the history of Icelanders previous to the introduction of Christianity had passed from the oral into the written shape. Of all those Sagas, none were so interesting as Njal, whether as regarded the length of the story, the number and rank of the chiefs who appeared in it as actors, and the graphic way in which the tragic tale was told. As a rounded whole, in which each part is finely and beautifully polished, in which the two great divisions of the story are kept in perfect balance and counterpoise, in which each person who appears is left free to speak in a way which stamps him with a character of his own, while all unite in working towards a common end, no Saga had such claims on public attention as Njala, and it is certain none would sooner have been committed to writing. The latest period, therefore, that we can assign as the date at which our Saga was moulded into its present shape is the year 1200....

It was a foster-father's duty, in old times, to rear and cherish the child which he had taken from the arms of its natural parents, his superiors in rank. And so may this work, which the translator has taken from the house of Icelandic scholars, his masters in knowledge, and which he has reared and fostered so many years under an English roof, go forth and fight the battle of life for itself, and win fresh fame for those who gave it birth. It will be reward enough for him who has first clothed it in an English dress if his foster-child adds another leaf to that evergreen wreath of glory which crowns the brows of Iceland's ancient worthies.

BROAD SANCTUARY.

Christmas Eve, 1860.

It will be seen that in most cases the names of places throughout the Saga have been turned into English, either in whole or in part, as "Lithend" for "Lfaðrendi," and "Bergthorsknoll" for "Bergthorshvól". The translator adopted this course to soften the ruggedness of the original names for the English reader, but in every case the Icelandic name, with its English rendering, will be found in the maps. The surnames and nicknames have also been turned into English—an attempt which has not a little increased the toil of translation. Great allowance must be made for these renderings, as those nicknames often arose out of circumstances of which we know little or nothing. Of some, such as "Thorgeir Craggeir," and "Thorkel foulmouth," the Saga itself explains the origin. In a state of society where so many men bore the same name, any circumstance or event in a man's life, as well as any peculiarity in form or feature, or in temper and turn of mind, gave rise to a surname or nickname, which clung to him through life as a distinguishing mark. The Post Office in the United States is said to give persons in the same district, with similar names, an initial of identification, which answers the same purpose, as the Icelandic nickname, thus: "John *P* Smith."—"John *Q* Smith". As a general rule the translator has withstood the temptation to use old English words. "Busk" and "boun" he pleads guilty to, because both still linger in the language understood by few. "Busk" is a reflective formed from 'eat búa sik,' "to get oneself ready," and "boun" is the past participle of the active form "búa, búinn," to get ready. When the leader in Old Ballads says—

"Busk ye, busk ye,
My bonny, bonny men,"

he calls on his followers to equip themselves; when they are thus equipped they are "boun". A bride "busks" herself for the bridal; when she is dressed she is "boun". In old times a ship was "busked" for a voyage; when she was filled and ready for sea she was "boun"—whence come our outward "bound" and homeward "bound". These with "redes" for counsels or plans are almost the only words in the translation which are not still in everyday use.

SIR GEORGE DASENT'S INTRODUCTION.

(ABRIDGED).

THE NORTHMEN IN ICELAND.

The men who colonized Iceland towards the end of the ninth century of the Christian æra, were of no savage or servile race. They fled from the overbearing power of the king, from that new and strange doctrine of government put forth by Harold Fairhair, 860-933, which made them the king's men at all times, instead of his only at certain times for special service, which laid scatts and taxes on their lands, which interfered with vested rights and world-old laws, and allowed the monarch to meddle and make with the freemen's allodial holdings. As we look at it now, and from another point of view, we see that what to them was unbearable tyranny was really a step in the great march of civilization and progress, and that the centralization and consolidation of the royal authority, according to Charlemagne's system, was in time to be a blessing to the kingdoms of the north. But to the freeman it was a curse. He fought against it as long as he could; worsted over and over again, he renewed the struggle, and at last, when the isolated efforts, which were the key-stone of his edifice of liberty, were fruitless, he sullenly withdrew from the field, and left the land of his fathers, where, as he thought, no free-born man could now care to live. Now it is that we hear of him in Iceland, where Ingolf was the first settler in the year 874, and was soon followed by many of his countrymen. Now, too, we hear of him in all lands. Now France—now Italy—now Spain, feel the fury of his wrath, and the weight of his arm. After a time, but not until nearly a century has passed, he spreads his wings for a wider flight, and takes service under the great emperor at Byzantium, or Micklegarth—the great city, the town of towns—and fights his foes from whatever quarter they come. The Moslem in Sicily and Asia, the Bulgarians and Slavonians on the shores of the Black Sea and in Greece, well know the temper of the Northern steel, which has forced many of their chosen champions to bite the dust. Wherever he goes the Northman leaves his mark, and to this day the lion at the entrance to the arsenal at Venice is scored with runes which tell of his triumph.

But of all countries, what were called the Western Lands were his favourite haunt. England, where the Saxons were losing their old dash and daring, and settling down into a sluggish sensual race; Ireland, the flower of Celtic lands, in which a system of great age and undoubted civilization was then fast falling to pieces, afforded a tempting battlefield in the everlasting feuds between chief and chief; Scotland, where the power of the Picts was waning, while that of the Scots had not taken firm hold on the country, and most of all the islands in the Scottish Main, Orkney, Shetland, and the outlying Faroe Isles;—all these were his chosen abode. In those islands he took deep root, established himself on the old system, shared in the quarrels of the chiefs and princes of the Mainland, now helped Pict and now Scot, roved the seas and made all ships prizes, and kept alive his old grudge against Harold Fairhair and the new system by a long series of piratical incursions on the Norway coast. So worrying did these Viking cruises at last become, that Harold, who meantime had steadily pursued his policy at home, and forced all men to bow to his sway or leave the land, resolved to crush the wasps that stung him summer after summer in their own nest. First of all he sent Kettle flatnose, a mighty chief, to subdue the foe; but though Kettle waged successful war, he kept what he won for himself. It was the old story of setting a thief to catch a thief; and Harold found that if he was to have his work done to his mind he must do it himself. He called on his chiefs to follow him, levied a mighty force, and, sailing suddenly with a fleet which must have seemed an armada in those days, he fell upon the Vikings in Orkney and Shetland, in the Hebrides and Western Isles, in Man and Anglesey, in the Lewes and Faroe—wherever he could find them he followed them up with fire and sword. Not once, but twice he crossed the sea after them, and tore them out so thoroughly, root and branch, that we hear no more of these lands as a lair of Vikings, but as the abode of Norse Jarls and their udallers (freeholders) who look upon the new state of things at home as right and just, and acknowledge the authority of Harold and his successors by an allegiance more or less dutiful at different times, but which was never afterwards entirely thrown off.

It was just then, just when the unflinching will of Harold had taught this stern lesson to his old foes, and arising in most part out of that lesson, that the great rush of settlers to Iceland took place. We have already seen that Ingolf and others had settled in Iceland from 874 downwards, but it was not until nearly twenty years afterwards that the island began to be thickly peopled. More than half of the names of the first colonists contained in the venerable Landnáma Book—the Book of Lots, the Doomsday of Iceland, and far livelier reading than that of the Conqueror—are those of Northmen who had been before settled in the British Isles. Our own country then was the great stepping-stone between Norway and Iceland; and this one fact is enough to account for the close connection which the Icelanders ever afterwards kept up with their kinsmen who had remained behind in the islands of the west....

SUPERSTITIONS OF THE RACE.

The Northman had many superstitions. He believed in good giants and bad giants, in dark elves and bright elves, in superhuman beings who tilled the wide gulf which existed between himself and the gods. He believed, too, in wraiths and fetches and guardian spirits, who followed particular persons, and belonged to certain families—a belief which seems to have sprung from the habit of regarding body and soul as two distinct beings, which at certain times took each a separate bodily shape. Sometimes the guardian spirit or fylgja took a human shape; at others its form took that of some animal fancied to foreshadow the character of the man to whom it belonged. Thus it becomes a bear, a wolf, an ox, and even a fox, in men. The fylgjur of women were fond of taking the shape of swans. To see one's own fylgja was unlucky, and often a sign that a man was "fey," or death-doomed. So, when Thord Freedmanson tells Njal that he sees the goat wallowing in its gore in the "town" of Bergthorsknoll, the foresighted man tells him that he has seen his own fylgja, and that he must be doomed to die. Finer and nobler natures often saw the guardian spirits of others. Thus Njal saw the fylgjur of Gunnar's enemies, which gave him no rest the livelong night, and his weird feeling is soon confirmed by the news brought by his shepherd. From the fylgja of the individual it was easy to rise to the still more abstract notion of the guardian spirits of a family, who sometimes, if a great change in the house is about to begin, even show themselves as hurtful to some member of the house. He believed also that some men had more than one shape; that they could either take the shapes of animals, as bears or wolves, and so work mischief; or that, without undergoing bodily change, an access of rage and strength came over them, and more especially towards night, which made them more than a match for ordinary men. Such men were called hamrammir, "shape-strong," and it was remarked that when the fit left them they were weaker than they had been before.

This gift was looked upon as something "uncanny," and it leads us at once to another class of men, whose supernatural strength was regarded as a curse to the community. These were the Baresarks. What the hamrammir men were when they were in their fits the Baresarks almost always were. They are described as being always of exceeding, and when their fury rose high, of superhuman strength. They too, like the hamrammir men, were very tired when the fits passed off. What led to their fits is hard to say. In the case of the only class of men like them nowadays, that of the Malays running a-muck, the intoxicating fumes of bangh or arrack are said to be the cause of their fury. One thing, however, is certain, that the Baresark, like his Malay brother, was looked upon as a public pest, and the mischief which they caused, relying partly no doubt on their natural strength, and partly on the hold which the belief in their supernatural nature had on the mind of the people, was such as to render their killing a good work.

Again, the Northman believed that certain men were "fast" or "hard"; that no weapons would touch them or wound their skin; that the mere glance of some men's eyes would turn the edge of the best sword; and that some persons had the power of withstanding poison. He believed in omens and dreams and warnings, in signs and wonders and tokens; he believed in good luck and bad luck, and that the man on whom fortune smiled or frowned bore the marks of her favour or displeasure on his face; he believed also in magic and sorcery, though he loathed them as unholy rites. With one of his beliefs our story has much to do, though this was a belief in good rather than in evil. He believed firmly that some men had the inborn gift, not won by any black arts, of seeing things and events beforehand. He believed, in short, in what is called in Scotland "second sight". This was what was called being "forspár" or "framsýnn," "foretelling" and "foresighted ". Of such men it was said that their "words could not be broken". Njal was one of these men; one of the wisest and at the same time most just and honourable of men. This gift ran in families, for Helgi Njal's son had it, and it was beyond a doubt one of the deepest-rooted of all their superstitions.

SOCIAL PRINCIPLES.

Besides his creed and these beliefs the new settler brought with him certain fixed social principles, which we shall do well to consider carefully in the outset. First and foremost came the father's right of property in his children. This right is common to the infancy of all communities, and exists before all law. We seek it in vain in codes which belong to a later period, but it has left traces of itself in all codes, and, abrogated in theory, still often exists in practice. We find it in the Roman law, and we find it among the Northmen. Thus it was the father's right to rear his children or not at his will. As soon as it was born, the child was laid upon the bare ground; and until the father came and looked at it, heard and saw that it was strong in lung and limb, lifted it in his arms, and handed it over to the women to be reared, its fate hung in the balance, and life or death depended on the sentence of its sire. After it had passed safely through that ordeal, it was duly washed, signed with Thor's holy hammer, and solemnly received into the family. If it were a weakly boy, and still more often, if it were a girl, no matter whether she were strong or weak, the infant was exposed to die by ravening beasts, or the inclemency of the climate. Many instances occur of children so exposed, who, saved by some kindly neighbour, and fostered beneath a stranger's roof, thus contracted ties reckoned still more binding than blood itself. So long as his children remained under his roof, they were their father's own. When the sons left the paternal roof, they were emancipated, and when the daughters were married they were also free, but the marriage itself remained till the latest times a matter of sale and barter in deed as well as name. The wife came into the house, in the patriarchal state, either stolen or bought from her nearest male relations; and though in later times when the sale took place it was softened by settling part of the dower and portion on the wife, we shall do well to bear in mind, that originally dower was only the price paid by the suitor to the father for his good will; while portion, on the other hand, was the sum paid by the father to persuade a suitor to take a daughter off his hands. Let us remember, therefore, that in those times, as Odin was supreme in Asgard as the Great Father of Gods and men, so in his own house every father of the race that revered Odin was also sovereign and supreme.

In the second place, as the creed of the race was one that adored the Great Father as the God of Battles; as it was his will that turned the fight; nay, as that was the very way in which he chose to call his own to himself,—it followed, that any appeal to arms was looked upon as an appeal to God. Victory was indeed the sign of a rightful cause, and he that won the day remained behind to enjoy the rights which he had won in fair fight, but he that lost it, if he fell bravely and like a man, if he truly believed his quarrel just, and brought it without guile to the issue of the sword, went by the very manner of his death to a better place. The Father of the Slain wanted him, and he was welcomed by the Valkyries, by Odin's corse-choosers, to the festive board in Valhalla. In every point of view, therefore, war and battle was a holy thing, and the Northman went to the battlefield in the firm conviction that right would prevail. In modern times, while we appeal in declarations of war to the God of Battles, we do it with the feeling that war is often an unholy thing, and that Providence is not always on the side of strong battalions. The Northman saw Providence on both sides. It was good to live, if one fought bravely, but it was also good to die, if one fell bravely. To live bravely and to die bravely, trusting in the God of Battles, was the warrior's comfortable creed.

But this feeling was also shown in private life. When two tribes or peoples rushed to war, there Odin, the warrior's god, was sure to be busy in the fight, turning the day this way or that at his will; but he was no less present in private war, where in any quarrel man met man to claim or to defend a right. There, too, he turned the scale and swayed the day, and there too an appeal to arms was regarded as an appeal to heaven. Hence arose another right older than all law, the right of duel—of wager of battle, as the old English law called it. Among the Northmen it underlaid all their early legislation, which, as we shall see, aimed rather at regulating and guiding it, by making it a part and parcel of the law, than at attempting to check at once a custom which had grown up with the whole faith of the people, and which was regarded as a right at once so time-honoured and so holy.

Thirdly, we must never forget that, as it is the Christian's duty to forgive his foes, and to be patient and long-suffering under the most grievous wrongs so it was the heathen's bounden duty to avenge all wrongs, and most of all those offered to blood relations, to his kith and kin, to the utmost limit of his power. Hence arose the constant blood-feuds between families, of which we shall hear so much in our story, but which we shall fail fully to understand, unless we keep in view, along with this duty of revenge, the right or property which all heads of houses had in their relations. Out of these twofold rights, of the right of revenge and the right of property, arose that strange medley of forbearance and blood-thirstiness which stamps the age. Revenge was a duty and a right, but property was no less a right; and so it rested with the father of a family either to take revenge, life for life, or to forego his vengeance, and take a compensation in goods or money for the loss he had sustained in his property. Out of this latter view arose those arbitrary tariffs for wounds or loss of life, which were gradually developed more or less completely in all the Teutonic and Scandinavian races, until every injury to life or limb had its proportionate price, according to the rank which the injured person bore in the social scale. These tariffs, settled by the heads of houses, are, in fact, the first elements of the law of nations; but it must be clearly understood that it always rested with the injured family either to follow up the quarrel by private war, or to call on the man who had inflicted the injury to pay a fitting fine. If he refused, the feud might be followed up on the battlefield, in the earliest times, or in later days, either by battle or by law. Of the latter mode of proceeding, we shall have to speak at greater length farther on; for the present, we content ourselves with indicating these different modes of settling a quarrel in what we have called the patriarchal state.

A fourth great principle of his nature was the conviction of the worthlessness and fleeting nature of all worldly goods. One thing alone was firm and unshaken, the stability of well-earned fame. "Goods perish, friends perish, a man himself perishes, but fame never dies to him that hath won it worthily." "One thing I know that never dies, the judgment passed on every mortal man." Over all man's life hung a blind, inexorable fate, a lower fold of the same gloomy cloud that brooded over Odin and the Æsir. Nothing could avert this doom. When his hour came, a man must meet his death, and until his hour came he was safe. It might strike in the midst of the highest happiness, and then nothing could avert the evil, but until it struck he would come safe through the direst peril. This fatalism showed itself among this vigorous pushing race in no idle resignation. On the contrary, the Northman went boldly to meet the doom which he felt sure no effort of his could turn aside, but which he knew, if he met it like a man, would secure him the only lasting thing on earth—a name famous in songs and story. Fate must be met then, but the way in which it was met, that rested with a man himself, that, at least, was in his own power; there he might show his free will; and thus this principle, which might seem at first to be calculated to blunt his energies and weaken his strength of mind, really sharpened and hardened them in a wonderful way, for it left it still worth everything to a man to fight this stern battle of life well and bravely, while its blind inexorable nature allowed no room for any careful weighing of chances or probabilities, or for any anxious prying into the nature of things doomed once for all to come to pass. To do things like a man, without looking to the right or left, as Kari acted when he smote off Gunnar's head in Earl Sigurd's hall, was the Northman's pride. He must do them openly too, and show no shame for what he had done. To kill a man and say that you had killed him, was manslaughter; to kill him and not to take it on your hand was murder. To kill men at dead of night was also looked on as murder. To kill a foe and not bestow the rights of burial on his body by throwing sand or gravel over him, was also looked on as murder. Even the wicked Thiostolf throws gravel over Glum in our Saga, and Thord Freedmanson's complaint against Brynjolf the unruly was that he had buried Atli's body badly. Even in killing a foe there was an open gentlemanlike way of doing it, to fail in which was shocking to the free and outspoken spirit of the age. Thorgeir Craggeir and the gallant Kari wake their foes and give them time to arm themselves before they fall upon them; and Hrapp, too, the thorough Icelander of the common stamp, "the friend of his friends and the foe of his foes," stalks before Gudbrand and tells him to his face the crimes which he has committed. Robbery and piracy in a good straightforward wholesale way were honoured and respected; but to steal, to creep to a man's abode secretly at dead of night and spoil his goods, was looked upon as infamy of the worst kind. To do what lay before him openly and like a man, without fear of either foes, fiends, or fate; to hold his own and speak his mind, and seek fame without respect of persons; to be free and daring in all his deeds; to be gentle and generous to his friends and kinsmen; to be stern and grim to his foes, but even towards them to feel bound to fulfil all bounden duties; to be as forgiving to some as he was unyielding and unforgiving to others. To be no truce-breaker, nor talebearer nor backbiter. To utter nothing against any man that he would not dare to tell him to his face. To turn no man from his door who sought food or shelter, even though he were a foe—these were other broad principles of the Northman's life, further features of that steadfast faithful spirit which he brought with him to his new home....

DAILY LIFE IN NJAL'S TIME.

In the tenth century the homesteads of the Icelanders consisted of one main building, in which the family lived by day and slept at night, and of out-houses for offices and farm-buildings, all opening on a yard. Sometimes these out-buildings touched the main building, and had doors which opened into it, but in most cases they stood apart, and for purposes of defence, no small consideration in those days, each might be looked upon as a separate house.

The main building of the house was the stofa, or sitting and sleeping room. In the abodes of chiefs and great men, this building had great dimensions, and was then called a skáli, or hall. It was also called eldhús, or eldáskáli, from the great fires which burned in it.... It had two doors, the men's or main door, and the women's or lesser door. Each of these doors opened into a porch of its own, andyri, which was often wide enough, in the case of that into which the men's door opened, as we see in Thrain's house at Grit water, to allow many men to stand in it abreast. It was sometimes called forskáli. Internally the hall consisted of three divisions, a nave and two low side aisles. The walls of these aisles were of stone, and low enough to allow of their being mounted with ease, as we see happened both with Gunner's skáli, and with Njal's. The centre division or nave on the other hand, rose high above the others on two rows of pillars. It was of timber, and had an open work timber roof. The roofs of the side aisles were supported by posts as well as by rafters and cross-beams leaning against the pillars of the nave. It was on one of these cross-beams, after it had fallen down from the burning roof, that Kari got on to the side wall and leapt out, while Skarphedinn, when the burnt beam snapped asunder under his weight, was unable to follow him. There were fittings of wainscot along the walls of the side aisles, and all round between the pillars of the inner row, supporting the roof of the nave, ran a wainscot panel. In places the wainscot was pierced by doors opening into sleeping places shut off from the rest of the hall on all sides for the heads of the family. In other parts of the passages were sleeping places and beds not so shut off, for the rest of the household. The women servants slept in the passage behind the dais at one end of the hall. Over some halls there were upper chambers or lofts, in one of which Gunnar of Lithend slept, and from which he made his famous defence.

We have hitherto treated only of the passages and recesses of the side aisles. The whole of the nave within the wainscot, between the inner round pillars, was filled by the hall properly so called. It had long hearths for fires in the middle, with louvres above to let out the smoke. On either side nearest to the wainscot, and in some cases touching it, was a row of benches; in each of these was a high seat, if the hall was that of a great man, that on the south side being the owner's seat. Before these seats were tables, boards, which, however, do not seem, any more than our early Middle Age tables, to have been always kept standing, but were brought in with, and cleared away after, each meal. On ordinary occasions, one row of benches on each side sufficed; but when there was a great feast, or a sudden rush of unbidden guests, as when Flosi paid his visit to Tongue to take down Asgrim's pride, a lower kind of seats, or stools were brought in, on which the men of lowest rank sat, and which were on the outside of the tables, nearest to the fire. At the end of the hall, over against the door, was a raised platform or dais, on which also was sometimes a high seat and benches. It was where the women eat at weddings, as we see from the account of Hallgerda's wedding, in our Saga, and from many other passages.

In later times the seat of honour was shifted from the upper bench to the dais; and this seems to have been the case occasionally with kings and earls In Njal's time, if we may judge from the passage in the Saga, where Hildigunna fits up a high seat on the dais for Flosi, which he spurns from under him with the words, that he was "neither king nor earl," meaning that he was a simple man, and would have nothing to do with any of those new-fashions. It was to the dais that Asgrim betook himself when Flosi paid him his visit, and unless Asgrim's hall was much smaller than we have any reason to suppose would be the case in the dwelling of so great a chief, Flosi must have eaten his meal not far from the dais, in order to allow of Asgrim's getting near enough to aim a blow at him with a pole-axe from the rail at the edge of the platform. On high days and feast days, part of the hall was hung with tapestry, often of great worth and beauty, and over the hangings all along the wainscot, were carvings such as those which ... our Saga tells us Thorkel Foulmouth had carved on the stool before his high seat and over his shut bed, in memory of those deeds of "derring do" which he had performed in foreign lands.

Against the wainscot in various parts of the hall, shields and weapons were hung up. It was the sound of Skarphedinn's axe against the wainscot that woke up Njal and brought him out of his shut bed, when his sons set out on their hunt after Sigmund the white and Skiolld.

Now let us pass out of the skáli by either door, and cast our eyes at the high gables with their carved projections, and we shall understand at a glance how it was that Mord's counsel to throw ropes round the ends of the timbers, and then to twist them tight with levers and rollers, could only end, if carried out, in tearing the whole roof off the house. It was then much easier work for Gunnar's foes to mount up on the side-roofs as the Easterling, who brought word that his bill was at home, had already done, and thence to attack him in his sleeping loft with safety to themselves, after his bowstring had been cut.

Some homesteads, like those of Gunnar at Lithend, and Gísli and his brother at Hol in Hawkdale, in the West Firths, had bowers, ladies' chambers, where the women eat and span, and where, in both the houses that we have named, gossip and scandal was talked with the worst results. These bowers stood away from the other buildings....

Every Icelandic homestead was approached by a straight road which led up to the yard round which the main building and its out-houses and farm-buildings stood. This was fenced in on each side by a wall of stones or turf. Near the house stood the "town" or home fields where meadow hay was grown, and in favoured positions where corn would grow, there were also enclosures of arable land near the house. On the uplands and marshes more hay was grown. Hay was the great crop in Iceland; for the large studs of horses and great herds of cattle that roamed upon the hills and fells in summer needed fodder in the stable and byre in winter, when they were brought home. As for the flocks of sheep, they seem to have been reckoned and marked every autumn, and milked and shorn in summer; but to have fought it out with nature on the hill-side all the year round as they best could. Hay, therefore, was the main staple, and haymaking the great end and aim of an Icelandic farmer.... Gunnar's death in our Saga may be set down to the fact that all his men were away in the Landisles finishing their haymaking. Again, Flosi, before the Burning, bids all his men go home and make an end of their haymaking, and when that is over, to meet and fall on Njal and his sons. Even the great duty of revenge gives way to the still more urgent duty of providing fodder for the winter store. Hayneed, to run short of hay, was the greatest misfortune that could befall a man, who with a fine herd and stud, might see both perish before his eyes in winter. Then it was that men of open heart and hand, like Gunnar, helped their tenants and neighbours, often, as we see in Gunnar's case, till they had neither hay nor food enough left for their own household, and had to buy or borrow from those that had. Then, too, it was that the churl's nature came out in Otkell and others, who having enough and to spare, would not part with their abundance for love or money.

These men were no idlers. They worked hard, and all, high and low, worked. In no land does the dignity of labour stand out so boldly. The greatest chiefs sow and reap, and drive their sheep, like Glum, the Speaker's brother, from the fells. The mightiest warriors were the handiest carpenters and smiths. Gísli Súr's son knew every corner of his foeman's house, because he had built it with his own hands while they were good friends. Njal's sons are busy at armourer's work, like the sons of the mythical Ragnar before them, when the news comes to them that Sigmund has made a mock of them in his songs. Gunnar sows his corn with his arms by his side, when Otkell rides over him; and Hauskuld the Whiteness priest is doing the same work when he is slain. To do something, and to do it well, was the Icelander's aim in life, and in no land does laziness like that of

Thorkell meet with such well deserved reproach. They were early risers and went early to bed, though they could sit up late if need were. They thought nothing of long rides before they broke their fast. Their first meal was at about seven o'clock, and though they may have taken a morsel of food during the day, we hear of no other regular daily meal till evening, when between seven and eight again they had supper. While the men laboured on the farm or in the smithy, threw nets for fish in the teeming lakes and rivers, or were otherwise at work during the day, the women, and the housewife, or mistress of the house, at their head, made ready the food for the meals, carded wool, and sewed or wove or span. At meal-time the food seems to have been set on the board by the women, who waited on the men, and at great feasts, such as Gunnar's wedding, the wives of his nearest kinsmen, and of his dearest friend, Thorhillda Skaldtongue, Thrain's wife, and Bergthora, Njal's wife, went about from board to board waiting on the guests.

In everyday life they were a simple sober people, early to bed and early to rise—ever struggling with the rigour of the climate. On great occasions, as at the Yule feasts in honour of the gods, held at the temples, or at "arvel," "heir-ale," feasts, when heirs drank themselves into their father's land and goods, or at the autumn feasts, which friends and kinsmen gave to one another, there was no doubt great mirth and jollity, much eating and hard drinking of mead and fresh-brewed ale; but these drinks are not of a very heady kind, and one glass of spirits in our days would send a man farther on the road to drunkenness than many a horn of foaming mead. They were by no means that race of drunkards and hard livers which some have seen fit to call them.

Nor were these people such barbarians as some have fancied, to whom it is easier to rob a whole people of its character by a single word than to take the pains to inquire into its history. They were bold warriors and bolder sailors. The voyage between Iceland and Norway, or Iceland and Orkney, was reckoned as nothing; but from the west firths of Iceland, Eric the Red—no ruffian as he has been styled, though he had committed an act of manslaughter—discovered Greenland; and from Greenland the hardy seafarers pushed on across the main, till they made the dreary coast of Labrador. Down that they ran until they came at last to Vineland the good, which took its name from the grapes that grew there. From the accounts given of the length of the days in that land, it is now the opinion of those best fitted to judge on such matters, that this Vineland was no other than some part of the North American continent near Rhode Island or Massachusetts, in the United States. Their ships were half-decked, high out of the water at stem and stern, low in the waist, that the oars might reach the water, for they were made for rowing as well as for sailing. The after-part had a poop. The fore-part seems to have been without deck, but loose planks were laid there for men to stand on. A distinction was made between long-ships or ships of war, made long for speed, and ... ships of burden, which were built to carry cargo. The common complement was thirty rowers, which in warships made sometimes a third and sometimes a sixth of the crew. All round the warships, before the fight began, shield was laid on shield, on a rim or rail, which ran all round the bulwarks, presenting a mark like the hammocks of our navy, by which a long-ship could be at once detected. The bulwarks in warships could be heightened at pleasure, and this was called "to girdle the ship for war". The merchant ships often carried heavy loads of meal and timber from Norway, and many a one of these half-decked yawls no doubt foundered, like Flosi's unseaworthy ship, under the weight of her heavy burden of beams and planks, when overtaken by the autumnal gales on that wild sea. The passages were often very long, more than one hundred days is sometimes mentioned as the time spent on a voyage between Norway and Iceland.

As soon as the ship reached the land, she ran into some safe bay or creek, the great landing places on the south and south-east coasts being Eyrar, "The Eres," as such spots are still called in some parts of the British Isles, that is, the sandy beaches opening into lagoons which line the shore of the marsh district called Flói; and Hornfirth, whence Flosi and the Burners put to sea after their banishment. There the ship was laid up in a slip, made for her, she was stripped and made snug for the winter, a roof of planks being probably thrown over her, while the lighter portions of her cargo were carried on pack-saddles up the country. The timber seems to have been floated up the firths and rivers as near as it could be got to its destination, and then dragged by trains of horses to the spot where it was to be used.

Some of the cargo—the meal, and cloth and arms—was wanted at home; some of it was sold to neighbours either for ready money or on trust, it being usual to ask for the debt either in coin or in kind, the spring after. Sometimes the account remained outstanding for a much longer time. Among these men whose hands were so swift to shed blood, and in that state of things which looks so lawless, but which in truth was based upon fixed principles of justice and law, the rights of property were so safe, that men like Njal went lending their money to overbearing fellows like Starkad under Threecorner for years, on condition that he should pay a certain rate of interest. So also Gunnar had goods and money out at interest, out of which he wished to supply Unna's wants. In fact the law of debtor and creditor, and of borrowing money at usance, was well understood in Iceland, from the very first day that the Northmen set foot on its shores.

If we examine the condition of the sexes in this state of society, we shall find that men and women met very nearly on equal terms. If any woman is shocked to read how Thrain Sigfus' son treated his wife, in parting from her, and marrying a new one, at a moment's warning, she must be told that Gudruna, in Laxdæla, threatened one of her three husbands with much the same treatment, and would have put her threat into execution if he had not behaved as she commanded him. In our Saga, too, the gudewife of Bjorn the boaster threatens him with a separation if he does not stand faithfully by Kari; and in another Saga of equal age and truthfulness, we hear of one great lady who parted from her husband, because, in playfully throwing a pillow of down at her, he unwittingly struck her with his finger. In point of fact, the customary law allowed great latitude to separations, at the will of either party, if good reason could be shown for the desired change. It thought that the worst service it could render to those whom it was intended to protect would be to force two people to live together against their will, or even against the will of only one of them, if that person considered him or herself, as the case might be, ill-treated or neglected. Gunnar no doubt could have separated himself from Hallgerda for her thieving, just as Hallgerda could have parted from Gunnar for giving her that slap in the face; but they lived on, to Gunnar's cost and Hallgerda's infamy. In marriage contracts the rights of brides, like Unna the great heiress of the south-west, or Hallgerda the flower of the western dales, were amply provided for. In the latter case it was a curious fact that this wicked woman retained possession of Laugarness, near Reykjavik, which was part of her second husband Glum's property, to her dying day, and there, according to constant tradition, she was buried in a cairn which is still shown at the present time, and which is said to be always green, summer and winter alike. Where marriages were so much matter of barter and bargain, the father's will went for so much and that of the children for so little, love matches were comparatively rare; and if the songs of Gunnlaugr snaketongue and Kormak have described the charms of their fair ones, and the warmth of their passion in glowing terms, the ordinary Icelandic marriage of the tenth century was much more a matter of business, in the first place, than of love. Though strong affection may have sprung up afterwards between husband and wife, the love was rather a consequence of the marriage than the marriage a result of the love.

When death came it was the duty of the next of kin to close the eyes and nostrils of the departed, and our Saga, in that most touching story of Rodny's behaviour after the death of her son Hauskuld, affords an instance of the custom. When Njal asks why she, the mother, as next of kin, had not closed the eyes and nostrils of the corpse, the mother answers, "That duty I meant for Skarphedinn". Skarphedinn then performs the duty, and, at the same time, undertakes the duty of revenge. In heathen times the burial took place on a "how" or cairn, in some commanding position near the abode of the dead, and now came another duty. This was the binding on of the "hellshoes," which the deceased was believed to need in heathen times on his way either to Valhalla's bright hall of warmth and mirth, or to Hell's dark realm of cold and sorrow. That duty over, the body was laid in the cairn with goods and arms, sometimes as we see was the case with Gunnar in a sitting posture; sometimes even in a ship, but always in a chamber formed of baulks of timber or blocks of stone, over which earth and gravel were piled....

Conclusion.

We are entitled to ask in what work of any age are the characters so boldly, and yet so delicately, drawn [as in this Saga]? Where shall we match the goodness and manliness of Gunnar, struggling with the storms of fate, and driven on by the wickedness of Hallgerda into quarrel after quarrel, which were none of his own seeking, but led no less surely to his own end? Where shall we match Hallgerda herself—that noble frame, so fair and tall, and yet with so foul a heart, the abode of all great crimes, and also the lurking place of tale-bearing and thieving? Where shall we find parallels to Skarphedinn's hastiness and readiness, as axe aloft he leapt twelve ells across Markfleet, and glided on to smite Thrain his death-blow on the slippery ice? where for Bergthora's love and tenderness for her husband, she who was given young to Njal, and could not find it in her heart to part from him when the house blazed over their heads? where for Kari's dash and gallantry, the man who dealt his blows straightforward, even in the Earl's hall, and never thought twice about them? where for Njal himself, the man who never dipped his hands in blood, who could unravel all the knotty points of the law; who foresaw all that was coming, whether for good or ill, for friend or for foe; who knew what his own end would be, though quite powerless to avert it; and when it came, laid him down to his rest, and never uttered sound or groan, though the flames roared loud around him? Nor are the minor characters less carefully drawn, the scolding tongue of Thrain's first wife, the mischief-making Thiostolf with his pole-axe, which divorced Hallgerda's first husband, Hrut's swordsmanship, Asgrim's dignity, Gizur's good counsel, Snorri's common sense and shrewdness, Gudmund's grandeur, Thorgeir's thirst for fame, Kettle's kindliness, Ingialld's heartiness, and, though last not least, Bjorn's boastfulness, which his gudewife is ever ready to cry down—are all sketched with a few sharp strokes which leave their mark for once and for ever on the reader's mind. Strange! were it not that human nature is herself in every age, that such forbearance and forgiveness as is shown by Njal and Hauskuld and Hall, should have shot up out of that social soil, so stained and steeped with the blood-shedding of revenge. Revenge was the great duty of Icelandic life, yet Njal is always ready to make up a quarrel, though he acknowledges the duty, when he refuses in his last moments to outlive his children, whom he feels himself unable to revenge. The last words of Hauskuld, when he was foully assassinated through the tale-bearing of Mord, were, "God help me and forgive you"; nor did the beauty of a Christian spirit ever shine out more brightly than in Hall, who, when his son Ljot, the flower of his flock, fell full of youth, and strength, and promise, in chance-medley at the battle on the Thingfield, at once for the sake of peace gave up the father's and the freeman's dearest rights, those of compensation and revenge, and allowed his son to fall unatoned in order that peace might be made. This struggle between the principle of an old system now turned to evil, and that of a new state of things which was still fresh and good, between heathendom as it sinks into superstition, and Christianity before it has had time to become superstitious, stands strongly forth in the latter part of the Saga; but as yet the new faith can only assert its forbearance and forgiveness in principle. It has not had time, except in some rare instances, to bring them into play in daily life. Even in heathen times such a deed as that by which Njal met his death, to hem a man in within his house and then to burn it and him together, to choke a freeman, as Skarphedinn says, like a fox in his earth, was quite against the free and open nature of the race; and though instances of such foul deeds occur besides those two great cases of Blundkettle and Njal, still they were always looked upon as atrocious crimes and punished accordingly. No wonder, therefore, then that Flosi, after the Change of Faith, when he makes up his mind to fire Njal's house, declares the deed to be one for which they would have to answer heavily before God, "seeing that we are Christian men ourselves"....

One word and we must bring this introduction to an end; it is merely to point out how calmly and peacefully the Saga ends, with the perfect reconciliation of Kari and Flosi, those generous foes, who throughout the bitter struggle in which they were engaged always treated each other with respect. It is a comfort to find, after the whole fitful story has been worked out, after passing from page to page, every one of which reeks with gore, to find that after all there were even in that bloodthirsty Iceland of the tenth century such things as peaceful old age and happy firesides, and that men like Flosi and Kari, who had both shed so much blood, one in a good and the other in a wicked cause, should after all die, Flosi on a trading voyage, an Icelandic Ulysses, in an unseaworthy ship, good enough, as he said, for an old and death-doomed man, Kari at home, well stricken in years, blessed with a famous and numerous offspring, and a proud but loving wife.

ICELANDIC CHRONOLOGY.

A.D. 850. Birth of Harold fairhair.

860. Harold fairhair comes to the throne.

870. Harold fairhair sole King in Norway.

871. Ingolf sets out for Iceland.

872. Battle of Hafrsfirth (Hafrsfjöðr).

874. Ingolf and Leif go to settle in Iceland.

877. Kettle hæng goes to Iceland.

880-884. Harold fairhair roots out the Vikings in the west.

888. Fall of Thorstein the red in Scotland.

890-900. Rush of settlers from the British Isles to Iceland.

892. Aud the deeply wealthy comes to Iceland.

900-920. The third period of the Landnámstide.

920. Harold fairhair shares the kingdom with his sons.

923. Hrut Hauskuld's brother born.

929. Althing established.

930. Hrafn Kettle hæng's son Speaker of the Law.

930-935. Njal born.

930. The Fleetlithe feud begins.

933. Death of Harold fairhair.

940. End of the Fleetlithe feud; Fiddle Mord a man of rank; Hamond Gunnar's son marries Mord's sister Rannveiga.

941. Fall of King Eric Bloodaxe.

c. 945. Gunnar of Lithend born.

955-960. Njal's sons born.

959. Glum marries Hallgerda.

960. Fall of King Hacon; Athelstane's foster-child, Harold Grayfell, King in Norway.

963. Hrut goes abroad.

965. Hrut returns to Iceland and marries Unna Mord's daughter.

968. Unna parts from Hrut.

969. Fiddle Mord and Hrut strive at the Althing; Fall of King Harold Grayfell; Earl Hacon rules in Norway.

970-971. Fiddle Mord's death; Gunnar and Hrut strive at the Althing.

972. Gunnar of Lithend goes abroad.

974. Gunnar returns to Iceland.

974. Gunnar's marriage with Hallgerda.

975. The slaying of Swart.

976. The slaying of Kol.

977. The slaying of Atli.

978. The slaying of Brynjolf the unruly and Thord Freedmanson.

979. The slaying of Sigmund the white.

983. Hallgerda steals from Otkell at Kirkby.

984. The suit for the theft settled at the Althing.

985. Otkell rides over Gunnar in the spring; fight at Rangriver just before the Althing; at the Althing Geir the priest and Gunnar strive; in the autumn Hauskuld Dale-Kolli's son, Gunnar's father-in-law, dies; birth of Hauskuld Thrain's son.

986. The fight at Knafahills, and death of Hjort Gunnar's brother.

987. The suit for those slain at Knafahills settled at the Althing.

988. Gunnar goes west to visit Olaf the peacock.

989. Slaying of Thorgeir Otkell's son before, and banishment of Gunnar at, the Althing; Njal's sons, Helgi and Grim, and Thrain Sigfus' son, go abroad.

990. Gunnar slain at Lithend.

992. Thrain returns to Iceland with Hrapp; Njal's sons ill-treated

by Earl Hacon for his sake.

994. Njal's sons return to Iceland, bringing Kari with them.

995. Death of Earl Hacon; Olaf Tryggvi's son King of Norway.

996. Skarphedinn slays Thrain.

997. Thangbrand sent by King Olaf to preach Christianity in Iceland.

998. Slaying of Arnor of Forswaterwood by Flosi's brothers at Skaptarfells Thing; Thangbrand's missionary journey; Gizur and Hjallti go abroad.

999. Hjallti Skeggi's son found guilty of blasphemy against the Gods at the Althing; Thangbrand returns to Norway.

1000. Gizur and Hjallti return to Iceland; the Change of Faith and Christianity brought into the law at the Althing on St. John's day, 24th June; fall of King Olaf Tryggvi's son at Svoldr, 9th September.

1001. Thorgeir the priest of Lightwater gives up the Speakership of the Law.

1002. Grim of Mossfell Speaker of the Law.

1003. Grim lays down the Speakership.

1003 or 1004. Skapti Thorod's son Speaker of the Law; the Fifth Court established; Hauskuld Thrain's son marries Hildigunna Flosi's niece and has one of the new priesthoods at Whiteness.

1006. Duels abolished in legal matters; slaying of Hauskuld Njal's son by Lyting and his brothers.

1009. Amund the blind slays Lyting; Valgard the guileful comes back to Iceland; his evil counsel to Mord; Mord begins to backbite and slander Hauskuld and Njal's sons to one another.

1111. Hauskald the Whiteness priest slain early in the spring; suit for his manslaughter at the Althing; Njal's Burning the autumn after.

1112. The suit for the Burning and battle at the Althing; Flosi and the Burners banished; Kari and Thorgeir Craggeir carry on the feud.

1113. Flosi goes abroad with the Burners, and Kari follows them; Flosi and Kari in Orkney.

1114. Brian's battle on Good Friday; Flosi goes to Rome.

1115. Flosi returns from Rome to Norway, and stays with Earl Eric, Earl Hacon's son.

1116. Flosi returns to Iceland; Kari goes to Rome and returns to Caithness; his wife Helga dies out in Iceland.

1117. Kari returns to Iceland, id reconciled with Flosi, and marries Hildigunna Hauskuld's widow.

CHAPTER I.

OF FIDDLE MORD.

There was a man named Mord whose surname was Fiddle; he was the son of Sigvat the Red, and he dwelt at the "Vale" in the Rangrivervales. He was a mighty chief, and a great taker up of suits, and so great a lawyer that no judgments were thought lawful unless he had a hand in them. He had an only daughter, named Unna. She was a fair, courteous and gifted woman, and that was thought the best match in all the Rangrivervales.

Now the story turns westward to the Broadfirth dales, where, at Hauskuldstede, in Laxriverdale, dwelt a man named Hauskuld, who was Dalakoll's son, and his mother's name was Thorgerda. He had a brother named Hrut, who dwelt at Hrutstede; he was of the same mother as Hauskuld, but his father's name was Heriolf. Hrut was handsome, tall and strong, well skilled in arms, and mild of temper; he was one of the wisest of men—stern towards his foes, but a good counsellor on great matters. It happened once that Hauskuld bade his friends to a feast, and his brother Hrut was there, and sat next him. Hauskuld had a daughter named Hallgerda, who was playing on the floor with some other girls. She was fair of face and tall of growth, and her hair was as soft as silk; it was so long, too, that it came down to her waist. Hauskuld called out to her, "Come hither to me, daughter". So she went up to him, and he took her by the chin, and kissed her; and after that she went away.

Then Hauskuld said to Hrut, "What dost thou think of this maiden? Is she not fair?" Hrut held his peace. Hauskuld said the same thing to him a second time, and then Hrut answered, "Fair enough is this maid, and many will smart for it, but this I know not, whence thief's eyes have come into our race". Then Hauskuld was wroth, and for a time the brothers saw little of each other.

CHAPTER II.

HRUT WOOS UNNA.

It happened once that those brothers, Hauskuld and Hrut, rode to the Althing, and there was much people at it. Then Hauskuld said to Hrut, "One thing I wish, brother, and that is, that thou wouldst better thy lot and woo thyself a wife."

Hrut answered, "That has been long on my mind, though there always seemed to be two sides to the matter; but now I will do as thou wishest; whither shall we turn our eyes?"

Hauskuld answered, "Here now are many chiefs at the Thing, and there is plenty of choice, but I have already set my eyes on a spot where a match lies made to thy hand. The woman's name is Unna, and she is a daughter of Fiddle Mord one of the wisest of men. He is here at the Thing, and his daughter too, and thou mayest see her if it pleases thee."

Now the next day, when men were going to the High Court, they saw some well-dressed women standing outside the booths of the men from the Rangrivervales, Then Hauskuld said to Hrut—

"Yonder now is Unna, of whom I spoke; what thinkest thou of her?"

"Well," answered Hrut; "but yet I do not know whether we should get on well together."

After that they went to the High Court, where Fiddle Mord was laying down the law as was his wont, and alter he had done he went home to his booth.

Then Hauskuld and Hrut rose, and went to Mord's booth. They went in and found Mord sitting in the innermost part of the booth, and they bade him "good day". He rose to meet them, and took Hauskuld by the hand and made him sit down by his side, and Hrut sat next to Hauskuld, So after they had talked much of this and that, at last Hauskuld said, "I have a bargain to speak to thee about; Hrut wishes to become thy son-in-law, and buy thy daughter, and I, for my part, will not be sparing in the matter".

Mord answered, "I know that thou art a great chief, but thy brother is unknown to me".

"He is a better man than I," answered Hauskuld.

"Thou wilt need to lay down a large sum with him, for she is heir to all I leave behind me," said Mord.

"There is no need," said Hauskuld, "to wait long before thou hearest what I give my word he shall have. He shall have Kamness and Hrutstede, up as far as Thrandargil, and a trading-ship beside, now on her voyage."

Then said Hrut to Mord, "Bear in mind, now, husband, that my brother has praised me much more than I deserve for love's sake; but if after what thou hast heard, thou wilt make the match, I am willing to let thee lay down the terms thyself".

Mord answered, "I have thought over the terms; she shall have sixty hundreds down, and this sum shall be increased by a third more in thine house, but if ye two have heirs, ye shall go halves in the goods".

Then said Hrut, "I agree to these terms, and now let us take witness". After that they stood up and shook hands, and Mord betrothed his daughter Unna to Hrut, and the bridal feast was to be at Mord's house, half a month after Midsummer.

Now both sides ride home from the Thing, and Hauskuld and Hrut ride westward by Hallbjorn's beacon. Then Thiostolf, the son of Biorn Gullbera of Reykiardale, rode to meet them, and told them how a ship had come out from Norway to the White River, and how aboard of her was Auzur, Hrut's father's brother, and he wished Hrut to come to him as soon as ever he could. When Hrut heard this, he asked Hauskuld to go with him to the ship, so Hauskuld went with his brother, and when they reached the ship, Hrut gave his kinsman Auzur a kind and hearty welcome. Auzur asked them into his booth to drink, so their horses were unsaddled, and they went in and drank, and while they were drinking, Hrut said to Auzur, "Now, kinsman, thou must ride west with me, and stay with me this winter."

"That cannot be, kinsman, for I have to tell thee the death of thy brother Eyvind, and he has left thee his heir at the Gula Thing, and now thy foes will seize thy heritage, unless thou comest to claim it."

"What's to be done now, brother?" said Hrut to Hauskuld, "for this seems a hard matter, coming just as I have fixed my bridal day."

"Thou must ride south," said Hauskuld, "and see Mord, and ask him to change the bargain which ye two have made, and to let his daughter sit for thee three winters as thy betrothed, but I will ride home and bring down thy wares to the ship."

Then said Hrut, "My wish is that thou shouldest take meal and timber, and whatever else thou needest out of the lading". So Hrut had his horses brought out, and he rode south, while Hauskuld rode home west. Hrut came east to the Rangrivervales to Mord, and had a good welcome, and he told Mord all his business, and asked his advice what he should do.

"How much money is this heritage?" asked Mord, and Hrut said it would come to a hundred marks, if he got it all.

"Well," said Mord, "that is much when set against what I shall leave behind me, and thou shalt go for it, if thou wilt."

After that they broke their bargain, and Unna was to sit waiting for Hrut three years as his betrothed. Now Hrut rides back to the ship, and stays by her during the summer, till she was ready to sail, and Hauskuld brought down all Hrut's wares and money to the ship, and Hrut placed all his other property in Hauskuld's hands to keep for him while he was away. Then Hauskuld rode home to his house, and a little while after they got a fair wind and sail away to sea. They were out three weeks, and the first land they made was Hern, near Bergen, and so sail eastward to the Bay.

CHAPTER III.

HRUT AND GUNNHILLDA, KINGS MOTHER.

At that time Harold Grayfell reigned in Norway; he was the son of Eric Bloodaxe, who was the son of Harold Fairhair; his mother's name was Gunnhillda, a daughter of Auzur Toti, and they had their abode east, at the King's Crag. Now the news was spread, how a ship had come thither east into the Bay, and as soon as Gunnhillda heard of it, she asked what men from Iceland were aboard, and they told her Hrut was the man's name, Auzur's brother's son. Then Gunnhillda said, "I see plainly that he means to claim his heritage, but there is a man named Soti, who has laid his hands on it".

After that she called her waiting-man, whose name was Augmund, and said—

"I am going to send thee to the Bay to find out Auzur and Hrut, and tell them that I ask them both to spend this winter with me. Say, too, that I will be their friend, and if Hrut will carry out my counsel, I will see after his suit, and anything else he takes in hand, and I will speak a good word, too, for him to the king."

After that he set off and found them; and as soon as they knew that he was Gunnhillda's servant, they gave him good welcome. He took them aside and told them his errand, and after that they talked over their plans by themselves. Then Auzur said to Hrut—

"Methinks, kinsman, here is little need for long talk, our plans are ready made for us; for I know Gunnhillda's temper; as soon as ever we say we will not go to her she will drive us out of the land, and take all our goods by force; but if we go to her, then she will do us such honour as she has promised."

Augmund went home, and when he saw Gunnhillda, he told her how his errand had ended, and that they would come, and Gunnhillda said—

"It is only what was to be looked for; for Hrut is said to be a wise and well-bred man; and now do thou keep a sharp look out, and tell me as soon as ever they come to the town."

Hrut and Auzur went east to the King's Crag, and when they reached the town, their kinsmen and friends went out to meet and welcome them. They asked, whether the king were in the town, and they told them he was. After that they met Augmund, and he brought them a greeting from Gunnhillda, saying, that she could not ask them to her house before they had seen the king, lest men should say, "I make too much of them". Still she would do all she could for them, and she went on, "tell Hrut to be outspoken before the king, and to ask to be made one of his body-guard"; "and here," said Augmund, "is a dress of honour which she sends to thee, Hrut, and in it thou must go in before the king". After that he went away.

The next day Hrut said—

"Let us go before the king."

"That may well be," answered Auzur.

So they went, twelve of them together, and all of them friends or kinsmen, and came into the hall where the king sat over his drink. Hrut went first and bade the king "good day," and the king, looking steadfastly at the man who was well-dressed, asked him his name. So he told his name.

"Art thou an Icelander?" said the king.

He answered, "Yes".

"What drove thee hither to seek us?"

Then Hrut answered—

"To see your state, lord; and, besides, because I have a great matter of inheritance here in the land, and I shall have need of your help, if I am to get my rights."

The king said—

"I have given my word that every man shall have lawful justice here in Norway; but hast thou any other errand in seeking me?"

"Lord!" said Hrut, "I wish you to let me live in your court, and become one of your men."

At this the king holds his peace, but Gunnhillda said—

"It seems to me as if this man offered you the greatest honour, for me thinks if there were many such men in the body-guard, it would be well filled."

"Is he a wise man?" asked the king.

"He is both wise and willing," said she.

"Well," said the king, "methinks my mother wishes that thou shouldst have the rank for which thou askest, but for the sake of our honour and the custom of the land, come to me in half a month's time, and then thou shalt be made one of my body-guard. Meantime, my mother will take care of thee, but then come to me."

Then Gunnhillda said to Augmund—

"Follow them to my house, and treat them well."

So Augmund went out, and they went with him, and he brought them to a hall built of stone, which was hung with the most beautiful tapestry, and there too was Gunnhillda's high-seat.

Then Augmund said to Hrut—

"Now will be proved the truth of all that I said to thee from Gunnhillda. Here is her high-seat, and in it thou shalt sit, and this seat thou shalt hold, though she comes herself into the hall."

After that he made them good cheer, and they had sat down but a little while when Gunnhillda came in. Hrut wished to jump up and greet her.

"Keep thy seat!" she says, "and keep it too all the time thou art my guest."

Then she sat herself down by Hrut, and they fell to drink, and at even she said—

"Thou shalt be in the upper chamber with me to-night, and we two together."

"You shall have your way," he answers.

After that they went to sleep, and she locked the door inside. So they slept that night, and in the morning fell to drinking again. Thus they spent their life all that half-month, and Gunnhillda said to the men who were there—

"Ye shall lose nothing except your lives if you say to any one a word of how Hrut and I are going on."

[When the half-month was over] Hrut gave her a hundred ells of household woollen and twelve rough cloaks, and Gunnhillda thanked him for his gifts. Then Hrut thanked her and gave her a kiss and went away. She bade him "farewell". And next day he went before the king with thirty men after him and bade the king "good-day". The king said—

"Now, Hrut, thou wilt wish me to carry out towards thee what I promised."

So Hrut was made one of the king's body-guard, and he asked, "Where shall I sit?"

"My mother shall settle that," said the king.

Then she got him a seat in the highest room, and he spent the winter with the king in much honour.

CHAPTER IV.

OF HRUT'S CRUISE.

When the spring came he asked about Soti, and found out he had gone south to Denmark with the inheritance. Then Hrut went to Gunnhillda and tells her what Soti had been about. Gunnhillda said—

"I will give thee two long-ships, full manned, and along with them the bravest men. Wolf the Unwashed, our overseer of guests; but still go and see the king before thou settest off."

Hrut did so; and when he came before the king, then he told the king of Soti's doings, and how he had a mind to hold on after him.

The king said, "What strength has my mother handed over to thee?"

"Two long-ships and Wolf the Unwashed to lead the men," says Hrut.

"Well given," says the king. "Now I will give thee other two ships, and even then thou'lt need all the strength thou'st got."

After that he went down with Hrut to the ship, and said "fare thee well". Then Hrut sailed away south with his crews.

CHAPTER V.

ATLI ARNVID SON'S SLAYING.

There was a man named Atli, son of Arnvid, Earl of East Gothland. He had kept back the taxes from Hacon Athelstane's foster child, and both father and son had fled away from Jemtland to Gothland. After that, Atli held on with his followers out of the Mælar by Stock Sound, and so on towards Denmark, and now he lies out in Öresound.[5] He is an outlaw both of the Dane-King and of the Swede-King. Hrut held on south to the Sound, and when he came into it he saw many ships in the Sound. Then Wolf said—

"What's best to be done now, Icelander?"

"Hold on our course," says Hrut, "'for nothing venture, nothing have'. My ship and Auzur's shall go first, but thou shalt lay thy ship where thou likest."

"Seldom have I had others as a shield before me," says Wolf, and lays his galley side by side with Hrut's ship; and so they hold on through the Sound. Now those who are in the Sound see that ships are coming up to them, and they tell Atli.

He answered, "Then maybe there'll be gain to be got".

After that men took their stand on board each ship; "but my ship," says Atli, "shall be in the midst of the fleet".

Meantime Hrut's ships ran on, and as soon as either side could hear the other's hail, Atli stood up and said—

"Ye fare unwarily. Saw ye not that war-ships were in the Sound? But what's the name of your chief?"

Hrut tells his name.

"Whose man art thou?" says Atli.

"One of king Harold Grayfell's body-guard."

Atli said, "'Tis long since any love was lost between us, father and son, and your Norway kings".

"Worse luck for thee," says Hrut.

"Well," says Atli, "the upshot of our meeting will be, that thou shalt not be left alive to tell the tale;" and with that he caught up a spear and hurled it at

Hrut's ship, and the man who stood before it got his death. After that the battle began, and they were slow in boarding Hrut's ship. Wolf, he went well forward, and with him it was now cut, now thrust. Atli's bowman's name was Asolf; he sprung up on Hrut's ship, and was four men's death before Hrut was ware of him; then he turned against him, and when they met, Asolf thrust at and through Hrut's shield, but Hrut cut once at Asolf, and that was his death-blow. Wolf the Unwashed saw that stroke, and called out—

"Truth to say, Hrut, thou dealest big blows, but thou'st much to thank Gunnhillda for."

"Something tells me," says Hrut, "that thou speakest with a 'fey' mouth."

Now Atli sees a bare place for a weapon on Wolf, and shot a spear through him, and now the battle grows hot: Atli leaps up on Hrut's ship, and clears it fast round about, and now Auzur turns to meet him, and thrust at him, but fell down full length on his back, for another man thrust at him. Now Hrut turns to meet Atli: he cut at once at Hrut's shield, and clove it all in two, from top to point; just then Atli got a blow on his hand from a stone, and down fell his sword. Hrut caught up the sword, and cut his foot from under him. After that he dealt him his death-blow. There they took much goods, and brought away with them two ships which were best, and stayed there only a little while. But meantime Soti and his crew had sailed past them, and he held on his course back to Norway, and made the land at Limgard's side. There Soti went on shore, and there he met Augmund, Gunnhillda's page; he knew him at once, and asks—

"How long meanest thou to be here?"

"Three nights," says Soti.

"Whither away, then?" says Augmund.

"West, to England," says Soti, "and never to come back again to Norway while Gunnhillda's rule is in Norway."

Augmund went away, and goes and finds Gunnhillda, for she was a little way off at a feast, and Gudred, her son, with her. Augmund told Gunnhillda what Soti meant to do, and she begged Gudred to take his life. So Gudred set off at once, and came unawares on Soti, and made them lead up the country, and hang him there. But the goods he took, and brought them to his mother, and she got men to carry them all down to the King's Crag, and after that she went thither herself.

Hrut came back towards autumn, and had gotten great store of goods. He went at once to the king, and had a hearty welcome. He begged them to take whatever they pleased of his goods, and the king took a third. Gunnhillda told Hrut how she had got hold of the inheritance, and had Soti slain. He thanked her, and gave her half of all he had.

CHAPTER VI.

HRUT SAILS OUT TO ICELAND.

Hrut stayed with the king that winter in good cheer, but when spring came he grew very silent. Gunnhillda finds that out, and said to him when they two were alone together—

"Art thou sick at heart?"

"So it is," said Hrut, "as the saying runs—'Ill goes it with those who are born on a barren land'."

"Wilt thou to Iceland?" she asks.

"Yes," he answered.

"Hast thou a wife out there?" she asked; and he answers, "No".

"But I am sure that is true," she says; and so they ceased talking about the matter.

[Shortly after] Hrut went before the king and bade him "good day"; and the king said, "What dost thou want now, Hrut?"

"I am come to ask, lord, that you give me leave to go to Iceland."

"Will thine honour be greater there than here?" asks the king.

"No, it will not," said Hrut; "but every one must win the work that is set before him."

"It is pulling a rope against a strong man," said Gunnhillda, "so give him leave to go as best suits him."

There was a bad harvest that year in the land, yet Gunnhillda gave Hrut as much meal as he chose to have; and now he busks him to sail out to Iceland, and Auzur with him; and when they were all-boun, Hrut went to find the king and Gunnhillda. She led him aside to talk alone, and said to him—

"Here is a gold ring which I will give thee;" and with that she clasped it round his wrist.

"Many good gifts have I had from thee," said Hrut.

Then she put her hands round his neck and kissed him, and said—

"If I have as much power over thee as I think, I lay this spell on thee that thou mayest never have any pleasure in living with that woman on whom thy heart is set in Iceland, but with other women thou mayest get on well enough, and now it is like to go well with neither of us;—but thou hast not believed what I have been saying."

Hrut laughed when he heard that, and went away; after that he came before the king and thanked him; and the king spoke kindly to him, and bade him "farewell". Hrut went straight to his ship, and they had a fair wind all the way until they ran into Borgarfirth.

As soon as the ship was made fest to the land, Hrut rode west home, but Auzur stayed by the ship to unload her, and lay her up. Hrut rode straight to Hauskuldstede, and Hauskuld gave him a hearty welcome, and Hrut told him all about his travels. After that they sent men east across the rivers to tell Fiddle Mord to make ready for the bridal feast; but the two brothers rode to the ship, and on the way Hauskuld told Hrut how his money matters stood, and his goods had gained much since he was away. Then Hrut said—

"The reward is less worth than it ought to be, but I will give thee as much meal as thou needst for thy household next winter."

Then they drew the ship on land on rollers, and made her snug in her shed, but all the wares on board her they carried away into the Dales westward. Hrut stayed at home at Hrutstede till winter was six weeks off, and then the brothers made ready, and Auzur with them, to ride to Hrut's wedding. Sixty men ride with them, and they rode east till they came to Rangriver plains. There they found a crowd of guests, and the men took their seats on benches down the length of the hall, but the women were seated on the cross benches on the dais, and the bride was rather downcast. So they drank out the feast and it went off well. Mord pays down his daughter's portion, and she rides west with her husband and his train. So they ride till they reach home. Hrut gave over everything into her hands inside the house, and all were pleased at that; but for all that she and Hrut did not pull well together as man and wife, and so things went on till spring, and when spring came Hrut had a journey to make to the Westfirths, to get in the money for which he had sold his wares; but before he set off his wife says to him—

"Dost thou mean to be back before men ride to the Thing?"

"Why dost thou ask?" said Hrut.

"I will ride to the Thing," she said, "to meet my father."

"So it shall be," said he, "and I will ride to the Thing along with thee."

"Well and good," she says.

After that Hrut rode from home west to the Firths, got in all his money, and laid it out anew, and rode home again. When he came home he busked him to ride to the Thing, and made all his neighbours ride with him. His brother Hauskuld rode among the rest. Then Hrut said to his wife—

"If thou hast as much mind now to go to the Thing as thou saidst a while ago, busk thyself and ride along with me."

She was not slow in getting herself ready, and then they all rode to the Thing. Unna went to her father's booth, and he gave her a hearty welcome, but she seemed somewhat heavy-hearted, and when he saw that he said to her—

"I have seen thee with a merrier face. Hast thou anything on thy mind?"

She began to weep, and answered nothing. Then he said to her again, "Why dost thou ride to the Thing, if thou wilt not tell me thy secret? Dost thou dislike living away there in the west?"

Then she answered him—

"I would give all I own in the world that I had never gone thither."

"Well!" said Mord, "I'll soon get to the bottom of this." Then he sends men to fetch Hauskuld and Hrut, and they came straightway; and when they came in to see Mord, he rose up to meet them and gave them a hearty welcome, and asked them to sit down. Then they talked a long time in a friendly way, and at last Mord said to Hauskuld—

"Why does my daughter think so ill of life in the west yonder?"

"Let her speak out," said Hrut, "if she has anything to lay to my charge."

But she brought no charge against him. Then Hrut made them ask his neighbours and household how he treated her, and all bore him good witness, saying that she did just as she pleased in the house.

Then Mord said, "Home thou shalt go, and be content with thy lot; for all the witness goes better for him than for thee".

After that Hrut rode home from the Thing, and his wife with him, and all went smoothly between them that summer; but when spring came it was the old story over again, and things grew worse and worse as the spring went on. Hrut had again a journey to make west to the Firths, and gave out that he would not ride to the Althing, but Unna his wife said little about it. So Hrut went away west to the Firths.

CHAPTER VII.

UNNA SEPARATES FROM HRUT.

Now the time for the Thing was coming on, Unna spoke to Sigmund Auzur's son, and asked if he would ride to the Thing with her; he said he could not ride if his kinsman Hrut set his face against it.

"Well!" says she, "I spoke to thee because I have better right to ask this from thee than from any one else."

He answered, "I will make a bargain with thee: thou must promise to ride back west with me, and to have no underhand dealings against Hrut or myself".

So she promised that, and then they rode to the Thing. Her father Mord was at the Thing, and was very glad to see her, and asked her to stay in his booth white the Thing lasted, and she did so.

"Now," said Mord, "what hast thou to tell me of thy mate, Hrut?"

Then she sung him a song, in which she praised Hrut's liberality, but said he was not master of himself. She herself was ashamed to speak out.

Mord was silent a short time, and then said—

"Thou hast now that on thy mind I see, daughter, which thou dost not wish that any one should know save myself, and thou wilt trust to me rather than any one else to help thee out of thy trouble."

Then they went aside to talk, to a place where none could overhear what they said; and then Mord said to his daughter—

"Now tell me all that is between you two, and don't make more of the matter than it is worth."

"So it shall be," she answered, and sang two songs, in which she revealed the cause of their misunderstanding; and when Mord pressed her to speak out, she told him how she and Hrut could not live together, because he was spell-bound, and that she wished to leave him.

"Thou didst right to tell me all this," said Mord, "and now I will give thee a piece of advice, which will stand thee in good stead, if thou canst carry it out to the letter. First of all, thou must ride home from the Thing, and by that time thy husband will have come back, and will be glad to see thee; thou must he blithe and buxom to him, and he will think a good change has come over thee, and thou must show no signs of coldness or ill-temper, but when spring comes thou must sham sickness, and take to thy bed. Hrut will not lose time in guessing what thy sickness can be, nor will he scold thee at all, but he will rather beg every one to take all the care they can of thee. After that he will set off west to the Firths, and Sigmund with him, for he will have to flit all his goods home from the Firths west, and he will be away till the summer is far spent. But when men ride to the Thing, and after all have ridden from the Dales that mean to ride thither, then thou must rise from thy bed and summon men to go along with thee to the Thing; and when thou art all-boun, then shalt thou go to thy bed, and the men with thee who are to bear thee company, and thou shalt take witness before thy husband's bed, and declare thyself separated from him by such a lawful separation as may hold good according to the judgment of the Great Thing, and the laws of the land; and at the man's door [the main door of the house] thou shalt take the same witness. After that ride away, and ride over Laxriverdale Heath, and so on over Holtbeacon Heath; for they will look for thee by way of Hrutfirth. And so ride on till thou comest to me; then I will see after the matter. But into his hands thou shalt never come more."

Now she rides home from the Thing, and Hrut had come back before her, and made her hearty welcome. She answered him kindly, and was blithe and forbearing towards him. So they lived happily together that half-year; but when spring came she fell sick, and kept her bed. Hrut set off west to the Firths, and bade them tend her well before he went. Now, when the time for the Thing comes, she busked herself to ride away, and did in every way as had been laid down for her; and then she rides away to the Thing. The country folk looked for her, but could not find her. Mord made his daughter welcome, and asked her if she had followed his advice; and she says, "I have not broken one tittle of it".

Then she went to the Hill of Laws, and declared herself separated from Hrut; and men thought this strange news. Unna went home with her father, and never went west from that day forward.

CHAPTER VIII.

MORD CLAIMS HIS GOODS FROM HRUT.

Hrut came home, and knit his brows when he heard his wife was gone, but yet kept his feelings well in hand, and stayed at home all that half-year, and spoke to no one on the matter. Next summer he rode to the Thing, with his brother Hauskuld, and they had a great following. But when he came to the Thing, he asked whether Fiddle Mord were at the Thing, and they told him he was; and all thought they would come to words at once about their matter, but it was not so. At last, one day when the brothers and others who were at the Thing went to the Hill of Laws, Mord took witness and declared that he had a money-suit against Hrut for his daughter's dower, and reckoned the amount at ninety hundreds in goods, calling on Hrut at the same time to pay and hand it over to him, and asking for a fine of three marks. He laid the suit in the Quarter Court, into which it would come by law, and gave lawful notice, so that all who stood on the Hill of Laws might hear.

But when he had thus spoken, Hrut said—

"Thou hast undertaken this suit, which belongs to thy daughter, rather for the greed of gain and love of strife than in kindliness and manliness. But I shall have something to say against it; for the goods which belong to me are not yet in thy hands. Now, what I have to say is this, and I say it out, so that all who hear me on this hill may bear witness: I challenge thee to fight on the island; there on one side shall be laid all thy daughter's dower, and on the other I will lay down goods worth as much, and whoever wins the day shall have both dower and goods; but if thou wilt not fight with me, then thou shalt give up all claim to these goods."

Then Mord held his peace, and took counsel with his friends about going to fight on the island, and Jorund the priest gave him an answer.

"There is no need for thee to come to ask us for counsel in this matter, for thou knowest if thou fightest with Hrut thou wilt lose both life and goods. He has a good cause, and is besides mighty in himself and one of the boldest of men."

Then Mord spoke out, that he would not fight with Hrut, and there arose a great shout and hooting on the hill, and Mord got the greatest shame by his suit.

After that men ride home from the Thing, and those brothers Hauskuld and Hrut ride west to Reykiardale, and turned in as guests at Lund, where Thiostolf, Biorn Gullbera's son, then dwelt. There had been much rain that day, and men got wet, so long-fires were made down the length of the hall. Thiostolf, the master of the house, sat between Hauskuld and Hrut, and two boys, of whom Thiostolf had the rearing, were playing on the floor, and a girl was playing with them. They were great chatterboxes, for they were too young to know better. So one of them said—

"Now, I will be Mord, and summon thee to lose thy wife because thou hast not been a good husband to her."

Then the other answered—

"I will be Hrut, and I call on thee to give up all claim to thy goods, if thou darest not to fight with me."

This they said several times, and all the household burst out laughing. Then Hauskuld got wroth, and struck the boy who called himself Mord with a switch, and the blow fell on his face, and graced the skin.

"Get out with thee," said Hauskuld to the boy, "and make no game of us;" but Hrut said, "Come hither to me," and the boy did so. Then Hrut drew a ring from his finger and gave it to him, and said—

"Go away, and try no man's temper henceforth."

Then the boy went away saying—

"Thy manliness I will bear in mind all my life."

From this matter Hrut got great praise, and after that they went home; and that was the end of Mord's and Hrut's quarrel.

CHAPTER IX.

THORWALD GETS HALLGERDA TO WIFE.

Now, it must be told how Hallgerda, Hauskuld's daughter, grows up, and is the fairest of women to look on; she was tall of stature, too, and therefore she was called "Longcoat". She was fair-haired, and had so much of it that she could hide herself in it; but she was lavish and hard-hearted. Her foster-father's name was Thiostolf; he was a South islander[6] by stock; he was a strong man, well skilled in arms, and had slain many men, and made no atonement in money for one of them. It was said, too, that his rearing had not bettered Hallgerda's temper.

There was a man named Thorwald; he was Oswif's son, and dwelt out on Middlefells strand, under the Fell. He was rich and well to do, and owned the islands called Bear-isles, which lie out in Broadfirth, whence he got meal and stock fish. This Thorwald was a strong and courteous man, though somewhat hasty in temper. Now, it fell out one day that Thorwald and his father were talking together of Thorwald's marrying, and where he had best look for a wife, and it soon came out that he thought there wasn't a match fit for him far or near.

"Well," said Oswif, "wilt thou ask for Hallgerda Longcoat, Hauskuld's daughter?"

"Yes! I will ask for her," said Thorwald.

"But that is not a match that will suit either of you," Oswif went on to say, "for she has a will of her own, and thou art stern-tempered and unyielding."

"For all that I will try my luck there," said Thorwald, "so it's no good trying to hinder me."

"Ay!" said Oswif, "and the risk is all thine own."

After that they set off on a wooing journey to Hauskuldstede, and had a hearty welcome. They were not long in telling Hauskuld their business, and began to woo; then Hauskuld answered—

"As for you, I know how you both stand in the world, but for my own part I will use no guile towards you. My daughter has a hard temper, but as to her looks and breeding you can both see for yourselves."

"Lay down the terms of the match," answered Thorwald, "for I will not let her temper stand in the way of our bargain."

Then they talked over the terms of the bargain, and Hauskuld never asked his daughter what she thought of it, for his heart was set on giving her away, and so they came to an understanding as to the terms of the match. After that Thorwald betrothed himself to Hallgerda, and rode away home when the matter was settled.

CHAPTER X.

HALLGERDA'S WEDDING.

Hauskuld told Hallgerda of the bargain he had made, and she said—

"Now that has been put to the proof which I have all along been afraid of, that thou lovest me not so much as thou art always saying, when thou hast not thought it worth while to tell me a word of all this matter. Besides, I do not think the match as good a one as thou hast always promised me."

So she went on, and let them know in every way that she thought she was thrown away.

Then Hauskuld said—

"I do not set so much store by thy pride as to let it stand in the way of my bargains; and my will, not thine, shall carry the day if we fell out on any point."

"The pride of all you kinsfolk is great," she said, "and so it is not wonderful if I have some of it."

With that she went away, and found her foster-father Thiostolf, and told him what was in store for her, and was very heavy-hearted. Then Thiostolf said—

"Be of good cheer, for thou wilt be married a second time, and then they will ask thee what thou thinkest of the match; for I will do in all things as thou wishest, except in what touches thy father or Hrut."

After that they spoke no more of the matter, and Hauskuld made ready the bridal feast, and rode off to ask men to it. So he came to Hrutstede and called Hrut out to speak with him. Hrut went out, and they began to talk, and Hauskuld told him the whole story of the bargain, and bade him to the feast, saying—

"I should be glad to know that thou dost not feel hurt though I did not tell thee when the bargain was being made."

"I should be better pleased," said Hrut, "to have nothing at all to do with it; for this match will bring luck neither to him nor to her; but still I will come to the feast if thou thinkest it will add any honour to thee."

"Of course I think so," said Hauskuld, and rode off home.

Oswif and Thorwald also asked men to come, so that no fewer than one hundred guests were asked.

There was a man named Swan, who dwelt in Bearfirth, which lies north from Steingrimsfirth. This Swan was a great wizard, and he was Hallgerda's mother's brother. He was quarrelsome, and hard to deal with, but Hallgerda asked him to the feast, and sends Thiostolf to him; so he went, and it soon got to friendship between him and Swan.

Now men come to the feast, and Hallgerda sat upon the cross-bench, and she was a very merry bride. Thiostolf was always talking to her, though he sometimes found time to speak to Swan, and men thought their talking strange. The feast went off well, and Hauskuld paid down Hallgerda's portion with the greatest readiness. After he had done that, he said to Hrut—

"Shall I bring out any gifts beside?"

"The day will come," answered Hrut, "when thou wilt have to waste thy goods for Hallgerda's sake, so hold thy hand now."

CHAPTER XI.

THORWALD'S SLAYING.

Thorwald rode home from the bridal feast, and his wife with him, and Thiostolf, who rode by her horse's side, and still talked to her in a low voice. Oswif turned to his son and said—

"Art thou pleased with thy match? and how went it when ye talked together?"

"Well," said he, "she showed all kindness to me. Thou mightst see that by the way she laughs at every word I say."

"I don't think her laughter so hearty as thou dost," answered Oswif, "but this will be put to the proof by and by."

So they ride on till they come home, and at night she took her seat by her husband's side, and made room for Thiostolf next herself on the inside. Thiostolf and Thorwald had little to do with each other, and few words were thrown away between them that winter, and so time went on. Hallgerda was prodigal and grasping, and there was nothing that any of their neighbours had that she must not have too, and all that she had, no matter whether it were her own or belonged to others, she waited. But when the spring came there was a scarcity in the house, both of meal and stock fish, so Hallgerda went up to Thorwald and said—

"Thou must not be sitting indoors any longer, for we want for the house both meal and fish."

"Well," said Thorwald, "I did not lay in less for the house this year than I laid in before, and then it used to last till summer."

"What care I," said Hallgerda, "if thou and thy father have made your money by starving yourselves."

Then Thorwald got angry and gave her a blow on the face and drew blood, and went away and called his men and ran the skiff down to the shore. Then six of them jumped into her and rowed out to the Bear-isles, and began to load her with meal and fish.

Meantime it is said that Hallgerda sat out of doors heavy at heart. Thiostolf went up to her and saw the wound on her face, and said—

"Who has been playing thee this sorry trick?"

"My husband Thorwald," she said, "and thou stoodst aloof, though thou wouldst not if thou hadst cared at all for me."

"Because I knew nothing about it," said Thiostolf, "but I will avenge it."

Then he went away down to the shore and ran out a six-oared boat, and held in his hand a great axe that he had with a haft overlaid with iron. He steps into the boat and rows out to the Bear-isles, and when he got there all the men had rowed away but Thorwald and his followers, and he stayed by the skiff to load her, while they brought the goods down to him. So Thiostolf came up just then and jumped into the skiff and began to load with him, and after a while he said—

"Thou canst do but little at this work, and that little thou dost badly."

"Thinkest thou thou canst do it better?" said Thorwald.

"There's one thing to be done which I can do better than thou," said Thiostolf, and then he went on—

"The woman who is thy wife has made a bad match, and you shall not live much longer together."

Then Thorwald snatched up a fishing-knife that lay by him, and made a stab at Thiostolf; he had lifted his axe to his shoulder and dashed it down. It came on Thorwald's arm and crushed the wrist, but down fell the knife. Then Thiostolf lifted up his axe a second time and gave Thorwald a blow on the head, and he fell dead on the spot.

CHAPTER XII.

THIOSTOLF'S FLIGHT.

While this was going on, Thorwald's men came down with their load, but Thiostolf was not slow in his plans. He hewed with both hands at the gunwale of the skiff and cut it down about two planks; then he leapt into his boat, but the dark blue sea poured into the skiff, and down she went with all her freight. Down too sank Thorwald's body, so that his men could not see what had been done to him, but they knew well enough that he was dead, Thiostolf rowed away up the firth, but they shouted after him wishing him ill luck. He made them no answer, but rowed on till he got home, and ran the boat up on the beach, and went up to the house with his axe, all bloody as it was, on his shoulder. Hallgerda stood out of doors, and said—

"Thine axe is bloody; what hast thou done?"

"I have done now what will cause thee to be wedded a second time."

"Thou tellest me then that Thorwald is dead?" she said.

"So it is," said he, "and now look out for my safety."

"So I will," she said; "I will send thee north to Bearfirth, to Swanshol, and Swan, my kinsman, will receive thee with open arms. He is so mighty a man that no one will seek thee thither."

So he saddled a horse that she had, and jumped on his back, and rode off north to Bearfirth, to Swanshol, and Swan received him with open arms, and said—

"That's what I call a man who does not stick at trifles! And now I promise thee if they seek thee here, they shall get nothing but the greatest shame."

Now, the story goes back to Hallgerda, and how she behaved. She called on Liot the black, her kinsman, to go with her, and bade him saddle their horses, for she said—"I will ride home to my father".

While he made ready for their journey, she went to her chests and unlocked them, and called all the men of her house about her, and gave each of them some gift; but they all grieved at her going. Now she rides home to her father; and he received her well, for as yet he had not heard the news. But Hrut said to Hallgerda—

"Why did not Thorwald come with thee?" and she answered—

"He is dead."

Then Said Hauskuld—

"That was Thiostolf's doing?"

"It was," she said.

"Ah!" said Hauskuld, "Hrut was not for wrong when he told me that this bargain would draw mickle misfortune after it. But there's no good in troubling one's self about a thing that's done and gone."

Now the story must go back to Thorwald's mates, how there they ate, and how they begged the loan of a boat to get to the mainland. So a boat was lent them at once, and they rowed up the firth to Reykianess, and found Oswif, and told him these tidings.

He said, "Ill luck is the end of ill redes, and now I see how it has all gone. Hallgerda must have sent Thiostolf to Bearfirth, but she herself must have ridden home to her father. Let us now gather folk and follow him up thither north." So they did that, and went about asking for help, and got together many men. And then they all rode off to Steingrims river, and so on to Liotriverdale and Selriverdale, till they came to Bearfirth.

Now Swan began to speak, and gasped much. "Now Oswif's fetches are seeking us out." Then up sprung Thiostolf, but Swan said, "Go thou out with me, there won't be need of much". So they went out both of them, and Swan took a goatskin and wrapped it about his own head, and said, "Become mist and fog, become fright and wonder mickle to all those who seek thee".

Now, it must be told how Oswif, his friends, and his men are riding along the ridge; then came a great mist against them, and Oswif said, "This is Swan's doing; 'twere well if nothing worse followed". A little after a mighty darkness came before their eyes, so that they could see nothing, and then they fell off their horses' backs, and lost their horses, and dropped their weapons, and went over head and ears into bogs, and some went astray into the wood, till they were on the brink of bodily harm. Then Oswif said, "If I could only find my horse and weapons, then I'd turn back"; and he had scarce spoken these words than they saw somewhat, and found their horses and weapons. Then many still egged the others on to look after the chase once more; and so they did, and at once the same wonders befell them, and so they fared thrice. Then Oswif said, "Though the course be not good, let us still turn back. Now, we will take counsel a second time, and what now pleases my mind best, is to go and find Hauskuld, and ask atonement for my son; for there's hope of honour where there's good store of it."

So they rode thence to the Broadfirth dales, and there is nothing to be told about them till they come to Hauskuldstede, and Hrut was there before them. Oswif called out Hauskuld and Hrut, and they both went out and bade him good-day. After that they began to talk. Hauskuld asked Oswif whence he came. He said he had set out to search for Thiostolf, but couldn't find him. Hauskuld said he must have gone north to Swanshol, "and thither it is not every man's lot to go to find him".

"Well," says Oswif, "I am come hither for this, to ask atonement for my son from thee."

Hauskuld answered—"I did not slay thy son, nor did I plot his death; still it may be forgiven thee to look for atonement somewhere".

"Nose is next of kin, brother, to eyes," said Hrut, "and it is needful to stop all evil tongues, and to make him atonement for his son, and so mend thy daughter's state, for that will only be the case when this suit is dropped, and the less that is said about it the better it will be."

Hauskuld said—"Wilt thou undertake the award?"

"That I will," says Hrut, "nor will I shield thee at all in my award; for if the truth must be told thy daughter planned his death."

Then Hrut held his peace some little while, and afterwards he stood up, and said to Oswif—"Take now my hand in handsel as a token that thou lettest the suit drop".

So Oswif stood up and said—"This is not an atonement on equal terms when thy brother utters the award, but still thou (speaking to Hrut) hast behaved so well about it that I trust thee thoroughly to make it" Then he stood up and took Hauskuld's hand, and came to an atonement in the matter, on the understanding that Hrut was to make up his mind and utter the award before Oswif went away. After that, Hrut made his award, and said—"For the slaying of Thorwald I award two hundred in silver"—that was then thought a good price for a man—"and thou shalt pay it down at once, brother, and pay it too with an open hand".

Hauskuld did so, and then Hrut said to Oswif—"I will give thee a good cloak which I brought with me from foreign lands".

He thanked him for his gift, and went home well pleased at the way in which things had gone.

After that Hauskuld and Hrut came to Oswif to share the goods, and they and Oswif came to a good agreement about that too, and they went home with their share of the goods, and Oswif is now out of our story. Hallgerda begged Hauskuld to let her come back home to him, and he gave her leave, and for a long time there was much talk about Thorwald's slaying. As for Hallgerda'a goods they went on growing till they were worth a great sum.

CHAPTER XIII.

GLUM'S WOOING.

Now three brothers are named in the story. One was called Thorarin, the second Ragi, and the third Glum. They were the sons of Olof the Halt, and were men of much worth and of great wealth in goods. Thorarin's surname was Ragi's brother; he had the Speakership of the Law after Rafn Heing's son. He was a very wise man, and lived at Varmalek, and he and Glum kept house together. Glum had been long abroad; he was a tall, strong, handsome man. Ragi their brother was a great man-slayer. Those brothers owned in the south Engey and Laugarness. One day the brothers Thorarin and Glum were talking together, and Thorarin asked Glum whether he meant to go abroad, as was his wont.

He answered—"I was rather thinking now of leaving off trading voyages".

"What hast thou then in thy mind? Wilt thou woo thee a wife?"

"That I will," says he, "if I could only get myself well matched."

Then Thorarin told off all the women who were unwedded in Borgarfirth, and asked him if he would have any of these—"Say the word, and I will ride with thee!"

But Glum answered—"I will have none of these".

"Say then the name of her thou wishest to have," says Thorarin.

Glum answered—"If thou must know, her name is Hallgerda, and she is Hauskuld's daughter away west in the dales".

"Well," says Thorarin, "'tis not with thee as the saw says, 'be warned by another's woe'; for she was wedded to a man, and she plotted his death."

Glum said—"May be such ill-luck will not befall her a second time, and sure I am she will not plot my death. But now, if thou wilt show me any honour, ride along with me to woo her."

Thorarin said—"There's no good striving against it, for what must be is sure to happen". Glum often talked the matter over with Thorarin, but he put it off a long time. At last it came about that they gathered men together and rode off ten in company, west to the dales, and came to Hauskuldstede. Hauskuld gave them a hearty welcome, and they stayed there that night. But early next morning, Hauskuld sends Hrut, and he came thither at once;

and Hauskuld was out of doors when he rode into the "town". Then Hauskuld told Hrut what men had come thither.

"What may it be they want?" asked Hrut

"As yet," says Hauskuld, "they have not let out to me that they have any business."

"Still," says Hrut, "their business must be with thee. They will ask the hand of thy daughter, Hallgerda. If they do, what answer wilt thou make?"

"What dost thou advise me to say?" says Hauskuld.

"Thou shalt answer well," says Hrut; "but still make a clean breast of all the good and all the ill thou knowest of the woman."

But while the brothers were talking thus, out came the guests. Hauskuld greeted them well, and Hrut bade both Thorarin and his brothers good morning. After that they all began to talk, and Thorarin said—

"I am come hither, Hauskuld, with my brother Glum on this errand, to ask for Hallgerda thy daughter, at the hand of my brother Glum. Thou must know that he is a man of worth."

"I know well," says Hauskuld, "that ye are both of you powerful and worthy men; but I must tell you right out, that I chose a husband for her before, and that turned out most unluckily for us."

Thorarin answered—"We will not let that stand in the way of the bargain; for one oath shall not become all oaths, and this may prove to be a good match, though that turned out ill; besides Thiostolf had most hand in spoiling it".

Then Hrut spoke: "Now I will give you a bit of advice—this: if ye will not let all this that has already happened to Hallgerda stand in the way of the match, mind you do not let Thiostolf go south with her if the match comes off, and that he is never there longer than three nights at a time, unless Glum gives him leave, but fall an outlaw by Glum's hand without atonement if he stay there longer. Of course, it shall be in Glum's power to give him leave; but he will not if he takes my advice. And now this match, shall not be fulfilled, as the other was, without Hallgerda's knowledge. She shall now know the whole course of this bargain, and see Glum, and herself settle whether she will have him or not; and then she will not be able to lay the blame on others if it does not turn out well. And all this shall be without craft or guile."

Then Thorarin said—"Now, as always, it will prove best if thy advice be taken".

Then they sent for Hallgerda, and she came thither, and two women with her. She had on a cloak of rich blue wool, and under it a scarlet kirtle, and a silver girdle round her waist, but her hair came down on both sides of her bosom, and she had turned the locks up under her girdle. She sat down between Hrut and her father, and she greeted them all with kind words, and spoke well and boldly, and asked what was the news. After that she ceased speaking.

Then Glum said—"There has been some talk between thy father and my brother Thorarin and myself about a bargain. It was that I might get thee, Hallgerda, if it be thy will, as it is theirs; and now, if thou art a brave woman, thou wilt say right out whether the match is at all to thy mind; but if thou hast anything in thy heart against this bargain with us, then we will not say anything more about it."

Hallgerda said—"I know well that you are men of worth and might, ye brothers. I know too that now I shall be much better wedded than I was before; but what I want to know is, what you have said already about the match, and how far you have given your words in the matter. But so far as I now see of thee, I think I might love thee well if we can but hit it off as to temper."

So Glum himself told her all about the bargain, and left nothing out, and then he asked Hauskuld and Hrut whether he had repeated it right. Hauskuld said he had; and then Hallgerda said—"Ye have dealt so well with me in this matter, my father and Hrut, that I will do what ye advise, and this bargain shall be struck as ye have settled it".

Then Hrut said—"Methinks it were best that Hauskuld and I should name witnesses, and that Hallgerda should betroth herself, if the Lawman thinks that right and lawful".

"Right and lawful it is," says Thorarin.

After that Hallgerda's goods were valued, and Glum was to lay down as much against them, and they were to go shares, half and half, in the whole. Then Glum bound himself to Hallgerda as his betrothed, and they rode away home south; but Hauskuld was to keep the wedding-feast at his house. And now all is quiet till men ride to the wedding.

CHAPTER XIV.

GLUM'S WEDDING.

Those brothers gathered together a great company, and they were all picked men. They rode west to the dales and came to Hauskuldstede, and there they found a great gathering to meet them. Hauskuld and Hrut, and their friends, filled one bench, and the bridegroom the other. Hallgerda sat upon the cross-bench on the dais, and behaved well. Thiostolf went about with his axe raised in air, and no one seemed to know that he was there, and so the wedding went off well. But when the feast was over, Hallgerda went away south with Glum and his brothers. So when they came south to Varmalek, Thorarin asked Hallgerda if she would undertake the housekeeping, "No, I will not," she said. Hallgerda kept her temper down that winter, and they liked her well enough. But when the spring came, the brothers talked about their property, and Thorarin said—"I will give up to you the house at Varmalek, for that is readiest to your hand, and I will go down south to Laugarness and live there, but Engey we will have both of us in common".

Glum was willing enough to do that. So Thorarin went down to the south of that district, and Glum and his wife stayed behind there, and lived in the house at Varmalek.

Now Hallgerda got a household about her; she was prodigal in giving, and grasping in getting. In the summer she gave birth to a girl. Glum asked her what name it was to have.

"She shall be called after my father's mother, and her name shall be Thorgerda," for she came down from Sigurd Fafnir's-bane on the father's side, according to the family pedigree.

So the maiden was sprinkled with water, and had this name given her, and there she grew up, and got like her mother in looks and feature. Glum and Hallgerda agreed well together, and so it went on for a while. About that time these tidings were heard from the north and Bearfirth, how Swan had rowed out to fish in the spring, and a great storm came down on him from the east, and how he was driven ashore at Fishless, and he and his men were there lost. But the fishermen who were at Kalback thought they saw Swan go into the fell at Kalbackshorn, and that he was greeted well; but some spoke against that story, and said there was nothing in it.

But this all knew that he was never seen again either alive or dead. So when Hallgerda heard that, she thought she had a great loss in her mother's brother. Glum begged Thorarin to change lands with him, but he said he would not; "but," said he, "if I outlive you, I mean to have Varmalek to myself". When Glum told this to Hallgerda, she said, "Thorarin has indeed a right to expect this from us".

CHAPTER XV.

THIOSTOLF GOES TO GLUM'S HOUSE.

Thiostolf had beaten one of Hauskuld's house-carles, so he drove him away. He took his horse and weapons, and said to Hauskuld—

"Now, I will go away and never come back."

"All will be glad at that," says Hauskuld.

Thiostolf rode till he came to Varmalek, and there he got a hearty welcome from Hallgerda, and not a bad one from Glum. He told Hallgerda how her father had driven him away, and begged her to give him her help and countenance. She answered him by telling him she could say nothing about his staying there before she had seen Glum about it.

"Does it go well between you?" he says.

"Yes," she says, "our love runs smooth enough."

After that she went to speak to Glum, and threw her arms round his neck and said—

"Wilt thou grant me a boon which I wish to ask of thee?"

"Grant it I will," he says, "if it be right and seemly; but what is it thou wishest to ask?"

"Well," she said, "Thiostolf has been driven away from the west, and what I want thee to do is to let him stay here; but I will not take it crossly if it is not to thy mind."

Glum said—"Now that thou behavest so well, I will grant thee thy boon; but I tell thee, if he takes to any ill he shall be sent off at once".

She goes then to Thiostolf and tells him, and he answered—

"Now, thou art still good, as I had hoped."

After that he was there, and kept himself down a little while, but then it was the old story, he seemed to spoil all the good he found; for he gave way to no one save to Hallgerda alone, but she never took his side in his brawls with others. Thorarin, Glum's brother, blamed him for letting him be there, and said ill luck would come of it, and all would happen as had happened before if he were there. Glum answered him well and kindly, but still kept on in his own way.

CHAPTER XVI.

GLUM'S SHEEP HUNT.

Now once on a time when autumn came, it happened that men had hard work to get their flocks home, and many of Glum's wethers were missing. Then Glum said to Thiostolf—

"Go thou up on the fell with my house-carles and see if ye cannot find out anything about the sheep."

"'Tis no business of mine," says Thiostolf, "to hunt up sheep, and this one thing is quite enough to hinder it. I won't walk in thy thralls' footsteps. But go thyself, and then I'll go with thee."

About this they had many words. The weather was good, and Hallgerda was sitting out of doors. Glum went up to her and said—

"Now Thiostolf and I have had a quarrel, and we shall not live much longer together." And so he told her all that they had been talking about.

Then Hallgerda spoke up for Thiostolf, and they had many words about him. At last Glum gave her a blow with his hand, and said—

"I will strive no longer with thee," and with that he went away.

Now she loved him much, and could not calm herself, but wept out loud. Thiostolf went up to her and said—

"This is sorry sport for thee, and so it must not be often again."

"Nay," she said, "but thou shalt not avenge this, nor meddle at all whatever passes between Glum and me."

He went off with a spiteful grin.

CHAPTER XVII.

GLUM'S SLAYING.

Now Glum called men to follow him, and Thiostolf got ready and went with them. So they went up South Reykiardale and then up along by Baugagil and so south to Crossfell. But some of his band he sent to the Sulafells, and they all found very many sheep. Some of them, too, went by way of Scoradale, and it came about at last that those twain, Glum and Thiostolf, were left alone together. They went south from Crossfell and found there a flock of wild sheep, and they went from the south towards the fell, and tried to drive them down; but still the sheep got away from them up on the fell. Then each began to scold the other, and Thiostolf said at last that Glum had no strength save to tumble about in Hallgerda's arms.

Then Glum said—

"'A man's foes are those of his own house.' Shall I take upbraiding from thee, runaway thrall as thou art?"

Thiostolf said—

"Thou shalt soon have to own that I am no thrall, for I will not yield an inch to thee."

Then Glum got angry, and cut at him with his hand-axe, but he threw his axe in the way, and the blow fell on the haft with a downward stroke and bit into it about the breadth of two fingers. Thiostolf cut at him at once with his axe, and smote him on the shoulder, and the stroke hewed asunder the shoulderbone and collarbone, and the wound bled inwards. Glum grasped at Thiostolf with his left hand so fast that he fell; but Glum could not hold him, for death came over him. Then Thiostolf covered his body with stones, and took off his gold ring. Then he went straight to Varmalek. Hallgerda was sitting out of doors, and saw that his axe was bloody. He said—

"I know not what thou wilt think of it, but I tell thee Glum is slain."

"That must be thy deed?" she says.

"So it is," he says.

She laughed and said—

"Thou dost not stand for nothing in this sport."

"What thinkest thou is best to be done now?" he asked.

"Go to Hrut, my father's brother," she said, "and let him see about thee."

"I do not know," says Thiostolf, "whether this is good advice; but still I will take thy counsel in this matter."

So he took his horse, and rode west to Hrutstede that night. He binds his horse at the back of the house, and then goes round to the door, and gives a great knock. After that he walks round the house, north about. It happened that Hrut was awake. He sprang up at once, and put on his jerkin and pulled on his shoes. Then he took up his sword, and wrapped a cloak about his left arm, up as far as the elbow. Men woke up just as he went out; there he saw a tall stout man at the back of the house, and knew it was Thiostolf. Hrut asked him what news.

"I tell thee Glum is slain," says Thiostolf.

"Who did the deed?" says Hrut.

"I slew him," says Thiostolf.

"Why rodest thou hither?" says Hrut.

"Hallgerda sent me to thee," says Thiostolf.

"Then she has no hand in this deed," says Hrut, and drew his sword. Thiostolf saw that, and would not be behind hand, so he cuts at Hrut at once. Hrut got out of the way of the stroke by a quick turn, and at the same time struck the back of the axe so smartly with a side-long blow of his left hand, that it flew out of Thiostolf's grasp. Then Hrut made a blow with the sword in his right hand at Thiostolf's leg, just above the knee, and cut it almost off so that it hung by a little piece, and sprang in upon him at the same time, and thrust him hard back. After that he smote him on the head, and dealt him his death-blow. Thiostolf fell down on his back at full length, and then out came Hrut's men, and saw the tokens of the deed. Hrut made them take Thiostolf away, and throw stones over his body, and then he went to find Hauskuld, and told him of Glum's slaying, and also of Thiostolf's. He thought it harm that Glum was dead and gone, but thanked him for killing Thiostolf. A little while after, Thorarin Ragi's brother hears of his brother Glum's death, then he rides with eleven men behind him west to Hauskuldstede, and Hauskuld welcomed him with both hands, and he is there the night. Hauskuld sent at once for Hrut to come to him, and he went at once, and next day they spoke much of the slaying of Glum, and Thorarin said—"Wilt thou make me any atonement for my brother, for I have had a great loss?"

Hauskuld answered—"I did not slay thy brother, nor did my daughter plot his death; but as soon as ever Hrut knew it he slew Thiostolf".

Then Thorarin held his peace, and thought the matter had taken a bad turn. But Hrut said—"Let us make his journey good; he has indeed had a heavy loss, and if we do that we shall be well spoken of. So let us give him gifts, and then he will be our friend ever afterwards."

So the end of it was that those brothers gave him gifts, and he rode back south. He and Hallgerda changed homesteads in the spring, and she went south to Laugarness and he to Varmalek. And now Thorarin is out of the story.

CHAPTER XVIII.

FIDDLE MORD'S DEATH.

Now it must be told how Fiddle Mord took a sickness and breathed his last; and that was thought great scathe. His daughter Unna took all the goods he left behind him. She was then still unmarried the second time. She was very lavish, and unthrifty of her property; so that her goods and ready money wasted away, and at last she had scarce anything left but land and stock.

CHAPTER XIX.

GUNNAR COMES INTO THE STORY.

There was a man whose name was Gunnar. He was one of Unna's kinsmen, and his mother's name was Rannveig. Gunnar's father was named Hamond. Gunnar Hamond's son dwelt at Lithend, in the Fleetlithe. He was a tall man in growth, and a strong man—best skilled in arms of all men. He could cut or thrust or shoot if he chose as well with his left as with his right hand, and he smote so swiftly with his sword, that three seemed to flash through the air at once. He was the best shot with the bow of all men, and never missed his mark. He could leap more than his own height, with all his war-gear, and as far backwards as forwards. He could swim like a seal, and there was no game in which it was any good for anyone to strive with him; and so it has been said that no man was his match. He was handsome of feature, and fair skinned. His nose was straight, and a little turned up at the end. He was blue-eyed and bright-eyed, and ruddy-cheeked. His hair thick, and of good hue, and hanging down in comely curls. The most courteous of men was he, of sturdy frame and strong will, bountiful and gentle, a fast friend, but hard to please when making them. He was wealthy in goods. His brother's name was Kolskegg; he was a tall strong man, a noble fellow, and undaunted in everything. Another brother's name was Hjort; he was then in his childhood. Orm Skogarnef was a base-born brother of Gunnar's; he does not come into this story. Arnguda was the name of Gunnar's sister. Hroar, the priest at Tongue, had her to wife.

CHAPTER XX.

OF NJAL AND HIS CHILDREN.

There was a man whose name was Njal. He was the son of Thorgeir Gelling, the son of Thorolf. Njal's mother's name was Asgerda. Njal dwelt at Bergthorsknoll in the land-isles; he had another homestead on Thorolfsfell. Njal was wealthy in goods, and handsome of face; no beard grew on his chin. He was so great a lawyer, that his match was not to be found. Wise too he was, and foreknowing and foresighted.[7] Of good counsel, and ready to give it, and all that he advised men was sure to be the best for them to do. Gentle and generous, he unravelled every man's knotty points who came to see him about them. Bergthora was his wife's name; she was Skarphedinn's daughter, a very high-spirited, brave-hearted woman, but somewhat hard-tempered. They had six children, three daughters and three sons, and they all come afterwards into this story.

CHAPTER XXI.

UNNA GOES TO SEE GUNNAR.

Now it must be told how Unna had lost all her ready money. She made her way to Lithend, and Gunnar greeted his kinswoman well. She stayed there that night, and the next morning they sat out of doors and talked. The end of their talk was that she told him how heavily she was pressed for money.

"This is a bad business," he said.

"What help wilt thou give me out of my distress?" she asked.

He answered—"Take as much money as thou needest from what I have out at interest".

"Nay," she said, "I will not waste thy goods."

"What then dost thou wish?"

"I wish thee to get back my goods out of Hrut's hands," she answered.

"That, methinks, is not likely," said he, "when thy father could not get them back, and yet he was a great lawyer, but I know little about law."

She answered—"Hrut pushed that matter through rather by boldness than by law; besides, my father was old, and that was why men thought it better not to drive things to the uttermost. And now there is none of my kinsmen to take this suit up if thou hast not daring enough."

"I have courage enough," he replied, "to get these goods back; but I do not know how to take the suit up."

"Well!" she answered, "go and see Njal of Bergthorsknoll, he will know how to give thee advice. Besides, he is a great friend of thine."

"'Tis like enough he will give me good advice, as he gives it to every one else," says Gunnar.

So the end of their talk was, that Gunnar undertook her cause, and gave her the money she needed for her housekeeping, and after that she went home.

Now Gunnar rides to see Njal, and he made him welcome, and they began to talk at once.

Then Gunnar said—"I am come to seek a bit of good advice from thee".

Njal replied—"Many of my friends are worthy of this, but still I think I would take more pains for none than for thee".

Gunnar said—"I wish to let thee know that I have undertaken to get Unna's goods back from Hrut".

"A very hard suit to undertake," said Njal, "and one very hazardous how it will go; but still I will get it up for thee in the way I think likeliest to succeed, and the end will be good if thou breakest none of the rules I lay down; if thou dost, thy life is in danger."

"Never fear; I will break none of them," said Gunnar.

Then Njal held his peace for a little while, and after that he spoke as follows:—

CHAPTER XXII.

NJAL'S ADVICE.

"I have thought over the suit, and it will do so. Thou shalt ride from home with two men at thy back. Over all thou shalt have a great rough cloak, and under that, a russet kirtle of cheap stuff, and under all, thy good clothes. Thou must take a small axe in thy hand, and each of you must have two horses, one fat, the other lean. Thou shalt carry hardware and smith's work with thee hence, and ye must ride off early to-morrow morning, and when ye are come across Whitewater westwards, mind and slouch thy hat well over thy brows. Then men will ask who is this tall man, and thy mates shall say—'Here is Huckster Hedinn the Big, a man from Eyjafirth, who is going about with smith's work for sale'. This Hedinn is ill-tempered and a chatterer—a fellow who thinks he alone knows everything. Very often he snatches back his wares, and flies at men if everything is not done as he wishes. So thou shalt ride west to Borgarfirth offering all sorts of wares for sale, and be sure often to cry off thy bargains, so that it will be noised abroad that Huckster Hedinn is the worst of men to deal with, and that no lies have been told of his bad behaviour. So thou shalt ride to Northwaterdale, and to Hrutfirth, and Laxriverdale, till thou comest to Hauskuldstede. There thou must stay a night, and sit in the lowest place, and hang thy head down. Hauskuld will tell them all not to meddle nor make with Huckster Hedinn, saying he is a rude unfriendly fellow. Next morning thou must be off early and go to the farm nearest Hrutstede. There thou must offer thy goods for sale, praising up all that is worst, and tinkering up the faults. The master of the house will pry about and find out the faults. Thou must snatch the wares away from him, and speak ill to him. He will say—'Twas not to be hoped that thou wouldst behave well to him, when thou behavest ill to every one else. Then thou shalt fly at him, though it is not thy wont, but mind and spare thy strength, that thou mayest not be found out. Then a man will be sent to Hrutstede to tell Hrut he had best come and part you. He will come at once and ask thee to his house, and thou must accept his offer. Thou shalt greet Hrut, and he will answer well. A place will be given thee on the lower bench over against Hrut's high-seat. He will ask if thou art from the North, and thou shalt answer that thou art a man of Eyjafirth. He will go on to ask if there are very many famous men there. 'Shabby fellows enough and to spare,' thou must answer. 'Dost thou know Reykiardale and the parts about?' he will ask. To which thou must answer—'I know all Iceland by heart'.

"Are there any stout champions left in Reykiardale?' he will ask. 'Thieves and scoundrels,' thou shalt answer. Then Hrut will smile and think it sport to listen. You two will go on to talk of the men in the Eastfirth Quarter, and thou must always find something to say against them. At last your talk will come to Rangrivervale, and then thou must say, there is small choice of men left in those parts since Fiddle Mord died. At the same time sing some stave to please Hrut, for I know thou art a skald. Hrut will ask what makes thee say there is never a man to come in Mord's place; and then thou must answer, that he was so wise a man and so good a taker up of suits, that he never made a false step in upholding his leadership. He will ask—'Dost thou know how matters fared between me and him?'

"'I know all about it,' thou must reply, 'he took thy wife from thee, and thou hadst not a word to say.'

"Then Hrut will ask—'Dost thou not think it was some disgrace to him when he could not get back his goods, though he set the suit on foot?'

"'I can answer thee that well enough,' thou must say, 'Thou challengedst him to single combat; but he was old, and so his friends advised him not to fight with thee, and then they let the suit fall to the ground.'

"'True enough," Hrut will say. 'I said so, and that passed for law among foolish men; but the suit might have been taken up again at another Thing if he had the heart.'

"'I know all that,' thou must say.

"Then he will ask—'Dost thou know anything about law?"

"'Up in the North I am thought to know something about it,' thou shalt say. 'But still I should like thee to tell me how this suit should be taken up.'

"'What suit dost thou mean?' he will ask.

"'A suit,' thou must answer, 'which does not concern me. I want to know how a man must set to work who wishes to get back Unna's dower.'

"Then Hrut will say—'In this suit I must be summoned so that I can hear the summons, or I must be summoned here in my lawful house'.

"'Recite the summons, then,' thou must say, and I will say it after thee.'

"Then Hrut will summon himself; and mind and pay great heed to every word he says. After that Hrut will bid thee repeat the summons, and thou must do so, and say it all wrong, so that no more than every other word is right.

"Then Hrut will smile and not mistrust thee, but say that scarce a word is right. Thou must throw the blame on thy companions, and say they put thee out, and then thou must ask him to say the words first, word by word, and to let thee say the words after him. He will give thee leave, and summon himself in the suit, and thou shalt summon after him there and then, and this time say every word right. When it is done, ask Hrut if that were rightly summoned, and he will answer 'there is no flaw to be found in it'. Then thou shalt say in a loud voice, so that thy companions may hear—

"'I summon thee in the suit which Unna Mord's daughter has made over to me with her plighted hand.'

"But when men are sound asleep, you shall rise and take your bridles and saddles, and tread softly, and go out of the house, and put your saddles on your fat horses in the fields, and so ride off on them, but leave the others behind you. You must ride up into the hills away from the home pastures and stay there three nights, for about so long will they seek you. After that ride home south, riding always by night and resting by day. As for us we will then ride this summer to the Thing, and help thee in thy suit." So Gunnar thanked Njal, and first of all rode home.

CHAPTER XXIII.

HUCKSTER HEDINN.

Gunnar rode from home two nights afterwards, and two men with him; they rode along until they got on Bluewoodheath, and then men on horseback met them and asked who that tall man might be of whom so little was seen. But his companions said it was Huckster Hedinn. Then the others said a worse was not to be looked for behind, when such a man as he went before. Hedinn at once made as though he would have set upon them, but yet each went their way. So Gunnar went on doing everything as Njal had laid it down for him, and when he came to Hauskuldstede he stayed there the night, and thence he went down the dale till he came to the next farm to Hrutstede. There he offered his wares for sale, and Hedinn fell at once upon the farmer. This was told to Hrut, and he sent for Hedinn, and Hedinn went at once to see Hrut, and had a good welcome. Hrut seated him over against himself, and their talk went pretty much as Njal had guessed; but when they came to talk of Rangrivervale, and Hrut asked about the men there, Gunnar sung this stave—

Men in sooth are slow to find,—
So the people speak by stealth,
Often this hath reached my ears,—
All through Rangar's rolling vales.
Still I trow that Fiddle Mord,
Tried his hand in fight of yore;
Sure was never gold-bestower,
Such a man for might and wit.

Then Hrut said, "Thou art a skald, Hedinn. But hast thou never heard how things went between me and Mord?" Then Hedinn sung another stave—

Once I ween I heard the rumour,
How the Lord of rings[8] bereft thee;
From thine arms earth's offspring[9] tearing,
Trickful he and trustful thou.
Then the men, the buckler-bearers,
Begged the mighty gold-begetter,
Sharp sword oft of old he reddened,
Not to stand in strife with thee.

So they went on, till Hrut, in answer told him how the suit must be taken up, and recited the summons. Hedinn repeated it all wrong, and Hrut burst out laughing, and had no mistrust. Then he said, Hrut must summon once more, and Hrut did so. Then Hedinn repeated the summons a second time, and this time right, and called his companions to witness how he summoned Hrut in a suit which Unna Mord's daughter had made over to him with her plighted hand. At night he went to sleep like other men, but as soon as ever Hrut was sound asleep, they took their clothes and arms, and went out and came to their horses, and rode off across the river, and so up along the bank by Hiardarholt till the dale broke off among the hills, and so there they are upon the fells between Laxriverdale and Hawkdale, having got to a spot where no one could find them unless he had fallen on them by chance.

Hauskuld wakes up that night at Hauskuldstede, and roused all his household, "I will tell you my dream," he said. "I thought I saw a great bear go out of this house, and I knew at once this beast's match was not to be found; two cubs followed him, wishing well to the bear, and they all made for Hrutstede, and went into the house there. After that I woke. Now I wish to ask if any of you saw aught about yon tall man."

Then one man answered him—"I saw how a golden fringe and a bit of scarlet cloth peeped out at his arm, and on his right arm he had a ring of gold".

Hauskuld said—"This beast is no man's fetch, but Gunnar's of Lithend, and now methinks I see all about it. Up! let us ride to Hrutstede." And they did so. Hrut lay in his locked bed, and asks who have come there? Hauskuld tells who he is, and asked what guests might be there in the house.

"Only Huckster Hedinn is here," says Hrut.

"A broader man across the back, it will be, I fear," says Hauskuld, "I guess here must have been Gunnar of Lithend."

"Then there has been a pretty trial of cunning," says Hrut.

"What has happened?" says Hauskuld.

"I told him how to take up Unna's suit, and I summoned myself and he summoned after, and now he can use this first step in the suit, and it is right in law."

"There has, indeed, been a great falling off of wit on one side," said Hauskuld, "and Gunnar cannot have planned it all by himself; Njal must be at the bottom of this plot, for there is not his match for wit in all the land."

Now they look for Hedinn, but he is already off and away; after that they gathered folk, and looked for them three days, but could not find them.

Gunnar rode south from the fell to Hawkdale and so east of Skard, and north to Holtbeaconheath, and so on until he got home.

CHAPTER XXIV.

GUNNAR AND HRUT STRIVE AT THE THING.

Gunnar rode to the Althing, and Hrut and Hauskuld rode thither too with a very great company. Gunnar pursues his suit, and began by calling on his neighbours to bear witness, but Hrut and his brother had it in their minds to make an onslaught on him, but they mistrusted their strength.

Gunnar next went to the court of the men of Broadfirth, and bade Hrut listen to his oath and declaration of the cause of the suit, and to all the proofs which he was about to bring forward. After that he took his oath, and declared his case. After that he brought forward his witnesses of the summons, along with his witnesses that the suit had been handed over to him. All this time Njal was not at the court. Now Gunnar pursued his suit till he called on the defendant to reply. Then Hrut took witness, and said the suit was naught, and that there was a flaw in the pleading; he declared that it had broken down because Gunnar had failed to call those three witnesses which ought to have been brought before the court. The first, that which was taken before the marriage-bed, the second, before the man's door, the third, at the Hill of Laws. By this time Njal was come to the court and said the suit and pleading might still be kept alive if they chose to strive in that way.

"No," says Gunnar, "I will not have that; I will do the same to Hrut as he did to Mord my kinsman;—or, are those brothers Hrut and Hauskuld so near that they may hear my voice?"

"Hear it we can," says Hrut. "What dost thou wish?"

Gunnar said—"Now all men here present be ear-witnesses, that I challenge thee Hrut to single combat, and we shall fight to-day on the holm, which is here in Axewater. But if thou wilt not fight with me, then pay up all the money this very day."

After that Gunnar sung a stave—

Yes, so must it be, this morning—
Now my mind is full of fire—
Hrut with me on yonder island
Raises roar of helm and shield.
All that hear my words bear witness,
Warriors grasping Woden's guard,
Unless the wealthy wight down payeth

Dower of wife with flowing veil.

After that Gunnar went away from the court with all his followers. Hrut and Hauskuld went home too, and the suit was never pursued nor defended from that day forth. Hrut said, as soon as he got inside the booth, "This has never happened to me before, that any man has offered me combat and I have shunned it".

"Then thou must mean to fight," says Hauskuld, "but that shall not be if I have my way; for thou comest no nearer to Gunnar than Mord would have come to thee, and we had better both of us pay up the money to Gunnar."

After that the brothers asked the householders of their own country what they would lay down, and they one and all said they would lay down as much as Hrut wished.

"Let us go then," says Hauskuld, "to Gunnar's booth, and pay down the money out of hand." That was told to Gunnar, and he went out into the doorway of the booth, and Hauskuld said—

"Now it is thine to take the money."

Gunnar said—

"Pay it down, then, for I am ready to take it."

So they paid down the money truly out of hand, and then Hauskuld said— "Enjoy it now, as thou hast gotten it". Then Gunnar sang another stave—

Men who wield the blade of battle
Hoarded wealth may well enjoy,
Guileless gotten this at least,
Golden meed I fearless take;
But if we for woman's quarrel,
Warriors born to brandish sword,
Glut the wolf with manly gore,
Worse the lot of both would be.

Hrut answered—"Ill will be thy meed for this".

"Be that as it may," says Gunnar.

Then Hauskuld and his brother went home to their booth, and he had much upon his mind, and said to Hrut—

"Will this unfairness of Gunnar's never be avenged?"

"Not so," says Hrut; "'twill be avenged on him sure enough, but we shall have no share nor profit in that vengeance. And after all it is most likely that he will turn to our stock to seek for friends."

After that they left off speaking of the matter. Gunnar showed Njal the money, and he said—"The suit has gone off well".

"Ay," says Gunnar, "but it was all thy doing."

Now men rode home from the Thing, and Gunnar got very great honour from the suit. Gunnar handed over all the money to Unna, and would have none of it, but said he thought he ought to look for more help from her and her kin hereafter than from other men. She said, so it should be.

CHAPTER XXV.

UNNA'S SECOND WEDDING.

There was a man named Valgard, he kept house at Hof by Rangriver, he was the son of Jorund the Priest, and his brother was Wolf Aurpriest. Those brothers. Wolf Aurpriest, and Valgard the guileful, set off to woo Unna, and she gave herself away to Valgard without the advice of any of her kinsfolk. But Gunnar and Njal, and many others thought ill of that, for he was a cross-grained man and had few friends. They begot between them a son, whose name was Mord, and he is long in this story. When he was grown to man's estate, he worked ill to his kinsfolk, but worst of all to Gunnar. He was a crafty man in his temper, but spiteful in his counsels.

Now we will name Njal's sons. Skarphedinn was the eldest of them. He was a tall man in growth and strong withal; a good swordsman; he could swim like a seal, the swiftest-footed of men, and bold and dauntless; he had a great flow of words and quick utterance; a good skald too; but still for the most part he kept himself well in hand; his hair was dark brown, with crisp curly locks; he had good eyes; his features were sharp, and his face ashen pale, his nose turned up and his front teeth stuck out, and his mouth was very ugly. Still he was the most soldier-like of men.

Grim was the name of Njal's second son. He was fair of face and wore his hair long. His hair was dark, and he was comelier to look on than Skarphedinn. A tall strong man.

Helgi was the name of Njal's third son. He too was fair of face and had fine hair. He was a strong man and well-skilled in arms. He was a man of sense and knew well how to behave. They were all unwedded at that time, Njal's sons.

Hauskuld was the fourth of Njal's sons. He was base-born. His mother was Rodny, and she was Hauskuld's daughter, the sister of Ingialld of the Springs.

Njal asked Skarphedinn one day if he would take to himself a wife. He bade his father settle the matter. Then Njal asked for his hand Thorhilda, the daughter of Ranvir of Thorolfsfell, and that was why they had another homestead there after that. Skarphedinn got Thorhilda, but he stayed still with his father to the end. Grim wooed Astrid of Deepback; she was a widow and very wealthy. Grim got her to wife, and yet lived on with Njal.

CHAPTER XXVI.

OF ASGRIM AND HIS CHILDREN.

There was a man named Asgrim. He was Ellidagrim's son. The brother of Asgrim Ellidagrim's son was Sigfus.

Asgrim had two sons, and both of them were named Thorhall. They were both hopeful men. Grim was the name of another of Asgrim's sons, and Thorhalla was his daughter's name. She was the fairest of women, and well behaved.

Njal came to talk with his son Helgi, and said, "I have thought of a match for thee, if thou wilt follow my advice".

"That I will surely," says he, "for I know that thou both meanest me well, and canst do well for me; but whither hast thou turned thine eyes?"

"We will go and woo Asgrim Ellidagrim's son's daughter, for that is the best choice we can make."

CHAPTER XXVII.

HELGI NJAL'S SON'S WOOING.

A little after they rode out across Thurso water, and fared till they came into Tongue. Asgrim was at home, and gave them a hearty welcome; and they were there that night. Next morning they began to talk, and then Njal raised the question of the wooing, and asked for Thorhalla for his son Helgi's hand. Asgrim answered that well, and said there were no men with whom he would be more willing to make this bargain than with them. They fell a-talking then about terms, and the end of it was that Asgrim betrothed his daughter to Helgi, and the bridal day was named. Gunnar was at that feast, and many other of the best men. After the feast Njal offered to foster in his house Thorhall, Asgrim's son, and he was with Njal long after. He loved Njal more than his own father. Njal taught him law, so that he became the greatest lawyer in Iceland in those days.

CHAPTER XXVIII.

HALLVARD COMES OUT TO ICELAND.

There came a ship out from Norway, and ran into Arnbæl's Oyce,[10] and the master of the ship was Hallvard, the white, a man from the Bay.[11] He went to stay at Lithend, and was with Gunnar that winter, and was always asking him to fare abroad with him. Gunnar spoke little about it, but yet said more unlikely things might happen; and about spring he went over to Bergthorsknoll to find out from Njal whether he thought it a wise step in him to go abroad.

"I think it is wise," says Njal; "they will think thee there an honourable man, as thou art."

"Wilt thou perhaps take my goods into thy keeping while I am away, for I wish my brother Kolskegg to fare with me; but I would that thou shouldst see after my household along with my mother."

"I will not throw anything in the way of that," says Njal; "lean on me in this thing as much as thou likest."

"Good go with thee for thy words," says Gunnar, and he rides then home.

The Easterling [the Norseman Hallvard] fell again to talk with Gunnar that he should fare abroad. Gunnar asked if he had ever sailed to other lands? He said he had sailed to every one of them that lay between Norway and Russia, and so, too, I have sailed to Biarmaland.[12]

"Wilt thou sail with me eastward ho?" says Gunnar.

"That I will of a surety," says he.

Then Gunnar made up his mind to sail abroad with him. Njal took all Gunnar's goods into his keeping.

CHAPTER XXIX.

GUNNAR GOES ABROAD.

So Gunnar fared abroad, and Kolskegg with him. They sailed first to Tönsberg,[13] and were there that winter. There had then been a shift of rulers in Norway, Harold Grayfell was then dead, and so was Gunnhillda. Earl Hacon the Bad, Sigurd's son, Hacon's son, Gritgarth's son, then ruled the realm. The mother of Hacon was Bergliot, the daughter of Earl Thorir. Her mother was Olof harvest-heal. She was Harold Fair-hair's daughter.

Hallvard asks Gunnar if he would make up his mind to go to Earl Hacon?

"No; I will not do that," says Gunnar. "Hast thou ever a long-ship?"

"I have two," he says.

"Then I would that we two went on warfare; and let us get men to go with us."

"I will do that," says Hallvard.

After that they went to the Bay, and took with them two ships, and fitted them out thence. They had good choice of men, for much praise was said of Gunnar.

"Whither wilt thou first fare?" says Gunnar.

"I wish to go south-east to Hisingen, to see my kinsman Oliver," says Hallvard.

"What dost thou want of him?" says Gunnar.

He answered—"He is a fine brave fellow, and he will be sure to get us some more strength for our voyage".

"Then let us go thither," says Gunnar.

So, as soon as they were "boun," they held on east to Hisingen, and had there a hearty welcome. Gunnar had only been there a short time ere Oliver made much of him. Oliver asks about his voyage, and Hallvard says that Gunnar wishes to go a-warfaring to gather goods for himself.

"There's no use thinking of that," says Oliver, "when ye have no force."

"Well," says Hallvard, "then you may add to it."

"So I do mean to strengthen Gunnar somewhat," says Oliver; "and though thou reckonest thyself my kith and kin, I think there is more good in him."

"What force, now, wilt thou add to ours?" he asks.

"Two long-ships, one with twenty, and the other with thirty seats for rowers."

"Who shall man them?" asks Hallvard.

"I will man one of them with my own house-carles, and the freemen around shall man the other. But still I have found out that strife has come into the river, and I know not whether ye two will be able to get away; for *they* are in the river."

"Who?" says Hallvard.

"Brothers twain," says Oliver; "one's name is Vandil and the other's Karli, sons of Sjolf the Old, east away out of Gothland."

Hallvard told Gunnar that Oliver had added some ships to theirs, and Gunnar was glad at that. They busked them for their voyage thence, till they were "all-boun". Then Gunnar and Hallvard went before Oliver, and thanked him; he bade them fare warily for the sake of those brothers.

CHAPTER XXX.

GUNNAR GOES A-SEA-ROVING.

So Gunnar held on out of the river, and he and Kolskegg were both on board one ship. But Hallvard was on board another. Now, they see the ships before them, and then Gunnar spoke, and said—

"Let us be ready for anything if they turn towards us! but else let us have nothing to do with them."

So they did that, and made all ready on board their ships. The others patted their ships asunder, and made a fareway between the ships. Gunnar fared straight on between the ships, but Vandil caught up a grappling-iron, and cast it between their ships and Gunnar's ship, and began at once to drag it towards him.

Oliver had given Gunnar a good sword; Gunnar now drew it, and had not yet put on his helm. He leapt at once on the forecastle of Vandil's ship, and gave one man his death-blow. Karli ran his ship alongside the other side of Gunnar's ship, and hurled a spear athwart the deck, and aimed at him about the waist. Gunnar sees this, and turned him about so quickly, that no eye could follow him, and caught the spear with his left hand, and hurled it back at Karli's ship, and that man got his death who stood before it. Kolskegg snatched up a grapnel and casts it at Karli's ship, and the fluke fell inside the hold, and went out through one of the planks, and in rushed the coal-blue sea, and all the men sprang on board other ships.

Now Gunnar leapt back to his own ship, and then Hallvard came up, and now a great battle arose. They saw now that their leader was unflinching, and every man did as well as he could. Sometimes Gunnar smote with the sword, and sometimes he hurled the spear, and many a man had his bane at his hand. Kolskegg backed him well. As for Karli, he hastened in a ship to his brother Vandil, and thence they fought that day. During the day Kolskegg took a rest on Gunnar's ship, and Gunnar sees that. Then he sung a song—

For the eagle ravine-eager,
Raven of my race, to-day
Better surely hast thou catered,
Lord of gold, than for thyself;
Here the morn come greedy ravens,
Many a rill of wolf[14] to sup,

But thee burning thirst down-beareth,
Prince of battle's Parliament!

After that Kolskegg took a beaker full of mead, and drank it off and went on fighting afterwards; and so it came about that those brothers sprang up on the ship of Vandil and his brother, and Kolskegg went on one side, and Gunnar on the other. Against Gunnar came Vandil, and smote at once at him with his sword, and the blow fell on his shield. Gunnar gave the shield a twist as the sword pierced it, and broke it short off at the hilt. Then Gunnar smote back at Vandil, and three swords seemed to be aloft, and Vandil could not see how to shun the blow. Then Gunnar cut both his legs from under him, and at the same time Kolskegg ran Karli through with a spear. After that they took great war spoil.

Thence they held on south to Denmark, and thence east to Smoland,[15] and had victory wherever they went. They did not come back in autumn. The next summer they held on to Reval, and fell in there with sea-rovers, and fought at once, and won the fight. After that they steered east to Osel,[16] and lay there somewhile under a ness. There they saw a man coming down from the ness above them; Gunnar went on shore to meet the man, and they had a talk. Gunnar asked him his name, and he said it was Tofi. Gunnar asked again what he wanted.

"Thee I want to see," says the man. "Two warships lie on the other side under the ness, and I will tell thee who command them: two brothers are the captains—one's name is Hallgrim, and the other's Kolskegg. I know them to be mighty men of war; and I know too that they have such good weapons that the like are not to be had. Hallgrim has a bill which he had made by seething-spells; and this is what the spells say, that no weapon shall give him his death-blow save that bill. That thing follows it too that it is known at once when a man is to be slain with that bill, for something sings in it so loudly that it may be heard a long way off—such a strong nature has that bill in it."

Then Gunnar sang a song—

Soon shall I that spearhead seize,
And the bold sea-rover slay,
Him whose blows on headpiece ring,
Heaper up of piles of dead.
Then on Endil's courser[17] bounding,
O'er the sea-depths I will ride,
While the wretch who spells abuseth,
Life shall lose in Sigar's storm.[18]

"Kolskegg has a short sword; that is also the best of weapons. Force, too, they have—a third more than ye. They have also much goods, and have stowed them away on land, and I know clearly where they are. But they have sent a spy-ship off the ness, and they know all about you. Now they are getting themselves ready as fast as they can; and as soon as they are 'boun,' they mean to run out against you. Now you have either to row away at once, or to busk yourselves as quickly as ye can; but if ye win the day, then I will lead you to all their store of goods."

Gunnar gave him a golden finger-ring, and went afterwards to his men and told them that war-ships lay on the other side of the ness, "and they know all about us; so let us take to our arms, and busk us well, for now there is gain to be got".

Then they busked them; and just when they were boun they see ships coming up to them. And now a fight sprung up between them, and they fought long, and many men fell. Gunnar slew many a man. Hallgrim and his men leapt on board Gunnar's ship, Gunnar turns to meet him, and Hallgrim thrust at him with his bill. There was a boom athwart the ship, and Gunnar leapt nimbly back over it, Gunnar's shield was just before the boom, and Hallgrim thrust his bill into it, and through it, and so on into the boom. Gunnar cut at Hallgrim's arm hard, and lamed the forearm, but the sword would not bite. Then down fell the bill, and Gunnar seized the bill, and thrust Hallgrim through, and then sang a song—

Slain is he who spoiled the people,
Lashing them with flashing steel:
Heard have I how Hallgrim's magic
Helm-rod forged in foreign land;
All men know, of heart-strings doughty,
How this bill hath come to me,
Deft in fight, the wolf's dear feeder.
Death alone us two shall part.

And that vow Gunnar kept, in that he bore the bill while he lived. Those namesakes [the two Kolskeggs] fought together, and it was a near thing which would get the better of it. Then Gunnar came up, and gave the other Kolskegg his death-blow. After that the sea-rovers begged for mercy. Gunnar let them have that choice, and he let them also count the slain, and take the goods which the dead men owned, but he gave the others whom he spared their arms and their clothing, and bade them be off to the lands that fostered them. So they went off and Gunnar took all the goods that were left behind.

Tofi came to Gunnar after the battle, and offered to lead him to that store of goods which the sea-rovers had stowed away, and said that it was both better and larger than that which they had already got.

Gunnar said he was willing to go, and so he went ashore, and Tofi before him, to a wood, and Gunnar behind him. They came to a place where a great heap of wood was piled together. Tofi says the goods were under there, then they tossed off the wood, and found under it both gold and silver, clothes and good weapons. They bore those goods to the ships, and Gunnar asks Tofi in what way he wished him to repay him.

Tofi answered, "I am a Dansk man by race, and I wish thou wouldst bring me to my kinsfolk".

Gunnar asks why he was there away east?

"I was taken by sea-rovers," says Tofi, "and they put me on land here in Osel, and here I have been ever since."

CHAPTER XXXI.

GUNNAR GOES TO KING HAROLD GORM'S SON AND EARL HACON.

Gunnar took Tofi on board, and said to Kolskegg and Hallvard, "Now we will hold our course for the north lands".

They were well pleased at that, and bade him have his way. So Gunnar sailed from the east with much goods. He had ten ships, and ran in with them to Heidarby in Denmark. King Harold Gorm's son was there up the country, and he was told about Gunnar, and how too that there was no man his match in all Iceland. He sent men to him to ask him to come to him, and Gunnar went at once to see the king, and the king made him a hearty welcome, and sat him down next to himself. Gunnar was there half a month. The king made himself sport by letting Gunnar prove himself in divers feats of strength against his men, and there were none that were his match even in one feat.

Then the king said to Gunnar, "It seems to me as though thy peer is not to be found far or near," and the king offered to get Gunnar a wife, and to raise him to great power if he would settle down there.

Gunnar thanked the king for his offer and said—"I will first of all sail back to Iceland to see my friends and kinsfolk".

"Then thou wilt never come back to us," says the king.

"Fate will settle that, lord," says Gunnar.

Gunnar gave the king a good long-ship, and much goods besides, and the king gave him a robe of honour, and golden-seamed gloves, and a fillet with a knot of gold on it, and a Russian hat.

Then Gunnar fared north to Hisingen. Oliver welcomed him with both hands, and he gave back to Oliver his ships, with their lading, and said that was his share of the spoil. Oliver took the goods, and said Gunnar was a good man and true, and bade him stay with him some while. Hallvard asked Gunnar if he had a mind to go to see Earl Hacon. Gunnar said that was near his heart, "for now I am somewhat proved, but then I was not tried at all when thou badest me do this before".

After that they fared north to Drontheim to see Earl Hacon, and he gave Gunnar a hearty welcome, and bade him stay with him that winter, and

Gunnar took that offer, and every man thought him a man of great worth. At Yule the Earl gave him a gold ring.

Gunnar set his heart on Bergliota, the Earl's kinswoman, and it was often to be seen from the Earl's way, that he would have given her to him to wife if Gunnar had said anything about that.

CHAPTER XXXII.

GUNNAR COMES OUT TO ICELAND.

When the spring came, the Earl asks Gunnar what course he meant to take. He said he would go to Iceland. The Earl said that had been a bad year for grain, "and there will be little sailing out to Iceland, but still thou shalt have meal and timber both in thy ship".

Gunnar fitted out his ship as early as he could, and Hallvard fared out with him and Kolskegg. They came out early in the summer, and made Arnbæl's Oyce before the Thing met.

Gunnar rode home from the ship, but got men to strip her and lay her up. But when they came home all men were glad to see them. They were blithe and merry to their household, nor had their haughtiness grown while they were away.

Gunnar asks if Njal were at home; and he was told that he was at home; then he let them saddle his horse, and those brothers rode over to Bergthorsknoll.

Njal was glad at their coming, and begged them to stay there that night, and Gunnar told him of his voyages.

Njal said he was a man of the greatest mark, "and thou hast been much proved; but still thou wilt be more tried hereafter; for many will envy thee".

"With all men I would wish to stand well," says Gunnar.

"Much bad will happen," says Njal, "and thou wilt always have some quarrel to ward off."

"So be it, then," says Gunnar, "so that I have a good ground on my side."

"So will it be too," says Njal, "if thou hast not to smart for others."

Njal asked Gunnar if he would ride to the Thing. Gunnar said he was going to ride thither, and asks Njal whether he were going to ride; but he said he would not ride thither, "and if I had my will thou wouldst do the like".

Gunnar rode home, and gave Njal good gifts, and thanked him for the care he had taken of his goods, Kolskegg urged him on much to ride to the Thing, saying, "There thy honour will grow, for many will flock to see thee there".

"That has been little to my mind," says Gunnar, "to make a show of myself; but I think it good and right to meet good and worthy men."

Hallvard by this time was also come thither, and offered to ride to the Thing with them.

CHAPTER XXXIII.

GUNNAR'S WOOING.

So Gunnar rode, and they all rode. But when they came to the Thing they were so well arrayed that none could match them in bravery; and men came out of every booth to wonder at them. Gunnar rode to the booths of the men of Rangriver, and was there with his kinsmen. Many men came to see Gunnar, and ask tidings of him; and he was easy and merry to all men, and told them all they wished to hear.

It happened one day that Gunnar went away from the Hill of Laws, and passed by the booths of the men from Mossfell; then he saw a woman coming to meet him, and she was in goodly attire; but when they met she spoke to Gunnar at once. He took her greeting well, and asks what woman she might be. She told him her name was Hallgerda, and said she was Hauskuld's daughter, Dalakoll's son. She spoke up boldly to him, and bade him tell her of his voyages; but he said he would not gainsay her a talk. Then they sat them down and talked. She was so clad that she had on a red kirtle, and had thrown over her a scarlet cloak trimmed with needlework down to the waist. Her hair came down to her bosom, and was both fair and full. Gunnar was clad in the scarlet clothes which King Harold Gorm's son had given him; he had also the gold ring on his arm which Earl Hacon had given him.

So they talked long out loud, and at last it came about that he asked whether she were unmarried. She said, so it was, "and there are not many who would run the risk of that".

"Thinkest thou none good enough for thee?"

"Not that," she says, "but I am said to be hard to please in husbands."

"How wouldst thou answer were I to ask for thee?"

"That can not be in thy mind," she says.

"It is though," says he.

"If thou hast any mind that way, go and see my father."

After that they broke off their talk.

Gunnar went straightway to the Dalesmen's booths, and met a man outside the doorway, and asks whether Hauskuld were inside the booth?

The man says that he was. Then Gunnar went in, and Hauskuld and Hrut made him welcome. He sat down between them, and no one could find out from their talk that there had ever been any misunderstanding between them. At last Gunnar's speech turned thither; how these brothers would answer if he asked for Hallgerda?

"Well," says Hauskuld, "if that is indeed thy mind."

Gunnar says that he is in earnest, "but we so parted last time, that many would think it unlikely that we should ever be bound together".

"How thinkest thou, kinsman Hrut?" says Hauskuld.

Hrut answered, "Methinks this is no even match".

"How dost thou make that out?" says Gunnar.

Hrut spoke—"In this wise will I answer thee about this matter, as is the very truth. Thou art a brisk brave man, well to do, and unblemished; but she is much mixed up with ill report, and I will not cheat thee in anything."

"Good go with thee for thy words," says Gunnar, "but still I shall hold that for true, that the old feud weighs with ye, if ye will not let me make this match."

"Not so," says Hrut, "'tis more because I see that thou art unable to help thyself; but though we make no bargain, we would still be thy friends."

"I have talked to her about it," says Gunnar, "and it is not far from her mind."

Hrut says—"I know that you have both set your hearts on this match; and, besides, ye two are those who run the most risk as to how it turns out".

Hrut told Gunnar unasked all about Hallgerda's temper, and Gunnar at first thought that there was more than enough that was wanting; but at last it came about that they struck a bargain.

Then Hallgerda was sent for, and they talked over the business when she was by, and now, as before, they made her betroth herself. The bridal feast was to be at Lithend, and at first they were to set about it secretly; but the end after all was that every one knew of it.

Gunnar rode home from the Thing, and came to Bergthorsknoll, and told Njal of the bargain he had made. He took it heavily.

Gunnar asks Njal why he thought this so unwise?

"Because from her," says Njal, "will arise all kind of ill if she comes hither east."

"Never shall she spoil our friendship," says Gunnar.

"Ah! but yet that may come very near," says Njal; "and, besides, thou wilt have always to make atonement for her."

Gunnar asked Njal to the wedding, and all those as well whom he wished should be at it from Njal's house.

Njal promised to go; and after that Gunnar rode home, and then rode about the district to bid men to his wedding.

CHAPTER XXXIV.

OF THRAIN SIGFUS' SON.

There was a man named Thrain, he was the son of Sigfus, the son of Sighvat the Red. He kept house at Gritwater on Fleetlithe. He was Gunnar's kinsman, and a man of great mark. He had to wife Thorhilda Skaldwife; she had a sharp tongue of her own, and was giving to jeering. Thrain loved her little. He and his wife were bidden to the wedding, and she and Bergthora, Skarphedinn's daughter, Njal's wife, waited on the guests with meat and drink.

Kettle was the name of the second son of Sigfus; he kept house in the Mark, east of Markfleet. He had to wife Thorgerda, Njal's daughter. Thorkell was the name of the third son of Sigfus; the fourth's name was Mord; the fifth's Lambi; the sixth's Sigmund; the seventh's Sigurd. These were all Gunnar's kinsmen, and great champions. Gunnar bade them all to the wedding.

Gunnar had also bidden Valgard the guileful, and Wolf Aurpriest, and their sons Runolf and Mord.

Hauskuld and Hrut came to the wedding with a very great company, and the sons of Hauskuld, Torleik, and Olof, were there; the bride, too, came along with them, and her daughter Thorgerda came also, and she was one of the fairest of women; she was then fourteen winters old. Many other women were with her, and besides there were Thorkatla Asgrim Ellidagrim's son's daughter, and Njal's two daughters, Thorgerda and Helga.

Gunnar had already many guests to meet them, and he thus arranged his men. He sat on the middle of the bench, and on the inside, away from him, Thrain Sigfus' son, then Wolf Aurpriest, then Valgard the guileful, then Mord and Runolf, then the other sons of Sigfus, Lambi sat outermost of them.

Next to Gunnar on the outside, away from him, sat Njal, then Skarphedinn, then Helgi, then Grim, then Hauskuld Njal's son, then Hafr the Wise, then Ingialld from the Springs, then the sons of Thorir from Holt away east. Thorir would sit outermost of the men of mark, for every one was pleased with the seat he got.

Hauskuld, the bride's father, sat on the middle of the bench over against Gunnar, but his sons sat on the inside away from him; Hrut sat on the outside away from Hauskuld, but it is not said how the others were placed. The bride sat in the middle of the cross-bench on the dais; but on one hand of her sat her daughter Thorgerda, and on the other Thorkatla Asgrim Ellidagrim's son's daughter.

Thorhillda went about waiting on the guests, and Bergthora bore the meat on the board.

Now Thrain Sigfus' son kept staring at Thorgerda Glum's daughter; his wife Thorhillda saw this, and she got wroth, and made a couplet upon him.

"Thrain," she says,

"Gaping mouths are no wise good,
Goggle eyne are in thy head,"

He rose at once up from the board, and said he would put Thorhillda away, "I will not bear her jibes and jeers any longer;" and he was so quarrelsome about this, that he would not be at the feast unless she were driven away. And so it was, that she went away; and now each man sat in his place, and they drank and were glad.

Then Thrain began to speak—"I will not whisper about that which is in my mind. This I will ask thee, Hauskuld Dalakoll's son, wilt thou give me to wife Thorgerda, thy kinswoman?"

"I do not know that," says Hauskuld; "methinks thou art ill parted from the one thou hadst before. But what kind of man is he, Gunnar?"

Gunnar answers—"I will not say aught about the man, because he is near of kin; but say thou about him, Njal," says Gunnar, "for all men will believe it".

Njal spoke, and said—"That is to be said of this man, that the man is well to do for wealth, and a proper man in all things. A man, too, of the greatest mark; so that ye may well make this match with him."

Then Hauskuld spoke—"What thinkest thou we ought to do, kinsman Hrut?"

"Thou mayst make the match, because it is an even one for her," says Hrut.

Then they talk about the terms of the bargain, and are soon of one mind on all points.

Then Gunnar stands up, and Thrain too, and they go to the cross-bench. Gunnar asked that mother and daughter whether they would say yes to this bargain. They said they would find no fault with it, and Hallgerda betrothed her daughter. Then the places of the women were shifted again, and now Thorhalla sate between the brides. And now the feast sped on well, and when it was over, Hauskuld and his company ride west, but the men of Rangriver rode to their own abode. Gunnar gave many men gifts, and that made him much liked.

Hallgerda took the housekeeping under her, and stood up for her rights in word and deed. Thorgerda took to housekeeping at Gritwater, and was a good housewife.

CHAPTER XXXV.

THE VISIT TO BERGTHORSKNOLL.

Now it was the custom between Gunnar and Njal, that each made the other a feast, winter and winter about, for friendship's sake; and it was Gunnar's turn to go to feast at Njal's. So Gunnar and Hallgerda set off for Bergthorsknoll, and when they got there Helgi and his wife were not at home. Njal gave Gunnar and his wife a hearty welcome, and when they had been there a little while, Helgi came home with Thorhalla his wife. Then Bergthora went up to the cross-bench, and Thorhalla with her, and Bergthora said to Hallgerda—

"Thou shalt give place to this woman."

She answered—"To no one will I give place, for I will not be driven into the corner for any one".

"I shall rule here," said Bergthora, After that Thorhalla sat down, and Bergthora went round the table with water to wash the guests' hands. Then Hallgerda took hold of Bergthora's hand, and said—

"There's not much to choose, though, between you two. Thou hast hangnails on every finger, and Njal is beardless."

"That's true," says Bergthora, "yet neither of us finds fault with the other for it; but Thorwald, thy husband, was not beardless, and yet thou plottedst his death."

Then Hallgerda said—"It stands me in little stead to have the bravest man in Iceland if thou dost not avenge this, Gunnar!"

He sprang up and strode across away from the board, and said—"Home I will go, and it were more seemly that thou shouldest wrangle with those of thine own household, and not under other men's roofs; but as for Njal, I am his debtor for much honour, and never will I be egged on by thee like a fool".

After that they set off home.

"Mind this, Bergthora," said Hallgerda, "that we shall meet again."

Bergthora said she should not be better off for that. Gunnar said nothing at all, but went home to Lithend, and was there at home all the winter. And now the summer was running on towards the Great Thing.

CHAPTER XXXVI.

KOL SLEW SWART.

Gunnar rode away to the Thing, but before he rode from home he said to Hallgerda—"Be good now while I am away, and show none of thine ill temper in anything with which my friends have to do".

"The trolls take thy friends," says Hallgerda.

So Gunnar rode to the Thing, and saw it was not good to come to words with her. Njal rode to the Thing too, and all his sons with him.

Now it must be told of what tidings happened at home. Njal and Gunnar owned a wood in common at Redslip; they had not shared the wood, but each was wont to hew in it as he needed, and neither said a word to the other about that. Hallgerda's grieve's[19] name was Kol; he had been with her long, and was one of the worst of men. There was a man named Swart; he was Njal's and Bergthora's house-carle; they were very fond of him. Now Bergthora told him that he must go up into Redslip and hew wood; but she said—"I will get men to draw home the wood".

He said he would do the work She set him to win; and so he went up into Redslip, and was to be there a week.

Some gangrel men came to Lithend from the east across Markfleet, and said that Swart had been in Redslip, and hewn wood, and done a deal of work.

"So," says Hallgerda, "Bergthora must mean to rob me in many things, but I'll take care that he does not hew again."

Rannveig, Gunnar's mother, heard that, and said—"There have been good housewives before now, though they never set their hearts on manslaughter".

Now the night wore away, and early next morning Hallgerda came to speak to Kol, and said—"I have thought of some work for thee"; and with that she put weapons into his hands, and went on to say—"Fare thou to Redslip; there wilt thou find Swart".

"What shall I do to him?" he says.

"Askest thou that when thou art the worst of men?" she says. "Thou shalt kill him."

"I can get that done," he says, "but 'tis more likely that I shall lose my own life for it."

"Everything grows big in thy eyes," she says, "and thou behavest ill to say this after I have spoken up for thee in everything. I must get another man to do this if thou darest not."

He took the axe, and was very wroth, and takes a horse that Gunnar owned, and rides now till he comes east of Markfleet. There he got off and bided in the wood, till they had carried down the firewood, and Swart was left alone behind. Then Kol sprang on him, and said—"More folk can hew great strokes than thou alone"; and so he laid the axe on his head, and smote him his death-blow, and rides home afterwards, and tells Hallgerda of the slaying.

She said—"I shall take such good care of thee, that no harm shall come to thee".

"May be so," says he, "but I dreamt all the other way as I slept ere I did the deed."

Now they come up into the wood, and find Swart slain, and bear him home. Hallgerda sent a man to Gunnar at the Thing to tell him of the slaying. Gunnar said no hard words at first of Hallgerda to the messenger, and men knew not at first whether he thought well or ill of it. A little after he stood up, and bade his men go with him: they did so, and fared to Njal's booth. Gunnar sent a man to fetch Njal, and begged him to come out. Njal went out at once, and he and Gunnar fell a-talking, and Gunnar said—

"I have to tell thee of the slaying of a man, and my wife and my grieve Kol were those who did it; but Swart, thy house-carle, fell before them."

Njal held his peace while he told him the whole story. Then Njal spoke—

"Thou must take heed not to let her have her way in everything."

Gunnar said—"Thou thyself shall settle the terms".

Njal spoke again—"'Twill be hard work for thee to atone for all Hallgerda's mischief; and somewhere else there will be a broader trail to follow than this which we two now have a share in, and yet, even here there will be much awanting before all be well; and herein we shall need to bear in mind the friendly words that passed between us of old; and something tells me that thou wilt come well out of it, but still thou wilt be sore tried".

Then Njal took the award into his own hands from Gunnar, and said—

"I will not push this matter to the uttermost; thou shalt pay twelve ounces of silver; but I will add this to my award, that if anything happens from our homestead about which thou hast to utter an award, thou wilt not be less easy in thy terms".

Gunnar paid up the money out of hand, and rode home afterwards. Njal, too, came home from the Thing, and his sons. Bergthora saw the money, and said—

"This is very justly settled; but even as much money shall be paid for Kol as time goes on."

Gunnar came home from the Thing and blamed Hallgerda. She said, better men lay unatoned in many places, Gunnar said, she might have her way in beginning a quarrel, "but how the matter is to be settled rests with me".

Hallgerda was for ever chattering of Swart's slaying, but Bergthora liked that ill. Once Njal and her sons went up to Thorolfsfell to see about the housekeeping there, but that selfsame day this thing happened when Bergthora was out of doors: she sees a man ride up to the house on a black horse. She stayed there and did not go in, for she did not know the man. That man had a spear in his hand, and was girded with a short sword. She asked this man his name.

"Atli is my name," says he.

She asked whence he came.

"I am an Eastfirther," he says.

"Whither shalt thou go?" she says.

"I am a homeless man," says he, "and I thought to see Njal and Skarphedinn, and know if they would take me in."

"What work is handiest to thee?" says she.

"I am a man used to field-work," he says, "and many things else come very handy to me; but I will not hide from thee that I am a man of hard temper and it has been many a man's lot before now to bind up wounds at my hand."

"I do not blame thee," she says, "though thou art no milksop."

Atli said—"Hast thou any voice in things here?"

"I am Njal's wife," she says, "and I have as much to say to our housefolk as he."

"Wilt thou take me in then?" says he.

"I will give thee thy choice of that," says she. "If thou wilt do all the work that I set before thee, and that though I wish to send thee where a man's life is at stake."

"Thou must have so many men at thy beck," says he, "that thou wilt not need me for such work."

"That I will settle as I please," she says.

"We will strike a bargain on these terms," says he.

Then she took him into the household. Njal and his sons came home and asked Bergthora what man that might be?

"He is thy house-carle," she says, "and I took him in." Then she went on to say he was no sluggard at work.

"He will be a great worker enough, I daresay," says Njal, "but I do not know whether he will be such a good worker."

Skarphedinn was good to Atli.

Njal and his sons ride to the Thing in the course of the summer; Gunnar was also at the Thing.

Njal took out a purse of money.

"What money is that, father?"

"Here is the money that Gunnar paid me for our house-carle last summer."

"That will come to stand thee in some stead," says Skarphedinn, and smiled as he spoke.

CHAPTER XXXVII.

THE SLAYING OF KOL, WHOM ATLI SLEW.

Now we must take up the story, and say that Atli asked Bergthora what work he should do that day.

"I have thought of some work for thee," she says; "thou shall go and look for Kol until thou find him; for now shalt thou slay him this very day, if thou wilt do my will."

"This work is well fitted," says Atli, "for each of us two are bad fellows; but still I will so lay myself out for him that one or other of us shall die."

"Well mayest thou fare," she says, "and thou shalt not do this deed for nothing."

He took his weapons and his horse, and rode up to Fleetlithe, and there met men who were coming down from Lithend. They were at home east in the Mark. They asked Atli whither he meant to go? He said he was riding to look for an old jade. They said that was a small errand for such a workman, "but still 'twould be better to ask those who have been about last night".

"Who are they?" says he.

"Killing-Kol," say they, "Hallgerda's house-carle, fared from the fold just now, and has been awake all night."

"I do not know whether I dare to meet him," says Atli, "he is bad-tempered, and may be that I shall let another's wound be my warning."

"Thou bearest that look beneath the brows as though thou wert no coward," they said, and showed him where Kol was.

Then he spurred his horse and rides fast, and when he meets Kol, Atli said to him—

"Go the pack-saddle bands well?"

"That's no business of thine, worthless fellow, nor of any one else whence thou comest."

Atli said—"Thou hast something behind that is earnest work, but that is to die".

After that Atli thrust at him with his spear, and struck him about his middle. Kol swept at him with his axe, but missed him, and fell off his horse, and died at once.

Atli rode till he met some of Hallgerda's workmen, and said, "Go ye up to the horse yonder, and look to Kol, for he has fallen off, and is dead".

"Hast thou slain him?" say they.

"Well, 'twill seem to Hallgerda as though he has not fallen by his own hand."

After that Atli rode home and told Bergthora; she thanked him for this deed, and for the words which he had spoken about it.

"I do not know," says he, "what Njal will think of this."

"He will take it well upon his hands," she says, "and I will tell thee one thing as a token of it, that he has earned away with him to the Thing the price of that thrall which we took last spring, and that money will now serve for Kol; but though peace be made thou must still beware of thyself, for Hallgerda will keep no peace."

"Wilt thou send at all a man to Njal to tell him of the slaying?"

"I will not," she says, "I should like it better that Kol were unatoned."

Then they stopped talking about it.

Hallgerda was told of Kol's slaying, and of the words that Atli had said. She said Atli should be paid off for them. She sent a man to the Thing to tell Gunnar of Kol's slaying; he answered little or nothing, and sent a man to tell Njal. He too made no answer, but Skarphedinn said—

"Thralls are men of more mettle than of yore; they used to fly at each other and fight, and no one thought much harm of that; but now they will do naught but kill," and as he said this he smiled.

Njal pulled down the purse of money which hung up in the booth, and went out; his sons went with him to Gunnar's booth.

Skarphedinn said to a man who was in the doorway of the booth—

"Say thou to Gunnar that my father wants to see him."

He did so, and Gunnar went out at once and gave Njal a hearty welcome. After that they began to talk.

"'Tis ill done," says Njal, "that my housewife should have broken the peace, and let thy house-carle be slain."

"She shall not have blame for that," says Gunnar.

"Settle the award thyself," says Njal.

"So I will do," say Gunnar, "and I value those two men at an even price, Swart and Kol. Thou shalt pay me twelve ounces in silver."

Njal took the purse of money and handed it to Gunnar. Gunnar knew the money, and saw it was the same that he had paid Njal. Njal went away to his booth, and they were just as good friends as before. When Njal came home, he blamed Bergthora; but she said she would never give way to Hallgerda. Hallgerda was very cross with Gunnar, because he had made peace for Kol's slaying, Gunnar told her he would never break with Njal or his sons, and she flew into a great rage; but Gunnar took no heed of that, and so they sat for that year, and nothing noteworthy happened.

CHAPTER XXXVIII.

THE KILLING OF ATLI THE THRALL.

Next spring Njal said to Atli—"I wish that thou wouldst change thy abode to the east firths, so that Hallgerda may not put an end to thy life".

"I am not afraid of that," says Atli, "and I will willingly stay at home if I have the choice."

"Still that is less wise," says Njal.

"I think it better to lose my life in thy house than to change my master; but this I will beg of thee, if I am slain, that a thrall's price shall not be paid for me."

"Thou shalt be atoned for as a free man; but perhaps Bergthora will make thee a promise which she will fulfil, that revenge, man for man, shall be taken for thee."

Then he made up his mind to be a hired servant there.

Now it must be told of Hallgerda that she sent a man west to Bearfirth, to fetch Brynjolf the Unruly, her kinsman. He was a base son of Swan, and he was one of the worst of men. Gunnar knew nothing about it. Hallgerda said he was well fitted to be a grieve. So Brynjolf came from the west, and Gunnar asked what he was to do there? He said he was going to stay there.

"Thou wilt not better our household," says Gunnar, "after what has been told me of thee, but I will not turn away any of Hallgerda's kinsmen, whom she wishes to be with her."

Gunnar said little, but was not unkind to him, and so things went on till the Thing. Gunnar rides to the Thing and Kolskegg rides too, and when they came to the Thing they and Njal met, for he and his sons were at the Thing, and all went well with Gunnar and them.

Bergthora said to Atli—"Go thou up into Thorolfsfell and work there a week".

So he went up thither, and was there on the sly, and burnt charcoal in the wood.

Hallgerda said to Brynjolf—"I have been told Atli is not at home, and he must be winning work on Thorolfsfell".

"What thinkest thou likeliest that he is working at?" says he.

"At something in the wood," she says.

"What shall I do to him?" he asks.

"Thou shalt kill him," says she.

He was rather slow in answering her, and Hallgerda said—

"'Twould grow less in Thiostolf's eyes to kill Atli if he were alive."

"Thou shalt have no need to goad me on much more," he says, and then he seized his weapons, and takes his horse and mounts, and rides to Thorolfsfell. There he saw a great reek of coal smoke east of the homestead, so he rides thither, and gets off his horse and ties him up, but he goes where the smoke was thickest. Then he sees where the charcoal pit is, and a man stands by it. He saw that he had thrust his spear in the ground by him. Brynjolf goes along with the smoke right up to him, but he was eager at his work, and saw him not. Brynjolf gave him a stroke on the head with his axe, and he turned so quick round that Brynjolf loosed his hold of the axe, and Atli grasped the spear, and hurled it after him. Then Brynjolf cast himself down on the ground, but the spear flew away over him.

"Lucky for thee that I was not ready for thee," says Atli, "but now Hallgerda will be well pleased, for thou wilt tell her of my death; but it is a comfort to know that thou wilt have the same fate soon; but come now, take thy axe which has been here."

He answered him never a word, nor did he take the axe before he was dead. Then he rode up to the house on Thorolfsfell, and told of the slaying, and after that rode home and told Hallgerda. She sent men to Bergthorsknoll, and let them tell Bergthora, that now Kol's slaying was paid for.

After that Hallgerda sent a man to the Thing to tell Gunnar of Atli's killing.

Gunnar stood up, and Kolskegg with him, and Kolskegg said—

"Unthrifty will Hallgerda's kinsmen be to thee."

Then they go to see Njal, and Gunnar said—

"I have to tell thee of Atli's killing." He told him also who slew him, and went on, "and now I will bid thee atonement for the deed, and thou shall make the award thyself".

Njal said—"We two have always meant never to come to strife about anything; but still I cannot make him out a thrall".

Gunnar said that was all right, and stretched out his hand.

Njal named his witnesses, and they made peace on those terms.

Skarphedinn said, "Hallgerda does not let our house-carles die of old age".

Gunnar said—"Thy mother will take care that blow goes for blow between the houses".

"Ay, ay," says Njal, "there will be enough of that work."

After that Njal fixed the price at a hundred in silver, but Gunnar paid it down at once. Many who stood by said that the award was high; Gunnar got wroth, and said that a full atonement was often paid for those who were no brisker men than Atli.

With that they rode home from the Thing.

Bergthora said to Njal when she saw the money—"Thou thinkest thou hast fulfilled thy promise, but now my promise is still behind".

"There is no need that thou shouldst fulfil it," says Njal.

"Nay," says she, "thou hast guessed it would be so; and so it shall be."

Hallgerda said to Gunnar—

"Hast thou paid a hundred in silver for Atli's slaying, and made him a free man?"

"He was free before," says Gunnar, "and besides, I will not make Njal's household outlaws who have forfeited their rights."

"There's not a pin to choose between you," she said, "for both of you are so blate."

"That's as things prove," says he.

Then Gunnar was for a long time very short with her, till she gave way to him; and now all was still for the rest of that year; in the spring Njal did not increase his household, and now men ride to the Thing about summer.

CHAPTER XXXIX.

THE SLAYING OF BRYNJOLF THE UNRULY.

There was a man named Thord, he was surnamed Freedmanson. Sigtrygg was his father's name, and he had been the freedman of Asgerd, and he was drowned in Markfleet. That was why Thord was with Njal afterwards. He was a tall man and a strong, and he had fostered all Njal's sons. He had set his heart on Gudfinna Thorolf's daughter, Njal's kinswoman; she was housekeeper at home there, and was then with child.

Now Bergthora came to talk with Thord Freedmanson; she said—

"Thou shalt go to kill Brynjolf, Hallgerda's kinsman."

"I am no man-slayer," he says, "but still I will do what ever thou wilt."

"This is my will," she says.

After that he went up to Lithend, and made them call Hallgerda out, and asked where Brynjolf might be.

"What's thy will with him?" she says.

"I want him to tell me where he has hidden Atli's body; I have heard say that he has buried it badly."

She pointed to him, and said he was down yonder in Acretongue.

"Take heed," says Thord, "that the same thing does not befall him as befell Atli."

"Thou art no man-slayer," she says, "and so nought will come of it even if ye two do meet."

"Never have I seen man's blood, nor do I know how I should feel if I did," he says, and gallops out of the "town" and down to Acretongue.

Rannveig, Gunnar's mother, had heard their talk.

"Thou goadest his mind much, Hallgerda," she says, "but I think him a dauntless man, and that thy kinsman will find."

They met on the beaten way, Thord and Brynjolf; and Thord said—"Guard thee, Brynjolf, for I will do no dastard's deed by thee".

Brynjolf rode at Thord, and smote at him with his axe. He smote at him at the same time with his axe, and hewed in sunder the haft just above Brynjolf's hands, and then hewed at him at once a second time, and struck him on the collarbone, and the blow went straight into his trunk. Then he fell from horseback, and was dead on the spot.

Thord met Hallgerda'a herdsman, and gave out the slaying as done by his hand, and said where he lay, and bade him tell Hallgerda of the slaying. After that he rode home to Bergthorsknoll, and told Bergthora of the slaying, and other people too.

"Good luck go with thy hands," she said.

The herdsman told Hallgerda of the slaying; she was snappish at it, and said much ill would come of it, if she might have her way.

CHAPTER XL.

GUNNAR AND NJAL MAKE PEACE ABOUT BRYNJOLF'S SLAYING.

Now these tidings come to the Thing, and Njal made them tell him the tale thrice, and then he said—

"More men now become man-slayers than I weened."

Skarphedinn spoke—"That man, though, must have been twice fey," he says, "who lost his life by our foster-father's hand, who has never seen man's blood. And many would think that we brothers would sooner have done this deed with the turn of temper that we have."

"Scant apace wilt thou have," says Njal, "ere the like befalls thee; but need will drive thee to it."

Then they went to meet Gunnar, and told him of the slaying. Gunnar spoke and said that was little manscathe, "but yet he was a free man".

Njal offered to make peace at once, and Gunnar said yes, and he was to settle the terms himself. He made his award there and then, and laid it at one hundred in silver. Njal paid down the money on the spot, and they were at peace after that.

CHAPTER XLI.

SIGMUND COMES OUT TO ICELAND.

There was a man whose name was Sigmund. He was the son of Lambi, the son of Sighvat the Red. He was a great voyager, and a comely and a courteous man; tall too, and strong. He was a man of proud spirit, and a good skald, and well trained in most feats of strength. He was noisy and boisterous, and given to jibes and mocking. He made the land east in Hornfirth. Skiolld was the name of his fellow-traveller; he was a Swedish man, and ill to do with. They took horse and rode from the east out of Hornfirth, and did not draw bridle before they came to Lithend, in the Fleetlithe. Gunnar gave them a hearty welcome, for the bonds of kinship were close between them. Gunnar begged Sigmund to stay there that winter, and Sigmund said he would take the offer if Skiolld his fellow might be there too.

"Well, I have been so told about him," said Gunnar, "that he is no better of thy temper; but as it is, thou rather needest to have it bettered. This, too, is a bad house to stay at, and I would just give both of you a bit of advice, my kinsmen, not to fire up at the egging on of my wife Hallgerda; for she takes much in hand that is far from my will."

"His hands are clean who warns another," says Sigmund.

"Then mind the advice given thee," says Gunnar, "for thou art sure to be sore tried; and go along always with me, and lean upon my counsel."

After that they were in Gunnar's company. Hallgerda was good to Sigmund; and it soon came about that things grew so warm that she loaded him with money, and tended him no worse than her own husband; and many talked about that, and did not know what lay under it.

One day Hallgerda said to Gunnar—"It is not good to be content with that hundred in silver which thou tookest for my kinsman Brynjolf. I shall avenge him if I may," she says.

Gunnar said he had no mind to bandy words with her, and went away. He met Kolskegg, and said to him, "Go and see Njal; and tell him that Thord must beware of himself though peace has been made, for, methinks, there is faithlessness somewhere".

He rode off and told Njal, but Njal told Thord, and Kolskegg rode home, and Njal thanked them for their faithfulness.

Once on a time they two were out in the "town," Njal and Thord; a he-goat was wont to go up and down in the "town," and no one was allowed to drive him away. Then Thord spoke and said—

"Well, this *is* a wondrous thing!"

"What is it that thou see'st that seems after a wondrous fashion?" says Njal.

"Methinks the goat lies here in the hollow, and he is all one gore of blood."

Njal said that there was no goat there, nor anything else.

"What is it then?" says Thord.

"Thou must be a 'fey' man," says Njal, "and thou must have seen the fetch that follows thee, and now be ware of thyself."

"That will stand me in no stead," says Thord, "if death is doomed for me."

Then Hallgerda came to talk with Thrain Sigfus' son, and said—"I would think thee my son-in-law indeed," she says, "if thou slayest Thord Freedmanson".

"I will not do that," he says, "for then I shall have the wrath of my kinsman Gunnar; and besides, great things hang on this deed, for this slaying would soon be avenged."

"Who will avenge it?" she asks; "is it the beardless carle?"

"Not so," says he; "his sons will avenge it."

After that they talked long and low, and no man knew what counsel they took together.

Once it happened that Gunnar was not at home, but those companions were. Thrain had come in from Gritwater, and then he and they and Hallgerda sat out of doors and talked. Then Hallgerda said—

"This have ye two brothers in arms, Sigmund and Skiolld, promised to slay Thord Freedmanson; but Thrain thou hast promised me that thou wouldst stand by them when they did the deed."

They all acknowledged that they had given her this promise.

"Now I will counsel you how to do it," she says: "Ye shall ride east into Hornfirth after your goods, and come home about the beginning of the Thing, but if ye are at home before it begins, Gunnar will wish that ye should ride to the Thing with him. Njal will be at the Thing and his sons and Gunnar, but then ye two shall slay Thord."

They all agreed that this plan should be carried out. After that they busked them east to the Firth, and Gunnar was not aware of what they were about, and Gunnar rode to the Thing. Njal sent Thord Freedmanson away east under Eyjafell, and bade him be away there one night. So he went east, but he could not get back from the east, for the Fleet had risen so high that it could not be crossed on horseback ever so far up. Njal waited for him one night, for he had meant him to have ridden with him; and Njal said to Bergthora, that she must send Thord to the Thing as soon as ever he came home. Two nights after, Thord came from the east, and Bergthora told him that he must ride to the Thing, "but first thou shalt ride up into Thorolfsfell and see about the farm there, and do not be there longer than one or two nights."

CHAPTER XLII.

THE SLAYING OF THORD FREEDSMANSON.

Then Sigmund came from the east and those companions. Hallgerda told them that Thord was at home, but that he was to ride straightway to the Thing after a few nights' space. "Now ye will have a fair chance at him," he says, "but if this goes off, ye will never get nigh him". Men came to Lithend from Thorolfsfell, and told Hallgerda that Thord was there. Hallgerda went to Thrain Sigfus' son, and his companions, and said to him, "Now is Thord on Thorolfsfell, and now your best plan is to fall on him and kill him as he goes home".

"That we will do," says Sigmund. So they went out, and took their weapons and horses and rode on the way to meet him. Sigmund said to Thrain, "Now thou shalt have nothing to do with it; for we shall not need all of us".

"Very well, so I will," says he.

Then Thord rode up to them a little while after, and Sigmund said to him—

"Give thyself up," he says, "for now shalt thou die."

"That shall not be," says Thord, "come thou to single combat with me."

"That shall not be either," says Sigmund, "we will make the most of our numbers; but it is not strange that Skarphedinn is strong, for it is said that a fourth of a foster-child's strength comes from the foster-father."

"Thou wilt feel the force of that," says Thord, "for Skarphedinn will avenge me."

After that they fall on him, and he breaks a spear of each of them, so well did he guard himself. Then Skiolld cut off his hand, and he still kept them off with his other hand for some time, till Sigmund thrust him through. Then he fell dead to earth. They threw over him turf and stones; and Thrain said—"We have won an ill work, and Njal's sons will take this slaying ill when they hear of it".

They ride home and tell Hallgerda. She was glad to hear of the slaying, but Rannveig, Gunnar's mother, said—

"It is said 'but a short while is hand fain of blow,' and so it will be here; but still Gunnar will set thee free from this matter. But if Hallgerda makes thee take another fly in thy mouth, then that will be thy bane."

Hallgerda sent a man to Bergthorsknoll, to tell the slaying, and another man to the Thing, to tell it to Gunnar. Bergthora said she would not fight against Hallgerda with ill worth about such a matter; "that," quoth she, "would be no revenge for so great a quarrel".

CHAPTER XLIII.

NJAL AND GUNNAR MAKE PEACE FOR THE SLAYING OF THORD.

But when the messenger came to the Thing to tell Gunnar of the slaying, then Gunnar said—

"This has happened ill, and no tidings could come to my ears which I should think worse; but yet we will now go at once and see Njal. I still hope he may take it well, though he be sorely tried."

So they went to see Njal, and called him to come out and talk to them. He went out at once to meet Gunnar, and they talked, nor were there any more men by at first than Kolskegg.

"Hard tidings have I to tell thee," says Gunnar; "the slaying of Thord Freedmanson, and I wish to offer thee self-doom for the slaying."

Njal held his peace some while, and then said—

"That is well offered, and I will take it; but yet it is to be looked for, that I shall have blame from my wife or from my sons for that, for it will mislike them much; but still I will run the risk, for I know that I have to deal with a good man and true; nor do I wish that any breach should arise in our friendship on my part."

"Wilt thou let thy sons be by, pray?" says Gunnar.

"I will not," says Njal, "for they will not break the peace which I make, but if they stand by while we make it, they will not pull well together with us."

"So it shall be," says Gunnar. "See thou to it alone."

Then they shook one another by the hand, and made peace well and quickly.

Then Njal said—"The award that I make is two hundred in silver, and that thou wilt think much".

"I do not think it too much," says Gunnar, and went home to his booth.

Njal's sons came home, and Skarphedinn asked whence that great sum of money came, which his father held in his hand.

Njal said—"I tell you of your foster-father's Thord's slaying, and we two, Gunnar and I, have now made peace in the matter, and he has paid an atonement for him as for two men".

"Who slew him?" says Skarphedinn.

"Sigmund and Skiolld, but Thrain was standing near too," says Njal.

"They thought they had need of much strength," says Skarphedinn, and sang a song—

Bold in deeds of derring-do,
Burdeners of ocean's steeds,
Strength enough it seems they needed
All to slay a single man;
When shall we our hands uplift?
We who brandish burnished steel—
Famous men erst reddened weapons,
When? if now we quiet sit?

"Yes! when shall the day come when we shall lift our hands?"

"That will not be long off," says Njal, "and then thou shalt not be baulked; but still, methinks, I set great store on your not breaking this peace that I have made."

"Then we will not break it," says Skarphedinn, "but if anything arises between us, then we will bear in mind the old feud."

"Then I will ask you to spare no one," says Njal.

CHAPTER XLIV.

SIGMUND MOCKS NJAL AND HIS SONS.

Now men ride home from the Thing; and when Gunnar came home, he said to Sigmund—

"Thou art a more unlucky man than I thought, and turnest thy good gifts to thine own ill. But still I have made peace for thee with Njal and his sons; and now, take care that thou dost not let another fly come into thy mouth. Thou art not at all after my mind, thou goest about with jibes and jeers, with scorn and mocking; but that is not my turn of mind. That is why thou gettest on so well with Hallgerda, because ye two have your minds more alike."

Gunnar scolded him a long time, and he answered him well, and said he would follow his counsel more for the time to come than he had followed it hitherto. Gunnar told him then they might get on together. Gunnar and Njal kept up their friendship though the rest of their people saw little of one another. It happened once that some gangrel women came to Lithend from Bergthorsknoll; they were great gossips and rather spiteful tongued. Hallgerda had a bower, and sate often in it, and there sate with her daughter Thorgerda, and there too were Thrain and Sigmund, and a crowd of women. Gunnar was not there nor Kolskegg. These gangrel women went into the bower, and Hallgerda greeted them, and made room for them; then she asked them for news, but they said they had none to tell. Hallgerda asked where they had been over night; they said at Bergthorsknoll.

"What was Njal doing?" she says.

"He was hard at work sitting still," they said.

"What were Njal's sons doing?" she says; "they think themselves men at any rate."

"Tall men they are in growth," they say, "but as yet they are all untried; Skarphedinn whetted an axe, Grim fitted a spearhead to the shaft, Helgi rivetted a hilt on a sword, Hauskuld strengthened the handle of a shield."

"They must be bent on some great deed," says Hallgerda.

"We do not know that," they say.

"What were Njal's house-carles doing?" she asks.

"We don't know what some of them were doing, but one was carting dung up the hill-side."

"What good was there in doing that?" she asks.

"He said it made the swathe better there than any where else," they reply. "Witless now is Njal," says Hallgerda, "though he knows how to give counsel on every thing."

"How so?" they ask.

"I will only bring forward what is true to prove it," says she; "why doesn't he make them cart dung over his beard that he may be like other men? Let us call him 'the beardless carle': but his sons we will call 'dung-beardlings'; and now do pray give some stave about them, Sigmund, and let us get some good by thy gift of song."

"I am quite ready to do that," says he, and sang these verses—

Lady proud with hawk in hand.
Prithee why should dungbeard boys,
Reft of reason, dare to hammer
Handle fast on battle shield?
For these lads of loathly feature—
Lady scattering swanbath's beams[20]—
Shall not shun this ditty shameful
Which I shape upon them now.

He the beardless carle shall listen
While I lash him with abuse,
Loon at whom our stomachs sicken.
Soon shall hear these words of scorn;
Far too nice for such base fellows
Is the name my bounty gives,
Eën my muse her help refuses,
Making mirth of dungbeard boys.

Here I find a nickname fitting
For those noisome dungbeard boys—
Loath am I to break my bargain
Linked with such a noble man—
Knit we all our taunts together—
Known to me is mind of man—
Call we now with outburst common,
Him, that churl, the beardless carle.

"Thou art a jewel indeed," says Hallgerda; "how yielding thou art to what I ask!"

Just then Gunnar came in. He had been standing outside the door of the bower, and heard all the words that had passed. They were in a great fright when they saw him come in, and then all held their peace, but before there had been bursts of laughter.

Gunnar was very wroth, and said to Sigmund, "thou art a foolish man, and one that cannot keep to good advice, and thou revilest Njal's sons, and Njal himself who is most worth of all; and this thou doest in spite of what thou hast already done. Mind, this will be thy death. But if any man repeats these words that thou hast spoken, or these verses that thou hast made, that man shall be sent away at once, and have my wrath beside."

But they were all so sore afraid of him, that no one dared to repeat those words. After that he went away, but the gangrel women talked among themselves, and said that they would get a reward from Bergthora if they told her all this. They went then away afterwards down thither, and took Bergthora aside and told her the whole story of their own free will.

Bergthora spoke and said, when men sate down to the board, "Gifts have been given to all of you, father and sons, and ye will be no true men unless ye repay them somehow".

"What gifts are these?" asks Skarphedinn.

"You, my sons," says Bergthora, "have got one gift between you all. Ye are nick-named 'Dung-beardlings,' but my husband 'the beardless carle'."

"Ours is no woman's nature," says Skarphedinn, "that we should fly into a rage at every little thing."

"And yet Gunnar was wroth for your sakes," says she, "and he is thought to be good-tempered. But if ye do not take vengeance for this wrong, ye will avenge no shame."

"The carline, our mother, thinks this fine sport," says Skarphedinn, and smiled scornfully as he spoke, but still the sweat burst out upon his brow, and red flecks came over his cheeks, but that was not his wont. Grim was silent and bit his lip. Helgi made no sign, and he said never a word. Hauskuld went off with Bergthora; she came into the room again, and fretted and foamed much.

Njal spoke and said, "'slow and sure,' says the proverb, mistress! and so it is with many things, though they try men's tempers, that there are always two sides to a story, even when vengeance is taken".

But at even when Njal was come into his bed, he heard that an axe came against the panel and rang loudly, but there was another shut bed, and there the shields were hung up, and he sees that they are away. He said, "who have taken down our shields?"

"Thy sons went out with them," says Bergthora.

Njal pulled his shoes on his feet, and went out at once, and round to the other side of the house, and sees that they were taking their course right up the slope; he said, "whither away, Skarphedinn?"

"To look after thy sheep," he answers.

"You would not then be armed," said Njal, "if you meant that, and your errand must be something else."

Then Skarphedinn sang a song—

Squanderer of hoarded wealth,
Some there are that own rich treasure,
Ore of sea that clasps the earth,
And yet care to count their sheep;
Those who forge sharp songs of mocking,
Death songs, scarcely can possess
Sense of sheep that crop the grass;
Such as these I seek in fight;

and said afterwards—

"We shall fish for salmon, father."

"'Twould be well then if it turned out so that the prey does not get away from you."

They went their way, but Njal went to his bed, and he said to Bergthora, "Thy sons were out of doors all of them, with arms, and now thou must have egged them on to something".

"I will give them my heartfelt thanks," said Bergthora, "if they tell me the slaying of Sigmund."

CHAPTER XLV.

THE SLAYING OF SIGMUND AND SKIOLLD.

Now they, Njal's sons, fare up to Fleetlithe, and were that night under the Lithe, and when the day began to break, they came near to Lithend. That same morning both Sigmund and Skiolld rose up and meant to go to the stud-horses; they had bits with them, and caught the horses that were in the "town" and rode away on them. They found the stud-horses between two brooks. Skarphedinn caught sight of them, for Sigmund was in bright clothing. Skarphedinn said, "See you now the red elf yonder, lads?" They looked that way, and said they saw him.

Skarphedinn spoke again: "Thou, Hauskuld, shalt have nothing to do with it, for thou wilt often be sent about alone without due heed; but I mean Sigmund for myself; methinks that is like a man; but Grim and Helgi, they shall try to slay Skiolld".

Hauskuld sat him down, but they went until they came up to them. Skarphedinn said to Sigmund—

"Take thy weapons and defend thyself; that is more needful now, than to make mocking songs on me and my brothers."

Sigmund took up his weapons, but Skarphedinn waited the while. Skiolld turned against Grim and Helgi, and they fell hotly to fight. Sigmund had a helm on his head, and a shield at his side, and was girt with a sword, his spear was in his hand; now he turns against Skarphedinn, and thrusts at once at him with his spear, and the thrust came on his shield. Skarphedinn dashes the spearhaft in two, and lifts up his axe and hews at Sigmund, and cleaves his shield down to below the handle. Sigmund drew his sword and cut at Skarphedinn, and the sword cuts into his shield, so that it stuck fast. Skarphedinn gave the shield such a quick twist, that Sigmund let go his sword. Then Skarphedinn hews at Sigmund with his axe, the "Ogress of war". Sigmund had on a corselet, the axe came on his shoulder. Skarphedinn cleft the shoulder-blade right through, and at the same time pulled the axe towards him, Sigmund fell down on both knees, but sprang up again at once.

"Thou hast lifted low to me already," says Skarphedinn, "but still thou shalt fall upon thy mother's bosom ere we two part."

"Ill is that then," says Sigmund.

Skarphedinn gave him a blow on his helm, and after that dealt Sigmund his death-blow.

Grim cut off Skiolld's foot at the ankle-joint, but Helgi thrust him through with his spear, and he got his death there and then.

Skarphedinn saw Hallgerda's shepherd, just as he had hewn off Sigmund's head; he handed the head to the shepherd, and bade him bear it to Hallgerda, and said she would know whether that head had made jeering songs about them, and with that he sang a song.

Here! this head shall thou, that heapest
Hoards from ocean-caverns won,[21]
Bear to Hallgerd with my greeting,
Her that hurries men to fight;
Sure am I, O firewood splitter!
That yon spendthrift knows it well,
And will answer if it ever
Uttered mocking songs on us.

The shepherd casts the head down as soon as ever they parted, for he dared not do so while their eyes were on him. They fared along till they met some men down by Markfleet, and told them the tidings. Skarphedinn gave himself out as the slayer of Sigmund; and Grim and Helgi as the slayers of Skiolld; then they fared home and told Njal the tidings. He answers them—

"Good luck to your hands! Here no self-doom will come to pass as things stand."

Now we must take up the story, and say that the shepherd came home to Lithend. He told Hallgerda the tidings.

"Skarphedinn put Sigmund's head into my hands," he says, "and bade me bring it thee; but I dared not do it, for I knew not how thou wouldst like that."

"'Twas ill that thou didst not do that," she says; "I would have brought it to Gunnar, and then he would have avenged his kinsman, or have to bear every man's blame."

After that she went to Gunnar and said, "I tell thee of thy kinsman Sigmund's slaying: Skarphedinn slew him, and wanted them to bring me the head".

"Just what might be looked for to befall him," says Gunnar, "for ill redes bring ill luck, and both you and Skarphedinn have often done one another spiteful turns".

Then Gunnar went away; he let no steps be taken towards a suit for manslaughter, and did nothing about it. Hallgerda often put him in mind of it, and kept saying that Sigmund had fallen unatoned. Gunnar gave no heed to that.

Now three Things passed away, at each of which men thought that he would follow up the suit: then a knotty point came on Gunnar's hands, which he knew not how to set about, and then he rode to find Njal. He gave Gunnar a hearty welcome. Gunnar said to Njal, "I am come to seek a bit of good counsel at thy hands about a knotty point".

"Thou art worthy of it," says Njal, and gave him counsel what to do. Then Gunnar stood up and thanked him. Njal then spoke and said, and took Gunnar by the hand, "Over long hath thy kinsman Sigmund been unatoned". "He has been long ago atoned," says Gunnar, "but still I will not fling back the honour offered me."

Gunnar had never spoken an ill word of Njal's sons. Njal would have nothing else than that Gunnar should make his own award in the matter. He awarded two hundred in silver, but let Skiolld fall without a price. They paid down all the money at once.

Gunnar declared this their atonement at the Thingskala Thing, when most men were at it, and laid great weight on the way in which they (Njal and his sons) had behaved; he told too those bad words which cost Sigmund his life, and no man was to repeat them or sing the verses, but if any sung them, the man who uttered them was to fall without atonement.

Both Gunnar and Njal gave each other their words that no such matters should ever happen that they would not settle among themselves; and this pledge was well kept ever after, and they were always friends.

CHAPTER XLVI.

OF GIZUR THE WHITE AND GEIR THE PRIEST.

There was a man named Gizur the White; he was Teit's son; Kettlebjorn the Old's son, of Mossfell. Gizur the White kept house at Mossfell, and was a great chief. That man is also named in this story, whose name was Geir the priest; his mother was Thorkatla, another daughter of Kettlebjorn the Old of Mossfell. Geir kept house at Lithe. He and Gizur backed one another in every matter. At that time Mord Valgard's son kept house at Hof on the Rangrivervales; he was crafty and spiteful. Valgard his father was then abroad, but his mother was dead. He was very envious of Gunnar of Lithend. He was wealthy, so far as goods went, but had not many friends.

CHAPTER XLVII.

OF OTKELL IN KIRKBY.

There was a man named Otkell; he was the son of Skarf, the son of Hallkell, who fought with Gorm of Gormness, and felled him on the holm.[22] This Hallkell and Kettlebjorn the Old were brothers.

Otkell kept house at Kirkby; his wife's name was Thorgerda; she was a daughter of Mar, the son of Runolf, the son of Naddad of the Faroe isles. Otkell was wealthy in goods. His son's name was Thorgeir; he was young in years, and a bold dashing man.

Skamkell was the name of another man; he kept house at another farm called Hof; he was well off for money, but he was a spiteful man and a liar; quarrelsome too, and ill to deal with. He was Otkell's friend. Hallkell was the name of Otkell's brother; he was a tall strong man, and lived there with Otkell; their brother's name was Hallbjorn the White; he brought out to Iceland a thrall, whose name was Malcolm; he was Irish and had not many friends.

Hallbjorn went to stay with Otkell, and so did his thrall Malcolm. The thrall was always saying that he should think himself happy if Otkell owned him. Otkell was kind to him, and gave him a knife and belt, and a full suit of clothes, but the thrall turned his hand to any work that Otkell wished.

Otkell wanted to make a bargain with his brother for the thrall; he said he would give him the thrall, but said too, that he was a worse treasure than he thought. And as soon as Otkell owned the thrall, then he did less and less work. Otkell often said outright to Hallbjorn, that he thought the thrall did little work; and he told Otkell that there was worse in him yet to come.

At that time came a great scarcity, so that men fell short both of meat and hay, and that spread over all parts of Iceland. Gunnar shared his hay and meat with many men; and all got them who came thither, so long as his stores lasted. At last it came about that Gunnar himself fell short both of hay and meat. Then Gunnar called on Kolskegg to go along with him; he called too on Thrain Sigfus' son, and Lambi Sigurd's son. They fared to Kirkby, and called Otkell out. He greeted them, and Gunnar said, "It so happens that I am come to deal with thee for hay and meat, if there be any left".

Otkell answers, "There is store of both, but I will sell thee neither".

"Wilt thou give me them then," says Gunnar, "and run the risk of my paying thee back somehow?"

"I will not do that either," says Otkell.

Skamkell all the while was giving him bad counsel.

Then Thrain Sigfus' son said, "It would serve him right if we take both hay and meat and lay down the worth of them instead".

Skamkell answered, "All the men of Mossfell must be dead and gone then, if ye, sons of Sigfus, are to come and rob them".

"I will have no hand in any robbery," says Gunnar.

"Wilt thou buy a thrall of me?" says Otkell.

"I'll not spare to do that," says Gunnar. After that Gunnar bought the thrall, and fared away as things stood.

Njal hears of this, and said, "Such things are ill done, to refuse to let Gunnar buy; and it is not a good outlook for others if such men as he cannot get what they want".

"What's the good of thy talking so much about such a little matter?" says Bergthora; "far more like a man would it be to let him have both meat and hay, when thou lackest neither of them."

"That is clear as day," says Njal, "and I will of a surety supply his need somewhat."

Then he fared up to Thorolfsfell, and his sons with him, and they bound hay on fifteen horses; but on five horses they had meat. Njal came to Lithend, and called Gunnar out. He greeted them kindly.

"Here is hay and meat," said Njal, "which I will give thee; and my wish is, that thou shouldst never look to any one else than to me if thou standest in need of any thing."

"Good are thy gifts," says Gunnar, "but methinks thy friendship is still more worth, and that of thy sons."

After that Njal fared home, and now the spring passes away.

CHAPTER XLVIII.

HOW HALLGERDA MAKES MALCOLM STEAL FROM KIRKBY.

Now Gunnar is about to ride to the Thing, but a great crowd of men from the Side east turned in as guests at his house.

Gunnar bade them come and be his guests again, as they rode back from the Thing; and they said they would do so.

Now they ride to the Thing, and Njal and his sons were there. That Thing was still and quiet.

Now we must take up the story, and say that Hallgerda comes to talk with Malcolm the thrall.

"I have thought of an errand to send thee on," she says; "thou shalt go to Kirkby."

"And what shall I do there?" he says.

"Thou shalt steal from thence food enough to load two horses, and mind and have butter and cheese; but thou shalt lay fire in the storehouse, and all will think that it has arisen out of heedlessness, but no one will think that there has been theft."

"Bad have I been," said the thrall, "but never have I been a thief."

"Hear a wonder!" says Hallgerda, "thou makest thyself good, thou that hast been both thief and murderer; but thou shalt not dare to do aught else than go, else will I let thee be slain."

He thought he knew enough of her to be sure that she would so do if he went not; so he took at night two horses and laid pack-saddles on them, and went his way to Kirkby. The house-dog knew him and did not bark at him, and ran and fawned on him. After that he went to the storehouse and loaded the two horses with food out of it, but the storehouse he burnt, and the dog he slew.

He went up along by Rangriver, and his shoe-thong snapped; so he takes his knife and makes the shoe right, but he leaves the knife and belt lying there behind him.

He fares till he comes to Lithend; then he misses the knife, but dares not to go back.

Now he brings Hallgerda the food, and she showed herself well pleased at it.

Next morning when men came out of doors at Kirkby there they saw great scathe. Then a man was sent to the Thing to tell Otkell, he bore the loss well, and said it must have happened because the kitchen was next to the storehouse; and all thought that that was how it happened.

Now men ride home from the Thing, and many rode to Lithend. Hallgerda set food on the board, and in came cheese and butter. Gunnar knew that such food was not to be looked for in his house, and asked Hallgerda whence it came?

"Thence," she says, "whence thou mightest well eat of it; besides, it is no man's business to trouble himself with housekeeping."

Gunnar got wroth and said, "Ill indeed is it if I am a partaker with thieves"; and with that he gave her a slap on the cheek.

She said she would bear that slap in mind and repay it if she could.

So she went off and he went with her, and then all that was on the board was cleared away, but flesh-meat was brought in instead, and all thought that was because the flesh was thought to have been got in a better way.

Now the men who had been at the Thing fare away.

CHAPTER XLIX.

OF SKAMKELL'S EVIL COUNSEL.

Now we must tell of Skamkell. He rides after some sheep up along Rangriver, and he sees something shining in the path. He finds a knife and belt, and thinks he knows both of them. He fares with them to Kirkby; Otkell was out of doors when Skamkell came. He spoke to him and said—

"Knowest thou aught of these pretty things?"

"Of a surety," says Otkell, "I know them."

"Who owns them?" asks Skamkell.

"Malcolm the thrall," says Otkell.

"Then more shall see and know them than we two," says Skamkell, "for true will I be to thee in counsel."

They showed them to many men, and all knew them. Then Skamkell said—

"What counsel wilt thou now take?"

"We shall go and see Mord Valgard's son," answers Otkell, "and seek counsel of him."

So they went to Hof, and showed the pretty things to Mord, and asked him if he knew them?

He said he knew them well enough, but what was there in that? "Do you think you have a right to look for anything at Lithend?"

"We think it hard for us," says Skamkell, "to know what to do, when such mighty men have a hand in it."

"That is so, sure enough," says Mord, "but yet I will get to know those things out of Gunnar's household, which none of you will ever know."

"We would give thee money," they say, "if thou wouldst search out this thing."

"That money I shall buy full dear," answered Mord, "but still, perhaps, it may be that I will look at the matter."

They gave him three marks of silver for lending them his help.

Then he gave them this counsel, that women should go about from house to house with small wares, and give them to the housewives, and mark what was given them in return.

"For," he says, "'tis the turn of mind of all men first to give away what has been stolen, if they have it in their keeping, and so it will be here also, if this hath happened by the hand of man. Ye shall then come and show me what has been given to each in each house, and I shall then be free from further share in this matter, if the truth comes to light."

To this they agreed, and went home afterwards.

Mord sends women about the country, and they were away half a month. Then they came back, and had big bundles. Mord asked where they had most given them?

They said that at Lithend most was given them, and Hallgerda had been most bountiful to them.

He asked what was given them there?

"Cheese," say they.

He begged to see it, and they showed it to him, and it was in great slices. These he took and kept.

A little after, Mord fared to see Otkell, and bade that he would bring Thorgerda's cheese-mould; and when that was done, he laid the slices down in it, and lo! they fitted the mould in every way.

Then they saw, too, that a whole cheese had been given to them.

Then Mord said, "Now may ye see that Hallgerda must have stolen the cheese"; and they all passed the same judgment; and then Mord said, that now he thought he was free of this matter.

After that they parted.

Shortly after Kolskegg fell to talking with Gunnar, and said—

"Ill is it to tell, but the story is in every man's mouth, that Hallgerda must have stolen, and that she was at the bottom of all that great scathe that befell at Kirkby."

Gunnar said that he too thought that must be so. "But what is to be done now?"

Kolskegg answered, "That wilt think it thy most bounden duty to make atonement for thy wife's wrong, and methinks it were best that thou farest to see Otkell, and makest him a handsome offer."

"This is well spoken," says Gunnar, "and so it shall be."

A little after Gunnar sent after Thrain Sigfus' son, and Lambi Sigurd's son, and they came at once.

Gunnar told them whither he meant to go, and they were well pleased. Gunnar rode with eleven men to Kirkby, and called Otkell out. Skamkell was there too, and said, "I will go out with thee, and it will be best now to have the balance of wit on thy side. And I would wish to stand closest by thee when thou needest it most, and now this will be put to the proof. Methinks it were best that thou puttest on an air of great weight."

Then they, Otkell and Skamkell, and Hallkell and Hallbjorn, went out all of them.

They greeted Gunnar, and he took their greeting well. Otkell asks whither he meant to go?

"No farther than here," says Gunnar, "and my errand hither is to tell thee about that bad mishap—how it arose from the plotting of my wife and that thrall whom I bought from thee."

"'Tis only what was to be looked for," says Hallbjorn.

"Now I will make thee a good offer," says Gunnar, "and the offer is this, that the best men here in the country round settle the matter."

"This is a fair-sounding offer," said Skamkell, "but an unfair and uneven one. Thou art a man who has many friends among the householders, but Otkell has not many friends."

"Well," says Gunnar, "then I will offer thee that I shall make an award, and utter it here on this spot, and so we will settle the matter, and my good-will shall follow the settlement. But I will make thee an atonement by paying twice the worth of what was lost."

"This choice shalt thou not take," said Skamkell; "and it is unworthy to give up to him the right to make his own award, when thou oughtest to have kept it for thyself."

So Otkell said, "I will not give up to thee, Gunnar, the right to make thine own award."

"I see plainly," said Gunnar, "the help of men who will be paid off for it one day I daresay; but come now, utter an award for thyself."

Otkell leant toward Skamkell and said, "What shall I answer now?"

"This thou shalt call a good offer, but still put thy suit into the hands of Gizur the white, and Geir the priest, and then many will say this, that thou behavest like Hallkell, thy grandfather, who was the greatest of champions."

"Well offered is this, Gunnar," said Otkell, "but still my will is thou wouldst give me time to see Gizur the white."

"Do now whatever thou likest in the matter," said Gunnar; "but men will say this, that thou couldst not see thine own honour when thou wouldst have none of the choices I offer thee."

Then Gunnar rode home, and when he had gone away, Hallbjorn said, "Here I see how much man differs from man. Gunnar made thee good offers, but thou wouldst take none of them; or how dost thou think to strive with Gunnar in a quarrel, when no one is his match in fight. But now he is still so kind-hearted a man that it may be he will let these offers stand, though thou art only ready to take them afterwards. Methinks it were best that thou farest to see Gizur the white and Geir the priest now this very hour."

Otkell let them catch his horse, and made ready in every way. Otkell was not sharpsighted, and Skamkell walked on the way along with him, and said to Otkell—

"Methought it strange that thy brother would not take this toil from thee, and now I will make thee an offer to fare instead of thee, for I know that the journey is irksome to thee."

"I will take that offer," says Otkell, "but mind and be as truthful as ever thou canst."

"So it shall be," says Skamkell.

Then Skamkell took his horse and cloak, but Otkell walks home.

Hallbjorn was out of doors, and said to Otkell—

"Ill is it to have a thrall for one's bosom friend, and we shall rue this for ever that thou hast turned back, and it is an unwise step to send the greatest liar on an errand, of which one may so speak that men's lives hang on it."

"Thou wouldst be sore afraid," says Otkell, "if Gunnar had his bill aloft, when thou art so scared now."

"No one knows who will be most afraid then," said Hallbjorn; "but this thou wilt have to own, that Gunnar does not lose much time in brandishing his bill when he is wroth."

"Ah!" said Otkell, "ye are all of you for yielding but Skamkell."

And then they were both wroth.

CHAPTER L.

OF SKAMKELL'S LYING.

Skamkell came to Mossfell, and repeated all the offers to Gizur.

"It so seems to me," says Gizur, "as though these have been bravely offered; but why took he not these offers?"

"The chief cause was," answers Skamkell, "that all wished to show thee honour, and that was why he waited for thy utterance; besides, that is best for all."

So Skamkell stayed there the night over, but Gizur sent a man to fetch Geir the priest; and he came there early. Then Gizur told him the story and said—

"What course is to be taken now?"

"As thou no doubt hast already made up thy mind—to make the best of the business for both sides."

"Now we will let Skamkell tell his tale a second time, and see how he repeats it."

So they did that, and Gizur said—

"Thou must have told this story right; but still I have seen thee to be the wickedest of men, and there is no faith in faces if thou turnest out well."

Skamkell fared home, and rides first to Kirkby and calls Otkell out. He greets Skamkell well, and Skamkell brought him the greeting of Gizur and Geir.

"But about this matter of the suit," he says, "there is no need to speak softly, how that it is the will of both Gizur and Geir that this suit should not be settled in a friendly way. They gave that counsel that a summons should be set on foot, and that Gunnar should be summoned for having partaken of the goods, but Hallgerda for stealing them."

"It shall be done," said Otkell, "in everything as they have given counsel."

"They thought most of this," says Skamkell, "that thou hadst behaved so proudly; but as for me, I made as great a man of thee in everything as I could."

Now Otkell tells all this to his brothers, and Hallbjorn said—

"This must be the biggest lie."

Now the time goes on until the last of the summoning days before the Althing came.

Then Otkell called on his brothers and Skamkell to ride on the business of the summons to Lithend.

Hallbjorn said he would go, but said also that they would rue this summoning as time went on.

Now they rode twelve of them together to Lithend, but when they came into the "town," there was Gunnar out of doors, and knew naught of their coming till they had ridden right up to the house.

He did not go indoors then, and Otkell thundered out the summons there and then; but when they had made an end of the summoning Skamkell said—

"Is it all right, master?"

"Ye know that best," says Gunnar, "but I will put thee in mind of this journey one of these days, and of thy good help."

"That will not harm us," says Skamkell, "if thy bill be not aloft."

Gunnar was very wroth and went indoors, and told Kolskegg, and Kolskegg said—

"Ill was it that we were not out of doors; they should have come here on the most shameful journey, if we had been by."

"Everything bides its time," says Gunnar; "but this journey will not turn out to their honour."

A little after Gunnar went and told Njal.

"Let it not worry thee a jot," said Njal, "for this will be the greatest honour to thee, ere this Thing comes to an end. As for us, we will all back thee with counsel and force."

Gunnar thanked him and rode home.

Otkell rides to the Thing, and his brothers with him and Skamkell.

CHAPTER LI.

OF GUNNAR.

Gunnar rode to the Thing and all the sons of Sigfus; Njal and his sons too, they all went with Gunnar; and it was said that no band was so well knit and hardy as theirs.

Gunnar went one day to the booth of the Dalemen; Hrut was by the booth and Hauskuld, and they greeted Gunnar well. Now Gunnar tells them the whole story of the suit up to that time.

"What counsel gives Njal?" asks Hrut.

"He bade me seek you brothers," says Gunnar, "and said he was sure that he and you would look at the matter in the same light."

"He wishes then," says Hrut, "that I should say what I think for kinship's sake; and so it shall be. Thou shalt challenge Gizur the white to combat on the island, if they do not leave the whole award to thee; but Kolskegg shall challenge Geir the Priest. As for Otkell and his crew, men must be got ready to fall on them; and now we have such great strength all of us together, that thou mayst carry out whatever thou wilt."

Gunnar went home to his booth and told Njal.

"Just what I looked for," said Njal.

Wolf Aurpriest got wind of this plan, and told Gizur, and Gizur said to Otkell—

"Who gave thee that counsel that thou shouldst summon Gunnar?"

"Skamkell told me that was the counsel of both Geir the priest and thyself."

"But where is that scoundrel," says Gizur, "who has thus lied?"

"He lies sick up at our booth," says Otkell.

"May he never rise from his bed," says Gizur, "Now we must all go to see Gunnar, and offer him the right to make his own award; but I know not whether he will take that now."

Many men spoke ill of Skamkell, and he lay sick all through the Thing.

Gizur and his friends went to Gunnar's booth; their coming was known, and Gunnar was told as he sat in his booth, and then they all went out and stood in array.

Gizur the white came first, and after a while he spoke and said—

"This is our offer—that thou, Gunnar, makest thine own award in this suit."

"Then," says Gunnar, "it was no doubt far from thy counsel that I was summoned."

"I gave no such counsel," says Gizur, "neither I nor Geir."

"Then thou must clear thyself of this charge by fitting proof."

"What proof dost thou ask?" says Gizur.

"That thou takest an oath," says Gunnar.

"That I will do," says Gizur, "if thou wilt take the award into thine own hands."

"That was the offer I made a while ago," says Gunnar; "but now, methinks, I have a greater matter to pass judgment on."

"It will not be right to refuse to make thine own award," said Njal; "for the greater the matter, the greater the honour in making it."

"Well," said Gunnar, "I will do this to please my friends, and utter my award; but I give Otkell this bit of advice, never to give me cause for quarrel hereafter."

Then Hrut and Hauskuld were sent for, and they came thither, and then Gizur the White and Geir the priest took their oaths; but Gunnar made his award, and spoke with no man about it, and afterwards he uttered it as follows:—

"This is my award," he says; "first, I lay it down that the storehouse must be paid for, and the food that was therein; but for the thrall, I will pay thee no fine, for that thou hiddest his faults; but I award him back to thee; for as the saying is, 'Birds of a feather flock most together'. Then, on the other hand, I see that thou hast summoned me in scorn and mockery, and for that I award to myself no less a sum than what the house that was burnt and the stores in it were worth; but if ye think it better that we be not set at one again, then I will let you have your choice of that, but if so I have already made up my mind what I shall do, and then I will fulfil my purpose."

"What we ask," said Gizur, "is that thou shouldst not be hard on Otkell, but we beg this of thee, on the other hand, that thou wouldst be his friend."

"That shall never be," said Gunnar, "so long as I live; but he shall have Skamkell's friendship; on that he has long leant."

"Well," answers Gizur, "we will close with thee in this matter, though thou alone layest down the terms."

Then all this atonement was made and hands were shaken on it, and Gunnar said to Otkell—

"It were wiser to go away to thy kinsfolk; but if thou wilt be here in this country, mind that thou givest me no cause of quarrel."

"That is wholesome counsel," said Gizur; "and so he shall do."

So Gunnar had the greatest honour from that suit, and afterwards men rode home from the Thing.

Now Gunnar sits in his house at home, and so things are quiet for a while.

CHAPTER LII.

OF RUNOLF, THE SON OF WOLF AURPRIEST.

There was a man named Runolf, the son of Wolf Aurpriest, he kept house at the Dale, east of Markfleet. He was Otkell's guest once when he rode from the Thing. Otkell gave him an ox, all black, without a spot of white, nine winters old. Runolf thanked him for the gift, and bade him come and see him at home whenever he chose to go; and this bidding stood over for some while, so that he had not paid the visit. Runolf often sent men to him and put him in mind that he ought to come; and he always said he would come, but never went.

Now Otkell had two horses, dun coloured, with a black stripe down the back; they were the best steeds to ride in all the country round, and so fond of each other, that whenever one went before, the other ran after him.

There was an Easterling staying with Otkell, whose name was Audulf; he had set his heart on Signy Otkell's daughter. Audulf was a tall man in growth, and strong.

CHAPTER LIII.

HOW OTKELL RODE OVER GUNNAR.

It happened next spring that Otkell said that they would ride east to the Dale, to pay Runolf a visit, and all showed themselves well pleased at that. Skamkell and his two brothers, and Audulf and three men more, went along with Otkell. Otkell rode one of the dun horses, but the other ran loose by his side. They shaped their course east towards Markfleet; and now Otkell gallops ahead, and now the horses race against each other, and they break away from the path up towards the Fleetlithe.

Now, Otkell goes faster than he wished, and it happened that Gunnar had gone away from home out of his house all alone; and he had a corn-sieve in one hand, but in the other a hand-axe. He goes down to his seed field and sows his corn there, and had laid his cloak of fine stuff and his axe down by his aide, and so he sows the corn a while.

Now, it must be told how Otkell rides faster than he would. He had spurs on his feet, and so he gallops down over the ploughed field, and neither of them sees the other; and just as Gunnar stands upright, Otkell rides down upon him, and drives one of the spurs into Gunnar's ear, and gives him a great gash, and it bleeds at once much.

Just then Otkell's companions rode up.

"Ye may see, all of you," says Gunnar, "that thou hast drawn my blood, and it is unworthy to go on so. First thou hast summoned me, but now thou treadest me under foot, and ridest over me."

Skamkell said, "Well it was no worse, master, but thou wast not one whit less wroth at the Thing, when thou tookest the self-doom and clutchedst thy bill."

Gunnar said, "When we two next meet thou shalt see the bill." After that they part thus, and Skamkell shouted out and said, "Ye ride hard, lads!"

Gunnar went home, and said never a word to any one about what had happened, and no one thought that this wound could have come by man's doing.

It happened, though, one day that he told it to his brother Kolskegg, and Kolskegg said—

"This thou shalt tell to more men, so that it may not be said that thou layest blame on dead men; for it will be gainsaid if witnesses do not know beforehand what has passed between you."

Then Gunnar told it to his neighbours, and there was little talk about it at first.

Otkell comes east to the Dale, and they get a hearty welcome there, and sit there a week.

Skamkell told Runolf all about their meeting with Gunnar, and how it had gone off; and one man had happened to ask how Gunnar behaved.

"Why," said Skamkell, "if it were a low-born man it would have been said that he had wept."

"Such things are ill spoken," says Runolf, "and when ye two next meet, thou wilt have to own that there is no voice of weeping in his frame of mind; and it will be well if better men have not to pay for thy spite. Now it seems to me best when ye wish to go home that I should go with you, for Gunnar will do me no harm."

"I will not have that," says Otkell; "but I will ride across the Fleet lower down."

Runolf gave Otkell good gifts, and said they should not see one another again.

Otkell bade him then to bear his sons in mind if things turned out so.

CHAPTER LIV.

THE FIGHT AT RANGRIVER.

Now we must take up the story, and say that Gunnar was out of doors at Lithend, and sees his shepherd galloping up to the yard. The shepherd rode straight into the "town"; and Gunnar said, "Why ridest thou so hard?"

"I would be faithful to thee," said the man; "I saw men riding down along Markfleet, eight of them together, and four of them were in coloured clothes."

Gunnar said, "That must be Otkell".

The lad said, "I have often heard many temper-trying words of Skamkell's; for Skamkell spoke away there East at Dale, and said that thou sheddest tears when they rode over thee; but I tell it thee because I cannot bear to listen to such speeches of worthless men".

"We must not be word-sick," says Gunnar, "but from this day forth thou shalt do no other work than what thou choosest for thyself."

"Shall I say aught of this to Kolskegg thy brother?" asked the shepherd.

"Go thou and sleep," says Gunnar; "I will tell Kolskegg."

The lad laid him down and fell asleep at once, but Gunnar took the shepherd's horse and laid his saddle on him; he took his shield, and girded him with his sword, Oliver's gift; he sets his helm on his head; takes his bill, and something sung loud in it, and his mother, Rannveig, heard it. She went up to him and said, "Wrathful art thou now, my son, and never saw I thee thus before".

Gunnar goes out, and drives the butt of his spear into the earth, and throws himself into the saddle, and rides away.

His mother, Rannveig, went into the sitting-room, where there was a great noise of talking.

"Ye speak loud," she says, "but yet the bill gave a louder sound when Gunnar went out."

Kolskegg heard what she said, and spoke, "This betokens no small tidings".

"That is well," says Hallgerda, "now they will soon prove whether he goes away from them weeping."

Kolskegg takes his weapons and seeks him a horse, and rides after Gunnar as fast as he could.

Gunnar rides across Acretongue, and so to Geilastofna, and thence to Rangriver, and down the stream to the ford at Hof. There were some women at the milking-post there. Gunnar jumped off his horse and tied him up. By this time the others were riding up towards him; there were flat stones covered with mud in the path that led down to the ford.

Gunnar called out to them and said, "Now is the time to guard yourselves; here now is the bill, and here now ye will put it to the proof whether I shed one tear for all of you".

Then they all of them sprang off their horses' backs and made towards Gunnar. Hallbjorn was the foremost.

"Do not thou come on," says Gunnar; "thee last of all would I harm; but I will spare no one if I have to fight to my life."

"That I cannot do," says Hallbjorn; "thou wilt strive to kill my brother for all that, and it is a shame if I sit idly by." And as he said this he thrust at Gunnar with a great spear which he held in both hands.

Gunnar threw his shield before the blow, but Hallbjorn pierced the shield through. Gunnar thrust the shield down so hard that it stood fast in the earth,[23] but he brandished his sword so quickly that no eye could follow it, and he made a blow with the sword, and it fell on Hallbjorn's arm above the wrist, so that it cut it off.

Skamkell ran behind Gunnar's back and makes a blow at him with a great axe. Gunnar turned short round upon him and parries the blow with the bill, and caught the axe under one of its horns with such a wrench that it flew out of Skamkell's hand away into the river.

Then Gunnar sang a song.

Once thou askedst, foolish fellow,
Of this man, this sea-horse racer,
When as fast as feet could foot it
Forth ye fled from farm of mine,
Whether that were rightly summoned?
Now with gore the spear we redden,
Battle-eager and avenge us
Thus on thee, vile source of strife.

Gunnar gives another thrust with his bill, and through Skamkell, and lifts him up and casts him down in the muddy path on his head.

Audulf the Easterling snatches up a spear and launches it at Gunnar. Gunnar caught the spear with his hand in the air, and hurled it back at once, and it flew through the shield and the Easterling too, and so down into the earth.

Otkell smites at Gunnar with his sword, and aims at his leg just below the knee, but Gunnar leapt up into the air and he misses him. Then Gunnar thrusts at him the bill, and the blow goes through him.

Then Kolskegg comes up, and rushes at once at Hallkell and dealt him his death-blow with his short sword. There and then they slay eight men.

A woman who saw all this, ran home and told Mord, and besought him to part them.

"They alone will be there," he says, "of whom I care not though they slay one another."

"Thou canst not mean to say that," she says, "for thy kinsman Gunnar, and thy friend Otkell will be there."

"Baggage that thou art," he says, "thou art always chattering," and so he lay still indoors while they fought.

Gunnar and Kolskegg rode home after this work, and they rode hard up along the river bank, and Gunnar slipped off his horse and came down on his feet.

Then Kolskegg said, "Hard now thou ridest, brother!"

"Ay," said Gunnar, "that was what Skamkell said when he uttered those very words when they rode over me."

"Well! thou hast avenged that now," says Kolskegg.

"I would like to know," says Gunnar, "whether I am by so much the less brisk and bold than other men, because I think more of killing men than they?"

CHAPTER LV.

NJAL'S ADVICE TO GUNNAR.

Now those tidings are heard far and wide, and many say that they thought they had not happened before it was likely. Gunnar rode to Bergthorsknoll and told Njal of these deeds.

Njal said, "Thou hast done great things, but thou hast been sorely tried."

"How will it now go henceforth?" says Gunnar.

"Wilt thou that I tell thee what hath not yet come to pass?" asks Njal. "Thou wilt ride to the Thing, and thou wilt abide by my counsel and get the greatest honour from this matter. This will be the beginning of thy manslayings."

"But give me some cunning counsel," says Gunnar.

"I will do that," says Njal: "never slay more than one man in the same stock, and never break the peace which good men and true make between thee and others, and least of all in such a matter as this."

Gunnar said, "I should have thought there was more risk of that with others than with me."

"Like enough," says Njal, "but still thou shalt so think of thy quarrels that, if that should come to pass of which I have warned thee, then thou wilt have but a little while to live; but otherwise, thou wilt come to be an old man."

Gunnar said, "Dost thou know what will be thine own death?"

"I know it," says Njal.

"What?" asks Gunnar.

"That," says Njal, "which all would be the last to think."

After that Gunnar rode home.

A man was sent to Gizur the white and Geir the priest, for they had the blood-feud after Otkell. Then they had a meeting, and had a talk about what was to be done; and they were of one mind that the quarrel should be followed up at law. Then some one was sought who would take the suit up, but no one was ready to do that.

"It seems to me," says Gizur, "that now there are only two courses, that one of us two undertakes the suit, and then we shall have to draw lots who it shall be, or else the man will be unatoned. We may make up our minds, too, that this will be a heavy suit to touch; Gunnar has many kinsmen and is much beloved; but that one of us who does not draw the lot shall ride to the Thing and never leave it until the suit comes to an end."

After that they drew lots, and Geir the priest drew the lot to take up the suit.

A little after, they rode from the west over the river, and came to the spot where the meeting had been by Rangriver, and dug up the bodies, and took witness to the wounds. After that they gave lawful notice and summoned nine neighbours to bear witness in the suit.

They were told that Gunnar was at home with about thirty men; then Geir the priest asked whether Gizur would ride against him with one hundred men.

"I will not do that," says he, "though the balance of force is great on our side."

After that they rode back home. The news that the suit was set on foot was spread all over the country, and the saying ran that the Thing would be very noisy and stormy.

CHAPTER LVI.

GUNNAR AND GEIR THE PRIEST STRIVE AT THE THING.

There was a man named Skapti. He was the son of Thorod. That father and son were great chiefs, and very well skilled in law. Thorod was thought to be rather crafty and guileful. They stood by Gizur the white in every quarrel.

As for the Lithemen and the dwellers by Rangriver, they came in a great body to the Thing. Gunnar was so beloved that all said with one voice that they would back him.

Now they all come to the Thing and fit up their booths. In company with Gizur the white were these chiefs: Skapti Thorod's son, Asgrim Ellidagrim's son, Oddi of Kidberg, and Halldor Ornolf's son.

Now one day men went to the Hill of Laws, and then Geir the priest stood up and gave notice that he had a suit of manslaughter against Gunnar for the slaying of Otkell. Another suit of manslaughter he brought against Gunnar for the slaying of Hallbjorn the white; then too he went on in the same way as to the slaying of Audulf, and so too as to the slaying of Skamkell. Then too he laid a suit of manslaughter against Kolskegg for the slaying of Hallkell.

And when he had given due notice of all his suits of manslaughter it was said that he spoke well. He asked, too, in what Quarter court the suits lay, and in what house in the district the defendants dwelt. After that men went away from the Hill of Laws, and so the Thing goes on till the day when the courts were to be set to try suits. Then either side gathered their men together in great strength.

Geir the priest and Gizur the white stood at the court of the men of Rangriver looking north, and Gunnar and Njal stood looking south towards the court.

Geir the priest bade Gunnar to listen to his oath, and then he took the oath, and afterwards declared his suit.

Then he let men bear witness of the notice given of the suit; then he called upon the neighbours who were to form the inquest to take their seats; then he called on Gunnar to challenge the inquest; and then he called on the inquest to utter their finding. Then the neighbours who were summoned on the inquest went to the court and took witness, and said that there was a bar to their finding in the suit as to Audulf's slaying, because the next of kin who ought to follow it up was in Norway, and so they had nothing to do with that suit.

After that they uttered their finding in the suit as to Otkell, and brought in Gunnar as truly guilty of killing him.

Then Geir the priest called on Gunnar for his defence, and took witness of all the steps in the suit which had been proved.

Then Gunnar, in his turn, called on Geir the priest to listen to his oath, and to the defence which he was about to bring forward in the suit. Then he took the oath and said—

"This defence I make to this suit, that I took witness and outlawed Otkell before my neighbours for that bloody wound which I got when Otkell gave me a hurt with his spur; but thee, Geir the priest, I forbid by a lawful protest made before a priest to pursue this suit, and so, too, I forbid the judges to hear it; and with this I make all the steps hitherto taken in this suit void and of none-effect. I forbid thee by a lawful protest, a full, fair, and binding protest, as I have a right to forbid thee by the common custom of the Thing and by the law of the land.

"Besides, I will tell thee something else which I mean to do," says Gunnar.

"What!" says Geir, "wilt thou challenge me to the island as thou art wont, and not bear the law?"

"Not that," says Gunnar; "I shall summon thee at the Hill of Laws for that thou calledst those men on the inquest who had no right to deal with Audulf's slaying, and I will declare thee for that guilty of outlawry."

Then Njal said, "Things must not take this turn, for the only end of it will be that this strife will be carried to the uttermost. Each of you, as it seems to me, has much on his side. There are some of these manslaughters, Gunnar, about which thou canst say nothing to hinder the court from finding thee guilty; but thou hast set on foot a suit against Geir, in which he, too, must be found guilty. Thou too, Geir the priest, shalt know that this suit of outlawry which hangs over thee shall not fall to the ground if thou wilt not listen to my words."

Thorod the priest said, "It seems to us as though the most peaceful way would be that a settlement and atonement were come to in the suit. But why sayest thou so little, Gizur the white?"

"It seems to me," says Gizur, "as though we shall need to have strong props for our suit; we may see, too, that Gunnar's friends stand near him, and so the best turn for us that things can take will be that good men and true should utter an award on the suit, if Gunnar so wills it."

"I have ever been willing to make matters up," says Gunnar; "and, besides, ye have much wrong to follow up, but still I think I was hard driven to do as I did."

And now the end of those suits was, by the counsel of the wisest men, that all the suits were put to arbitration; six men were to make this award, and it was uttered there and then at the Thing.

The award was that Skamkell should be unatoned. The blood money for Otkell's death was to be set off against the hurt Gunnar got from the spur; and as for the rest of the manslaughters, they were paid for after the worth of the men, and Gunnar's kinsmen gave money so that all the fines might be paid up at the Thing.

Then Geir the priest and Gizur the white went up and gave Gunnar pledges that they would keep the peace in good faith.

Gunnar rode home from the Thing, and thanked men for their help, and gave gifts to many, and got the greatest honour from the suit.

Now Gunnar sits at home in his honour.

CHAPTER LVII.

OF STARKAD AND HIS SONS.

There was a man named Starkad; he was a son of Bork the waxytoothed-blade, the son of Thorkell clubfoot, who took the land round about Threecorner as the first settler. His wife's name was Hallbera. The sons of Starkad and Hallbera were these: Thorgeir and Bork and Thorkell. Hildigunna the leech was their sister.

They were very proud men in temper, hard-hearted and unkind. They treated men wrongfully.

There was a man named Egil; he was a son of Kol, who took land as a settler between Storlek and Reydwater. The brother of Egil was Aunund of Witchwood, father of Hall the strong, who was at the slaying of Holt-Thorir with the sons of Kettle the smooth-tongued.

Egil kept house at Sandgil; his sons were these: Kol and Ottar and Hauk. Their mother's name was Steinvor; she was Starkad's sister.

Egil's sons were tall and strifeful; they were most unfair men. They were always on one side with Starkad's sons. Their sister was Gudruna nightsun, and she was the best-bred of women.

Egil had taken into his house two Easterlings; the one's name was Thorir and the other's Thorgrim. They were not long come out hither for the first time, and were wealthy and beloved by their friends; they were well skilled in arms, too, and dauntless in everything.

Starkad had a good horse of chesnut hue, and it was thought that no horse was his match in fight. Once it happened that these brothers from Sandgil were away under the Threecorner. They had much gossip about all the householders in the Fleetlithe, and they fell at last to asking whether there was any one that would fight a horse against them.

But there were some men there who spoke so as to flatter and honour them, that not only was there no one who would dare do that, but that there was no one that had such a horse.

Then Hildigunna answered, "I know that man who will dare to fight horses with you".

"Name him," they say.

"Gunnar has a brown horse," she says, "and he will dare to fight his horse against you, and against any one else."

"As for you women," they say, "you think no one can be Gunnar's match; but though Geir the priest or Gizur the white have come off with shame from before him, still it is not settled that we shall fare in the same way."

"Ye will fare much worse," she says; and so there arose out of this the greatest strife between them. Then Starkad said—

"My will is that ye try your hands on Gunnar last of all; for ye will find it hard work to go against his good luck."

"Thou wilt give us leave, though, to offer him a horse-fight?"

"I will give you leave, if ye play him no trick."

They said they would be sure to do what their father said.

Now they rode to Lithend; Gunnar was at home, and went out, and Kolskegg and Hjort went with him, and they gave them a hearty welcome, and asked whither they meant to go?

"No farther than hither," they say. "We are told that thou hast a good horse, and we wish to challenge thee to a horse-fight."

"Small stories can go about my horse," says Gunnar; "he is young and untried in every way."

"But still thou wilt be good enough to have the fight, for Hildigunna guessed that thou wouldst be easy in matching thy horse."

"How came ye to talk about that?" says Gunnar.

"There were some men," say they, "who were sure that no one would dare to fight his horse with ours."

"I would dare to fight him," says Gunnar; "but I think that was spitefully said."

"Shall we look upon the match as made, then?" they asked.

"Well, your journey will seem to you better if ye have your way in this; but still I will beg this of you, that we so fight our horses that we make sport for each other, but that no quarrel may arise from it, and that ye put no shame upon me; but if ye do to me as ye do to others, then there will be no help for it but that I shall give you such a buffet as it will seem hard to you to put up with. In a word, I shall do then just as ye do first."

Then they ride home. Starkad asked how their journey had gone off; they said that Gunnar had made their going good.

"He gave his word to fight his horse, and we settled when and where the horse-fight should be; but it was plain in everything that he thought he fell short of us, and he begged and prayed to get off."

"It will often be found," says Hildigunna, "that Gunnar is slow to be drawn into quarrels, but a hard hitter if he cannot avoid them."

Gunnar rode to see Njal, and told him of the horse-fight, and what words had passed between them, "But how dost thou think the horse-fight will turn out?"

"Thou wilt be uppermost," says Njal, "but yet many a man's bane will arise out of this fight."

"Will my bane perhaps come out of it?" asks Gunnar.

"Not out of this," says Njal; "but still they will bear in mind both the old and the new feud who fate against thee, and thou wilt have naught left, for it but to yield."

Then Gunnar rode home.

CHAPTER LVIII.

HOW GUNNAR'S HORSE FOUGHT.

Just then Gunnar heard of the death of his father-in-law Hauskuld; a few nights after, Thorgerda, Thrain's wife, was delivered at Gritwater, and gave birth to a boy child. Then she sent a man to her mother, and bade her choose whether it should be called Glum or Hauskuld. She bade call it Hauskuld. So that name was given to the boy.

Gunnar and Hallgerda had two sons, the one's name was Hogni and the other's Grani. Hogni was a brave man of few words, distrustful and slow to believe, but truthful.

Now men ride to the horse-fight, and a very great crowd is gathered together there. Gunnar was there and his brothers, and the sons of Sigfus. Njal and all his sons. There too was come Starkad and his sons, and Egil and his sons, and they said to Gunnar that now they would lead the horses together.

Gunner said, "That was well".

Skarphedinn said, "Wilt thou that I drive thy horse, kinsman Gunnar?"

"I will not have that," says Gunnar.

"It wouldn't be amiss though," says Skarphedinn; "we are hot-headed on both sides."

"Ye would say or do little," says Gunnar, "before a quarrel would spring up; but with me it will take longer, though it will be all the same in the end."

After that the horses were led together; Gunnar busked him to drive his horse, but Skarphedinn led him out. Gunnar was in a red kirtle, and had about his loins a broad belt, and a great riding-rod in his hand.

Then the horses run at one another, and bit each other long, so that there was no need for any one to touch them, and that was the greatest sport.

Then Thorgeir and Kol made up their minds that they would push their horse forward just as the horses rushed together, and see if Gunnar would fall before him.

Now the horses ran at one another again, and both Thorgeir and Kol ran alongside their horse's flank.

Gunnar pushes his horse against them, and what happened in a trice was this, that Thorgeir and his brother fall down flat on their backs, and their horse a-top of them.

Then they spring up and rush at Gunnar, Gunnar swings himself free and seizes Kol, casts him down on the field, so that he lies senseless, Thorgeir Starkad's son smote Gunnar's horse such a blow that one of his eyes started out. Gunnar smote Thorgeir with his riding-rod, and down falls Thorgeir senseless; but Gunnar goes to his horse, and said to Kolskegg, "Cut off the horse's head; he shall not live a maimed and blemished beast".

So Kolskegg cut the head off the horse.

Then Thorgeir got on his feet and took his weapons, and wanted to fly at Gunnar, but that was stopped, and there was a great throng and crush.

Skarphedinn said, "This crowd wearies me, and it is far more manly that men should fight it out with weapons"; and so he sang a song,—

At the Thing there is a throng;
Past all bounds the crowding comes;
Hard 'twill be to patch up peace
'Twixt the men: this wearies me;
Worthier is it far for men
Weapons red with gore to stain;
I for one would sooner tame
Hunger huge of cub of wolf.

Gunnar was still, so that one man held him, and spoke no ill words.

Njal tried to bring about a settlement, or to get pledges of peace; but Thorgeir said he would neither give nor take peace; far rather, he said, would he see Gunnar dead for the blow.

Kolskegg said, "Gunnar has before now stood too fast than that he should have fallen for words alone, and so it will be again".

Now men ride away from the horse-field, every one to his home. They make no attack on Gunnar, and so that half-year passed away. At the Thing, the summer after, Gunnar met Olaf the peacock, his cousin, and he asked him to come and see him, but yet bade him beware of himself; "For," says he, "they will do us all the harm they can, and mind and fare always with many men at thy back".

He gave him much good counsel beside, and they agreed that there should be the greatest friendship between them.

CHAPTER LIX.

OF ASGRIM AND WOLF UGGIS' SON.

Asgrim Ellidagrim's son had a suit to follow up at the Thing against Wolf Uggis' son. It was a matter of inheritance, Asgrim took it up in such a way as was seldom his wont; for there was a bar to his suit, and the bar was this, that he had summoned five neighbours to bear witness, when he ought to have summoned nine. And now they have this as their bar.

Then Gunnar spoke and said, "I will challenge thee to single combat on the island, Wolf Uggis' son, if men are not to get their rights by law; and Njal and my friend Helgi would like that I should take some share in defending thy cause, Asgrim, if they were not here themselves."

"But," says Wolf, "this quarrel is not one between thee and me."

"Still it shall be as good as though it were," says Gunnar.

And the end of the suit was, that Wolf had to pay down all the money.

Then Asgrim said to Gunnar, "I will ask thee to come and see me this summer, and I will ever be with thee in lawsuits, and never against thee".

Gunnar rides home from the Thing, and a little while after, he and Njal met, Njal besought Gunnar to be ware of himself, and said he had been told that those away under the Threecorner meant to fall on him, and bade him never go about with a small company, and always to have his weapons with him. Gunnar said so it should be, and told him that Asgrim had asked him to pay him a visit, "and I mean to go now this harvest."

"Let no men know before thou farest how long thou wilt be away," said Njal; "but, besides, I beg thee to let my sons ride with thee, and then no attack will be made on thee."

So they settled that among themselves.

"Now the summer wears away till it was eight weeks to winter," and then Gunnar says to Kolskegg, "Make thee ready to ride, for we shall ride to a feast at Tongue".

"Shall we say anything about it to Njal's sons?" said Kolskegg.

"No," says Gunnar; "they shall fall into no quarrels for me."

CHAPTER LX.

AN ATTACK AGAINST GUNNAR AGREED ON.

They rode three together, Gunnar and his brothers. Gunnar had the bill and his sword, Oliver's gift; but Kolskegg had his short sword; Hjort, too, had proper weapons.

Now they rode to Tongue, and Asgrim gave them a hearty welcome, and they were there some while. At last they gave it out that they meant to go home there and then. Asgrim gave them good gifts, and offered to ride east with them, but Gunnar said there was no need of any such thing; and so he did not go.

Sigurd Swinehead was the name of a man who dwelt by Thurso water. He came to the farm under the Threecorner, for he had given his word to keep watch on Gunnar's doings, and so he went and told them of his journey home; "and," quoth he, "there could never be a finer chance than just now, when he has only two men with him".

"How many men shall we need to have to lie in wait for him?" says Starkad.

"Weak men shall be as nothing before him," he says; "and it is not safe to have fewer than thirty men."

"Where shall we lie in wait?"

"By Knafahills," he says; "there he will not see us before he comes on us."

"Go thou to Sandgil and tell Egil that fifteen of them must busk themselves thence, and now other fifteen will go hence to Knafahills."

Thorgeir said to Hildigunna, "This hand shall show thee Gunnar dead this very night".

"Nay, but I guess," says she, "that thou wilt hang thy head after ye two meet."

So those four, father and sons, fare away from the Threecorner, and eleven men besides, and they fared to Knafahills, and lay in wait there.

Sigurd Swinehead came to Sandgil and said, "Hither am I sent by Starkad and his sons to tell thee, Egil, that ye, father and sons, must fare to Knafahills to lie in wait for Gunnar".

"How many shall we fare in all?" says Egil.

"Fifteen, reckoning me," he says.

Kol said, "Now I mean to try my hand on Kolskegg".

"Then I think thou meanest to have a good deal on thy hands," says Sigurd.

Egil begged his Easterlings to fare with them. They said they had no quarrel with Gunnar; "and besides," says Thorir, "ye seem to need much help here, when a crowd of men shall go against three men".

Then Egil went away and was wroth.

Then the mistress of the house said to the Easterling: "In an evil hour hath my daughter Gudruna humbled herself, and broken the point of her maidenly pride, and lain by thy side as thy wife, when thou wilt not dare to follow thy father-in-law, and thou must be a coward," she says.

"I will go," he says, "with thy husband, and neither of us two shall come back."

After that he went to Thorgrim his messmate, and said, "Take thou now the keys of my chests; for I shall never unlock them again. I bid thee take for thine own whatever of our goods thou wilt; but sail away from Iceland, and do not think of revenge for me. But if thou dost not leave the land, it will be thy death."

So the Easterling joined himself to their band.

CHAPTER LXI.

GUNNAR'S DREAM.

Now we must go back and say that Gunnar rides east over Thurso water, but when he had gone a little way from the river he grew very drowsy, and bade them lie down and rest there.

They did so. He fell fast asleep, and struggled much as he slumbered.

Then Kolskegg said, "Gunnar dreams now". But Hjort said, "I would like to wake him".

"That shall not be," said Kolskegg, "but he shall dream his dream out".

Gunnar lay a very long while, and threw off his shield from him, and he grew very warm. Kolskegg said, "What hast thou dreamt, kinsman?"

"That have I dreamt," says Gunnar, "which if I had dreamt it there I would never have ridden with so few men from Tongue."

"Tell us thy dream," says Kolskegg.

Then Gunnar sang a song.

Chief, that chargest foes in fight!
Now I fear that I have ridden
Short of men from Tongue, this harvest;
Raven's fast I sure shall break.
Lord, that scatters Ocean's fire![24]
This at least, I long to say,
Kite with wolf shall fight for marrow,
Ill I dreamt with wandering thought.

"I dreamt, methought, that I was riding on by Knafahills, and there I thought I saw many wolves, and they all made at me; but I turned away from them straight towards Rangriver, and then methought they pressed hard on me on all sides, but I kept them at bay, and shot all those that were foremost, till they came so close to me that I could not use my bow against them. Then I took my sword, and I smote with it with one hand, but thrust at them with my bill with the other. Shield myself then I did not, and methought then I knew not what shielded me. Then I slew many wolves, and thou, too, Kolskegg; but Hjort methought they pulled down, and tore open his breast, and one methought had his heart in his maw; but I grew so wroth that I hewed that wolf asunder just below the brisket, and after that methought the wolves turned and fled. Now my counsel is, brother Hjort, that thou ridest back west to Tongue."

"I will not do that," says Hjort; "though I know my death is sure, I will stand by thee still."

Then they rode and came east by Knafahills, and Kolskegg said—

"Seest thou, kinsman! many spears stand up by the hills, and men with weapons."

"It does not take me unawares," says Gunnar, "that my dream comes true."

"What is best to be done now?" says Kolskegg; "I guess thou wilt not run away from them."

"They shall not have that to jeer about," says Gunnar, "but we will ride on down to the ness by Rangriver; there is some vantage ground there."

Now they rode on to the ness, and made them ready there, and as they rode on past them Kol called out and said—

"Whither art thou running to now, Gunnar?"

But Kolskegg said, "Say the same thing farther on when this day has come to an end".

CHAPTER LXII.

THE SLAYING OF HJORT AND FOURTEEN MEN.

After that Starkad egged on his men, and then they turn down upon them into the ness. Sigurd Swinehead came first and had a red targe, but in his other hand he held a cutlass. Gunnar sees him and shoots an arrow at him from his bow; he held the shield up aloft when he saw the arrow flying high, and the shaft passes through the shield and into his eye, and so came out at the nape of his neck, and that was the first man slain.

A second arrow Gunnar shot at Ulfhedinn, one of Starkad's men, and that struck him about the middle and he fell at the feet of a yeoman, and the yeoman over him. Kolskegg cast a stone and struck the yeoman on the head, and that was his death-blow.

Then Starkad said, "'Twill never answer our end that he should use his bow, but let us come on well and stoutly". Then each man egged on the other, and Gunnar guarded himself with his bow and arrows as long as he could; after that he throws them down, and then he takes his bill and sword and fights with both hands. There is long the hardest fight, but still Gunnar and Kolskegg slew man after man.

Then Thorgeir Starkad's son said, "I vowed to bring Hildigunna thy head, Gunnar."

Then Gunnar sang a song—

Thou, that battle-sleet down bringeth,
Scarce I trow thou speakest truth;
She, the girl with golden armlets,
Cannot care for such a gift;
But, O serpent's hoard despoiler!
If the maid must have my head—
Maid whose wrist Rhine's fire[25] wreatheth,
Closer come to crash of spear.

"She will not think that so much worth having," says Gunnar; "but still to get it thou wilt have to come nearer!"

Thorgeir said to his brothers—

"Let us run all of us upon him at once; he has no shield and we shall have his life in our hands."

So Bork and Thorkel both ran forward and were quicker than Thorgeir. Bork made a blow at Gunnar, and Gunnar threw his bill so hard in the way that the sword flew out of Bork's hand; then he sees Thorkel standing on his other hand within stroke of sword. Gunnar was standing with his body swayed a little on one side, and he makes a sweep with his sword, and caught Thorkel on the neck, and off flew his head.

Kol Egil's son said, "Let me get at Kolskegg," and turning to Kolskegg he said, "This I have often said, that we two would be just about an even match in fight".

"That we can soon prove," says Kolskegg.

Kol thrust at him with his spear; Kolskegg had just slain a man and had his hands full, and so he could not throw his shield before the blow, and the thrust came upon his thigh, on the outside of the limb and went through it.

Kolskegg turned sharp round, and strode towards him, and smote him with his short sword on the thigh, and cut off his leg, and said, "Did it touch thee or not?"

"Now," says Kol, "I pay for being bare of my shield."

So he stood a while on his other leg and looked at the stump.

"Thou needest not to look at it," said Kolskegg; "'tis even as thou seest, the leg is off."

Then Kol fell down dead.

But when Egil sees this, he runs at Gunnar and makes a cut at him; Gunnar thrusts at him with the bill and struck him in the middle, and Gunnar hoists him up on the bill and hurls him out into Rangriver.

Then Starkad said, "Wretch that thou art indeed, Thorir Easterling, when thou sittest by; but thy host and father-in-law Egil is slain."

Then the Easterling sprung up and was very wroth. Hjort had been the death of two men, and the Easterling leapt on him and smote him full on the breast. Then Hjort fell down dead on the spot.

Gunnar sees this and was swift to smite at the Easterling, and cuts him asunder at the waist.

A little while after Gunnar hurls the bill at Bork, and struck him in the middle, and the bill went through him and stuck in the ground.

Then Kolskegg cut off Hauk Egil's son's head, and Gunnar smites off Otter's hand at the elbow-joint. Then Starkad said—

"Let us fly now. We have not to do with men!"

Gunnar said, "Ye two will think it a sad story if there is naught on you to show that ye have both been in the battle".

Then Gunnar ran after Starkad and Thorgeir, and gave them each a wound. After that they parted; and Gunnar and his brothers had then wounded many men who got away from the field, but fourteen lost their lives, and Hjort the fifteenth.

Gunnar brought Hjort home, laid out on his shield, and he was buried in a cairn there. Many men grieved for him, for he had many dear friends.

Starkad came home, too, and Hildigunna dressed his wounds and Thorgeir's, and said, "Ye would have given a great deal not to have fallen out with Gunnar".

"So we would," says Starkad.

CHAPTER LXIII.

NJAL'S COUNSEL TO GUNNAR.

Steinvor, at Sandgil, besought Thorgrim the Easterling to take in hand the care of her goods, and not to sail away from Iceland, and so to keep in mind the death of his messmate and kinsman.

"My messmate Thorir," said he, "foretold that I should fall by Gunnar's hand if I stayed here in the land, and he must have foreseen that when he foreknew his own death."

"I will give thee," she says, "Gudruna my daughter to wife, and all my goods into the bargain."

"I knew not," he said, "that thou wouldest pay such a long price."

After that they struck the bargain that he shall have her, and the wedding feast was to be the next summer.

Now Gunnar rides to Bergthorsknoll, and Kolskegg with him. Njal was out of doors and his sons, and they went to meet Gunnar and gave them a hearty welcome. After that they fell a-talking, and Gunnar said—

"Hither am I come to seek good counsel and help at thy hand."

"That is thy due," said Njal.

"I have fallen into a great strait," says Gunnar, "and slain many men, and I wish to know what thou wilt make of the matter?"

"Many will say this," said Njal, "that thou hast been driven into it much against thy will; but now thou shalt give me time to take counsel with myself."

Then Njal went away all by himself, and thought over a plan, and came back and said—

"Now have I thought over the matter somewhat, and it seems to me as though this must be carried through—if it be carried through at all—with hardihood and daring. Thorgeir has got my kinswoman Thorfinna with child, and I will hand over to thee the suit for seduction. Another suit of outlawry against Starkad I hand over also to thee, for having hewn trees in my wood on the Threecorner ridge. Both these suits shalt thou take up. Thou shalt fare too to the spot where ye fought, and dig up the dead, and name witnesses to the wounds, and make all the dead outlaws, for that they came against thee with that mind to give thee and thy brothers wounds or swift death. But if this be tried at the Thing, and it be brought up against thee that thou first gave Thorgeir a blow, and so mayest neither plead thine own cause nor that of others, then I will answer in that matter, and say that I gave thee back thy rights at the Thingskala-Thing, so that thou shouldest be able to plead thine own suit as well as that of others, and then there will be an answer to that point. Thou shalt also go to see Tyrfing of Berianess, and he must hand over to thee a suit against Aunund of Witchwood, who has the blood feud after his brother Egil."

Then first of all Gunnar rode home; but a few nights after Njal's sons and Gunnar rode thither where the bodies were, and dug them up that were buried there. Then Gunnar summoned them all as outlaws for assault and treachery, and rode home after that.

CHAPTER LXIV.

OF VALGARD AND MORD.

That same harvest Valgard the guileful came out to Iceland, and fared home to Hof. Then Thorgeir went to see Valgard and Mord, and told them what a strait they were in if Gunnar were to be allowed to make all those men outlaws whom he had slain.

Valgard said that must be Njal's counsel, and yet every thing had not come out yet which he was likely to have taught him.

Then Thorgeir begged those kinsmen for help and backing, but they held out a long while, and at last asked for and got a large sum of money.

That, too, was part of their plan, that Mord should ask for Thorkatla, Gizur the white's daughter, and Thorgeir was to ride at once west across the river with Valgard and Mord.

So the day after they rode twelve of them together and came to Mossfell. There they were heartily welcomed, and they put the question to Gizur about the wooing, and the end of it was that the match should be made, and the wedding feast was to be in half a month's space at Mossfell.

They ride home, and after that they ride to the wedding, and there was a crowd of guests to meet them, and it went off well. Thorkatla went home with Mord and took the housekeeping in hand but Valgard went abroad again the next summer.

Now Mord eggs on Thorgeir to set his suit on foot against Gunnar, and Thorgeir went to find Aunund; he bids him now to begin a suit for manslaughter for his brother Egil and his sons; "but I will begin one for the manslaughter of my brothers, and for the wounds of myself and my father".

He said he was quite ready to do that, and then they set out, and give notice of the manslaughter, and summon nine neighbours who dwelt nearest to the spot where the deed was done. This beginning of the suit was heard of at Lithend; and then Gunnar rides to see Njal, and told him, and asked what he wished them to do next.

"Now," says Njal, "thou shalt summon those who dwell next to the spot, and thy neighbours; and call men to witness before the neighbours, and choose out Kol as the slayer in the manslaughter of Hjort thy brother: for that is lawful and right; then thou shalt give notice of the suit for manslaughter at Kol's hand, though he be dead. Then shall thou call men to witness, and summon the neighbours to ride to the Althing to bear witness of the fact, whether they, Kol and his companions, were on the spot, and in onslaught when Hjort was slain. Thou shalt also summon Thorgeir for the suit of seduction, and Aunund at the suit of Tyrfing."

Gunnar now did in everything as Njal gave him counsel. This men thought a strange beginning of suits, and now these matters come before the Thing. Gunnar rides to the Thing, and Njal's sons and the sons of Sigfus. Gunnar had sent messengers to his cousins and kinsmen, that they should ride to the Thing, and come with as many men as they could, and told them that this matter would lead to much strife. So they gathered together in a great band from the west.

Mord rode to the Thing and Runolf of the Dale, and those under the Threecorner, and Aunund of Witchwood. But when they come to the Thing, they join them in one company with Gizur the white and Geir the priest.

CHAPTER LXV.

OF FINES AND ATONEMENTS.

Gunnar, and the sons of Sigfus, and Njal's sons, went altogether in one band, and they marched so swiftly and closely that men who came in their way had to take heed lest they should get a fall; and nothing was so often spoken about over the whole Thing as these great lawsuits.

Gunnar went to meet his cousins, and Olaf and his men greeted him well. They asked Gunnar about the fight, but he told them all about it, and was just in all he said; he told them, too, what steps he had taken since.

Then Olaf said, "'Tis worth much to see how close Njal stands by thee in all counsel".

Gunnar said he should never be able to repay that, but then he begged them for help; and they said that was his due.

Now the suits on both sides came before the court, and each pleads his cause.

Mord asked—"How it was that a man could have the right to set a suit on foot who, like Gunnar, had already made himself an outlaw by striking Thorgeir a blow?"

"Wast thou," answered Njal, "at Thingskala-Thing last autumn?"

"Surely I was," says Mord.

"Heardest thou," asks Njal, "how Gunnar offered him full atonement? Then I gave back Gunnar his right to do all lawful deeds."

"That is right and good law," says Mord, "but how does the matter stand if Gunnar has laid the slaying of Hjort at Kol's door, when it was the Easterling that slew him?"

"That was right and lawful," says Njal, "when he chose him as the slayer before witnesses."

"That was lawful and right, no doubt," says Mord; "but for what did Gunnar summon them all as outlaws?"

"Thou needest not to ask about that," says Njal, "when they went out to deal wounds and manslaughter."

"Yes," says Mord, "but neither befell Gunnar."

"Gunnar's brothers," said Njal, "Kolskegg and Hjort, were there, and one of them got his death and the other a flesh wound."

"Thou speakest nothing but what is law," says Mord, "though it is hard to abide by it."

Then Hjallti Skeggis son of Thursodale, stood forth and said—

"I have had no share in any of your lawsuits; but I wish to know whether thou wilt do something, Gunnar, for the sake of my words and friendship."

"What askest thou?" says Gunnar.

"This," he says, "that ye lay down the whole suit to the award and judgment of good men and true."

"If I do so," said Gunnar, "then thou shalt never be against me, whatever men I may have to deal with."

"I will give my word to that," says Hjallti.

After that he tried his best with Gunnar's adversaries, and brought it about that they were all set at one again. And after that each side gave the other pledges of peace; but for Thorgeir's wound came the suit for seduction, and for the hewing in the wood, Starkad's wound. Thorgeir's brothers were atoned for by half fines, but half fell away for the onslaught on Gunnar. Egil's staying and Tyrfing's lawsuit were set off against each other. For Hjort's slaying, the slaying of Kol and of the Easterling were to come, and as for all the rest, they were atoned for with half fines.

Njal was in this award, and Asgrim Ellidagrim's son, and Hjallti Skeggi's son.

Njal had much money out at interest with Starkad, and at Sandgil too, and he gave it all to Gunnar to make up these fines.

So many friends had Gunnar at the Thing, that he not only paid up there and then all the fines on the spot, but gave besides gifts to many chiefs who had lent him help; and he had the greatest honour from the suit; and all were agreed in this, that no man was his match in all the South Quarter.

So Gunnar rides home from the Thing and sits there in peace, but still his adversaries envied him much for his honour.

CHAPTER LXVI.

OF THORGEIR OTKELL'S SON.

Now we must tell of Thorgeir Otkell's son; he grew up to be a tall strong man, true-hearted and guileless, but rather too ready to listen to fair words. He had many friends among the best men, and was much beloved by his kinsmen.

Once on a time Thorgeir Starkad's son had been to see his kinsman Mord.

"I can ill brook," he says, "that settlement of matters which we and Gunnar had, but I have bought thy help so long as we two are above ground; I wish thou wouldest think out some plan and lay it deep; this is why I say it right out, because I know that thou art Gunnar's greatest foe, and he too thine. I will much increase thine honour if thou takest pains in this matter."

"It will always seem as though I were greedy of gain, but so it must be. Yet it will be hard to take care that thou mayest not seem to be a truce-breaker, or peace-breaker, and yet carry out thy point. But now I have been told that Kolskegg means to try a suit, and regain a fourth part of Moeidsknoll, which was paid to thy father as an atonement for his son. He has taken up this suit for his mother, but this too is Gunnar's counsel, to pay in goods and not to let the land go. We must wait till this comes about, and then declare that he has broken the settlement made with you. He has also taken a cornfield from Thorgeir Otkell's son, and so broken the settlement with him too. Thou shalt go to see Thorgeir Otkell's son, and bring him into the matter with thee, and then fall on Gunnar; but if ye fail in aught of this, and cannot get him hunted down, still ye shall set on him over and over again, I must tell thee that Njal has 'spaed' his fortune, and foretold about his life, if he slays more than once in the same stock, that it would lead him to his death, if it so fell out that he broke the settlement made after the deed. Therefore shalt thou bring Thorgeir into the suit, because he has already slain his father; and now, if ye two are together in an affray, thou shalt shield thyself; but he will go boldly on, and then Gunnar will slay him. Then he has slain twice in the same stock, but thou shalt fly from the fight. And if this is to drag him to his death he will break the settlement afterwards, and so we may wait till then."

After that Thorgeir goes home and tells his father secretly. Then they agreed among themselves that they should work out this plot by stealth.

CHAPTER LXVII.

OF THORGEIR STARKAD'S SON.

Sometime after Thorgeir Starkad's son fared to Kirkby to see his namesake, and they went aside to speak, and talked secretly all day; but at the end Thorgeir Starkad's son, gave his namesake a spear inlaid with gold, and rode home afterwards; they made the greatest friendship the one with the other.

At the Thingskala-Thing in the autumn, Kolskegg laid claim to the land at Moeidsknoll, but Gunnar took witness, and offered ready money, or another piece of land at a lawful price to those under the Threecorner.

Thorgeir took witness also, that Gunnar was breaking the settlement made between them.

After that the Thing was broken up, and so the next year wore away.

Those namesakes were always meeting, and there was the greatest friendship between them. Kolskegg spoke to Gunnar and said—

"I am told that there is great friendship between those namesakes, and it is the talk of many men that they will prove untrue, and I would that thou wouldst be ware of thyself."

"Death will come to me when it will come," says Gunnar, "wherever I may be, if that is my fate."

Then they left off talking about it.

About autumn, Gunnar gave out that they would work one week there at home, and the next down in the isles, and so make an end of their haymaking. At the same time, he let it be known that every man would have to leave the house, save himself and the women.

Thorgeir under Threecorner goes to see his namesake, but as soon as they met they began to talk after their wont, and Thorgeir Starkad's son, said—

"I would that we could harden our hearts and fall on Gunnar."

"Well," says Thorgeir Otkell's son, "every struggle with Gunnar has had but one end, that few have gained the day; besides, methinks it sounds ill to be called a peace-breaker."

"They have broken the peace, not we," says Thorgeir Starkad's son. "Gunnar took away from thee thy cornfield; and he has taken Moeidsknoll from my father and me."

And so they settle it between them to fall on Gunnar; and then Thorgeir said that Gunnar would be all alone at home in a few nights' space, "and then thou shalt come to meet me with eleven men, but I will have as many".

After that Thorgeir rode home.

CHAPTER LXVIII.

OF NJAL AND THOSE NAMESAKES.

Now when Kolskegg and the house-carles had been three nights in the isles, Thorgeir Starkad's son had news of that, and sends word to his namesake that he should come to meet him on Threecorner ridge.

After that Thorgeir of the Threecorner busked him with eleven men; he rides up on the ridge and there waits for his namesake.

And now Gunnar is at home in his house, and those namesakes ride into a wood hard by. There such a drowsiness came over them that they could do naught else but sleep. So they hung their shields up in the boughs, and tethered their horses, and laid their weapons by their sides.

Njal was that night up in Thorolfsfell, and could not sleep at all, but went out and in by turns.

Thorhilda asked Njal why he could not sleep?

"Many things now flit before my eyes," said he; "I see many fetches of Gunnar's bitter foes, and what is very strange is this, they seem to be mad with rage, and yet they fare without plan or purpose."

A little after, a man rode up to the door and got off his horse's back and went in, and there was come the shepherd of Thorhilda and her husband.

"Didst thou find the sheep?" she asked.

"I found what might be more worth," said he.

"What was that?" asked Njal.

"I found twenty-four men up in the wood yonder; they had tethered their horses, but slept themselves. Their shields they had hung up in the boughs."

But so closely had he looked at them that he told of all their weapons and war-gear and clothes, and then Njal knew plainly who each of them must have been, and said to him—

"'Twere good hiring if there were many such shepherds; and this shall ever stand to thy good; but still I will send thee on an errand."

He said at once he would go.

"Thou shalt go," says Njal, "to Lithend and tell Gunnar that he must fare to Gritwater, and then send after men; but I will go to meet with those who are in the wood and scare them away. This thing hath well come to pass, so that they shall gain nothing by this journey, but lose much."

The shepherd set off and told Gunnar as plainly as he could the whole story. Then Gunnar rode to Gritwater and summoned men to him.

Now it is to be told of Njal how he rides to meet these namesakes.

"Unwarily ye lie here," he says, "or for what end shall this journey have been made? And Gunnar is not a man to be trifled with. But if the truth must be told then, this is the greatest treason. Ye shall also know this, that Gunnar is gathering force, and he will come here in the twinkling of an eye, and slay you all, unless ye ride away home."

They bestirred them at once, for they were in great fear, and took their weapons, and mounted their horses and galloped home under the Threecorner.

Njal fared to meet Gunnar and bade him not to break up his company.

"But I will go and seek for an atonement; now they will be finely frightened; but for this treason no less a sum shall be paid when one has to deal with all of them, than shall be paid for the slaying of one or other of those namesakes, though such a thing should come to pass. This money I will take into my keeping, and so lay it out that it may be ready to thy hand when thou hast need of it."

CHAPTER LXIX.

OLAF THE PEACOCK'S GIFTS TO GUNNAR.

Gunnar thanked Njal for his aid, and Njal rode away under the Threecorner, and told those namesakes that Gunnar would not break up his band of men before he had fought it out with them.

They began to offer terms for themselves, and were full of dread, and bade Njal to come between them with an offer of atonement.

Njal said that could only be if there were no guile behind. Then they begged him to have a share in the award, and said they would hold to what he awarded.

Njal said he would make no award unless it were at the Thing, and unless the best men were by; and they agreed to that.

Then Njal came between them, so that they gave each other pledges of peace and atonement.

Njal was to utter the award, and to name as his fellows those whom he chose.

A little while after those namesakes met Mord Valgard's son, and Mord blamed them much for having laid the matter in Njal's hands, when he was Gunnar's great friend. He said that would turn out ill for them.

Now men ride to the Althing after their wont, and now both sides are at the Thing.

Njal begged for a hearing, and asked all the best men who were come thither, what right at law they thought Gunnar had against those namesakes for their treason. They said they thought such a man had great right on his side.

Njal went on to ask, whether he had a right of action against all of them, or whether the leaders had to answer for them all in the suit?

They say that most of the blame would fall on the leaders, but a great deal still on them all.

"Many will say this," said Mord, "that it was not without a cause when Gunnar broke the settlement made with those namesakes."

"That is no breach of settlement," says Njal, "that any man should take the law against another; for with law shall our land be built up and settled, and with lawlessness wasted and spoiled."

Then Njal tells them that Gunnar had offered land for Moeidsknoll, or other goods.

Then those namesakes thought they had been beguiled by Mord, and scolded him much, and said that this fine was all his doing.

Njal named twelve men as judges in the suit, and then every man paid a hundred in silver who had gone out, but each of those namesakes two hundred.

Njal took this money into his keeping, but either side gave the other pledges of peace, and Njal gave out the terms.

Then Gunnar rode from the Thing west to the Dales, till he came to Hjardarholt, and Olaf the peacock gave him a hearty welcome. There he sat half a month, and rode far and wide about the Dales, and all welcomed him with joyful hands. But at their parting Olaf said—

"I will give thee three things of price, a gold ring, and a cloak which Moorkjartan the Erse king owned, and a hound that was given me in Ireland; he is big, and no worse follower than a sturdy man. Besides, it is part of his nature that he has man's wit, and he will bay at every man whom he knows is thy foe, but never at thy friends; he can see, too, in any man's face, whether he means thee well or ill, and he will lay down his life to be true to thee. This hound's name is Sam."

After that he spoke to the hound, "Now shalt thou follow Gunnar, and do him all the service thou canst".

The hound went at once to Gunnar and laid himself down at his feet.

Olaf bade Gunnar to be ware of himself, and said he had many enviers, "For now thou art thought to be a famous man throughout all the land".

Gunnar thanked him for his gifts and good counsel, and rode home.

Now Gunnar sits at home for some time, and all is quiet.

CHAPTER LXX.

MORD'S COUNSEL.

A little after, those namesakes and Mord met, and they were not at all of one mind. They thought they had lost much goods for Mord's sake, but had got nothing in return; and they bade him set on foot some other plot which might do Gunnar harm.

Mord said so it should be. "But now this is my counsel, that thou, Thorgeir Otkell's son shouldest beguile Ormilda, Gunnar's kinswoman; but Gunnar will let his displeasure grow against thee at that, and then I will spread that story abroad that Gunnar will not suffer thee to do such things."

"Then ye two shall some time after make an attack on Gunnar, but still ye must not seek him at home, for there is no thinking of that while the hound is alive."

So they settled this plan among them that it should be brought about.

Thorgeir began to turn his steps towards Ormilda, and Gunnar thought that ill, and great dislike arose between them.

So the winter wore away. Now comes the summer, and their secret meetings went on oftener than before.

As for Thorgeir of the Threecorner and Mord, they were always meeting; and they plan an onslaught on Gunnar, when he rides down to the isles to see after the work done by his house-carles.

One day Mord was ware of it when Gunnar rode down to the isles, and sent a man off under the Threecorner to tell Thorgeir that then would be the likeliest time to try to fall on Gunnar.

They bestirred them at once, and fare thence twelve together, but when they came to Kirkby there they found thirteen men waiting for them.

Then they made up their minds to ride down to Rangriver and lie in wait there for Gunnar.

But when Gunnar rode up from the isles, Kolskegg rode with him. Gunnar had his bow and his arrows and his bill. Kolskegg had his short sword and weapons to match.

CHAPTER LXXI.

THE SLAYING OF THORGEIR OTKELL'S SON.

That token happened as Gunnar and his brother rode up towards Rangriver, that much blood burst out on the bill.

Kolskegg asked what that might mean.

Gunnar says, "If such tokens took place in other lands, it was called 'wound-drops,' and Master Oliver told me also that this only happened before great fights".

So they rode on till they saw men sitting by the river on the other side, and they had tethered their horses.

Gunnar said, "Now we have an ambush".

Kolskegg answered, "Long have they been faithless; but what is best to be done now?"

"We will gallop up alongside them to the ford," says Gunnar, "and there make ready for them."

The others saw that and turned at once towards them.

Gunnar strings his bow, and takes his arrows and throws them on the ground before him, and shoots as soon as ever they come within shot; by that Gunnar wounded many men, but some he slew.

Then Thorgeir Otkell's son spoke and said, "This is no use; let us make for him as hard as we can".

They did so, and first went Aunund the fair, Thorgeir's kinsman. Gunnar hurled the bill at him, and it fell on his shield and clove it in twain, but the bill rushed through Aunund. Augmund Shockhead rushed at Gunnar behind his back. Kolskegg saw that and cut off at once both Augmund's legs from under him, and hurled him out into Rangriver, and he was drowned there and then.

Then a hard battle arose; Gunnar cut with one hand and thrust with the other. Kolskegg slew some men and wounded many.

Thorgeir's Starkad's son called out to his namesake, "It looks very little as though thou hadst a father to avenge".

"True it is," he answers, "that I do not make much way, but yet thou hast not followed in my footsteps; still I will not bear thy reproaches."

With that he rushes at Gunnar in great wrath, and thrust his spear through his shield, and so on through his arm.

Gunnar gave the shield such a sharp twist that the spearhead broke short off at the socket. Gunnar sees that another man was come within reach of his sword, and he smites at him and deals him his death-blow. After that, he clutches his bill with both hands; just then Thorgeir Otkell's son had come near him with a drawn sword, and Gunnar turns on him in great wrath, and drives the bill through him, and lifts him up aloft, and casts him out into Rangriver, and he drifts down towards the ford, and stuck fast there on a stone; and the name of that ford has since been Thorgeir's ford.

Then Thorgeir Starkad's son said, "Let us fly now; no victory will be fated to us this time".

So they all turned and fled from the field.

"Let us follow them up now," says Kolskegg, "and take thou thy bow and arrows, and thou wilt come within bow-shot of Thorgeir Starkad's son."

Then Gunnar sang a song.

Reaver of rich river-treasure,
Plundered will our purses be,
Though to-day we wound no other
Warriors wight in play of spears;
Aye, if I for all these sailors
Lowly lying, fines must pay—
This is why I hold my hand,
Hearken, brother dear, to me.

"Our purses will be emptied," says Gunnar, "by the time that these are atoned for who now lie here dead."

"Thou wilt never lack money," says Kolskegg; "but Thorgier will never leave off before he compasses thy death."

Gunnar sung another song.

Lord of water-skates[26] that skim
Sea-king's fields, more good as he,
Shedding wounds' red stream, must stand
In my way ere I shall wince.
I, the golden armlets' warder,
Snakelike twined around my wrist,
Ne'er shall shun a foeman's faulchion
Flashing bright in din of fight.

"He, and a few more as good as he," says Gunnar, "must stand in my path ere I am afraid of them."

After that they ride home and tell the tidings.

Hallgerda was well pleased to hear them, and praised the deed much.

Rannveig said, "May be the deed is good; but somehow," she says, "I feel too downcast about it to think that good can come of it".

CHAPTER LXXII.

OF THE SUITS FOR MANSLAUGHTER AT THE THING.

These tidings were spread far and wide, and Thorgeir's death was a great grief to many a man. Gizur the white and his men rode to the spot and gave notice of the manslaughter, and called the neighbours on the inquest to the Thing. Then they rode home west.

Njal and Gunnar met and talked about the battle. Then Njal said to Gunnar—

"Now be ware of thyself! Now hast thou slain twice in the same stock; and so now take heed to thy behaviour, and think that it is as much as thy life is worth, if thou dost not hold to the settlement that is made."

"Nor do I mean to break it in any way," says Gunnar, "but still I shall need thy help at the Thing."

"I will hold to my faithfulness to thee," said Njal, "till my death day."

Then Gunnar rides home. Now the Thing draws near; and each side gather a great company; and it is a matter of much talk at the Thing how these suits will end.

Those two, Gizur the white, and Geir the priest, talked with each other as to who should give notice of the suit of manslaughter after Thorgeir, and the end of it was that Gizur took the suit on his hand, and gave notice of it at the Hill of Laws, and spoke in these words:—

"I gave notice of a suit for assault laid down by law against Gunnar Hamond's son; for that he rushed with an onslaught laid down by law on Thorgeir Otkell's son, and wounded him with a body wound, which proved a death wound, so that Thorgeir got his death.

"I say on this charge he ought to become a convicted outlaw, not to be fed, not to be forwarded, not to be helped or harboured in any need.

"I say that his goods are forfeited, half to me and half to the men of the Quarter, whose right it is by law to seize the goods of outlaws.

"I give notice of this charge in the Quarter Court, into which this suit ought by law to come.

"I give this lawful notice in the hearing of all men at the Hill of Laws.

"I give notice now of this suit, and of full forfeiture and outlawry against Gunnar Hamond's son."

A second time Gizur took witness, and gave notice of a suit against Gunnar Hamond's son, for that he had wounded Thorgeir Otkell's son with a body wound which was a death wound, and from which Thorgeir got his death, on such and such a spot when Gunnar first sprang on Thorgeir with an onslaught, laid down by law.

After that he gave notice of this declaration as he had done of the first. Then he asked in what Quarter Court the suit lay, and in what house in the district the defendant dwelt.

When that was over men left the Hill of Laws, and all said that he spoke well.

Gunnar kept himself well in hand and said little or nothing.

Now the Thing wears away till the day when the courts were to be set.

Then Gunnar stood looking south by the court of the men of Rangriver, and his men with him.

Gizur stood looking north, and calls his witnesses, and bade Gunnar to listen to his oath, and to his declaration of the suit, and to all the steps and proofs which he meant to bring forward. After that he took his oath, and then he brought forward the suit in the same shape before the court, as he had given notice of it before. Then he made them bring forward witness of the notice, then he bade the neighbours on the inquest to take their seats, and called upon Gunnar to challenge the inquest.

CHAPTER LXXIII.

OF THE ATONEMENT.

Then Njal spoke and said—

"Now I can no longer sit still and take no part. Let us go to where the neighbours sit on the inquest."

They went thither and challenged four neighbours out of the inquest, but they called on the five that were left to answer the following question in Gunnar's favour "whether those namesakes had gone out with that mind to the place of meeting to do Gunnar a mischief if they could?"

But all bore witness at once that so it was.

Then Njal called this a lawful defence to the suit, and said he would bring forward proof of it unless they gave over the suit to arbitration.

Then many chiefs joined in praying for an atonement, and so it was brought about that twelve men should utter an award in the matter.

Then either side went and handselled this settlement to the other. Afterwards the award was made, and the sum to be paid settled, and it was all to be paid down then and there at the Thing.

But besides, Gunnar was to go abroad and Kolskegg with him, and they were to be away three winters; but if Gunnar did not go abroad when he had a chance of a passage, then he was to be slain by the kinsmen of those whom he had killed.

Gunnar made no sign, as though he thought the terms of atonement were not good. He asked Njal for that money which he had handed over to him to keep. Njal had laid the money out at interest and paid it down all at once, and it just came to what Gunnar had to pay for himself.

Now they ride home. Gunnar and Njal rode both together from the Thing, and then Njal said to Gunnar—

"Take good care, messmate, that thou keepest to this atonement, and bear in mind what we have spoken about; for though thy former journey abroad brought thee to great honour, this will be a far greater honour to thee. Thou wilt come back with great glory, and live to be an old man, and no man here will then tread on thy heel; but if thou dost not fare away, and so breakest thy atonement, then thou wilt be slain here in the land, and that is ill knowing for those who are thy friends."

Gunnar said he had no mind to break the atonement, and he rides home and told them of the settlement.

Rannveig said it was well that he fared abroad, for then they must find some one else to quarrel.

CHAPTER LXXIV.

KOLSKEGG GOES ABROAD.

Thrain Sigfus' son said to his wife that he meant to fare abroad that summer. She said that was well. So he took his passage with Hogni the white.

Gunnar took his passage with Arnfin of the Bay; and Kolskegg was to go with him.

Grim And Helgi, Njal's sons, asked their father's leave to go abroad too, and Njal said—

"This foreign voyage ye will find hard work, so hard that it will be doubtful whether ye keep your lives; but still ye two will get some honour and glory, but it is not unlikely that a quarrel will arise out of your journey when ye come back."

Still they kept on asking their father to let them go, and the end of it was that he bade them go if they chose.

Then they got them a passage with Bard the black, and Olaf Kettle's son of Elda; and it is the talk of the whole country that all the better men in that district were leaving it.

By this time Gunnar's sons, Hogni and Grani, were grown up; they were men of very different turn of mind. Grani had much of his mother's temper, but Hogni was kind and good.

Gunnar made men bear down the wares of his brother and himself to the ship, and when all Gunnar's baggage had come down, and the ship was all but "boun," then Gunnar rides to Bergthorsknoll, and to other homesteads to see men, and thanked them all for the help they had given him.

The day after he gets ready early for his journey to the ship, and told all his people that he would ride away for good and all, and men took that much to heart, but still they said that they looked to his coming back afterwards.

Gunnar threw his arms round each of the household when he was "boun," and every one of them went out of doors with him; he leans on the butt of his spear and leaps into the saddle, and he and Kolskegg ride away.

They ride down along Markfleet, and just then Gunnar's horse tripped and threw him off. He turned with his face up towards the Lithe and the homestead at Lithend, and said—

"Fair is the Lithe; so fair that it has never seemed to me so fair; the corn fields are white to harvest, and the home mead is mown; and now I will ride back home, and not fare abroad at all."

"Do not this joy to thy foes," says Kolskegg, "by breaking thy atonement, for no man could think thou wouldst do thus, and thou mayst be sure that all will happen as Njal has said."

"I will not go away any whither," says Gunnar, "and so I would thou shouldest do too."

"That shall not be," says Kolskegg; "I will never do a base thing in this, nor in anything else which is left to my good faith; and this is that one thing that could tear us asunder; but tell this to my kinsmen and to my mother, that I never mean to see Iceland again, for I shall soon learn that thou art dead, brother, and then there will be nothing left to bring me back."

So they parted there and then. Gunnar rides home to Lithend, but Kolskegg rides to the ship, and goes abroad.

Hallgerda was glad to see Gunnar when he came home, but his mother said little or nothing.

Now Gunnar sits at home that fall and winter, and had not many men with him.

Now the winter leaves the farmyard. Olaf the peacock asked Gunnar and Hallgerda to come and stay with him; but as for the farm, to put it into the hands of his mother and his son Hogni.

Gunnar thought that a good thing at first, and agreed to it, but when it came to the point he would not do it.

But at the Thing next summer, Gizur the white, and Geir the priest, gave notice of Gunnar's outlawry at the Hill of Laws; and before the Thing broke up Gizur summoned all Gunnar's foes to meet in the "Great Rift".[27] He summoned Starkad under the Threecorner, and Thorgeir his son; Mord and Valgard the guileful; Geir the priest and Hjalti Skeggi's son; Thorbrand and Asbrand, Thorleik's sons; Eyjulf, and Aunund his son, Aunund of Witchwood and Thorgrim the Easterling of Sandgil.

Then Gizur spoke and said, "I will make you all this offer, that we go out against Gunnar this summer and slay him".

"I gave my word to Gunnar," said Hjalti, "here at the Thing, when he showed himself most willing to yield to my prayer, that I would never be in any attack upon him; and so it shall be."

Then Hjalti went away, but those who were left behind made up their minds to make an onslaught on Gunnar, and shook hands on the bargain, and laid a fine on any one that left the undertaking.

Mord was to keep watch and spy out when there was the best chance of falling on him, and they were forty men in this league, and they thought it would be a light thing for them to hunt down Gunnar, now that Kolskegg was away, and Thrain and many other of Gunnar's friends.

Men ride from the Thing, and Njal went to see Gunnar, and told him of his outlawry, and how an onslaught was planned against him.

"Me thinks thou art the best of friends," says Gunnar; "thou makest me aware of what is meant."

"Now," says Njal, "I would that Skarphedinn should come to thy house, and my son Hauskuld; they will lay down their lives for thy life."

"I will not," says Gunnar, "that thy sons should be slain for my sake, and thou hast a right to look for other things from me."

"All thy care will come to nothing," says Njal; "quarrels will turn thitherward where my sons are as soon as thou art dead and gone."

"That is not unlikely," says Gunnar, "but still it would mislike me that they fell into them for me; but this one thing I will ask of thee, that ye see after my son Hogni, but I say naught of Grani, for he does not behave himself much after my mind."

Njal rode home, and gave his word to do that.

It is said that Gunnar rode to all meetings of men, and to all lawful Things, and his foes never dared to fall on him.

And so some time went on that he went about as a free and guiltless man.

CHAPTER LXXV.

THE RIDING TO LITHEND.

Next autumn Mord Valgard's son, sent word that Gunnar would be all alone at home, but all his people would be down in the isles to make an end of their haymaking. Then Gizur the white and Geir the priest rode east over the rivers as soon as ever they heard that, and so east across the sands to Hof. Then they sent word to Starkad under the Threecorner, and there they all met who were to fall on Gunnar, and took counsel how they might best bring it about.

Mord said that they could not come on Gunnar unawares, unless they seized the farmer who dwelt at the next homestead, whose name was Thorkell, and made him go against his will with them to lay hands on the hound Sam, and unless he went before them to the homestead to do this.

Then they set out east for Lithend, but sent to fetch Thorkell. They seized him and bound him, and gave him two choices—one that they would slay him, or else he must lay hands on the hound; but he chooses rather to save his life, and went with them.

There was a beaten sunk road, between fences, above the farm yard at Lithend, and there they halted with their band. Master Thorkell went up to the homestead, and the tyke lay on the top of the house, and he entices the dog away with him into a deep hollow in the path. Just then the hound sees that there are men before them, and he leaps on Thorkell and tears his belly open.

Aunund of Witchwood smote the hound on the head with his axe, so that the blade sunk into the brain. The hound gave such a great howl that they thought it passing strange, and he fell down dead.

CHAPTER LXXVI.

GUNNAR'S SLAYING.

Gunnar woke up in his hall and said—

"Thou hast been sorely treated, Sam, my fosterling, and this warning is so meant that our two deaths will not be far apart."

Gunnar's hall was made all of wood, and roofed with beams above, and there were window-slits under the beams that carried the roof, and they were fitted with shutters.

Gunnar slept in a loft above the hall, and so did Hallgerda and his mother.

Now when they were come near to the house they knew not whether Gunnar were at home, and bade that some one would go straight up to the house and see if he could find out. But the rest sat them down on the ground.

Thorgrim the Easterling went and began to climb up on the hall; Gunnar sees that a red kirtle passed before the windowslit, and thrusts out the bill, and smote him on the middle. Thorgrim's feet slipped from under him, and he dropped his shield, and down he toppled from the roof.

Then he goes to Gizur and his band as they sat on the ground.

Gizur looked at him and said—

"Well, is Gunnar at home?"

"Find that out for yourselves," said Thorgrim; "but this I am sure of, that his bill is at home," and with that he fell down dead.

Then they made for the buildings. Gunnar shot out arrows at them, and made a stout defence, and they could get nothing done. Then some of them got into the out-houses and tried to attack him thence, but Gunnar found them out with his arrows there also, and still they could get nothing done.

So it went on for while, then they took a rest, and made a second onslaught. Gunnar still shot out at them, and they could do nothing, and fell off the second time. Then Gizur the white said-

"Let us press on harder; nothing comes of our onslaught."

Then they made a third bout of it, and were long at it, and then they fell off again.

Gunnar said, "There lies on arrow outside on the wall, and it is one of their shafts; I will shoot at them with it, and it will be a shame to them if they get a hurt from their own weapons".

His mother said, "Do not so, my son; nor rouse them again when they have already fallen off from the attack".

But Gunnar caught up the arrow and shot it after them, and struck Eylif Aunund's son, and he got a great wound; he was standing all by himself, and they knew not that he was wounded.

"Out came an arm yonder," says Gizur, "and there was a gold ring on it, and took an arrow from the roof and they would not look outside for shafts if there were enough in doors; and now ye shall make a fresh onslaught."

"Let us burn him house and all," said Mord.

"That shall never be," says Gizur, "though I knew that my life lay on it; but it is easy for thee to find out some plan, such a cunning man as thou art said to be."

Some ropes lay there on the ground, and they were often used to strengthen the roof. Then Mord said—"Let us take the ropes and throw one end over the end of the carrying beams, but let us fasten the other end to these rocks and twist them tight with levers, and so pull the roof off the hall."

So they took the ropes and all lent a hand to carry this out, and before Gunnar was aware of it, they had pulled the whole roof off the hall.

Then Gunnar still shoots with his bow so that they could never come nigh him. Then Mord said again that they must burn the house over Gunnar's head. But Gizur said—

"I know not why thou wilt speak of that which no one else wishes, and that shall never be."

Just then Thorbrand Thorleik's son sprang up on the roof, and cuts asunder Gunnar's bowstring. Gunnar clutches the bill with both hands, and turns on him quickly and drives it through him, and hurls him down on the ground.

Then up sprung Asbrand his brother. Gunnar thrusts at him with the bill, and he threw his shield before the blow, but the bill passed clean through the shield and broke both his arms, and down he fell from the wall.

Gunnar had already wounded eight men and slain those twain.[28] By that time Gunnar had got two wounds, and all men said that he never once winced either at wounds or death.

Then Gunnar said to Hallgerda, "Give me two locks of thy hair, and ye two, my mother and thou, twist them together into a bowstring for me."

"Does aught lie on it?" she says.

"My life lies on it," he said; "for they will never come to close quarters with me if I can keep them off with my bow."

"Well!" she says, "now I will call to thy mind that slap on the face which thou gavest me; and I care never a whit whether thou holdest out a long while or a short."

Then Gunnar sang a song—

Each who hurls the gory javelin
Hath some honour of his own,
Now my helpmeet wimple-hooded
Hurries all my fame to earth.
No one owner of a war-ship
Often asks for little things,
Woman, fond of Frodi's flour,[29]
Wends her hand as she is wont.

"Every one has something to boast of," says Gunnar, "and I will ask thee no more for this."

"Thou behavest ill," said Rannveig, "and this shame shall long be had in mind."

Gunnar made a stout and bold defence, and now wounds other eight men with such sore wounds that many lay at death's door. Gunnar keeps them all off until he fell worn out with toil. Then they wounded him with many and great wounds, but still he got away out of their hands, and held his own against them a while longer, but at last it came about that they slew him.

Of this defence of his, Thorkell the Skald of Göta-Elf sang in the verses which follow—

We have heard how south in Iceland
Gunnar guarded well himself,
Boldly battle's thunder wielding,
Fiercest Iceman on the wave;
Hero of the golden collar,
Sixteen with the sword he wounded;

In the shock that Odin loveth,
Two before him lasted death.

But this is what Thormod Olaf's son sang—

None that scattered sea's bright sunbeams,[30]
Won more glorious fame than Gunnar,
So runs fame of old in Iceland,
Fitting fame of heathen men;
Lord of fight when helms were crashing,
Lives of foeman twain he took,
Wielding bitter steel he sorely
Wounded twelve, and four besides.

Then Gizur spoke and said: "We have now laid low to earth a mighty chief, and hard work has it been, and the fame of this defence of his shall last as long as men live in this land".

After that he went to see Rannveig and said, "Wilt thou grant us earth here for two of our men who are dead, that they may lie in a cairn here?"

"All the more willingly for two," she says, "because I wish with all my heart I had to grant it to all of you."

"It must be forgiven thee," he says, "to speak thus, for thou hast had a great loss."

Then he gave orders that no man should spoil or rob anything there.

After that they went away.

Then Thorgeir Starkad's son said, "We may not be in our house at home for the sons of Sigfus, unless thou Gizur or thou Geir be here south some little while".

"This shall be so," says Gizur, and they cast lots, and the lot fell on Geir to stay behind.

After that he came to the Point, and set up his house there; he had a son whose name was Hroald; he was base born, and his mother's name was Biartey; he boasted that he had given Gunnar his death-blow. Hroald was at the Point with his father.

Thorgeir Starkad's son boasted of another wound which he had given to Gunnar.

Gizur sat at home at Mossfell. Gunnar's slaying was heard of, and ill spoken of throughout the whole country, and his death was a great grief to many a man.

CHAPTER LXXVII.

GUNNAR SINGS A SONG DEAD.

Njal could ill brook Gunnar's death, nor could the sons of Sigfus brook it either.

They asked whether Njal thought they had any right to give notice of a suit of manslaughter for Gunnar, or to set the suit on foot.

He said that could not be done, as the man had been outlawed; but said it would be better worth trying to do something to wound their glory, by slaying some men in vengeance after him.

They cast a cairn over Gunnar, and made him sit upright in the cairn. Rannveig would not hear of his bill being buried in the cairn, but said he alone should have it as his own, who was ready to avenge Gunnar. So no one took the bill.

She was so hard on Hallgerda, that she was on the point of killing her; and she said that she had been the cause of her son's slaying.

Then Hallgerda fled away to Gritwater, and her son Grani with her, and they shared the goods between them; Hogni was to have the land at Lithend and the homestead on it, but Grani was to have the land let out on lease.

Now this token happened at Lithend, that the neat-herd and the serving-maid were driving cattle by Gunnar's cairn. They thought that he was merry, and that he was singing inside the cairn. They went home and told Rannveig, Gunnar's mother, of this token, but she bade them go and tell Njal.

Then they went over to Bergthorsknoll and told Njal, but he made them tell it three times over.

After that, he had a long talk all alone with Skarphedinn; and Skarphedinn took his weapons and goes with them to Lithend.

Rannveig and Hogni gave him a hearty welcome, and were very glad to see him. Rannveig asked him to stay there some time, and he said he would.

He and Hogni were always together, at home and abroad. Hogni was a brisk, brave man, well-bred and well-trained in mind and body, but distrustful and slow to believe what he was told, and that was why they dared not tell him of the token.

Now those two, Skarphedinn and Hogni, were out of doors one evening by Gunnar's cairn on the south side. The moon and stars were shining clear and bright, but every now and then the clouds drove over them. Then all at once they thought they saw the cairn standing open, and lo! Gunnar had turned himself in the cairn and looked at the moon. They thought they saw four lights burning in the cairn, and none of them threw a shadow. They saw that Gunnar was merry, and he wore a joyful face. He sang a song, and so loud, that it might have been heard though they had been farther off.

He that lavished rings in largesse,
When the fight's red rain-drops fell,
Bright of face, with heart-strings hardy,
Hogni's father met his fate;
Then his brow with helmet shrouding,
Bearing battle-shield, he spake,
"I will die the prop of battle,
Sooner die than yield an inch.
Yes, sooner die than yield an inch".

After that the cairn was shut up again.

"Wouldst thou believe these tokens if Njal or I told them to thee?" says Skarphedinn.

"I would believe them," he says, "if Njal told them, for it is said he never lies."

"Such tokens as these mean much," says Skarphedinn, "when he shows himself to us, he who would sooner die than yield to his foes; and see how he has taught us what we ought to do."

"I shall be able to bring nothing to pass," says Hogni, "unless thou wilt stand by me."

"Now," says Skarphedinn, "will I bear in mind how Gunnar behaved after the slaying of your kinsman Sigmund; now I will yield you such help as I may. My father gave his word to Gunnar to do that whenever thou or thy mother had need of it."

After that they go home to Lithend.

CHAPTER LXXVIII.

GUNNAR OF LITHEND AVENGED.

"Now we shall set off at once," says Skarphedinn, "this very night; for if they learn that I am here, they will be more wary of themselves."

"I will fulfil thy counsel," says Hogni.

After that they took their weapons when all men were in their beds. Hogni takes down the bill, and it gave a sharp ringing sound.

Rannveig sprang up in great wrath and said—

"Who touches the bill, when I forbade every one to lay hand on it?"

"I mean," says Hogni, "to bring it to my father, that he may bear it with him to Valhalla, and have it with him when the warriors meet."

"Rather shalt thou now bear it," she answered, "and avenge thy father; for the bill has spoken of one man's death or more."

Then Hogni went out, and told Skarphedinn all the words that his grandmother had spoken.

After that they fare to the Point, and two ravens flew along with them all the way. They came to the Point while it was still night. Then they drove the flock before them up to the house, and then Hroald and Tjorfi ran out and drove the flock up the hollow path, and had their weapons with them.

Skarphedinn sprang up and said, "Thou needest not to stand and think if it be really as it seems. Men are here."

Then Skarphedinn smites Tjorfi his death-blow. Hroald had a spear in his hand, and Hogni rushes at him; Hroald thrusts at him, but Hogni hewed asunder the spear-shaft with his bill, and drives the bill through him.

After that they left them there dead, and turn away thence under the Threecorner.

Skarphedinn jumps up on the house and plucks the grass, and those who were inside the house thought it was cattle that had come on the roof. Starkad and Thorgeir took their weapons and upper clothing, and went out and round about the fence of the yard. But when Starkad sees Skarphedinn he was afraid, and wanted to turn back.

Skarphedinn cut him down by the fence. Then Hogni comes against Thorgeir and slays him with the bill.

Thence they went to Hof, and Mord was outside in the field, and begged for mercy, and offered them full atonement.

Skarphedinn told Mord the slaying of those four men, and sang a song.

Four who wielded warlike weapons
We have slain, all men of worth,
Them at once, gold-greedy fellow,
Thou shalt follow on the spot;
Let us press this pinch-purse so,
Pouring fear into his heart;
Wretch! reach out to Gunnar's son
Right to settle all disputes.

"And the like journey," says Skarphedinn, "shalt thou also fare, or hand over to Hogni the right to make his own award, if he will take these terms."

Hogni said his mind had been made up not to come to any terms with the slayers of his father; but still at last he took the right to make his own award from Mord.

CHAPTER LXXIX.

HOGNI TAKES AN ATONEMENT FOR GUNNAR'S DEATH.

Njal took a share in bringing those who had the blood-feud after Starkad and Thorgeir to take an atonement, and a district meeting was called together, and men were chosen to make the award, and every matter was taken into account, even the attack on Gunnar, though he was an outlaw; but such a fine as was awarded, all that Mord paid; for they did not close their award against him before the other matter was already settled, and then they set off one award against the other.

Then they were all set at one again, but at the Thing there was great talk, and the end of it was, that Geir the priest and Hogni were set at one again, and that atonement they held to ever afterwards.

Geir the priest dwelt in the Lithe till his death-day, and he is out of the story.

Njal asked as a wife for Hogni Alfeida the daughter of Weatherlid the Skald, and she was given away to him. Their son was Ari, who sailed for Shetland, and took him a wife there; from him is come Einar the Shetlander, one of the briskest and boldest of men.

Hogni kept up his friendship with Njal, and he is now out of the story.

CHAPTER LXXX.

OF KOLSKEGG: HOW HE WAS BAPTISED.

Now it is to be told of Kolskegg how he comes to Norway, and is in the Bay east that winter. But the summer after he fares east to Denmark, and bound himself to Sweyn Forkbeard the Dane-king, and there he had great honour.

One night he dreamt that a man came to him; he was bright and glistening, and he thought he woke him up. He spoke, and said to him—

"Stand up and come with me."

"What wilt thou with me?" he asks.

"I will get thee a bride, and thou shalt be my knight."

He thought he said yea to that, and after that he woke up.

Then he went to a wizard and told him the dream, but he read it so that he should fare to southern lands and become God's knight.

Kolskegg was baptised in Denmark, but still he could not rest there, but fared east to Russia, and was there one winter. Then he fared thence out to Micklegarth,[31] and there took service with the Emperor. The last that was heard of him was, that he wedded a wife there, and was captain over the Varangians, and stayed there till his death-day; and he, too, is out of this story.

CHAPTER LXXXI.

OF THRAIN: HOW HE SLEW KOL.

Now we must take up the story, and say how Thrain Sigfus' son came to Norway. They made the land north in Helgeland, and held on south to Drontheim, and so to Hlada.[32] But as soon as Earl Hacon heard of that, he sent men to them, and would know what men were in the ship. They came back and told him who the men were. Then the Earl sent for Thrain Sigfus' son, and he went to see him. The Earl asked of what stock he might be. He said that he was Gunnar of Lithend's near kinsman. The Earl said—

"That shall stand thee in good stead; for I have seen many men from Iceland, but none his match."

"Lord," said Thrain, "is it your will that I should be with you this winter?"

The Earl took to him, and Thrain was there that winter, and was thought much of.

There was a man named Kol, he was a great sea-rover. He was the son of Asmund Ashside, east out of Smoland. He lay east in the Göta-Elf, and had five ships, and much force.

Thence Kol steered his course out of the river to Norway, and landed at Fold,[33] in the bight of the "Bay," and came on Hallvard Soti unawares, and found him in a loft. He kept them off bravely till they set fire to the house, then he gave himself up; but they slew him, and took there much goods, and sailed thence to Lödese.[34]

Earl Hacon heard these tidings, and made them make Kol an outlaw over all his realm, and set a price upon his head.

Once on a time it so happened that the Earl began to speak thus—

"Too far off from us now is Gunnar of Lithend. He would slay my outlaw if he were here; but now the Icelanders will slay him, and it is ill that he hath not fared to us."

Then Thrain Sigfus' son answered—

"I am not Gunnar, but still I am near akin to him, and I will undertake this voyage."

The Earl said, "I should be glad of that, and thou shalt be very well fitted out for the journey".

After that his son Eric began to speak, and said—

"Your word, father, is good to many men, but fulfilling it is quite another thing. This is the hardest undertaking; for this sea-rover is tough and ill to deal with, wherefore thou wilt need to take great pains, both as to men and ships for this voyage."

Thrain said, "I will set out on this voyage, though it looks ugly".

After that the Earl gave him five ships, and all well trimmed and manned. Along with Thrain was Gunnar Lambi's son, and Lambi Sigurd's son. Gunnar was Thrain's brother's son, and had come to him young, and each loved the other much.

Eric, the Earl's son, went heartily along with them, and looked after strength for them, both in men and weapons, and made such changes in them as he thought were needful. After they were "boun," Eric got them a pilot. Then they sailed south along the land; but wherever they came to land, the Earl allowed them to deal with whatever they needed as their own.

So they held on east to Lödese, and then they heard that Kol was gone to Denmark. Then they shaped their course south thither; but when they came south to Helsingborg, they met men in a boat, who said that Kol was there just before them, and would be staying there for a while.

One day when the weather was good, Kol saw the ships as they sailed up towards him, and said he had dreamt of Earl Hacon the night before, and told his people he was sure these must be his men, and bade them all to take their weapons.

After that they busked them, and a fight arose; and they fought long, so that neither side had the mastery.

Then Kol sprang up on Thrain's ship, and cleared the gangways fast, and slays many men. He had a gilded helm.

Now Thrain sees that this is no good, and now he eggs on his men to go along with him, but he himself goes first and meets Kol.

Kol hews at him, and the blow fell on Thrain's shield, and cleft it down from top to bottom. Then Kol got a blow on the arm from a stone, and then down fell his sword.

Thrain hews at Kol, and the stroke came on his leg so that it cut it off. After that they slew Kol, and Thrain cut off his head, and they threw the trunk over-board, but kept his head.

There they took much spoil, and then they held on north to Drontheim, and go to see the Earl.

The Earl gave Thrain a hearty welcome, and he showed the Earl Kol's head, but the Earl thanked him for that deed.

Eric said it was worth more than words alone, and the Earl said so it was, and bade them come along with him.

They went thither, where the Earl had made them make a good ship that was not made like a common long-ship. It had a vulture's head, and was much carved and painted.

"Thou art a great man for show, Thrain," said the Earl, "and so have both of you, kinsmen, been, Gunnar and thou; and now I will give thee this ship, but it is called the 'Vulture'. Along with it shall go my friendship; and my will is that thou stayest with me as long as thou wilt."

He thanked him for his goodness, and said he had no longing to go to Iceland just yet.

The Earl had a journey to make to the marches of the land to meet the Swede-king. Thrain went with him that summer, and was a shipmaster and steered the Vulture, and sailed so fast that few could keep up with him, and he was much envied. But it always came out that the Earl laid great store on Gunnar, for he set down sternly all who tried Thrain's temper.

So Thrain was all that winter with the Earl, but next spring the Earl asked Thrain whether he would stay there or fare to Iceland; but Thrain said he had not yet made up his mind, and said that he wished first to know tidings from Iceland.

The Earl said that so it should be as he thought it suited him best; and Thrain was with the Earl.

Then those tidings were heard from Iceland, which many thought great news, the death of Gunnar of Lithend. Then the Earl would not that Thrain should fare out to Iceland, and so there he stayed with him.

CHAPTER LXXXII.

NJAL'S SONS SAIL ABROAD.

Now it must be told how Njal's sons, Grim and Helgi, left Iceland the same summer that Thrain and his fellows went away; and in the ship with them were Olaf Kettle's son of Elda, and Bard the black. They got so strong a wind from the north that they were driven south into the main; and so thick a mist came over them that they could not tell whither they were driving, and they were out a long while. At last they came to where was a great ground sea, and thought then they must be near land. So then Njal's sons asked Bard if he could tell at all to what land they were likely to be nearest.

"Many lands there are," said he, "which we might hit with the weather we have had—the Orkneys, or Scotland, or Ireland."

Two nights after, they saw land on both boards, and a great surf running up in the firth. They cast anchor outside the breakers, and the wind began to fall; and next morning it was calm. Then they see thirteen ships coming out to them.

Then Bard spoke and said, "What counsel shall we take now, for these men are going to make an onslaught on us?"

So they took counsel whether they should defend themselves or yield, but before they could make up their minds, the Vikings were upon them. Then each side asked the other their names, and what their leaders were called. So the leaders of the chapmen told their names, and asked back who led that host. One called himself Gritgard, and the other Snowcolf, sons of Moldan of Duncansby in Scotland, kinsmen of Malcolm the Scot king.

"And now," says Gritgard, "we have laid down two choices, one that ye go on shore, and we will take your goods; the other is, that we fall on you and slay every man that we can catch."

"The will of the chapmen," answers Helgi, "is to defend themselves."

But the chapmen called out, "Wretch that thou art to speak thus! What defence can we make? Lading is less than life."

But Grim, he fell upon a plan to shout out to the Vikings, and would not let them hear the bad choice of the chapmen.

Then Bard and Olaf said, "Think ye not that these Icelanders will make game of you sluggards; take rather your weapons and guard your goods".

So they all seized their weapons, and bound themselves, one with another, never to give up so long as they had strength to fight.

CHAPTER LXXXIII.

OF KARI SOLMUND'S SON.

Then the Vikings shot at them and the fight began, and the chapmen guard themselves well. Snowcolf sprang aboard and at Olaf, and thrust his spear through his body, but Grim thrust at Snowcolf with his spear, and so stoutly, that he fell over-board. Then Helgi turned to meet Grim, and they too drove down all the Vikings as they tried to board, and Njal's sons were ever where there was most need. Then the Vikings called out to the chapmen and bade them give up, but they said they would never yield. Just then some one looked seaward, and there they see ships coming from the south round the Ness, and they were not fewer than ten, and they row hard and steer thitherwards. Along their sides were shield on shield, but on that ship that came first stood a man by the mast, who was clad in a silken kirtle, and had a gilded helm, and his hair was both fair and thick; that man had a spear inlaid with gold in his hand.

He asked, "Who have here such an uneven game?"

Helgi tells his name, and said that against them are Gritgard and Snowcolf.

"But who are your captains?" he asks.

Helgi answered, "Bard the black, who lives, but the other, who is dead and gone, was called Olaf".

"Are ye men from Iceland?" says he.

"Sure enough we are," Helgi answers.

He asked whose sons they were, and they told him, then he knew them and said—

"Well known names have ye all, father and sons both."

"Who art thou?" asks Helgi.

"My name is Kari, and I am Solmund's son."

"Whence comest thou?" says Helgi.

"From the Southern Isles."

"Then thou art welcome," says Helgi, "if thou wilt give us a little help."

"I'll give ye all the help ye need," says Kari; "but what do ye ask?"

"To fall on them," says Helgi.

Kari says that so it shall be. So they pulled up to them, and then the battle began the second time; but when they had fought a little while, Kari springs up on Snowcolf's ship; he turns to meet him and smites at him with his sword. Kari leaps nimbly backwards over a beam that lay athwart the ship, and Snowcolf smote the beam so that both edges of the sword were hidden. Then Kari smites at him, and the sword fell on his shoulder, and the stroke was so mighty that he cleft in twain shoulder, arm, and all, and Snowcolf got his death there and then. Gritgard hurled a spear at Kari, but Kari saw it and sprang up aloft, and the spear missed him. Just then Helgi and Grim came up both to meet Kari, and Helgi springs on Gritgard and thrusts his spear through him, and that was his death blow; after that they went round the whole ship on both boards, and then men begged for mercy. So they gave them all peace, but took all their goods. After that they ran all the ships out under the islands.

CHAPTER LXXXIV.

OF EARL SIGURD.

Sigurd was the name of an earl who ruled over the Orkneys; he was the son of Hlodver, the son of Thorfinn the scull-splitter, the son of Turf-Einar, the son of Rognvald, Earl of M[oe]ren, the son of Eystein the noisy. Kari was one of Earl Sigurd's body-guard, and had just been gathering scatts in the Southern Isles from Earl Gilli. Now Kari asks them to go to Hrossey,[35] and said the Earl would take to them well. They agreed to that, and went with Kari and came to Hrossey. Kari led them to see the Earl, and said what men they were.

"How came they," says the Earl, "to fall upon thee?"

"I found them," says Kari, "in Scotland's Firths, and they were fighting with the sons of Earl Moldan, and held their own so well that they threw themselves about between the bulwarks, from side to side, and were always there where the trial was greatest, and now I ask you to give them quarters among your body-guard."

"It shall be as thou choosest," says the Earl, "thou hast already taken them so much by the hand."

Then they were there with the Earl that winter, and were worthily treated, but Helgi was silent as the winter wore on. The Earl could not tell what was at the bottom of that, and asked why he was so silent, and what was on his mind.

"Thinkest thou it not good to be here?"

"Good, methinks, it is here," he says.

"Then what art thou thinking about?" asks the Earl.

"Hast thou any realm to guard in Scotland?" asks Helgi.

"So we think," says the Earl, "but what makes thee think about that, or what is the matter with it?"

"The Scots," says Helgi, "must have taken your steward's life, and stopped all the messengers; that none should cross the Pentland Firth."

"Hast thou the second sight?" said the Earl.

"That has been little proved," answers Helgi.

"Well," says the Earl, "I will increase thy honour if this be so, otherwise thou shalt smart for it."

"Nay," says Kari, "Helgi is not that kind of man, and like enough his words are sooth, for his father has the second sight."

After that the Earl sent men south to Straumey[36] to Arnljot, his steward there, and after that Arnljot sent them across the Pentland Firth, and they spied out and learnt that Earl Hundi and Earl Melsnati had taken the life of Havard in Thraswick, Earl Sigurd's brother-in-law. So Arnljot sent word to Earl Sigurd to come south with a great host and drive those earls out of his realm, and as soon as the Earl heard that, he gathered together a mighty host from all the isles.

CHAPTER LXXXV.

THE BATTLE WITH THE EARLS.

After that the Earl set out south with his host, and Kari went with him, and Njal's sons too. They came south to Caithness. The Earl had these realms in Scotland, Ross and Moray, Sutherland, and the Dales. There came to meet them men from those realms, and said that the Earls were a short way off with a great host. Then Earl Sigurd turns his host thither, and the name of that place is Duncansness, above which they met, and it came to a great battle between them. Now the Scots had let some of their host go free from the main battle, and these took the Earl's men in flank, and many men fell there till Njal's sons turned against the foe, and fought with them and put them to flight; but still it was a hard fight, and then Njal's sons turned back to the front by the Earl's standard, and fought well. Now Kari turns to meet Earl Melsnati, and Melsnati hurled a spear at him, but Kari caught the spear and threw it back and through the Earl. Then Earl Hundi fled, but they chased the fleers until they learnt that Malcolm was gathering a host at Duncansby. Then the Earl took counsel with his men, and it seemed to all the best plan to turn back, and not to fight with such a mighty land force; so they turned back. But when the Earl came to Straumey they shared the battle-spoil. After that he went north to Hrossey, and Njal's sons and Kari followed him. Then the Earl made a great feast, and at that feast he gave Kari a good sword, and a spear inlaid with gold; but he gave Helgi a gold ring and a mantle, and Grim a shield and sword. After that he took Helgi and Grim into his body-guard, and thanked them for their good help. They were with the Earl that winter and the summer after, till Kari went sea-roving; then they went with him, and harried far and wide that summer, and everywhere won the victory. They fought against Godred, King of Man, and conquered him; and after that they fared back, and had gotten much goods. Next winter they were still with the Earl, and when the spring came Njal's sons asked leave to go to Norway. The Earl said they should go or not as they pleased, and he gave them a good ship and smart men. As for Kari, he said he must come that summer to Norway with Earl Hacon's scatts, and then they would meet; and so it fell out that they gave each other their word to meet. After that Njal's sons put out to sea and sailed for Norway, and made the land north near Drontheim.

CHAPTER LXXXVI.

HRAPP'S VOYAGE FROM ICELAND.

There was a man named Kolbein, and his surname was Arnljot's son; he was a man from Drontheim; he sailed out to Iceland that same summer in which Kolskegg and Njal's sons went abroad. He was that winter east in Broaddale; but the spring after, he made his ship ready for sea in Gautawick; and when men were almost "boun," a man rowed up to them in a boat, and made the boat fast to the ship, and afterwards he went on board the ship to see Kolbein.

Kolbein asked that man for his name.

"My name is Hrapp," says he.

"What wilt thou with me?" says Kolbein.

"I wish to ask thee to put me across the Iceland main."

"Whose son art thou?" asks Kolbein.

"I am a son of Aurgunleid, the son of Geirolf the fighter."

"What need lies on thee," asked Kolbein, "to drive thee abroad?"

"I have slain a man," says Hrapp.

"What manslaughter was that," says Kolbein, "and what men have the blood-feud?"

"The men of Weaponfirth," says Hrapp, "but the man I slew was Aurlyg, the son of Aurlyg, the son of Roger the white."

"I guess this," says Kolbein, "that he will have the worst of it who bears thee abroad."

"I am the friend of my friend," said Hrapp, "but when ill is done to me I repay it. Nor am I short of money to lay down for my passage."

Then Kolbein took Hrapp on board, and a little while after a fair breeze sprung up, and they sailed away on the sea.

Hrapp ran short of food at sea, and then he sate him down at the mess of those who were nearest to him. They sprang up with ill words, and so it was that they came to blows, and Hrapp, in a trice, has two men under him.

Then Kolbein was told, and he bade Hrapp to come and share his mess, and he accepted that.

Now they come off the sea, and lie outside off Agdirness.

Then Kolbein asked where that money was which he had offered to pay for his fare?

"It is out in Iceland," answers Hrapp.

"Thou wilt beguile more men than me, I fear," says Kolbein; "but now I will forgive thee all the fare."

Hrapp bade him have thanks for that. "But what counsel dost thou give as to what I ought to do?"

"That first of all," he says, "that thou goest from the ship as soon as ever thou canst, for all Easterlings will bear thee bad witness; but there is yet another bit of good counsel which I will give thee, and that is, never to cheat thy master."

Then Hrapp went on shore with his weapons, and he had a great axe with an iron-bound haft in his hand.

He fares on and on till he comes to Gudbrand of the Dale. He was the greatest friend of Earl Hacon. They two had a shrine between them, and it was never opened but when the Earl came thither. That was the second greatest shrine in Norway, but the other was at Hlada.

Thrand was the name of Gudbrand's son, but his daughter's name was Gudruna.

Hrapp went in before Gudbrand, and hailed him well. He asked whence he came and what was his name. Hrapp told him about himself, and how he had sailed abroad from Iceland.

After that he asks Gudbrand to take him into his household as a guest.

"It does not seem," said Gudbrand, "to look on thee, as though thou wert a man to bring good luck."

"Methinks, then," says Hrapp, "that all I have heard about thee has been great lies; for it is said that thou takest every one into thy house that asks thee; and that no man is thy match for goodness and kindness, far or near; but now I shall have to speak against that saying, if thou dost not take me in."

"Well, thou shalt stay here," said Gudbrand.

"To what seat wilt thou show me?" says Hrapp.

"To one on the lower bench, over against my high seat."

Then Hrapp went and took his seat. He was able to tell of many things, and so it was at first that Gudbrand and many thought it sport to listen to him; but still it came about that most men thought him too much given to mocking, and the end of it was that he took to talking alone with Gudruna, so that many said that he meant to beguile her.

But when Gudbrand was aware of that, he scolded her much for daring to talk alone with him, and bade her beware of speaking aught to him if the whole household did not hear it. She gave her word to be good at first, but still it was soon the old story over again as to their talk. Then Gudbrand got Asvard, his overseer, to go about with her, out of doors and in, and to be with her wherever she went. One day it happened that she begged for leave to go into the nut-wood for a pastime, and Asvard went along with her. Hrapp goes to seek for them and found them, and took her by the hand, and led her away alone.

Then Asvard went to look for her, and found them both together stretched on the grass in a thicket.

He rushes at them, axe in air, and smote at Hrapp's leg, but Hrapp gave himself a second turn, and he missed him. Hrapp springs on his feet as quick as he can, and caught up his axe. Then Asvard wished to turn and get away, but Hrapp hewed asunder his backbone.

Then Gudruna said, "Now hast thou done that deed which will hinder thy stay any Longer with my father; but still there is something behind which he will like still less, for I go with child".

"He shall not learn this from others," says Hrapp, "but I will go home and tell him both these tidings."

"Then," she says, "thou will not come away with thy life."

"I will run the risk of that," he says.

After that he sees her back to the other women, but he went home. Gudbrand sat in his high seat, and there were few men in the hall.

Hrapp went in before him, and bore his axe high.

"Why is thine axe bloody?" asks Gudbrand.

"I made it so by doing a piece of work on thy overseer Asvard's back," says Hrapp.

"That can be no good work," says Gudbrand; "thou must have slain him."

"So it is, be sure," says Hrapp.

"What did ye fall out about?" asks Gudbrand.

"Oh!" says Hrapp, "what you would think small cause enough. He wanted to hew off my leg."

"What hast thou done first?" asked Gudbrand.

"What he had no right to meddle with," says Hrapp.

"Still thou wilt tell me what it was."

"Well!" said Hrapp, "if thou must know, I lay by thy daughter's side, and he thought that bad."

"Up men!" cried Gudbrand, "and take him. He shall be slain out of hand."

"Very little good wilt thou let me reap of my son-in-lawship," says Hrapp, "but thou hast not so many men at thy back as to do that speedily."

Up they rose, but he sprang out of doors. They run after him, but he got away to the wood, and they could not lay hold of him.

Then Gudbrand gathers people, and lets the wood be searched; but they find him not, for the wood was great and thick.

Hrapp fares through the wood till he came to a clearing; there he found a house, and saw a man outside cleaving wood.

He asked that man for his name, and he said his name was Tofi.

Tofi asked him for his name in turn, and Hrapp told him his true name.

Hrapp asked why the householder had set up his abode so far from other men?

"For that here," he says, "I think I am less likely to have brawls with other men."

"It is strange how we beat about the bush in out talk," says Hrapp, "but I will first tell thee who I am. I have been with Gudbrand of the Dale, but I ran away thence because I slew his overseer; but now I know that we are both of us bad men; for thou wouldst not have come hither away from other men unless thou wert some man's outlaw. And now I give thee two choices, either that I will tell where thou art,[37] or that we two have between us, share and share alike, all that is here."

"This is even as thou sayest," said the householder; "I seized and carried off this woman who is here with me, and many men have sought for me."

Then he led Hrapp in with him; there was a small house there, but well built.

The master of the house told his mistress that he had taken Hrapp into his company.

"Most men will get ill luck from this man," she says; "but thou wilt have thy way."

So Hrapp was there after that. He was a great wanderer, and was never at home. He still brings about meetings with Gudruna; her father and brother, Thrand and Gudbrand, lay in wait for him, but they could never get nigh him, and so all that year passed away.

Gudbrand sent and told Earl Hacon what trouble he had had with Hrapp, and the Earl let him be made an outlaw, and laid a price upon his head. He said too, that he would go himself to look after him; but that passed off, and the Earl thought it easy enough for them to catch him when he went about so unwarily.

CHAPTER LXXXVII.

THRAIN TOOK TO HRAPP.

That same summer Njal's sons fared to Norway from the Orkneys, as was before written, and they were there at the fair during the summer. Then Thrain Sigfus' son busked his ship for Iceland, and was all but "boun". At that time Earl Hacon went to a feast at Gudbrand's house. That night Killing-Hrapp came to the shrine of Earl Hacon and Gudbrand, and he went inside the house, and there he saw Thorgerda Shrinebride sitting, and she was as tall as a full-grown man. She had a great gold ring on her arm, and a wimple on her head; he strips her of her wimple, and takes the gold ring from off her. Then he sees Thor's car, and takes from him a second gold ring; a third he took from Irpa; and then dragged them all out, and spoiled them of all their gear.

After that he laid fire to the shrine, and burnt it down, and then he goes away just as it began to dawn. He walks across a ploughed field, and there six men sprung up with weapons, and fall upon him at once; but he made a stout defence, and the end of the business was that he slays three men, but wounds Thrand to the death, and drives two to the woods, so that they could bear no news to the Earl. He then went up to Thrand and said—

"It is now in my power to slay thee if I will, but I will not do that; and now I will set more store by the ties that are between us than ye have shown to me."

Now Hrapp means to turn back to the wood, but now he sees that men have come between him and the wood, so he dares not venture to turn thither, but lays him down in a thicket, and so lies there a while.

Earl Hacon and Gudbrand went that morning early to the shrine and found it burnt down; but the three gods were outside, stripped of all their bravery.

Then Gudbrand began to speak, and said—

"Much might is given to our gods, when here they have walked of themselves out of the fire!"

"The gods can have naught to do with it," says the Earl; "a man must have burnt the shrine, and borne the gods out; but the gods do not avenge everything on the spot. That man who has done this will no doubt be driven away out of Valhalla, and never come in thither."

Just then up ran four of the Earl's men, and told them ill tidings; for they said they had found three men slain in the field, and Thrand wounded to the death.

"Who can have done this?" says the Earl.

"Killing-Hrapp," they say.

"Then he must have burnt down the shrine," says the Earl.

They said they thought he was like enough to have done it.

"And where may he be now?" says the Earl.

They said that Thrand had told them that he had laid down in a thicket.

The Earl goes thither to look for him, but Hrapp was off and away. Then the Earl set his men to search for him, but still they could not find him. So the Earl was in the hue and cry himself, but first he bade them rest a while.

Then the Earl went aside by himself, away from other men, and bade that no man should follow him, and so he stays a while. He fell down on both his knees, and held his hands before his eyes; after that he went back to them, and then he said to them, "Come with me".

So they went along with him. He turns short away from the path on which they had walked before, and they came to a dell. There up sprang Hrapp before them, and there it was that he had hidden himself at first.

The Earl urges on his men to run after him, but Hrapp was so swift-footed that they never came near him. Hrapp made for Hlada. There both Thrain and Njal's sons lay "boun" for sea at the same time. Hrapp runs to where Njal's sons are.

"Help me, like good men and true," he said, "for the Earl will slay me."

Helgi looked at him and said—

"Thou lookest like an unlucky man, and the man who will not take thee in will have the best of it."

"Would that the worst might befall you from me," says Hrapp.

"I am the man," says Helgi, "to avenge me on thee for this as time rolls on."

Then Hrapp turned to Thrain Sigfus' son, and bade him shelter him.

"What hast thou on thy hand?" says Thrain.

"I have burnt a shrine under the Earl's eyes, and slain some men, and now he will be here speedily, for he has joined in the hue and cry himself."

- 215 -

"It hardly beseems me to do this," says Thrain, "when the Earl has done me so much good."

Then he showed Thrain the precious things which he had borne out of the shrine, and offered to give him the goods, but Thrain said he could not take them unless he gave him other goods of the same worth for them.

"Then," said Hrapp, "here will I take my stand, and here shall I be slain before thine eyes, and then thou wilt have to abide by every man's blame."

Then they see the Earl and his band of men coming, and then Thrain took Hrapp under his safeguard, and let them shove off the boat, and put out to his ship.

Then Thrain said, "Now this will be thy best hiding place, to knock out the bottoms of two casks, and then thou shalt get into them".

So it was done, and he got into the casks, and then they were lashed together, and lowered over-board.

Then comes the Earl with his band to Njal's sons, and asked if Hrapp had come there.

They said that he had come.

The Earl asked whither he had gone thence.

They said they had not kept eyes on him, and could not say.

"He," said the Earl, "should have great honour from me who would tell me where Hrapp was."

Then Grim said softly to Helgi—

"Why should we not say. What know I whether Thrain will repay us with any good?"

"We should not tell a whit more for that," says Helgi, "when his life lies at stake."

"Maybe," said Grim, "the Earl will turn his vengeance on us, for he is so wroth that some one will have to fall before him."

"That must not move us," says Helgi, "but still we will pull our ship out, and so away to sea as soon as ever we get a wind."

So they rowed out under an isle that lay there, and wait there for a fair breeze.

The Earl went about among the sailors, and tried them all, but they, one and all, denied that they knew aught of Hrapp.

Then the Earl said, "Now we will go to Thrain, my brother-in-arms, and he will give Hrapp up, if he knows anything of him".

After that they took a long-ship and went off to the merchant ship.

Thrain sees the Earl coming, and stands up and greets him kindly. The Earl took his greeting well and spoke thus—

"We are seeking for a man whose name is Hrapp, and he is an Icelander. He has done us all kind of ill; and now we will ask you to be good enough to give him up, or to tell us where he is."

"Ye know, Lord," said Thrain, "that I slew your outlaw, and then put my life in peril, and for that I had of you great honour."

"More honour shalt thou now have," says the Earl.

Now Thrain thought within himself, and could not make up his mind how the Earl would take it, so he denies that Hrapp is there, and bade the Earl to look for him. He spent little time on that, and went on land alone, away from other men, and was then very wroth, so that no man dared to speak to him.

"Show me to Njal's sons," said the Earl, "and I will force them to tell me the truth."

Then he was told that they had put out of the harbour.

"Then there is no help for it," says the Earl, "but still there were two water-casks alongside of Thrain's ship, and in them a man may well have been hid, and if Thrain has hidden him, there he must be; and now we will go a second time to see Thrain."

Thrain sees that the Earl means to put off again and said—

"However wroth the Earl was last time, now he will be half as wroth again, and now the life of every man on board the ship lies at stake."

They all gave their words to hide the matter, for they were all sore afraid. Then they took some sacks out of the lading, and put Hrapp down into the hold in their stead, and other sacks that were tight were laid over him.

Now comes the Earl, just as they were done stowing Hrapp away. Thrain greeted the Earl well. The Earl was rather slow to return it, and they saw that the Earl was very wroth.

Then said the Earl to Thrain—

"Give thou up Hrapp, for I am quite sure that thou hast hidden him."

"Where shall I have hidden him, Lord?" says Thrain.

"That thou knowest best," says the Earl; "but if I must guess, then I think that thou hiddest him in the water-casks a while ago."

"Well!" says Thrain, "I would rather not be taken for a liar, far sooner would I that ye should search the ship."

Then the Earl went on board the ship and hunted and hunted, but found him not.

"Dost thou speak me free now?" says Thrain. "Far from it," says the Earl, "and yet I cannot tell why we cannot find him, but methinks I see through it all when I come on shore, but when I come here, I can see nothing."

With that he made them row him ashore. He was so wroth that there was no speaking to him. His son Sweyn was there with him, and he said, "A strange turn of mind this to let guiltless men smart for one's wrath!"

Then the Earl went away alone aside from other men, and after that he went back to them at once, and said—

"Let us row out to them again," and they did so.

"Where can he have been hidden?" says Sweyn.

"There's not much good in knowing that," says the Earl, "for now he will be away thence; two sacks lay there by the rest of the lading, and Hrapp must have come into the lading in their place."

Then Thrain began to speak, and said—

"They are running off the ship again, and they must mean to pay us another visit. Now we will take him out of the lading, and stow other things in his stead, but let the sacks still lie loose. They did so, and then Thrain spoke—

"Now let us fold Hrapp in the sail."

It was then brailed up to the yard, and they did so.

Then the Earl comes to Thrain and his men, and he was very wroth, and said, "Wilt thou now give up the man, Thrain?" and he is worse now than before.

"I would have given him up long ago," answers Thrain, "if he had been in my keeping, or where can he have been?"

"In the lading," says the Earl.

"Then why did ye not seek him there?" says Thrain.

"That never came into our mind," says the Earl.

After that they sought him over all the ship, and found him not.

"Will you now hold me free?" says Thrain.

"Surely not," says the Earl, "for I know that thou hast hidden away the man, though I find him not; but I would rather that thou shouldest be a dastard to me than I to thee," says the Earl, and then they went on shore.

"Now," says the Earl, "I seem to see that Thrain has hidden away Hrapp in the sail."

Just then up sprung a fair breeze, and Thrain and his men sailed out to sea. He then spoke these words which have long been held in mind since—

Let us make the Vulture fly,
Nothing now gars Thrain flinch.

But when the Earl heard of Thrain's words, then he said—

"Tis not my want of foresight which caused this, but rather their ill-fellowship, which will drag them both to death."

Thrain was a short time out on the sea, and so came to Iceland, and fared home to his house. Hrapp went along with Thrain, and was with him that year; but the spring after, Thrain got him a homestead at Hrappstede, and he dwelt there; but yet he spent most of his time At Gritwater. He was thought to spoil everything there, and some men even said that he was too good friends with Hallgerda, and that he led her astray, but some spoke against that.

Thrain gave the Vulture to his kinsman, Mord the reckless; that Mord slew Oddi Haldor's son, east in Gautawick by Berufirth.

All Thrain's kinsmen looked on him as a chief.

CHAPTER LXXXVIII.

EARL HACON FIGHTS WITH NJAL'S SONS.

Now we must take up the story, and say how, when Earl Hacon missed Thrain, he spoke to Sweyn his son, and said—

"Let us take four long-ships, and let us fare against Njal's sons and slay them, for they must have known all about it with Thrain."

"'Tis not good counsel," says Sweyn, "to throw the blame on guiltless men, but to let him escape who is guilty."

"I shall have my way in this," says the Earl.

Now they hold on after Njal's sons, and seek for them, and find them under an island.

Grim first saw the Earl's ships and said to Helgi—

"Here are war ships sailing up, and I see that here is the Earl, and he can mean to offer us no peace."

"It is said," said Helgi, "that he is the boldest man who holds his own against all comers, and so we will defend ourselves."

They all bade him take the course he thought best, and then they took to their arms.

Now the Earl comes up and called out to them, And bade them give themselves up.

Helgi said that they would defend themselves so long as they could.

Then the Earl offered peace and quarter to all who would neither defend themselves nor Helgi; but Helgi was so much beloved that all said they would rather die with him.

Then the Earl and his men fall on them, but they defended themselves well, and Njal's sons were ever where there was most need. The Earl often offered peace, but they all made the same answer, and said they would never yield.

Then Aslak of Longisle pressed them hard, and came on board their ship thrice. Then Grim said—

"Thou pressest on hard, and 'twere well that thou gettest what thou seekest;" and with that he snatched up a spear and hurled it at him, and hit him under the chin, and Aslak got his death wound there and then.

A little after, Helgi slew Egil the Earl's banner-bearer.

Then Sweyn, Earl Bacon's son, fell on them, and made men hem them in and bear them down with shields, and so they were taken captive.

The Earl was for letting them all be slain at once, but Sweyn said that should not be, and said too that it was night.

Then the Earl said, "Well, then, slay them to-morrow, but bind them fast to-night".

"So, I ween, it must be," says Sweyn; "but never yet have I met brisker men than these, and I call it the greatest manscathe to take their lives."

"They have slain two of our briskest men," said the Earl, "and for that they shall be slain."

"Because they were brisker men themselves," says Sweyn; "but still in this it must be done as thou wiliest."

So they were bound and fettered.

After that the Earl fell asleep; but when all men slept, Grim spoke to Helgi, and said, "Away would I get if I could".

"Let us try some trick then," says Helgi.

Grim sees that there lies an axe edge up, so Grim crawled thither, and gets the bowstring which bound him cut asunder against the axe, but still he got great wounds on his arms.

Then he set Helgi loose, and after that they crawled over the ship's side, and got on shore, so that neither Hacon nor his men were ware of them. Then they broke off their fetters and walked away to the other side of the island. By that time it began to dawn. There they found a ship, and knew that there was come Kari Solmund's son. They went at once to meet him, and told him of their wrongs and hardships, and showed him their wounds, and said the Earl would be then asleep.

"Ill is it," said Karl, "that ye should suffer such wrongs for wicked men; but what now would be most to your minds?"

"To fall on the Earl," they say, "and slay him."

"This will not be fated," says Kari; "but still ye do not lack heart, but we will first know whether he is there now."

After that they fared thither, and then the Earl was up and away.

Then Kari sailed in to Hlada to meet the Earl, and brought him the Orkney scatts; so the Earl said—

"Hast thou taken Njal's sons into thy keeping?"

"So it is, sure enough," says Kari.

"Wilt thou hand Njal's sons over to me?" asks the Earl.

"No, I will not," said Kari.

"Wilt thou swear this," says the Earl, "that thou wilt not fall on me with Njal's sons?"

Then Eric, the Earl's son, spoke and said—

"Such things ought not to be asked. Kari has always been our friend, and things should not have gone as they have, had I been by. Njal's sons should have been set free from all blame, but they should have had chastisement who had wrought for it. Methinks now it would be more seemly to give Njal's sons good gifts for the hardships and wrongs which have been put upon them, and the wounds they have got."

"So it ought to be, sure enough," says the Earl, "but I know not whether they will take an atonement."

Then the Earl said that Kari should try the feeling of Njal's sons as to an atonement.

After that Kari spoke to Helgi, and asked whether he would take any amends from the Earl or not.

"I will take them," said Helgi, "from his son Eric, but I will have nothing to do with the Earl."

Then Kari told Eric their answer.

"So it shall be," says Eric. "He shall take the amends from me if he thinks it better; and tell them this too, that I bid them to my house, and my father shall do them no harm."

This bidding they took, and went to Eric's house, and were with him till Kari was ready to sail west across the sea to meet Earl Sigurd.

Then Eric made a feast for Kari, and gave him gifts, and Njal's sons gifts too. After that Kari fared west across the sea, and met Earl Sigurd, and he greeted them very well, and they were with the Earl that winter.

But when the spring came, Kari asked Njal's sons to go on warfare with him, but Grim said they would only do so if he would fare with them afterwards out to Iceland. Kari gave his word to do that, and then they fared with him a-sea-roving. They harried south about Anglesea and all the Southern isles. Thence they held on to Cantyre, and landed there, and fought with the landsmen, and got thence much goods, and so fared to their ships. Thence they fared south to Wales, and harried there. Then they held on for Man, and there they met Godred, and fought with him, and got the victory, and slew Dungal the king's son. There they took great spoil. Thence they held on north to Coll, and found Earl Gilli there, and he greeted them well, and there they stayed with him a while. The Earl fared with them to the Orkneys to meet Earl Sigurd, but next spring Earl Sigurd gave away his sister Nereida to Earl Gilli, and then he fared back to the Southern isles.

CHAPTER LXXXIX.

NJAL'S SONS AND KARI COME OUT TO ICELAND.

That summer Kari and Njal's sons busked them for Iceland, and when they were "all-boun" they went to see the Earl. The Earl gave them good gifts, and they parted with great friendship.

Now they put to sea and have a short passage, and they got a fine fair breeze, and made the land at Eyrar. Then they got them horses and ride from the ship to Bergthorsknoll, but when they came home all men were glad to see them. They flitted home their goods and laid up the ship, and Kari was there that winter with Njal.

But the spring after, Kari asked for Njal's daughter, Helga, to wife, and Helgi and Grim backed his suit; and so the end of it was that she was betrothed to Kari, and the day for the wedding-feast was fixed, and the feast was held half a month before mid-summer, and they were that winter with Njal.

Then Kari bought him land at Dyrholms, east away by Mydale, and set up a farm there; they put in there a grieve and housekeeper to see after the farm, but they themselves were ever with Njal.

CHAPTER XC.

THE QUARREL OF NJAL'S SONS WITH THRAIN SIGFUS' SON.

Hrapp owned a farm at Hrappstede, but for all that he was always at Gritwater, and he was thought to spoil everything there. Thrain was good to him.

Once on a time it happened that Kettle of the Mark was at Bergthorsknoll; then Njal's sons told him of their wrongs and hardships, and said they had much to lay at Thrain Sigfus' son's door, whenever they chose to speak about it.

Njal said it would be best that Kettle should talk with his brother Thrain about it, and he gave his word to do so.

So they gave Kettle breathing-time to talk to Thrain.

A little after they spoke of the matter again to Kettle, but he said that he would repeat few of the words that had passed between them, "for it was pretty plain that Thrain thought I set too great store on being your brother-in-law".

Then they dropped talking about it, and thought they saw that things looked ugly, and so they asked their father for his counsel as to what was to be done, but they told him they would not let things rest as they then stood.

"Such things," said Njal, "are not so strange. It will be thought that they are slain without a cause, if they are slain now, and my counsel is, that as many men as may be should be brought to talk with them about these things, that thus as many as we can find may be ear-witnesses if they answer ill as to these things. Then Kari shall talk about them too, for he is just the man with the right turn of mind for this; then the dislike between you will grow and grow, for they will heap bad words on bad words when men bring the matter forward, for they are foolish men. It may also well be that it may be said that my sons are slow to take up a quarrel, but ye shall bear that for the sake of gaining time, for there are two sides to everything that is done, and ye can always pick a quarrel; but still ye shall let so much of your purpose out, as to say that if any wrong be put upon you that ye do mean something. But if ye had taken counsel from me at first, then these things should never have been spoken about at all, and then ye would have gotten no disgrace from them; but now ye have the greatest risk of it, and so it will go on ever growing and growing with your disgrace, that ye will never get rid of it until ye bring yourselves into a strait, and have to fight your way out with weapons; but in that there is a long and weary night in which ye will have to grope your way."

After that they ceased speaking about it; but the matter became the daily talk of many men.

One day it happened that those brothers spoke to Kari and bade him go to Gritwater. Kari said he thought he might go elsewhither on a better journey, but still he would go if that were Njal's counsel. So after that Kari fares to meet Thrain, and then they talk over the matter, and they did not each look at it in the same way.

Kari comes home, and Njal's sons ask how things had gone between Thrain and him. Kari said he would rather not repeat the words that had passed, "but," he went on, "it is to be looked for that the like words will be spoken when ye yourselves can hear them".

Thrain had fifteen house-earles trained to arms in his house, and eight of them rode with him whithersoever he went. Thrain was very fond of show and dress, and always rode in a blue cloak, and had on a guilded helm, and the spear—the Earl's gift—in his hand, and a fair shield, and a sword at his belt. Along with him always went Gunnar Lambi's son, and Lambi Sigurd's son, and Grani, Gunnar of Lithend's son. But nearest of all to him went Killing-Hrapp. Lodinn was the name of his serving-man, he too went with Thrain when he journeyed; Tjorvi was the name of Loddin's brother, and he too was one of Thrain's band. The worst of all, in their words against Njal's sons, were Hrapp and Grani; and it was mostly their doing that no atonement was offered to them.

Njal's sons often spoke to Kari that he should ride with them; and it came to that at last, for he said it would be well that they heard Thrain's answer.

Then they busked them, four of Njal's sons, and Kari the fifth, and so they fare to Gritwater.

There was a wide porch in the homestead there, so that many men might stand in it side by side. There was a woman out of doors, and she saw their coming, and told Thrain of it; he bade them to go out into the porch, and take their arms, and they did so.

Thrain stood in mid-door, Killing-Hrapp and Grani Gunnar's son stood on either hand of him; then next stood Gunnar Lambi's son, then Lodinn and Tjorvi, then Lambi Sigurd's son; then each of the others took his place right and left; for the house-earles were all at home.

Skarphedinn and his men walk up from below, and he went first, then Kari, then Hauskuld, then Grim, then Helgi. But when they had come up to the door, then not a word of welcome passed the lips of those who stood before them.

"May we all be welcome here?" said Skarphedinn.

Hallgerda stood in the porch, and had been talking low to Hrapp, then she spoke out loud—

"None of those who are here will say that ye are welcome."

Then Skarphedinn sang a song.

Prop of sea-waves' fire,[38] thy fretting
Cannot cast a weight on us,
Warriors wight; yes, wolf and eagle
Willingly I feed to-day;
Carline thrust into the ingle,
Or a tramping whore, art thou;
Lord of skates that skim the sea-belt,[39]
Odin's mocking cup[40] I mix.

"Thy words," said Skarphedinn, "will not be worth much, for thou art either a hag, only fit to sit in the ingle, or a harlot."

"These words of thine thou shalt pay for," she says, "ere thou farest home."

"Thee am I come to see, Thrain," said Helgi, "and to know if thou will make me any amends for those wrongs and hardships which befell me for thy sake in Norway."

"I never knew," said Thrain, "that ye two brothers were wont to measure your manhood by money; or, how long shall such a claim for amends stand over?"

"Many will say," says Helgi, "that thou oughtest to offer us atonement, since thy life was at stake."

Then Hrapp said, "'Twas just luck that swayed the balance, when he got stripes who ought to bear them; and she dragged you under disgrace and hardship, but us away from them."

"Little good luck was there in that," says Helgi, "to break faith with the Earl, and to take to thee instead."

"Thinkest thou not that thou hast some amends to seek from me?" says Hrapp, "I will atone thee in a way that, methinks, were fitting."

"The only dealings we shall have," says Helgi, "will be those which will not stand thee in good stead."

"Don't bandy words with Hrapp," said Skarphedinn, "but give him a red skin for a grey."[41]

"Hold thy tongue, Skarphedinn," said Hrapp, "or I will not spare to bring my axe on thy head."

"'Twill be proved soon enough, I dare say," says Skarphedinn, "which of us is to scatter gravel over the other's head."

"Away with you home, ye 'Dung-beardlings!'" says Hallgerda, "and so we will call you always from this day forth; but your father we will call 'the Beardless Carle'."

They did not fare home before all who were there had made themselves guilty of uttering those words, save Thrain; he forbade men to utter them.

Then Njal's sons went away, and fared till they came home; then they told their father.

"Did ye call any men to witness of those words?" says Njal.

"We called none," says Skarphedinn; "we do not mean to follow that suit up except on the battlefield."

"No one will now think," says Bergthora, "that ye have the heart to lift your weapons."

"Spare thy tongue, mistress!" says Kari, "in egging on thy sons, for they will be quite eager enough."

After that they all talk long in secret, Njal and his sons, and Kari Solmund's son, their brother-in-law.

CHAPTER XCI.

THRAIN SIGFUS' SON'S SLAYING.

Now there was great talk about this quarrel of theirs, and all seemed to know that it would not settle down peacefully.

Runolf, the son of Wolf Aurpriest, east in the Dale, was a great friend of Thrain's, and had asked Thrain to come and see him, and it was settled that he should come east when about three weeks or a month were wanting to winter.

Thrain bade Hrapp, and Grani, and Gunnar Lambi's son, and Lambi Sigurd's son, and Lodinn, and Tjorvi, eight of them in all, to go on this journey with him. Hallgerda and Thorgerda were to go too. At the same time Thrain gave it out that he meant to stay in the Mark with his brother Kettle, and said how many nights he meant to be away from home.

They all of them had full arms. So they rode east across Markfleet, and found there some gangrel women, and they begged them to put them across the Fleet west on their horses, and they did so.

Then they rode into the Dale, and had a hearty welcome; there Kettle of the Mark met them, and there they sate two nights.

Both Runolf and Kettle besought Thrain that he would make up his quarrel with Njal's sons; but he said he would never pay any money, and answered crossly, for he said he thought himself quite a match for Njal's sons wherever they met.

"So it may be," says Runolf; "but so far as I can see, no man has been their match since Gunnar of Lithend died, and it is likelier that ye will both drag one another down to death."

Thrain said that was not to be dreaded.

Then Thrain fared up into the Mark, and was there two nights more; after that he rode down into the Dale, and was sent away from both houses with fitting gifts.

Now the Markfleet was then flowing between sheets of ice on both sides, and there were tongues of ice bridging it across every here and there.

Thrain said that he meant to ride home that evening, but Runolf said that he ought not to ride home; he said, too, that it would be more wary not to fare back as he had said he would before he left home.

"That is fear, and I will none of it," answers Thrain.

Now those gangrel women whom they had put across the Fleet came to Bergthorsknoll, and Bergthora asked whence they came, but they answered, "Away east under Eyjafell".

"Then, who put you across Markfleet?" said Bergthora.

"Those," said they, "who were the most boastful and bravest clad of men."

"Who?" asked Bergthora.

"Thrain Sigfus' son," said they, "and his company, but we thought it best to tell thee that they were so full-tongued and foul-tongued towards this house, against thy husband and his sons."

"Listeners do not often hear good of themselves," says Bergthora. After that they went their way, and Bergthora gave them gifts on their going, and asked them when Thrain might be coming home.

They said that he would be from home four or five nights.

After that Bergthora told her sons and her son-in-law Kari, and they talked long and low about the matter.

But that same morning, when Thrain and his men rode from the east, Njal woke up early and heard how Skarphedinn's axe came against the panel.

Then Njal rises up, and goes out, and sees that his sons are all there with their weapons, and Karl, his son-in-law too. Skarphedinn was foremost. He was in a blue cape, and had a targe, and his axe aloft on his shoulder. Next to him went Helgi; he was in a red kirtle, had a helm on his head, and a red shield, on which a hart was marked. Next to him went Kari; he had on a silken jerkin, a gilded helm and shield, and on it was drawn a lion. They were all in bright holiday clothes.

Njal called out to Skarphedinn—

"Whither art thou going, kinsman?"

"On a sheep hunt," he said.

"So it was once before," said Njal, "but then ye hunted men."

Skarphedinn laughed at that, and said—

"Hear ye what the old man says? He is not without his doubts."

"When was it that thou spokest thus before?" asks Kari.

"When I slew Sigmund the white," says Skarphedinn, "Gunnar of Lithend's kinsman."

"For what?" asks Kari.

"He had slain Thord Freedmanson, my foster-father."

Njal went home, but they fared up into the Redslips, and bided there; thence they could see the others as soon as ever they rode from the east out of the dale.

There was sunshine that day and bright weather.

Now Thrain and his men ride down out of the Dale along the river bank.

Lambi Sigurd's son said—

"Shields gleam away yonder in the Redslips when the sun shines on them, and there must be some men lying in wait there."

"Then," says Thrain, "we will turn our way lower down the Fleet, and then they will come to meet us if they have any business with us."

So they turn down the Fleet. "Now they have caught sight of us," said Skarphedinn, "for lo! they turn their path elsewhither, and now we have no other choice than to run down and meet them."

"Many men," said Kari, "would rather not lie in wait if the balance of force were not more on their side than it is on ours; they are eight, but we are five."

Now they turn down along the Fleet, and see a tongue of ice bridging the stream lower down and mean to cross there.

Thrain and his men take their stand upon the ice away from the tongue, and Thrain said—

"What can these men want? They are five, and we are eight."

"I guess," said Lambi Sigurd's son, "that they would still run the risk though more men stood against them."

Thrain throws off his cloak, and takes off his helm.

Now it happened to Skarphedinn, as they ran down along the Fleet, that his shoe-string snapped asunder, and he stayed behind.

"Why so slow, Skarphedinn?" quoth Grim.

"I am tying my shoe," he says.

"Let us get on ahead," says Kari; "methinks he will not be slower than we."

So they turn off to the tongue, and run as fast as they can. Skarphedinn sprang up as soon as he was ready, and had lifted his axe, "the ogress of war," aloft, and runs right down to the Fleet. But the Fleet was so deep that there was no fording it for a long way up or down.

A great sheet of ice had been thrown up by the flood on the other side of the Fleet as smooth and slippery as glass, and there Thrain and his men stood in the midst of the sheet.

Skarphedinn takes a spring into the air, and leaps over the stream between the icebanks, and does not check his course, but rushes still onwards with a slide. The sheet of ice was very slippery, and so he went as fast as a bird flies. Thrain was just about to put his helm on his head; and now Skarphedinn bore down on them, and hews at Thrain with his axe, "the ogress of war," and smote him on the head, and clove him down to the teeth, so that his jaw-teeth fell out on the ice. This feat was done with such a quick sleight that no one could get a blow at him; he glided away from them at once at full speed. Tjorvi, indeed, threw his shield before him on the ice, but he leapt over it, and still kept his feet, and slid quite to the end of the sheet of ice.

There Kari and his brothers came to meet him.

"This was done like a man," says Kari.

"Your share is still left," says Skarphedinn, and sang a song.

To the strife of swords not slower,
After all, I came than you,
For with ready stroke the sturdy
Squanderer of wealth I felled;
But since Grim's and Helgi's sea-stag[42]
Norway's Earl erst took and stripped,
Now 'tis time for sea-fire bearers[43]
Such dishonour to avenge.

And this other song he sang—

Swiftly down I dashed my weapon,
Gashing giant, byrnie-breacher,[44]
She, the noisy ogre's namesake,[45]
Soon with flesh the ravens glutted;
Now your words to Hrapp remember,
On broad ice now rouse the storm,
With dull crash war's eager ogress
Battle's earliest note hath sung.

"That befits us well, and we wilt do it well," says Helgi. Then they turn up towards them. Both Grim and Helgi see where Hrapp is, and they turned on him at once. Hrapp hews at Grim there and then with his axe; Helgi sees this and cuts at Hrapp's arm, and cut it off, and down fell the axe.

"In this," says Hrapp, "thou hast done a most needful work, for this hand hath wrought harm and death to many a man."

"And so here an end shall be put to it," says Grim; and with that he ran him through with a spear, and then Hrapp fell down dead.

Tjorvi turns against Kari and hurls a spear at him. Kari leapt up in the air, and the spear flew below his feet. Then Kari rushes at him, and hews at him on the breast with his sword, and the blow passed at once into his chest, and he got his death there and then.

Then Skarphedinn seizes both Gunnar Lambi's son, and Grani Gunnar's son, and said—

"Here have I caught two whelps! but what shall we do with them?"

"It is in thy power," says Helgi, "to slay both or either of them, if you wish them dead."

"I cannot find it in my heart to do both—help Hogni and slay his brother," says Skarphedinn.

"Then the day will once come," says Helgi, "when thou wilt wish that thou hadst slain him, for never will he be true to thee, nor will any one of the others who are now here."

"I shall not fear them," answers Skarphedinn.

After that they gave peace to Grani Gunnar's son, and Gunnar Lambi's son, and Lambi Sigurd's son, and Lodinn.

After that they went down to the Fleet where Skarphedinn had leapt over it, and Kari and the others measured the length of the leap with their spear-shafts, and it was twelve ells (about eighteen feet, according to the old Norse measure).

Then they turned homewards, and Njal asked what tidings.

They told him all just as it had happened, and Njal said—

"These are great tidings, and it is more likely that hence will come the death of one of my sons, if not more evil."

Gunnar Lambi's son bore the body of Thrain with him to Gritwater, and he was laid in a cairn there.

CHAPTER XCII.

KETTLE TAKES HAUSKULD AS HIS FOSTER-SON.

Kettle of the Mark had to wife Thorgerda, Njal's daughter, but he was Thrain's brother, and he thought he was come into a strait, so he rode to Njal's house, and asked whether he were willing to atone in any way for Thrain's slaying?

"I will atone for it handsomely," answered Njal; "and my wish is that thou shouldst look after the matter with thy brothers who have to take the price of the atonement, that they may be ready to join in it."

Kettle said he would do so with all his heart, and Kettle rode home first; a little after, he summoned all his brothers to Lithend, and then he had a talk with them; and Hogni was on his side all through the talk; and so it came about that men were chosen to utter the award; and a meeting was agreed on, and the fair price of a man was awarded for Thrain's slaying, and they all had a share in the blood-money who had a lawful right to it. After that pledges of peace and good faith were agreed to, and they were settled in the most sure and binding way.

Njal paid down all the money out of hand well and bravely; and so things were quiet for a while.

One day Njal rode up into the Mark, and he and Kettle talked together the whole day, Njal rode home at even, and no man knew of what they had taken counsel.

A little after Kettle fares to Gritwater, and he said to Thorgerda—

"Long have I loved my brother Thrain much, and now I will show it, for I will ask Hauskuld Thrain's son to be my foster-child."

"Thou shalt have thy choice of this," she says; "and thou shalt give this lad all the help in thy power when he is grown up, and avenge him if he is slain with weapons, and bestow money on him for his wife's dower; and besides, thou shalt swear to do all this."

Now Hauskuld fares home with Kettle, and is with him some time.

CHAPTER XCIII.

NJAL TAKES HAUSKULD TO FOSTER.

Once on a time Njal rides up into the Mark, and he had a hearty welcome. He was there that night, and in the evening Njal called out to the lad Hauskuld, and he went up to him at once.

Njal had a ring of gold on his hand, and showed it to the lad. He took hold of the gold, and looked at it, and put it on his finger.

"Wilt thou take the gold as a gift?" said Njal.

"That I will," said the lad.

"Knowest thou," says Njal, "what brought thy father to his death?"

"I know," answers the lad, "that Skarphedinn slew him; but we need not keep that in mind, when an atonement has been made for it, and a full price paid for him."

"Better answered than asked," said Njal; "and thou wilt live to be a good man and true," he adds.

"Methinks thy forecasting," says Hauskuld, "is worth having, for I know that thou art foresighted and unlying."

"Now I will offer to foster thee," said Njal, "if thou wilt take the offer."

He said he would be willing to take both that honour and any other good offer which he might make. So the end of the matter was, that Hauskuld fared home with Njal as his foster-son.

He suffered no harm to come nigh the lad, and loved him much. Njal's sons took him about with them, and did him honour in every way. And so things go on till Hauskuld is full grown. He was both tall and strong; the fairest of men to look on, and well-haired; blithe of speech, bountiful, well-behaved; as well trained to arms as the best; fairspoken to all men, and much beloved.

Njal's sons and Hauskuld were never apart, either in word or deed.

CHAPTER XCIV.

OF FLOSI THORD'S SON.

There was a man named Flosi, he was the son of Thord Freyspriest. Flosi had to wife Steinvora, daughter of Hall of the Side. She was base born, and her mother's name was Solvora, daughter of Herjolf the white. Flosi dwelt at Swinefell, and was a mighty chief. He was tall of stature, and strong withal, the most forward and boldest of men. His brother's name was Starkad; he was not by the same mother as Flosi.

The other brothers of Flosi were Thorgeir and Stein, Kolbein and Egil. Hildigunna was the name of the daughter of Starkad Flosi's brother. She was a proud, high-spirited maiden, and one of the fairest of women. She was so skilful with her hands, that few women were equally skilful. She was the grimmest and hardest-hearted of all women; but still a woman of open hand and heart when any fitting call was made upon her.

CHAPTER XCV.

OF HALL OF THE SIDE.

Hall was the name of a man who was called Hall of the Side. He was the son of Thorstein Baudvar's son. Hall had to wife Joreida, daughter of Thidrandi the wise. Thorstein was the name of Hall's brother, and he was nick-named broadpaunch. His son was Kol, whom Kari slays in Wales. The sons of Hall of the Side were Thorstein and Egil, Thorwald and Ljot, and Thidrandi, whom, it is said, the goddesses slew.

There was a man named Thorir, whose surname was Holt-Thorir; his sons were these: Thorgeir Craggeir, and Thorleif crow, from whom the Wood-dwellers are come, and Thorgrim the big.

CHAPTER XCVI.

OF THE CHANGE OF FAITH.

There had been a change of rulers in Norway, Earl Hacon was dead and gone, but in his stead was come Olaf Tryggvi's son. That was the end of Earl Hacon, that Kark, the thrall, cut his throat at Rimul in Gaulardale.

Along with that was heard that there had been a change of faith in Norway; they had cast off the old faith, but King Olaf had christened the western lands, Shetland, and the Orkneys, and the Faroe Isles.

Then many men spoke so that Njal heard it, that it was a strange and wicked thing to throw off the old faith.

Then Njal spoke and said—

"It seems to me as though this new faith must be much better, and he will be happy who follows this rather than the other; and if those men come out hither who preach this faith, then I will back them well."

He went often alone away from other men and muttered to himself.

That same harvest a ship came out into the firths east to Berufirth, at a spot called Gautawick. The captain's name was Thangbrand. He was a son of Willibald, a count of Saxony, Thangbrand was sent out hither by King Olaf Tryggvi's son, to preach the faith. Along with him came that man of Iceland whose name was Gudleif. Gudleif was a great man-slayer, and one of the strongest of men, and hardy and forward in everything.

Two brothers dwelt at Beruness; the name of the one was Thorleif, but the other was Kettle. They were sons of Holmstein, the son of Auzur of Broaddale. These brothers held a meeting, and forbade men to have any dealings with them. This Hall of the Side heard. He dwelt at Thvattwater in Alftafirth; he rode to the ship with twenty-nine men, and he fares at once to find Thangbrand, and spoke to him and asked him—

"Trade is rather dull, is it not?"

He answered that so it was.

"Now will I say my errand," says Hall; "it is, that I wish to ask you all to my house, and run the risk of my being able to get rid of your wares for you."

Thangbrand thanked him, and fared to Thvattwater that harvest.

It so happened one morning that Thangbrand was out early and made them pitch a tent on land, and sang mass in it, and took much pains with it, for it was a great high day.

Hall spoke to Thangbrand and asked, "In memory of whom keepest thou this day?"

"In memory of Michael the archangel," says Thangbrand.

"What follows that angel?" asks Hall.

"Much good," says Thangbrand. "He will weigh all the good that thou doest, and he is so merciful, that whenever any one pleases him, he makes his good deeds weigh more."

"I would like to have him for my friend," says Hall.

"That thou mayest well have," says Thangbrand, "only give thyself over to him by God's help this very day."

"I only make this condition," says Hall, "that thou givest thy word for him that he will then become my guardian angel."

"That I will promise," says Thangbrand.

Then Hall was baptised, and all his household.

CHAPTER XCVII.

OF THANGBRAND'S JOURNEYS.

The spring after Thangbrand set out to preach Christianity, and Hall went with him. But when they came west across Lonsheath to Staffell, there they found a man dwelling named Thorkell. He spoke most against the faith, and challenged Thangbrand to single combat. Then Thangbrand bore a rood-cross[46] before his shield, and the end of their combat was that Thangbrand won the day and slew Thorkell.

Thence they fared to Hornfirth and turned in as guests at Borgarhaven, west of Heinabergs sand. There Hilldir the old dwelt,[47] and then Hilldir and all his household took upon them the new faith.

Thence they fared to Fellcombe, and went in as guests to Calffell. There dwelt Kol Thorstein's son, Hall's kinsman, and he took upon him the faith and all his house.

Thence they fared to Swinefell, and Flosi only took the sign of the cross, but gave his word to back them at the Thing.

Thence they fared west to Woodcombe, and went in as guests at Kirkby. There dwelt Surt Asbjorn's son, the son of Thorstein, the son of Kettle the foolish. These had all of them been Christians from father to son.

After that they fared out of Woodcombe on to Headbrink. By that time the story of their journey was spread far and wide. There was a man named Sorcerer-Hedinn who dwelt in Carlinedale. There heathen men made a bargain with him that he should put Thangbrand to death with all his company. He fared upon Arnstacksheath, and there made a great sacrifice when Thangbrand was riding from the east. Then the earth burst asunder under his horse, but he sprang off his horse and saved himself on the brink of the gulf, but the earth swallowed up the horse and all his harness, and they never saw him more.

Then Thangbrand praised God.

CHAPTER XCVIII.

OF THANGBRAND AND GUDLEIF.

Gudleif now searches for Sorcerer-Hedinn and finds him on the heath, and chases him down into Carlinedale, and got within spearshot of him, and shoots a spear at him and through him.

Thence they fared to Dyrholms and held a meeting there, and preached the faith there, and there Ingialld, the son of Thorsteinn Highbankawk, became a Christian.

Thence they fared to the Fleetlithe and preached the faith there. There Weatherlid the Skald, and Ari his son, spoke most against the faith, and for that they slew Weatherlid, and then this song was sung about it—

He who proved his blade on bucklers,
South went through the land to whet
Brand that oft hath felled his foeman,
'Gainst the forge which foams with song;[48]
Mighty wielder of war's sickle
Made his sword's avenging edge
Hard on hero's helm-prop rattle,[49]
Skull of Weatherlid the Skald.

Thence Thangbrand fared to Bergthorsknoll, and Njal took the faith and all his house, but Mord and Valgard went much against it, and thence they fared out across the rivers; so they went on into Hawkdale and there they baptised Hall,[50] and he was then three winters old.

Thence Thangbrand fared to Grimsness, there Thorwald the scurvy gathered a band against him, and sent word to Wolf Uggi's son, that he must fare against Thangbrand and slay him, and made this song on him—

To the wolf in Woden's harness,
Uggi's worthy warlike son,
I, steel's swinger dearly loving,
This my simple bidding send;
That the wolf of Gods[51] he chaseth,—
Man who snaps at chink of gold—
Wolf who base our Gods blasphemeth,
I the other wolf[52] will crush.

Wolf sang another song in return—

Swarthy skarf from month that skimmeth
Of the man who speaks in song
Never will I catch, though surely
Wealthy warrior it hath sent;
Tender of the sea-horse snorting,
E'en though ill deeds are on foot,
Still to risk mine eyes are open;
Harmful 'tis to snap at flies.[53]

"And," says he, "I don't mean to be made a catspaw by him, but let him take heed lest his tongue twists a noose for his own neck."

And after that the messenger fared back to Thorwald the scurvy and told him Wolf's words. Thorwald had many men about him, and gave it out that he would lie in wait for them on Bluewoodheath.

Now those two, Thangbrand and Gudleif, ride out of Hawkdale, and there they came upon a man who rode to meet them. That man asked for Gudleif, and when he found him he said—

"Thou shalt gain by being the brother of Thorgil of Reykiahole, for I will let thee know that they have set many ambushes, and this too, that Thorwald the scurvy is now with his band At Heatbeck on Grimsness."

"We shall not the less for all that ride to meet him," says Gudleif, and then they turned down to Hestbeck. Thorwald was then come across the brook, and Gudleif said to Thangbrand—

"Here is now Thorwald; let us rush on him now." Thangbrand shot a spear through Thorwald, but Gudleif smote him on the shoulder and hewed his arm off, and that was his death.

After that they ride up to the Thing, and it was a near thing that the kinsmen of Thorwald had fallen on Thangbrand, but Njal and the eastfirthers stood by Thangbrand.

Then Hjallti Skeggi's son sang this rhyme at the Hill of Laws—

Ever will I Gods blaspheme
Freyja methinks a dog does seem,
Freyja a dog? Aye! let them be
Both dogs together Odin and she.[54]

Hjallti fared abroad that summer and Gizur the white with him, but Thangbrand's ship was wrecked away east at Bulandsness, and the ship's name was "Bison".

Thangbrand and his messmate fared right through the west country, and Steinvora, the mother of Ref the Skald, came against him; she preached the heathen faith to Thangbrand and made him a long speech. Thangbrand held his peace while she spoke, but made a long speech after her, and turned all that she had said the wrong way against her.

"Hast thou heard," she said, "how Thor challenged Christ to single combat, and how he did not dare to fight with Thor?"

"I have heard tell," says Thangbrand, "that Thor was naught but dust and ashes, if God had not willed that he should live."

"Knowest thou," she says, "who it was that shattered thy ship?"

"What hast thou to say about that?" he asks.

"That I will tell thee," she says.

He that giant's offspring[55] slayeth
Broke the new-field's bison stout,[56]
Thus the Gods, bell's warder[57] grieving.
Crushed the falcon of the strand;[58]
To the courser of the causeway[59]
Little good was Christ I ween,
When Thor shattered ships to pieces
Gylfi's hart[60] no God could help.

And again she sang another song—

Thangbrand's vessel from her moorings,
Sea-king's steed, Thor wrathful tore,
Shook and shattered all her timbers,
Hurled her broadside on the beach;
Ne'er again shall Viking's snow-shoe,[61]
On the briny billows glide,
For a storm by Thor awakened,
Dashed the bark to splinters small.

After that Thangbrand and Steinvora parted, and they fared west to Bardastrand.

CHAPTER XCIX.

OF GEST ODDLEIF'S SON.

Gest Oddleif's son dwelt at Hagi on Bardastrand, He was one of the wisest of men, so that he foresaw the fates and fortunes of men. He made a feast for Thangbrand and his men. They fared to Hagi with sixty men. Then it was said that there were two hundred heathen men to meet them, and that a Baresark was looked for to come thither, whose name was Otrygg, and all were afraid of him. Of him such great things as these were said, that he feared neither fire nor sword, and the heathen men were sore afraid at his coming. Then Thangbrand asked if men were willing to take the faith, but all the heathen men spoke against it.

"Well," says Thangbrand, "I will give you the means whereby ye shall prove whether my faith is better. We will hallow two fires. The heathen men shall hallow one and I the other, but a third shall he unhallowed; and if the Baresark is afraid of the one that I hallow, but treads both the others, then ye shall take the faith."

"That is well-spoken," says Gest, "and I will agree to this for myself and my household."

And when Gest had so spoken, then many more agreed to it.

Then it was said that the Baresark was coming up to the homestead, and then the fires were made and burned strong. Then men took their arms and sprang up on the benches, and so waited.

The Baresark rushed in with his weapons. He comes into the room, and treads at once the fire which the heathen men had hallowed, and so comes to the fire that Thangbrand had hallowed, and dares not to tread it, but said that he was on fire all over. He hews with his sword at the bench, but strikes a cross-beam as he brandished the weapon aloft. Thangbrand smote the arm of the Baresark with his crucifix, and so mighty a token followed that the sword fell from the Baresark's hand.

Then Thangbrand thrusts a sword into his breast, and Gudleif smote him on the arm and hewed it off. Then many went up and slew the Baresark.

After that Thangbrand asked if they would take the faith now?

Gest said he had only spoken what he meant to keep to.

Then Thangbrand baptised Gest and all his house and many others. Then Thangbrand took counsel with Gest whether he should go any further west among the firths, but Gest set his face against that, and said they were a hard race of men there, and ill to deal with, "but if it be foredoomed that this faith shall make its way, then it will be taken as law at the Althing, and then all the chiefs out of the districts will be there".

"I did all that I could at the Thing," says Thangbrand, "and it was very uphill work."

"Still thou hast done most of the work," says Gest, "though it may be fated that others shall make Christianity law; but it is here as the saying runs, 'No tree falls at the first stroke'."

After that Gest gave Thangbrand good gifts, and he fared back south. Thangbrand fared to the Southlander's Quarter, and so to the Eastfirths. He turned in as a guest at Bergthorsknoll, and Njal gave him good gifts. Thence he rode east to Alftafirth to meet Hall of the Side. He caused his ship to be mended, and heathen man called it "Iron-basket". On board that ship Thangbrand fared abroad, and Gudleif with him.

CHAPTER C.

OF GIZUR THE WHITE AND HJALLTI.

That same summer Hjallti Skeggi's son was outlawed at the Thing for blasphemy against the Gods.

Thangbrand told King Olaf of all the mischief that the Icelanders had done to him, and said that they were such sorcerers there that the earth burst asunder under his horse and swallowed up the horse.

Then King Olaf was so wroth that he made them seize all the men from Iceland and set them in dungeons, and meant to slay them.

Then they, Gizur the white and Hjallti, came up and offered to lay themselves in pledge for those men, and fare out to Iceland and preach the faith. The king took this well, and they got them all set free again.

Then Gizur and Hjallti busked their ship for Iceland, and were soon "boun". They made the land at Eyrar when ten weeks of summer had passed; they got them horses at once, but left other men to strip their ship. Then they ride with thirty men to the Thing, and sent word to the Christian men that they must be ready to stand by them.

Hjallti stayed behind at Reydarmull, for he had heard that he had been made an outlaw for blasphemy, but when they came to the "Boiling Kettle"[62] down below the brink of the Rift,[63] there came Hjallti after them, and said he would not let the heathen men see that he was afraid of them.

Then many Christian men rode to meet them, and they ride in battle array to the Thing. The heathen men had drawn up their men in array to meet them, and it was a near thing that the whole body of the Thing had come to blows, but still it did not go so far.

CHAPTER CI.

OF THORGEIR OF LIGHTWATER.

There was a man named Thorgeir who dwelt at Lightwater; he was the son of Tjorfi, the son of Thorkel the long, the son of Kettle Longneck. His mother's name was Thoruna, and she was the daughter of Thorstein, the son of Sigmund, the son of Bard of the Nip. Gudrida was the name of his wife; she was a daughter of Thorkel the black of Hleidrargarth. His brother was Worm wallet-back, the father of Hlenni the old of Saurby.

The Christian men set up their booths, and Gizur the white and Hjallti were in the booths of the men from Mossfell. The day after both sides went to the Hill of Laws, and each, the Christian men as well as the heathen, took witness, and declared themselves out of the other's laws, and then there was such an uproar on the Hill of Laws that no man could hear the other's voice.

After that men went away, and all thought things looked like the greatest entanglement. The Christian men chose as their Speaker Hall of the Side, but Hall went to Thorgeir, the priest of Lightwater, who was the old Speaker of the law, and gave him three marks of silver to utter what the law should be, but still that was most hazardous counsel, since he was an heathen.

Thorgeir lay all that day on the ground, and spread a cloak over his head, so that no man spoke with him; but the day after men went to the Hill of Laws, and then Thorgeir bade them be silent and listen, and spoke thus—

"It seems to me as though our matters were come to a dead lock, if we are not all to have one and the same law; for if there be a sundering of the laws, then there will be a sundering of the peace, and we shall never be able to live in the land. Now, I will ask both Christian men and heathen whether they will hold to those laws which I utter".

They all say they would.

He said he wished to take an oath of them, and pledges that they would hold to them, and they all said "yea" to that, and so he took pledges from them.

"This is the beginning of our laws," he said, "that all men shall be Christian here in the land, and believe in one God, the Father, the Son, and the Holy Ghost, but leave off all idol-worship, not expose children to perish, and not eat horseflesh. It shall be outlawry if such things are proved openly against any man; but if these things are done by stealth, then it shall be blameless."

But all this heathendom was all done away with within a few years' space, so that those things were not allowed to be done either by stealth or openly.

Thorgeir then uttered the law as to keeping the Lord's day and fast days, Yuletide and Easter, and all the greatest highdays and holidays.

The heathen men thought they had been greatly cheated; but still the true faith was brought into the law, and so all men became Christian here in the land.

After that men fare home from the Thing.

CHAPTER CII.

THE WEDDING OF HAUSKULD, THE PRIEST OF WHITENESS.

Now we must take up the story, and say that Njal spoke thus to Hauskuld, his foster-son, and said—

"I would seek thee a match."

Hauskuld bade him settle the matter as he pleased, and asked whether he was most likely to turn his eyes.

"There is a woman called Hildigunna," answers Njal, "and she is the daughter of Starkad, the son of Thord Freyspriest. She is the best match I know of."

"See thou to it, foster-father," said Hauskuld; "that shall be my choice which thou choosest."

"Then we will look thitherward," says Njal.

A little while after, Njal called on men to go along with him. Then the sons of Sigfus, and Njal's sons, and Kari Solmund's son, all of them fared with him and they rode east to Swinefell.

There they got a hearty welcome.

The day after, Njal and Flosi went to talk alone, and the speech of Njal ended thus, that he said—

"This is my errand here, that we have set out on a wooing-journey, to ask for thy kinswoman Hildigunna."

"At whose hand?" says Flosi.

"At the hand of Hauskuld my foster-son," says Njal.

"Such things are well meant," says Flosi, "but still ye run each of you great risk, the one from the other; but what hast thou to say of Hauskuld?"

"Good I am able to say of him," says Njal; "and besides, I will lay down as much money as will seem fitting to thy niece and thyself, if thou wilt think of making this match."

"We will call her hither," says Flosi, "and know how she looks on the man."

Then Hildigunna was called, and she came thither.

Flosi told her of the wooing, but she said she was a proud-hearted woman.

"And I know not how things will turn out between me and men of like spirit; but this, too, is not the least of my dislike, that this man has no priesthood or leadership over men, but thou hast always said that thou wouldest not wed me to a man who had not the priesthood."

"This is quite enough," says Flosi, "if thou wilt not be wedded to Hauskuld, to make me take no more pains about the match."

"Nay!" she says, "I do not say that I will not be wedded to Hauskuld if they can get him a priesthood or a leadership over men; but otherwise I will have nothing to say to the match."

"Then," said Njal, "I will beg thee to let this match stand over for three winters, that I may see what I can do."

Flosi said that so it should be.

"I will only bargain for this one thing," says Hildigunna, "if this match comes to pass, that we shall stay here away east."

Njal said he would rather leave that to Hauskuld, but Hauskuld said that he put faith in many men, but in none so much as his foster-father.

Now they ride from the east.

Njal sought to get a priesthood and leadership for Hauskuld, but no one was willing to sell his priesthood, and now the summer passes away till the Althing.

There were great quarrels at the Thing that summer, and many a man then did as was their wont, in faring to see Njal; but he gave such counsel in men's lawsuits as was not thought at all likely, so that both the pleadings and the defence came to naught, and out of that great strife arose, when the lawsuits could not be brought to an end, and men rode home from the Thing unatoned.

Now things go on till another Thing comes. Njal rode to the Thing, and at first all is quiet until Njal says that it is high time for men to give notice of their suits.

Then many said that they thought that came to little, when no man could get his suit settled, even though the witnesses were summoned to the Althing, "and so," say they, "we would rather seek our rights with point and edge."

"So it must not be," says Njal, "for it will never do to have no law in the land. But yet ye have much to say on your side in this matter, and it behoves us who know the law, and who are bound to guide the law, to set men at one again, and to ensue peace. 'Twere good counsel, then, methinks, that we call together all the chiefs and talk the matter over."

Then they go to the Court of Laws, and Njal spoke and said—

"Thee, Skapti Thorod's son and you other chiefs, I call on, and say, that methinks our lawsuits have come into a deadlock, if we have to follow up our suits in the Quarter Courts, and they get so entangled that they can neither be pleaded nor ended. Methinks, it were wiser if we had a Fifth Court, and there pleaded those suits which cannot be brought to an end in the Quarter Courts."

"How," said Skapti, "wilt thou name a Fifth Court, when the Quarter Court is named for the old priesthoods, three twelves in each quarter?"

"I can see help for that," says Njal, "by setting up new priesthoods, and filling them with the men who are best fitted in each Quarter, and then let those men who are willing to agree to it, declare themselves ready to join the new priest's Thing."

"Well," says Skapti, "we will take this choice; but what weighty suits shall come before the court?"

"These matters shall come before it," says Njal—"all matters of contempt of the Thing, such as if men bear false witness, or utter a false finding; hither, too, shall come all those suits in which the Judges are divided in opinion in the Quarter Court; then they shall be summoned to the Fifth Court; so, too, if men offer bribes, or take them, for their help in suits. In this court all the oaths shall be of the strongest kind, and two men shall follow every oath, who shall support on their words of honour what the others swear. So it shall be also, if the pleadings on one side are right in form, and the other wrong, that the judgment shall be given for those that are right in form. Every suit in this court shall be pleaded just as is now done in the Quarter Court, save and except that when four twelves are named in the Fifth Court, then the plaintiff shall name and set aside six men out of the court, and the defendant other six; but if he will not set them aside, then the plaintiff shall name them and set them aside as he has done with his own six; but if the plaintiff does not set them aside, then the suit comes to naught, for three twelves shall utter judgment on all suits. We shall also have this arrangement in the Court of Laws, that those only shall have the right to make or change laws who sit on the middle bench, and to this bench those only shall be chosen who are wisest and best. There, too, shall the Fifth Court sit; but if those who sit in the Court of Laws are not agreed as to what they shall allow or bring in as law, then they shall clear the court for a division, and the majority shall bind the rest; but if any man who has a seat in the Court be outside the Court of Laws and cannot get inside it, or thinks himself overborne in the suit, then he shall forbid them by a protest, so that they can hear it in the Court, and then he has made all their grants and all their decisions void and of none effect, and stopped them by his protest."

After that, Skapti Thorod's son brought the Fifth Court into the law, and all that was spoken of before. Then men went to the Hill of Laws, and men set up new priesthoods: in the Northlanders' Quarter were these new priesthoods. The priesthood of the Melmen in Midfirth, and the Laufesingers' priesthood in the Eyjafirth.

Then Njal begged for a hearing, and spoke thus—

"It is known to many men what passed between my sons and the men of Gritwater when they slew Thrain Sigfus' son. But for all that we settled the matter; and now I have taken Hauskuld into my house, and planned a marriage for him if he can get a priesthood anywhere; but no man will sell his priesthood, and so I will beg you to give me leave to set up a new priesthood at Whiteness for Hauskuld."

He got this leave from all, and after that he set up the new priesthood for Hauskuld; and he was afterwards called Hauskuld, the Priest of Whiteness.

After that, men ride home from the Thing, and Njal stayed but a short time at home ere he rides east to Swinefell, and his sons with him, and again stirs in the matter of the marriage with Flosi; but Flosi said he was ready to keep faith with them in everything.

Then Hildigunna was betrothed to Hauskuld, and the day for the wedding feast was fixed, and so the matter ended. They then ride home, but they rode again shortly to the bridal, and Flosi paid down all her goods and money after the wedding, and all went off well.

They fared home to Bergthorsknoll, and were there the next year, and all went well between Hildigunna and Bergthora. But the next spring Njal bought land in Ossaby, and hands it over to Hauskuld, and thither he fares to his own abode. Njal got him all his household, and there was such love between them all, that none of them thought anything that he said or did any worth unless the others had a share in it.

Hauskuld dwelt long at Ossaby, and each backed the other's honour, and Njal's sons were always in Hauskuld's company. Their friendship was so warm, that each house bade the other to a feast every harvest, and gave each other great gifts; and so it goes on for a long while.

CHAPTER CIII.

THE SLAYING OF HAUSKULD NJAL'S SON.

There was a man named Lyting; he dwelt at Samstede, and he had to wife a woman named Steinvora; she was a daughter of Sigfus, and Thrain's sister. Lyting was tall of growth and a strong man, wealthy in goods and ill to deal with.

It happened once that Lyting had a feast in his house at Samstede, and he had bidden thither Hauskuld and the sons of Sigfus, and they all came. There, too, was Grani Gunnar's son, and Gunnar Lambi's son, and Lambi Sigurd's son.

Hauskuld Njal's son and his mother had a farm at Holt, and he was always riding to his farm from Bergthorsknoll, and his path lay by the homestead at Samstede. Hauskuld had a son called Amund; he had been born blind, but for all that he was tall and strong. Lyting had two brothers—the one's name was Hallstein, and the other's Hallgrim. They were the most unruly of men, and they were ever with their brother, for other men could not bear their temper.

Lyting was out of doors most of that day, but every now and then he went inside his house. At last he had gone to his seat, when in came a woman who had been out of doors, and she said—

"You were too far off to see outside how that proud fellow rode by the farmyard!"

"What proud fellow was that," says Lyting, "of whom thou speakest?"

"Hauskuld Njal's son rode here by the yard," she says.

"He rides often here by the farmyard," said Lyting, "and I can't say that it does not try my temper; and now I will make thee an offer, Hauskuld [Sigfus' son], to go along with thee if thou wilt avenge thy father and slay Hauskuld Njal's son."

"That I will not do," says Hauskuld, "for then I should repay Njal, my foster father, evil for good, and mayst thou and thy feasts never thrive henceforth."

With that he sprang up away from the board, and made them catch his horses, and rode home.

Then Lyting said to Grani Gunnar's son—

"Thou wert by when Thrain was slain, and that will still be in thy mind; and thou, too, Gunnar Lambi's son, and thou, Lambi Sigurd's son. Now, my will is that we ride to meet him this evening, and slay him."

"No," says Grani, "I will not fall on Njal's son, and so break the atonement which good men and true have made."

With like words spoke each man of them, and so, too, spoke all the sons of Sigfus; and they took that counsel to ride away.

Then Lyting said, when they had gone away—

"All men know that I have taken no atonement for my brother-in-law Thrain, and I shall never be content that no vengeance—man for man—shall be taken for him."

After that he called on his two brothers to go with him, and three house-carles as well. They went on the way to meet Hauskuld [Njal's son] as he came back, and lay in wait for him north of the farmyard in a pit; and there they bided till it was about mid-even [six o'clock P.M.]. Then Hauskuld rode up to them. They jump up all of them with their arms, and fall on him. Hauskuld guarded himself well, so that for a long while they could not get the better of him; but the end of it was at last that he wounded Lyting on the arm, and slew two of his serving-men, and then fell himself. They gave Hauskuld sixteen wounds, but they hewed not off the head from his body. They fared away into the wood east of Rangriver, and hid themselves there.

That same evening, Rodny's shepherd found Hauskuld dead, and went home and told Rodny of her son's slaying.

"Was he surely dead?" she asks; "was his head off?"

"It was not," he says.

"I shall know if I see," she says; "so take thou my horse and driving gear."

He did so, and got all things ready, and then they went thither where Hauskuld lay.

She looked at the wounds, and said—

"'Tis even as I thought, that he could not be quite dead, and Njal no doubt can cure greater wounds."

After that they took the body and laid it on the sledge and drove to Bergthorsknoll, and drew it into the sheepcote, and made him sit upright against the wall.

Then they went both of them and knocked at the door, and a house-carle went to the door. She steals in by him at once, and goes till she comes to Njal's bed.

She asked whether Njal were awake? He said he had slept up to that time, but was then awake.

"But why art thou come hither so early?"

"Rise thou up," said Rodny, "from thy bed by my rival's side, and come out, and she too, and thy sons, to see thy son Hauskuld."

They rose and went out.

"Let us take our weapons," said Skarphedinn, "and have them with us."

Njal said naught at that, and they ran in and came out again armed.

She goes first till they come to the sheepcote; she goes in and bade them follow her. Then she lit a torch and held it up and said—

"Here, Njal, is thy son Hauskuld, and he hath gotten many wounds upon him, and now he will need leechcraft."

"I see death marks on him," said Njal, "but no signs of life; but why hast thou not closed his eyes and nostrils? see, his nostrils are still open!"

"That duty I meant for Skarphedinn," she says.

Then Skarphedinn went to close his eyes and nostrils, and said to his father—

"Who, sayest thou, hath slain him?"

"Lyting of Samstede and his brothers must have slain him," says Njal.

Then Rodny said, "Into thy hands, Skarphedinn, I leave it to take vengeance for thy brother, and I ween that thou wilt take it well, though he be not lawfully begotten, and that thou wilt not be slow to take it".

"Wonderfully do ye men behave," said Bergthora, "when ye slay men for small cause, but talk and tarry over such wrongs as this until no vengeance at all is taken; and now tidings of this will soon come to Hauskuld, the Priest of Whiteness, and he will be offering you atonement, and you will grant him that, but now is the time to act about it, if ye seek for vengeance."

"Our mother eggs us on now with a just goading," said Skarphedinn, and sang a song.

Well we know the warrior's temper,[64]
One and all, well, father thine,

But atonement to the mother,
Snake-land's stem[65] and thee were base;
He that hoardeth ocean's fire[66]
Hearing this will leave his home;
Wound of weapon us hath smitten,
Worse the lot of those that wait!

After that they all ran out of the sheepcote, but Rodny went indoors with Njal, and was there the rest of the night.

CHAPTER CIV.

THE SLAYING OF LYTING'S BROTHERS.

Now we must speak of Skarphedinn and his brothers, how they bend their course up to Rangriver. Then Skarphedinn said—

"Stand we here and listen, and let us go stilly, for I hear the voices of men up along the river's bank. But will ye, Helgi and Grim, deal with Lyting single-handed, or with both his brothers?"

They said they would sooner deal with Lyting alone.

"Still," says Skarphedinn, "there is more game in him, and methinks it were ill if he gets away, but I trust myself best for not letting him escape."

"We will take such steps," says Helgi, "if we get a chance at him, that he shall not slip through our fingers."

Then they went thitherward, Where they heard the voices of men, and see where Lyting and his brothers are by a stream.

Skarphedinn leaps over the stream at once, and alights on the sandy brink on the other side. There upon it stands Hallgrim and his brother. Skarphedinn smites at Hallgrim's thigh, so that he cut the leg clean off, but he grasps Hallstein with his left hand. Lyting thrust at Skarphedinn, but Helgi came up then and threw his shield before the spear, and caught the blow on it. Lyting took up a stone and hurled it at Skarphedinn, and he lost his hold on Hallstein. Hallstein sprang up the sandy bank, but could get up it in no other way than by crawling on his hands and knees. Skarphedinn made a side blow at him with his axe, "the ogress of war," and hews asunder his backbone. Now Lyting turns and flies, but Helgi and Grim both went after him, and each gave him a wound, but still Lyting got across the river away from them, and so to the horses, and gallops till he comes to Ossaby.

Hauskuld was at home, and meets him at once. Lyting told him of these deeds.

"Such things were to be looked for by thee," says Hauskuld. "Thou hast behaved like a madman, and here the truth of the old saw will be proved: 'but a short while is hand fain of blow'. Methinks what thou hast got to look to now is whether thou wilt be able to save thy life or not."

"Sure enough," says Lyting, "I had hard work to get away, but still I wish now that thou wouldest get me atoned with Njal and his sons, so that I might keep my farm."

"So it shall be," says Hauskuld.

After that Hauskuld made them saddle his horse, and rode to Bergthorsknoll with five men. Njal's sons were then come home and had laid them down to sleep.

Hauskuld went at once to see Njal, and they began to talk.

"Hither am I come," said Hauskuld to Njal, "to beg a boon on behalf of Lyting, my uncle. He has done great wickedness against you and yours, broken his atonement and slain thy son."

"Lyting will perhaps think," said Njal, "that he has already paid a heavy fine in the loss of his brothers, but if I grant him any terms, I shall let him reap the good of my love for thee, and I will tell thee before I utter the award of atonement, that Lyting's brothers shall fall as outlaws. Nor shall Lyting have any atonement for his wounds, but on the other hand, he shall pay the full blood-fine for Hauskuld."

"My wish," said Hauskuld, "is, that thou shouldest make thine own terms."

"Well," says Njal, "then I will utter the award at once if thou wilt."

"Wilt thou," says Hauskuld, "that thy sons should be by?"

"Then we should be no nearer an atonement than we were before," says Njal, "but they will keep to the atonement which I utter."

Then Hauskuld said, "Let us close the matter then, and handsel him peace on behalf of thy sons".

"So it shall be," says Njal. "My will then is that he pays two hundred in silver for the slaying of Hauskuld, but he may still dwell at Samstede; and yet I think it were wiser if he sold his land and changed his abode; but not for this quarrel; neither I nor my sons will break our pledges of peace to him: but methinks it may be that some one may rise up in this country against whom he may have to be on his guard. Yet, lest it should seem that I make a man an outcast from his native place, I allow him to be here in this neighbourhood, but in that case he alone is answerable for what may happen."

After that Hauskuld fared home, and Njal's sons woke up as he went, and asked their father who had come, but he told them that his foster-son Hauskuld had been there.

"He must have come to ask a boon for Lyting then," said Skarphedinn.

"So it was," says Njal

"Ill was it then," says Grim.

"Hauskuld could not have thrown his shield before him," says Njal, "if thou hadst slain him, as it was meant thou shouldst."

"Let us throw no blame on our father," says Skarphedinn.

Now it is to be said that this atonement was kept between them afterwards.

CHAPTER CV.

OF AMUND THE BLIND.

That event happened three winters after at the Thingskala-Thing that Amund the blind was at the Thing; he was the son of Hauskuld Njal's son. He made men lead him about among the booths, and so he came to the booth inside which was Lyting of Samstede. He made them lead him into the booth till he came before Lyting.

"Is Lyting of Samstede here?" he asked.

"What dost thou want?" says Lyting.

"I want to know," says Amund, "what atonement thou wilt pay me for my father, I am base-born, and I have touched no fine."

"I have atoned for the slaying of thy father," says Lyting, "with a full price, and thy father's father and thy father's brothers took the money; but my brothers fell without a price as outlaws; and so it was that I had both done an ill-deed, and paid dear for it."

"I ask not," says Amund, "as to thy having paid an atonement to them. I know that ye two are now friends, but I ask this, what atonement thou wilt pay to me?"

"None at all," says Lyting.

"I cannot see," says Amund, "how thou canst have right before God, when thou hast stricken me so near the heart; but all I can say is, that if I were blessed with the sight of both my eyes, I would have either a money fine for my father, or revenge man for man; and so may God judge between us."

After that he went out; but when he came to the door of the booth, he turned short round towards the inside. Then his eyes were opened, and he said—

"Praised be the Lord! now I see what His will is."

With that he ran straight into the booth until he comes before Lyting, and smites him with an axe on the head, so that it sunk in up to the hammer, and gives the axe a pull towards him.

Lyting fell forwards and was dead at once.

Amund goes out to the door of the booth, and when he got to the very same spot on which he had stood when his eyes were opened, lo! they were shut again, and he was blind all his life after.

Then he made them lead him to Njal and his sons, and he told them of Lyting's slaying.

"Thou mayest not be blamed for this," says Njal, "for such things are settled by a higher power; but it is worth while to take warning from such events, lest we cut any short who have such near claims as Amund had."

After that Njal offered an atonement to Lyting's kinsmen. Hauskuld the Priest of Whiteness had a share in bringing Lyting's kinsmen to take the fine, and then the matter was put to an award, and half the fines fell away for the sake of the claim which he seemed to have on Lyting.

After that men came forward with pledges of peace and good faith, and Lyting's kinsmen granted pledges to Amund. Men rode home from the Thing; and now all is quiet for a long while.

CHAPTER CVI.

OF VALGARD THE GUILEFUL.

Valgard the guileful came back to Iceland that summer; he was then still heathen. He fared to Hof to his son Mord's house, and was there the winter over. He said to Mord—

"Here I have ridden far and wide all over the neighbourhood, and methinks I do not know it for the same. I came to Whiteness, and there I saw many tofts of booths and much ground levelled for building, I came to Thingskala-Thing, and there I saw all our booths broken down. What is the meaning of such strange things?"

"New priesthoods," answers Mord, "have been set up here, and a law for a Fifth Court, and men have declared themselves out of my Thing, and have gone over to Hauskuld's Thing."

"Ill hast thou repaid me," said Valgard, "for giving up to thee my priesthood, when thou hast handled it so little like a man, and now my wish is that thou shouldst pay them off by something that will drag them all down to death; and this thou canst do by setting them by the ears by tale-bearing, so that Njal's sons may slay Hauskuld; but there are many who will have the blood-feud after him, and so Njal's sons will be slain in that quarrel."

"I shall never be able to get that done," says Mord.

"I will give thee a plan," says Valgard; "thou shalt ask Njal's sons to thy house, and send them away with gifts, but thou shalt keep thy tale-bearing in the back ground until great friendship has sprung up between you, and they trust thee no worse than their own selves. So wilt thou be able to avenge thyself on Skarphedinn for that he took thy money from thee after Gunnar's death; and in this wise, further on, thou wilt be able to seize the leadership when they are all dead and gone."

This plan they settled between them should be brought to pass; and Mord said—

"I would, father, that thou wouldst take on thee the new faith. Thou art an old man."

"I will not do that," says Valgard. "I would rather that thou shouldst cast off the faith, and see what follows then."

Mord said he would not do that. Valgard broke crosses before Mord's face, and all holy tokens. A little after Valgard took a sickness and breathed his last, and he was laid in a cairn by Hof.

CHAPTER CVII.

OF MORD AND NJAL'S SONS.

Some while after Mord rode to Bergthorsknoll and saw Skarphedinn there; he fell into very fair words with them, and so he talked the whole day, and said he wished to be good friends with them, and to see much of them.

Skarphedinn took it all well, but said he had never sought for anything of the kind before. So it came about that he got himself into such great friendship with them, that neither side thought they had taken any good counsel unless the other had a share in it.

Njal always disliked his coming thither, and it often happened that he was angry with him.

It happened one day that Mord came to Bergthorsknoll, and Mord said to Njal's sons—

"I have made up my mind to give a feast yonder, and I mean to drink in my heirship after my father, but to that feast I wish to bid you, Njal's sons, and Kari; and at the same time I give you my word that ye shall not fare away giftless."

They promised to go, and now he fares home and makes ready the feast. He bade to it many householders, and that feast was very crowded.

Thither came Njal's sons and Kari. Mord gave Skarphedinn a brooch of gold, and a silver belt to Kari, and good gifts to Grim and Helgi.

They come home and boast of these gifts, and show them to Njal. He said they would be bought full dear, "and take heed that ye do not repay the giver in the coin which he no doubt wishes to get".

CHAPTER CVIII.

OF THE SLANDER OF MORD VALGARD'S SON.

A little after Njal's sons and Hauskuld were to have their yearly feasts, and they were the first to bid Hauskuld to come to them.

Skarphedinn had a brown horse four winters old, both tall and sightly. He was a stallion, and had never yet been matched in fight. That horse Skarphedinn gave to Hauskuld, and along with him two mares. They all gave Hauskuld gifts, and assured him of their friendship.

After that Hauskuld bade them to his house at Ossaby, and had many guests to meet them, and a great crowd.

It happened that he had just then taken down his hall, but he had built three out-houses, and there the beds were made.

So all that were bidden came, and the feast went off very well. But when men were to go home Hauskuld picked out good gifts for them, and went a part of the way with Njal's sons.

The sons of Sigfus followed him and all the crowd, and both sides said that nothing should ever come between them to spoil their friendship.

A little while after Mord came to Ossaby and called Hauskuld out to talk with him, and they went aside and spoke.

"What a difference in manliness there is," said Mord, "between thee and Njal's sons! Thou gavest them good gifts, but they gave thee gifts with great mockery."

"How makest thou that out?" says Hauskuld.

"They gave thee a horse which they called a 'dark horse,' and that they did out of mockery at thee, because they thought thee too untried, I can tell thee also that they envy thee the priesthood, Skarphedinn took it up as his own at the Thing when thou camest not to the Thing at the summoning of the Fifth Court, and Skarphedinn never means to let it go."

"That is not true," says Hauskuld, "for I got it back at the Folkmote last harvest."

"Then that was Njal's doing," says Mord. "They broke, too, the atonement about Lyting."

"I do not mean to lay that at their door," says Hauskuld.

"Well," says Mord, "thou canst not deny that when ye two, Skarphedinn and thou, were going east towards Markfleet, an axe fell out from under his belt, and he meant to have slain thee then and there."

"It was his woodman's axe," says Hauskuld, "and I saw how he put it under his belt; and now, Mord, I will just tell thee this right out, that thou canst never say so much ill of Njal's sons as to make me believe it; but though there were aught in it, and it were true as thou sayest, that either I must slay them or they me, then would I far rather suffer death at their hands than work them any harm. But as for thee, thou art all the worse a man for having spoken this."

After that Mord fares home. A little after Mord goes to see Njal's sons, and he talks much with those brothers and Kari.

"I have been told," says Mord, "that Hauskuld has said that thou, Skarphedinn, hast broken the atonement made with Lyting; but I was made aware also that he thought that thou hadst meant some treachery against him when ye two fared to Markfleet. But still, methinks that was no less treachery when he bade you to a feast at his house, and stowed you away in an outhouse that was farthest from the house, and wood was then heaped round the outhouse all night, and he meant to burn you all inside; but it so happened that Hogni Gunnar's son came that night, and naught came of their onslaught, for they were afraid of him. After that he followed you on your way and great band of men with him, then he meant to make another onslaught on you, and set Grani Gunnar's son, and Gunnar Lambi's son to kill thee; but their hearts failed them, and they dared not to fall on thee."

But when he had spoken thus, first of all they spoke against it, but the end of it was that they believed him, and from that day forth a coldness sprung up on their part towards Hauskuld, and they scarcely ever spoke to him when they met; but Hauskuld showed them little deference, and so things went on for a while.

Next harvest Hauskuld fared east to Swinefell to a feast, and Flosi gave him a hearty welcome. Hildigunna was there too. Then Flosi spoke to Hauskuld and said—

"Hildigunna tells me that there is great coldness with you and Njal's sons, and methinks that is ill, and I will beg thee not to ride west, but I will get thee a homestead in Skaptarfell, and I will send my brother, Thorgeir, to dwell at Ossaby."

"Then some will say," says Hauskuld, "that I am flying thence for fear's sake, and that I will not have said."

"Then it is more likely that great trouble will arise," says Flosi.

"Ill is that then," says Hauskuld, "for I would rather fall unatoned, than that many should reap ill for my sake."

Hauskuld busked him to ride home a few nights after, but Flosi gave him a scarlet cloak, and it was embroidered with needlework down to the waist.

Hauskuld rode home to Ossaby, and now all is quiet for a while.

Hauskuld was so much beloved that few men were his foes, but the same ill-will went on between him and Njal's sons the whole winter through.

Njal had taken as his foster-child, Thord, the son of Kari. He had also fostered Thorhall, the son of Asgrim Ellidagrim's son. Thorhall was a strong man, and hardy both in body and mind, he had learnt so much law that he was the third greatest lawyer in Iceland.

Next spring was an early spring, and men are busy sowing their corn.

CHAPTER CIX.

OF MORD AND NJAL'S SONS.

It happened one day that Mord came to Bergthorsknoll. He and Kari and Njal's sons fell a-talking at once, and Mord slanders Hauskuld after his wont, and has now many new tales to tell, and does naught but egg Skarphedinn and them on to slay Hauskuld, and said he would be beforehand with them if they did not fall on him at once.

"I will let thee have thy way in this," says Skarphedinn, "if thou wilt fare with us, and have some hand in it."

"That I am ready to do," says Mord, and so they bound that fast with promises, and he was to come there that evening.

Bergthora asked Njal—

"What are they talking about out of doors?"

"I am not in their counsels," says Njal, "but I was seldom left out of them when their plans were good."

Skarphedinn did not lie down to rest that evening, nor his brothers, nor Kari.

That same night, when it was well-nigh spent, came Mord Valgard's son, and Njal's sons and Kari took their weapons and rode away. They fared till they came to Ossaby, and bided there by a fence. The weather was good, and the sun just risen.

CHAPTER CX.

THE SLAYING OF HAUSKULD, THE PRIEST OF WHITENESS.

About that time Hauskuld, the Priest of Whiteness, awoke; he put on his clothes, and threw over him his cloak, Flosi's gift. He took his corn-sieve, and had his sword in his other hand, and walks towards the fence, and sows the corn as he goes.

Skarphedinn and his band had agreed that they would all give him a wound. Skarphedinn sprang up from behind the fence, but when Hauskuld saw him he wanted to turn away, then Skarphedinn ran up to him and said—

"Don't try to turn on thy heel, Whiteness priest," and hews at him, and the blow came on his head, and he fell on his knees. Hauskuld said these words when he fell—

"God help me, and forgive you!"

Then they all ran up to him and gave him wounds.

After that Mord said—

"A plan comes into my mind."

"What is that?" says Skarphedinn.

"That I shall fare home as soon as I can, but after that I will fare up to Gritwater, and tell them the tidings, and say 'tis an ill deed; but I know surely that Thorgerda will ask me to give notice of the slaying, and I will do that, for that will be the surest way to spoil their suit. I will also send a man to Ossaby, and know how soon they take any counsel in the matter, and that man will learn all these tidings thence, and I will make believe that I have heard them from him."

"Do so by all means," says Skarphedinn.

Those brothers fared home, and Kari with them, and when they came home they told Njal the tidings.

"Sorrowful tidings are these," says Njal, "and such are ill to hear, for sooth to say this grief touches me so nearly, that methinks it were better to have lost two of my sons and that Hauskuld lived."

"It is some excuse for thee," says Skarphedinn, "that thou art an old man, and it is to be looked for that this touches thee nearly."

"But this," says Njal, "no less than old age, is why I grieve, that I know better than thou what will come after."

"What will come after?" says Skarphedinn.

"My death," says Njal, "and the death of my wife and of all my sons."

"What dost thou foretell for me?" says Kari.

"They will have hard work to go against thy good fortune, for thou wilt be more than a match for all of them."

This one thing touched Njal so nearly that he could never speak of it without shedding tears.

CHAPTER CXI.

OF HILDIGUNNA AND MORD VALGARD'S SON.

Hildigunna woke up and found that Hauskuld was away out of his bed.

"Hard have been my dreams," she said, "and not good; but go and search for *him*, Hauskuld."

So they searched for him about the homestead and found him not.

By that time she had dressed herself; then she goes and two men with her, to the fence, and there they find Hauskuld slain.

Just then, too, came up Mord Valgard's son's shepherd, and told her that Njal's sons had gone down thence, "and," he said, "Skarphedinn called out to me and gave notice of the slaying as done by him".

"It were a manly deed," she says, "if one man had been at it."

She took the cloak and wiped off all the blood with it, and wrapped the gouts of gore up in it, and so folded it together and laid it up in her chest.

Now she sent a man up to Gritwater to tell the tidings thither, but Mord was there before him, and had already told the tidings. There, too, was come Kettle of the Mark.

Thorgerda said to Kettle—

"Now is Hauskuld dead as we know, and now bear in mind what thou promisedst to do when thou tookest him for thy foster-child."

"It may well be," says Kettle, "that I promised very many things then, for I thought not that these days would ever befall us that have now come to pass; but yet I am come into a strait, for 'nose is next of kin to eyes,' since I have Njal's daughter to wife."

"Art thou willing, then," says Thorgerda, "that Mord should give notice of the suit for the slaying?"

"I know not that," says Kettle, "for methinks ill comes from him more often than good."

But as soon as ever Mord began to speak to Kettle he fared the same as others, in that he thought as though Mord would be true to him, and so the end of their council was that Mord should give notice of the slaying, and get ready the suit in every way before the Thing.

Then Mord fared down to Ossaby, and thither came nine neighbours who dwelt nearest the spot.

Mord had ten men with him. He shows the neighbours Hauskuld's wounds, and takes witness to the hurts, and names a man as the dealer of every wound save one; that he made as though he knew not who had dealt it, but that wound he had dealt himself. But the slaying he gave notice of at Skarphedinn's hand, and the wounds at his brothers' and Kari's.

After that he called on nine neighbours who dwelt nearest the spot to ride away from home to the Althing on the inquest.

After that he rode home. He scarce ever met Njal's sons, and when he did meet them, he was cross, and that was part of their plan.

The slaying of Hauskuld was heard over all the land, and was ill-spoken of. Njal's sons went to see Asgrim Ellidagrim's son, and asked him for aid.

"Ye very well know that ye may look that I shall help you in all great suits, but still my heart is heavy about this suit, for there are many who have the blood feud, and this slaying is ill-spoken of over all the land."

Now Njal's sons fare home.

CHAPTER CXII.

THE PEDIGREE OF GUDMUND THE POWERFUL.

There was a man named Gudmund the powerful, who dwelt at Modruvale in Eyjafirth. He was the son of Eyjolf the son of Einar. Gudmund was a mighty chief, wealthy in goods; he had in his house a hundred hired servants. He overbore in rank and weight all the chiefs in the north country, so that some left their homesteads, but some he put to death, and some gave up their priesthoods for his sake, and from him are come the greatest part of all the picked and famous families in the land, such as "the Point-dwellers" and the "Sturlungs" and the "Hvamdwellers," and the "Fleetmen," and Kettle the bishop, and many of the greatest men.

Gudmund was a friend of Asgrim Ellidagrim's son, and so he hoped to get his help.

CHAPTER CXIII.

OF SNORRI THE PRIEST, AND HIS STOCK.

There was a man named Snorri, who was surnamed the Priest. He dwelt at Helgafell before Gudruna Oswif's daughter bought the land of him, and dwelt there till she died of old age; but Snorri then went and dwelt at Hvamsfirth on Sælingdale's tongue. Thorgrim was the name of Snorri's father, and he was a son of Thorstein codcatcher. Snorri was a great friend of Asgrim Ellidagrim's son, and he looked for help there also. Snorri was the wisest and shrewdest of all these men in Iceland who had not the gift of foresight. He was good to his friends, but grim to his foes.

At that time there was a great riding to the Thing out of all the Quarters, and men had many suits set on foot.

CHAPTER CXIV.

OF FLOSI THORD'S SON.

Flosi hears of Hauskuld's slaying, and that brings him much grief and wrath, but still he kept his feelings well in hand. He was told how the suit had been set on foot, as has been said, for Hauskuld's slaying, and he said little about it. He sent word to Hall of the Side, his father-in-law, and to Ljot his son, that they must gather in a great company at the Thing. Ljot was thought the most hopeful man for a chief away there east. It had been foretold that if he could ride three summers running to the Thing, and come safe and sound home, that then he would be the greatest chief in all his family, and the oldest man. He had then ridden one summer to the Thing, and now he meant to ride the second time.

Flosi sent word to Kol Thorstein's son, and Glum the son of Hilldir the old, the son of Gerleif, the son of Aunund wallet-back, and to Modolf Kettle's son, and they all rode to meet Flosi.

Hall gave his word, too, to gather a great company, and Flosi rode till he came to Kirkby, to Surt Asbjorn's son. Then Flosi sent after Kolbein Egil's son, his brother's son, and he came to him there. Thence he rode to Headbrink. There dwelt Thorgrim the showy, the son of Thorkel the fair. Flosi begged him to ride to the Althing with him, and he said yea to the journey, and spoke thus to Flosi—

"Often hast thou been more glad, master, than thou art now, but thou hast some right to be so."

"Of a truth," said Flosi, "that hath now come on my hands, which I would give all my goods that it had never happened. Ill seed has been sown, and so an ill crop will spring from it."

Thence he rode over Arnstacksheath, and so to Solheim that evening. There dwelt Lodmund Wolf's son, but he was a great friend of Flosi, and there he stayed that night, and next morning Lodmund rode with him into the Dale.

There dwelt Runolf, the son of Wolf Aurpriest.

Flosi said to Runolf—

"Here we shall have true stories as to the slaying of Hauskuld, the Priest of Whiteness. Thou art a truthful man, and hast got at the truth by asking, and

I will trust to all that thou tellest me as to what was the cause of quarrel between them."

"There is no good in mincing the matter," said Runolf, "but we must say outright that he has been slain for less than no cause; and his death is a great grief to all men. No one thinks it so much a loss as Njal, his foster-father."

"Then they will be ill off for help from men," says Flosi; "and they will find no one to speak up for them."

"So it will be," says Runolf, "unless it be otherwise foredoomed."

"What has been done in the suit?" says Flosi.

"Now the neighbours have been summoned on the inquest," says Runolf, "and due notice given of the suit for manslaughter."

"Who took that step?" asks Flosi.

"Mord Valgard's son," says Runolf.

"How far is that to be trusted?" says Flosi.

"He is of my kin," says Runolf; "but still, if I tell the truth of him, I must say that more men reap ill than good from him. But this one thing I will ask of thee, Flosi, that thou givest rest to thy wrath, and takest the matter up in such a way as may lead to the least trouble. For Njal will make a good offer, and so will others of the best men."

"Ride thou then to the Thing, Runolf," said Flosi, "and thy words shall have much weight with me, unless things turn out worse than they should."

After that they cease speaking about it, and Runolf promised to go to the Thing.

Runolf sent word to Hatr the wise, his kinsman, and he rode thither at once.

Thence Flosi rode to Ossaby.

CHAPTER CXV.

OF FLOSI AND HILDIGUNNA.

Hildigunna was out of doors, and said, "Now shall all the men of my household be out of doors when Flosi rides into the yard; but the women shall sweep the house and deck it with hangings, and make ready the high-seat for Flosi."

Then Flosi rode into the town, and Hildigunna turned to him and said—

"Come in safe and sound and happy kinsman, and my heart is fain at thy coming hither."

"Here," says Flosi, "we will break our fast, and then we will ride on."

Then their horses were tethered, and Flosi went into the sitting-room and sat him down, and spurned the high-seat away from him on the dais, and said—

"I am neither king nor earl, and there is no need to make a high-seat for me to sit on, nor is there any need to make a mock of me."

Hildigunna was standing close by, and said—

"It is ill if it mislikes thee, for this we did with a whole heart."

"If thy heart is whole towards me, then what I do will praise itself if it be well done, but it will blame itself if it be ill done."

Hildigunna laughed a cold laugh, and said—

"There is nothing new in that, we will go nearer yet ere we have done."

She sat her down by Flosi, and they talked long and low. After that the board was laid, and Flosi and his band washed their hands. Flosi looked hard at the towel and saw that it was all in rags, and had one end torn off. He threw it down on the bench and would not wipe himself with it, but tore off a piece of the table-cloth, and wiped himself with that, and then threw it to his men.

After that Flosi sat down to the board and bade men eat.

Then Hildigunna came into the room and went before Flosi, and threw her hair off her eyes and wept.

"Heavy-hearted art thou now, kinswoman," said Flosi, "when thou weepest, but still it is well that thou shouldst weep for a good husband."

"What vengeance or help shall I have of thee?" she says.

"I will follow up thy suit," said Flosi, "to the utmost limit of the law, or strive for that atonement which good men and true shall say that we ought to have as full amends."

"Hauskuld would avenge thee," she said, "if he had the blood-feud after thee."

"Thou lackest not grimness," answered Flosi, "and what thou wantest is plain."

"Arnor Ornolf's son, of Forswaterwood," said Hildigunna, "had done less wrong towards Thord Frey's priest thy father; and yet thy brothers Kolbein and Egil slew him at Skaptarfells-Thing."

Then Hildigunna went back into the hall and unlocked her chest, and then she took out the cloak, Flosi's gift, and in it Hauskuld had been slain, and there she had kept it, blood and all. Then she went back into the sitting room with the cloak; she went up silently to Flosi. Flosi had just then eaten his full, and the board was cleared. Hildigunna threw the cloak over Flosi, and the gore rattled down all over him.

Then she spoke and said—

"This cloak, Flosi, thou gavest to Hauskuld, and now I will give it back to thee, he was slain in it, and I call God and all good men to witness, that I adjure thee, by all the might of thy Christ, and by thy manhood and bravery, to take vengeance for all those wounds which he had on his dead body, or else to be called every man's dastard."

Flosi threw the cloak off him and hurled it into her lap, and said—

"Thou art the greatest hell-hag, and thou wishest that we should take that course which will be the worst for all of us. But 'women's counsel is ever cruel'."

Flosi was so stirred at this, that sometimes he was bloodred in the face, and sometimes ashy pale as withered grass, and sometimes blue as death.

Flosi and his men rode away; he rode to Holtford, and there waits for the sons of Sigfus and other of his men.

Ingialld dwelt at the Springs; he was the brother of Rodny, Hauskuld Njal's son's mother. Ingialld had to wife Thraslauga, the daughter of Egil, the son of Thord Frey's priest. Flosi sent word to Ingialld to come to him, and Ingialld went at once, with fourteen men. They were all of his household. Ingialld was a tall man and a strong, and slow to meddle with other men's business, one of the bravest of men, and very bountiful to his friends.

Flosi greeted him well, and said to him, "Great trouble hath now come on me and my brothers-in-law, and it is hard to see our way out of it; I beseech thee not to part from my suit until this trouble is past and gone."

"I am come into a strait myself," said Ingialld, "for the sake of the ties that there are between me and Njal and his sons, and other great matters which stand in the way."

"I thought," said Flosi, "when I gave away my brother's daughter to thee, that thou gavest me thy word to stand by me in every suit."

"It is most likely," says Ingialld, "that I shall do so, but still I will now, first of all, ride home, and thence to the Thing."

CHAPTER CXVI.

OF FLOSI AND MORD AND THE SONS OF SIGFUS.

The sons of Sigfus heard how Flosi was at Holtford, and they rode thither to meet him, and there were Kettle of the Mark, and Lambi his brother, Thorkell and Mord, the sons of Sigfus, Sigmund their brother, and Lambi Sigurd's son, and Gunnar Lambi's son, and Grani Gunnar's son, and Vebrand Hamond's son.

Flosi stood up to meet them, and greeted them gladly. So they went down to the river. Flosi had the whole story from them about the slaying, and there was no difference between them and Kettle of the Mark's story.

Flosi spoke to Kettle of the Mark, and said—

"This now I ask of thee; how tightly are your hearts knit as to this suit, thou and the other sons of Sigfus?"

"My wish is," said Kettle, "that there should be peace between us, but yet I have sworn an oath not to part from this suit till it has been brought somehow to an end, and to lay my life on it."

"Thou art a good man and true," said Flosi, "and it is well to have such men with one."

Then Grani Gunnar's son and Lambi Sigurd's son both spoke together, and said—

"We wish for outlawry and death."

"It is not given us," said Flosi, "both to share and choose, we must take what we can get."

"I have had it in my heart," says Grani, "ever since they slew Thrain by Markfleet, and after that his son Hauskuld, never to be atoned with them by a lasting peace, for I would willingly stand by when they were all slain, every man of them."

"Thou hast stood so near to them," said Flosi, "that thou mightest have avenged these things hadst thou had the heart and manhood. Methinks thou and many others now ask for what ye would give much money hereafter never to have had a share in. I see this clearly, that though we slay Njal or his sons, still they are men of so great worth, and of such good family, that there will be such a blood feud and hue and cry after them, that we shall have to fall on our knees before many a man, and beg for help, ere we get an atonement and find our way out of this strait. Ye may make up your minds, then, that many will become poor who before had great goods, but some of you will lose both goods and life."

Mord Valgard's Son rode to meet Flosi, and said he would ride to the Thing with him with all his men. Flosi took that well, and raised a matter of a wedding with him, that he should give away Rannveiga his daughter to Starkad Flosi's brother's son, who dwelt at Staffell. Flosi did this because he thought he would so make sure both of his faithfulness and force.

Mord took the wedding kindly, but handed the matter over to Gizur the white, and bade him talk about it at the Thing.

Mord had to wife Thorkatla, Gizur the white's daughter.

They two, Mord and Flosi, rode both together to the Thing, and talked the whole day, and no man knew aught of their counsel.

CHAPTER CXVII.

NJAL AND SKARPHEDINN TALK TOGETHER.

Now, we must say how Njal said to Skarphedinn—

"What plan have ye laid down for yourselves, thou and thy brothers and Kari?"

"Little reck we of dreams in most matters," said Skarphedinn; "but if thou must know, we shall ride to Tongue to Asgrim Ellidagrim's son, and thence to the Thing; but what meanest thou to do about thine own journey, father?"

"I shall ride to the Thing," says Njal, "for it belongs to my honour not to be severed from your suit so long as I live. I ween that many men will have good words to say of me, and so I shall stand you in good stead, and do you no harm."

There, too, was Thorhall Asgrim's son, and Njal's foster-son. The sons of Njal laughed at him because he was clad in a coat of russet, and asked how long he meant to wear that?

"I shall have thrown it off," he said, "when I have to follow up the blood-feud for my foster father."

"There will ever be most good in thee," said Njal, "when there is most need of it."

So they all busked them to ride away from home, and were nigh thirty men in all, and rode till they came to Thursowater. Then came after them Njal's kinsmen, Thorleif crow, and Thorgrim the big; they were Holt-Thorir's sons, and offered their help and following to Njal's sons, and they took that gladly.

So they rode altogether across Thursowater, until they came on Laxwater bank, and took a rest and baited their horses there, and there Hjallti's Skeggi's son came to meet them, and Njal's sons fell to talking with him, and they talked long and low.

"Now, I will show," said Hjallti, "that I am not black-hearted; Njal has asked me for help, and I have agreed to it, and given my word to aid him; he has often given me and many others the worth of it in cunning counsel."

Hjallti tells Njal all about Flosi's doings. They sent Thorhall on to Tongue to tell Asgrim that they would be there that evening; and Asgrim made ready at once, and was out of doors to meet them when Njal rode into the town.

Njal was clad in a blue cape, and had a felt hat on his head, and a small axe in his hand. Asgrim helped Njal off his horse, and led him and sate him down in his own seat. After that they all went in, Njal's sons and Kari. Then Asgrim went out.

Hjallti wished to turn away, and thought there were too many there; but Asgrim caught hold of his reins, and said he should never have his way in riding off, and made men unsaddle their horses, and led Hjallti in and sate him down by Njal's aide; but Thorleif and his brother sat on the other bench and their men with them.

Asgrim sate him down on a stool before Njal, and asked—

"What says thy heart about our matter?"

"It speaks rather heavily," says Njal, "for I am afraid that we shall have no lucky men with us in the suit; but I would, friend, that thou shouldest send after all the men who belong to thy Thing, and ride to the Althing with me."

"I have always meant to do that," says Asgrim; "and this I will promise thee at the same time—that I will never leave thy cause while I can get any men to follow me."

But all those who were in the house thanked him, and said, that was bravely spoken. They were there that night, but the day after all Asgrim's band came thither.

And after that they all rode together till they come up on the Thingfield, and fit up their booths.

CHAPTER CXVIII.

ASGRIM AND NJAL'S SONS PRAY MEN FOR HELP.

By that time Flosi had come to the Thing, and filled all his booths. Runolf filled the Dale-dwellers' booths, and Mord the booths of the men from Rangriver. Hall of the Side had long since come from the east, but scarce any of the other men; but still Hall of the Side had come with a great band, and joined this at once to Flosi's company, and begged him to take an atonement and to make peace.

Hall was a wise man and good-hearted, Flosi answered him well in everything, but gave way in nothing.

Hall asked what men had promised him help? Flosi named Mord Valgard's son, and said he had asked for his daughter at the hand of his kinsman Starkad.

Hall said she was a good match, but it was ill dealing with Mord, "and that thou wilt put to the proof ere this Thing be over".

After that they ceased talking.

One day Njal and Asgrim had a long talk in secret.

Then all at once Asgrim sprang up and said to Njal's sons—

"We must set about seeking friends, that we may not be overborne by force; for this suit will be followed up boldly."

Then Asgrim went out, and Helgi Njal's son next; then Kari Solmund's son; then Grim Njal's son; then Skarphedinn; then Thorhall; then Thorgrim the big; then Thorleif crow.

They went to the booth of Gizur the white and inside it. Gizur stood up to meet them, and bade them sit down and drink.

"Not thitherward," says Asgrim, "tends our way, and we will speak our errand out loud, and not mutter and mouth about it. What help shall I have from thee, as thou art my kinsman?"

"Jorunn my sister," said Gizur, "would wish that I should not shrink from standing by thee; and so it shall be now and hereafter, that we will both of us have the same fate."

Asgrim thanked him, and went away afterwards.

Then Skarphedinn asked, "Whither shall we go now?"

"To the booths of the men of Olfus," says Asgrim.

So they went thither, and Asgrim asked whether Skapti Thorod's son were in the booth? He was told that he was. Then they went inside the booth.

Skapti sate on the cross bench, and greeted Asgrim, and he took the greeting well.

Skapti offered Asgrim a seat by his side, but Asgrim said he should only stay there a little while, "but still we have an errand to thee".

"Let me hear it," says Skapti.

"I wish to beg thee for thy help, that thou wilt stand by us in our suit."

"One thing I had hoped," says Skapti, "and that is, that neither you nor your troubles would ever come into my dwelling."

"Such things are ill-spoken," says Asgrim, "when a man is the last to help others, when most lies on his aid."

"Who is yon man," says Skapti, "before whom four men walk, a big burly man, and pale-faced, unlucky-looking, well-knit, and troll-like?"

"My name is Skarphedinn," he answers, "and thou hast often seen me at the Thing; but in this I am wiser than thou, that I have no need to ask what thy name is. Thy name is Skapti Thorod's son, but before thou calledst thyself 'Bristle-poll,' after thou hadst slain Kettle of Elda; then thou shavedst thy poll, and puttedst pitch on thy head, and then thou hiredst thralls to cut up a sod of turf, and thou creptest underneath it to spend the night. After that thou wentest to Thorolf Lopt's son of Eyrar, and he took thee on board, and bore thee out here in his meal sacks."

After that Asgrim and his band went out, and Skarphedinn asked—

"Whither shall we go now?"

"To Snorri the Priest's booth," says Asgrim.

Then they went to Snorri's booth. There was a man outside before the booth, and Asgrim asked whether Snorri were in the booth.

The man said he was.

Asgrim went into the booth, and all the others. Snorri was sitting on the cross bench, and Asgrim went and stood before him, and hailed him well.

Snorri took his greeting blithely, and bade him sit down.

Asgrim said he should be only a short time there, "but we have an errand with thee".

Snorri bade him tell it.

"I would," said Asgrim, "that thou wouldst come with me to the court, and stand by me with thy help, for thou art a wise man, and a great man of business."

"Suits fall heavy on us now," says Snorri the Priest, "and now many men push forward against us, and so we are slow to take up the troublesome suits of other men from other quarters."

"Thou mayest stand excused," says Asgrim, "for thou art not in our debt for any service."

"I know," says Snorri, "that thou art a good man and true, and I will promise thee this, that I will not be against thee, and not yield help to thy foes."

Asgrim thanked him, and Snorri the Priest asked—

"Who is that man before whom four go, pale-faced, and sharp-featured, and who shows his front teeth, and has his axe aloft on his shoulder?"

"My name is Hedinn," he says, "but some men call me Skarphedinn by my full name; but what more hast thou to say to me?"

"This," said Snorri the Priest, "that methinks thou art a well-knit, ready-handed man, but yet I guess that the best part of thy good fortune is past, and I ween thou hast not long to live."

"That is well," says Skarphedinn, "for that is a debt we all have to pay, but still it were more needful to avenge thy father than to foretell my fate in this way."

"Many have said that before," says Snorri, "and I will not be angry at such words."

After that they went out, and got no help there. Then they fared to the booths of the men of Skagafirth. There Hafr the wealthy had his booth. The mother of Hafr was named Thoruna, she was a daughter of Asbjorn baldpate of Myrka, the son of Hrosbjorn.

Asgrim and his band went into the booth, and Hafr sate in the midst of it, and was talking to a man.

Asgrim went up to him, and hailed him well; he took it kindly, and bade him sit down.

"This I would ask of thee," said Asgrim, "that thou wouldst grant me and my sons-in-law help."

Hafr answered sharp and quick, and said he would have nothing to do with their troubles.

"But still I must ask who that pale-faced man is before whom four men go, so ill-looking, as though he had come out of the sea-crags."

"Never mind, milksop that thou art!" said Skarphedinn, "who I am, for I will dare to go forward wherever thou standest before me, and little would I fear though such striplings were in my path. 'Twere rather thy duty, too, to get back thy sister Swanlauga, whom Eydis ironsword and his messmate Stediakoll took away out of thy house, but thou didst not dare to do aught against them."

"Let us go out," said Asgrim, "there is no hope of help here."

Then they went out to the booths of men of Modruvale, and asked whether Gudmund the powerful were in the booth, but they were told he was.

Then they went into the booth. There was a high seat in the midst of it, and there sate Gudmund the powerful.

Asgrim went and stood before him, and hailed him.

Gudmund took his greeting well, and asked him to sit down.

"I will not sit," said Asgrim, "but I wish to pray thee for help, for thou art a bold man and a mighty chief."

"I will not be against thee," said Gudmund, "but if I see fit to yield thee help, we may well talk of that afterwards," and so he treated them well and kindly in every way.

Asgrim thanked him for his words, and Gudmund said—

"There is one man in your band at whom I have gazed for awhile, and he seems to me more terrible than most men that I have seen."

"Which is he?" says Asgrim.

"Four go before him," says Gudmund; "dark brown is his hair, and pale is his face; tall of growth and sturdy. So quick and shifty in his manliness, that I would rather have his following than that of ten other men; but yet the man is unlucky-looking."

"I know," said Skarphedinn, "that thou speakest at me, but it does not go in the same way as to luck with me and thee. I have blame, indeed, from the slaying of Hauskuld, the Whiteness priest, as is fair and right; but both Thorkel foulmouth and Thorir Helgi's son spread abroad bad stories about thee, and that has tried thy temper very much."

Then they went out, and Skarphedinn said—

"Whither shall we go now?"

"To the booths of the men of Lightwater," said Asgrim.

There Thorkel foulmouth had set up his booth.

Thorkel foulmouth had been abroad and worked his way to fame in other lands. He had slain a robber east in Jemtland's wood, and then he fared on east into Sweden, and was a messmate of Saurkvir the churl, and they harried eastward ho; but to the east of Baltic side.[67] Thorkel had to fetch water for them one evening; then he met a wild man of the woods,[68] and struggled against him long; but the end of it was that he slew the wild man. Thence he fared east into Adalsyssla, and there he slew a flying fire-drake. After that he fared back to Sweden, and thence to Norway, and so out to Iceland, and let these deeds of derring do be carved over his shut bed, and on the stool before his high-seat. He fought, too, on Lightwater way with his brothers against Gudmund the powerful, and the men of Lightwater won the day. He and Thorir Helgi's son spread abroad bad stories about Gudmund. Thorkel said there was no man in Iceland with whom he would not fight in single combat, or yield an inch to, if need were. He was called Thorkel foulmouth, because he spared no one with whom he had to do either in word or deed.

CHAPTER CXIX.

OF SKARPHEDINN AND THORKEL FOULMOUTH.

Asgrim and his fellows went to Thorkel foulmouth's booth, and Asgrim said then to his companions, "This booth Thorkel foulmouth owns, a great champion, and it were worth much to us to get his help. We must here take heed in everything, for he is self-willed and bad tempered; and now I will beg thee, Skarphedinn, not to let thyself be led into our talk."

Skarphedinn smiled at that. He was so clad, he had on a blue kirtle and gray breeks, and black shoes on his feet, coming high up his leg; he had a silver belt about him, and that same axe in his hand with which he slew Thrain, and which he called the "ogress of war," a round buckler, and a silken band round his brow, and his hair was brushed back behind his ears. He was the most soldier-like of men, and by that all men knew him. He went in his appointed place, and neither before nor behind.

Now they went into the booth and into its inner chamber. Thorkel sate in the middle of the cross-bench, and his men away from him on all sides. Asgrim hailed him, and Thorkel took the greeting well, and Asgrim said to him—

"For this have we come hither, to ask help of thee, and that thou wouldst come to the court with us."

"What need can ye have of my help," said Thorkel, "when ye have already gone to Gudmund; he must surely have promised thee his help?"

"We could not get his help," says Asgrim.

"Then Gudmund thought the suit likely to make him foes," said Thorkel; "and so no doubt it will be, for such deeds are the worst that have ever been done; nor do I know what can have driven you to come hither to me, and to think that I should be easier to undertake your suit than Gudmund, or that I would back a wrongful quarrel."

Then Asgrim held his peace, and thought it would be hard work to win him over.

Then Thorkel went on and said, "Who is that big and ugly fellow, before whom four men go, pale-faced and sharp-featured, and unlucky-looking, and cross-grained?"

- 289 -

"My name is Skarphedinn," said Skarphedinn, "and thou hast no right to pick me out, a guiltless man, for thy railing. It never has befallen me to make my father bow down before me, or to have fought against him, as thou didst with thy father. Thou hast ridden little to the Althing, or toiled in quarrels at it, and no doubt it is handier for thee to mind thy milking pails at home than to be here at Axewater in idleness. But stay, it were as well if thou pickedst out from thy teeth that steak of mare's rump which thou atest ere thou rodest to the Thing, while thy shepherd looked on all the while, and wondered that thou couldst work such filthiness!"

Then Thorkel sprang up in mickle wrath, and clutched his short sword and said—

"This sword I got in Sweden when I slew the greatest champion, but since then I have slain many a man with it, and as soon as ever I reach thee I will drive it through thee, and thou shall take that for thy bitter words."

Skarphedinn stood with his axe aloft, and smiled scornfully and said—

"This axe I had in my hand when I leapt twelve ells across Markfleet, and slew Thrain Sigfus' son, and eight of them stood before me, and none of them could touch me. Never have I aimed weapon at man that I have not smitten him."

And with that he tore himself from his brothers, and Kari his brother-in-law, and strode forward to Thorkel.

Then Skarphedinn said—

"Now, Thorkel foulmouth, do one of these two things: sheathe thy sword and sit thee down, or I drive the axe into thy head and cleave thee down to the chine."

Then Thorkel sate him down and sheathed the sword, and such a thing never happened to him either before or since.

Then Asgrim and his band go out, and Skarphedinn said—

"Whither shall we now go?"

"Home to out booths," answered Asgrim.

"Then we fare hack to our booths wearied of begging," says Skarphedinn.

"In many places," said Asgrim, "hast thou been rather sharp-tongued, but here now, in what Thorkel had a share methinks thou hast only treated him as is fitting."

Then they went home to their booths, and told Njal, word for word, all that had been done.

"Things," he said, "draw on to what must be."

Now Gudmund the powerful heard what had passed between Thorkel and Skarphedinn, and said—

"Ye all know how things fared between us and the men of Lightwater, but I have never suffered such scorn and mocking at their hands as has befallen Thorkel from Skarphedinn, and this is just as it should be."

Then he said to Einar of Thvera, his brother, "Thou shalt go with all my band, and stand by Njal's sons when the courts go out to try suits; but if they need help next summer, then I myself will yield them help".

Einar agreed to that, and sent and told Asgrim, and Asgrim said—

"There is no man like Gudmund for nobleness of mind," and then he told it to Njal.

CHAPTER CXX.

OF THE PLEADING OF THE SUIT.

The next day Asgrim, and Gizur the white, and Hjallti Skeggi's son, and Einar of Thvera, met together. There too was Mord Valgard's son; he had then let the suit fall from his hand, and given it over to the sons of Sigfus.

Then Asgrim spoke.

"Thee first I speak to about this matter, Gizur the white, and thee Hjallti, and thee Einar, that I may tell you how the suit stands. It will be known to all of you that Mord took up the suit, but the truth of the matter is, that Mord was at Hauskuld's slaying, and wounded him with that wound, for giving which no man was named. It seems to me, then, that this suit must come to nought by reason of a lawful flaw."

"Then we will plead it at once," says Hjallti.

"It is not good counsel," said Thorhall Asgrim's son, "that this should not be hidden until the courts are set."

"How so?" asks Hjallti.

"If," said Thorhall, "they knew now at once that the suit has been wrongly set on foot, then they may still save the suit by sending a man home from the Thing, and summoning the neighbours from home over again, and calling on them to ride to the Thing, and then the suit will be lawfully set on foot."

"Thou art a wise man, Thorhall," say they, "and we will take thy counsel."

After that each man went to his booth.

The sons of Sigfus gave notice of their suits at the Hill of Laws, and asked in what Quarter Courts they lay, and in what house in the district the defendants dwelt. But on the Friday night the courts were to go out to try suits, and so the Thing was quiet up to that day.

Many sought to bring about an atonement between them, but Flosi was steadfast; but others were still more wordy, and things looked ill.

Now the time comes when the courts were to go out, on the Friday evening. Then the whole body of men at the Thing went to the courts. Flosi stood south at the court of the men of Rangriver, and his band with him. There with him was Hall of the Side, and Runolf of the Dale, Wolf Aurpriest's son, and those other men who had promised Flosi help.

But north of the court of the men of Rangriver stood Asgrim Ellidagrim's son, and Gizur the white, Hjallti Skeggi's son, and Einar of Thvera. But Njal's sons were at home at their booth, and Kari and Thorleif crow, and Thorgeir Craggeir, and Thorgrim the big. They sate all with their weapons, and their band looked safe from onslaught.

Njal had already prayed the judges to go into the court, and now the sons of Sigfus plead their suit. They took witness and bade Njal's sons to listen to their oath; after that they took their oath, and then they declared their suit; then they brought forward witness of the notice, then they bade the neighbours on the inquest to take their seats, then they called on Njal's sons to challenge the inquest.

Then up stood Thorhall Asgrim's son, and took witness, and forbade the inquest by a protest to utter their finding; and his ground was, that he who had given notice of the suit was truly under the ban of the law, and was himself an outlaw.

"Of whom speakest thou this?" says Flosi.

"Mord Valgard's son," said Thorhall, "fared to Hauslkuld's slaying with Njal's sons, and wounded him with that wound for which no man was named when witness was taken to the death-wounds; and ye can say nothing against this, and so the suit comes to naught."

CHAPTER CXXI.

OF THE AWARD OF ATONEMENT BETWEEN FLOSI AND NJAL.

Then Njal stood up and said—

"This I pray, Hall of the Side, and Flosi, and all the sons of Sigfus, and all our men too, that ye will not go away, but listen to my words."

They did so, and then he spoke thus—

"It seems to me as though this suit were come to naught, and it is likely it should, for it hath sprung from an ill root. I will let you all know that I loved Hauskuld more than my own sons, and when I heard that he was slain, methought the sweetest light of my eyes was quenched, and I would rather have lost all my sons, and that he were alive. Now I ask thee, Hall of the Side, and thee Runolf of the Dale, and thee Hjallti Skeggi's son, and thee Einar of Thvera, and thee Hafr the wise, that I may be allowed to make an atonement for the slaying of Hauskuld on my sons' behalf; and I wish that those men who are best fitted to do so shall utter the award."

Gizur, and Hafr, and Einar, spoke each on their own part, and prayed Flosi to take an atonement, and promised him their friendship in return.

Flosi answered them well in all things, but still did not give his word.

Then Hall of the Side said to Flosi—

"Wilt thou now keep thy word, and grant me my boon which thou hast already promised me, when I put beyond sea Thorgrim, the son of Kettle the fat, thy kinsman, when he had slain Halli the red."

"I will grant it thee, father-in-law," said Flosi, "for that alone wilt thou ask which will make my honour greater than it erewhile was."

"Then," said Hall, "my wish is that thou shouldst be quickly atoned, and lettest good men and true make an award, and so buy the friendship of good and worthy men."

"I will let you all know," said Flosi, "that I will do according to the word of Hall, my father-in-law, and other of the worthiest men, that he and others of the best men on each side, lawfully named, shall make this award. Methinks Njal is worthy that I should grant him this."

Njal thanked him and all of them, and others who were by thanked them too, and said that Flosi had behaved well.

Then Flosi said—

"Now will I name my daysmen [arbitrators]—First, I name Hall, my father-in-law; Auzur from Broadwater; Surt Asbjorn's son of Kirkby; Modolf Kettle's son"—he dwelt then at Asar—"Hafr the wise; and Runolf of the Dale; and it is scarce worth while to say that these are the fittest men out of all my company."

Now he bade Njal to name his daysmen, and then Njal stood up, and said—

"First of these I name, Asgrim Ellidagrim's son; and Hjallti Skeggi's son; Gizur the white; Einar of Thvera; Snorri the priest; and Gudmund the powerful."

After that Njal and Flosi, and the sons of Sigfus shook hands, and Njal pledged his hand on behalf of all his sons, and of Kari, his son-in-law, that they would hold to what those twelve men doomed; and one might say that the whole body of men at the Thing was glad at that.

Then men were sent after Snorri and Gudmund, for they were in their booths.

Then it was given out that the judges in this award would sit in the Court of Laws, but all the others were to go away.

CHAPTER CXXII.

OF THE JUDGES.

Then Snorri the priest spoke thus—"Now are we here twelve judges to whom these suits are handed over, now I will beg you all that we may have no stumbling-blocks in these suits, so that they may not be atoned".

"Will ye," said Gudmund, "award either the lesser or the greater outlawry? Shall they be banished from the district, or from the whole land?"

"Neither of them," says Snorri, "for those banishments are often ill fulfilled, and men have been slain for that sake, and atonements broken, but I will award so great a money fine that no man shall have had a higher price here in the land than Hauskuld."

They all spoke well of his words.

Then they talked over the matter, and could not agree which should first utter how great he thought the fine ought to be, and so the end of it was that they cast lots, and the lot fell on Snorri to utter it.

Then Snorri said, "I will not sit long over this, I will now tell you what my utterance is, I will let Hauskuld be atoned for with triple manfines, but that is six hundred in silver. Now ye shall change it, if ye think it too much or too little."

They said that they would change it in nothing.

"This too shall be added," he said, "that all the money shall be paid down here at the Thing."

Then Gizur the white spoke and said—

"Methinks that can hardly be, for they will not have enough money to pay their fines."

"I know what Snorri wishes," said Gudmund the powerful, "he wants that all we daysmen should give such a sum as our bounty will bestow, and then many will do as we do."

Hall of the Side thanked him, and said he would willingly give as much as any one else gave, and then all the other daysmen agreed to that.

After that they went away, and settled between them that Hall should utter the award at the Court of Laws.

So the bell was rung, and all men went to the Court of Laws, and Hall of the Side stood up and spoke—

"In this suit, in which we have come to an award, we have been all well agreed, and we have awarded six hundred in silver, and half this sum we the daysmen will pay, but it must all be paid up here at the Thing. But it is my prayer to all the people that each man will give something for God's sake."

All answered well to that, and then Hall took witness to the award, that no one should be able to break it.

Njal thanked them for their award, but Skarphedinn stood by, and held his peace, and smiled scornfully.

Then men went from the Court of Laws and to their booths, but the daysmen gathered together in the freeman's church-yard the money which they had promised to give.

Njal's sons handed over that money which they had by them, and Kari did the same, and that came to a hundred in silver.

Njal took out that money which he had with him, and that was another hundred in silver.

So this money was all brought before the Court of Laws, and then men gave so much, that not a penny was wanting.

Then Njal took a silken scarf and a pair of boots and laid them on the top of the heap.

After that, Hall said to Njal, that he should go to fetch his sons, "but I will go for Flosi, and now each must give the other pledges of peace".

Then Njal went home to his booth, and spoke to his sons and said, "Now, are our suits come into a fair way of settlement, now are we men atoned, for all the money has been brought together in one place; and now either side is to go and grant the other peace and pledges of good faith. I will therefore ask you this, my sons, not to spoil these things in any way."

Skarphedinn stroked his brow, and smiled scornfully. So they all go to the Court of Laws.

Hall went to meet Flosi and said—

"Go thou now to the Court of Laws, for now all the money has been bravely paid down, and it has been brought together in one place."

Then Flosi bade the sons of Sigfus to go up with him, and they all went out of their booths. They came from the east, but Njal went from the west to the Court of Laws, and the sons with him.

Skarphedinn went to the middle bench and stood there.

Flosi went into the Court of Laws to look closely at his money, and said—

"This money is both great and good, and well paid down, as was to be looked for."

After that he took up the scarf, and waved it, and asked—

"Who may have given this?"

But no man answered him.

A second time he waved the scarf, and asked—

"Who may have given this?" and laughed, but no man answered him.

Then Flosi said—

"How is it that none of you knows who has owned this gear, or is it that none dares to tell me?"

"Who?" said Skarphedinn, "dost thou think, has given it?"

"If thou must know," said Flosi, "then I will tell thee; I think that thy father the 'Beardless Carle' must have given it, for many know not who look at him whether he is more a man than a woman."

"Such words are ill-spoken," said Skarphedinn, "to make game of him, an old man, and no man of any worth has ever done so before. Ye may know, too, that he is a man, for he has had sons by his wife, and few of our kinsfolk have fallen unatoned by our house, so that we have not had vengeance for them."

Then Skarphedinn took to himself the silken scarf, but threw a pair of blue breeks to Flosi, and said he would need them more.

"Why," said Flosi, "should I need these more?"

"Because," said Skarphedinn, "thou art the sweetheart of the Swinefell's goblin, if, as men say, he does indeed turn thee into a woman every ninth night."

Then Flosi spurned the money, and said he would not touch a penny of it, and then he said he would only have one of two things: either that Hauskuld should fall unatoned, or they would have vengeance for him.

Then Flosi would neither give nor take peace, and he said to the sons of Sigfus—

"Go we now home; one fate shall befall us all."

Then they went home to their booth, and Hall said—

"Here most unlucky men have a share in this suit."

Njal and his sons went home to their booth, and Njal said—

"Now comes to pass what my heart told me long ago, that this suit would fall heavy on us."

"Not so," says Skarphedinn; "they can never pursue us by the laws of the land."

"Then that will happen," says Njal, "which will be worse for all of us."

Those men who had given the money spoke about it, and said that they should take it back; but Gudmund the powerful said—

"That shame I will never choose for myself, to take back what I have given away, either here or elsewhere."

"That is well spoken," they said; and then no one would take it back.

Then Snorri the priest said, "My counsel is, that Gizur the white and Hjallti Skeggi's son keep the money till the next Althing; my heart tells me that no long time will pass ere there may be need to touch this money".

Hjallti took half the money and kept it safe, but Gizur took the rest.

Then men went home to their booths.

CHAPTER CXXIII.

AN ATTACK PLANNED ON NJAL AND HIS SONS.

Flosi summoned all his men up to the "Great Rift," and went thither himself.

So when all his men were come, there were one hundred and twenty of them.

Then Flosi spake thus to the sons of Sigfus—

"In what way shall I stand by you in this quarrel, which will be most to your minds?"

"Nothing will please us," said Gunnar Lambi's son, "until those brothers, Njal's sons, are all slain."

"This," said Flosi, "will I promise to you, ye sons of Sigfus, not to part from this quarrel before one of us bites the dust before the other, I will also know whether there be any man here who will not stand by us in this quarrel."

But they all said they would stand by him.

Then Flosi said—

"Come now all to me, and swear an oath that no man will shrink from this quarrel."

Then all went up to Flosi and swore oaths to him; and then Flosi said—

"We will all of us shake hands on this, that he shall have forfeited life and land who quits this quarrel ere it be over."

These were the chiefs who were with Flosi:—Kol the son of Thorstein broadpaunch, the brother's son of Hall of the Side, Hroald Auzur's son from Broadwater, Auzur son of Anund wallet-back, Thorstein the fair the son of Gerleif, Glum Hilldir's son, Modolf Kettle's son, Thorir the son of Thord Illugi's son of Mauratongue, Kolbein and Egil Flosi's kinsmen, Kettle Sigfus' son, and Mord his brother, Ingialld of the Springs, Thorkel and Lambi, Grani Gunnar's son, Gunnar Lambi's son, and Sigmund Sigfus' son, and Hroar from Hromundstede.

Then Flosi said to the sons of Sigfus—

"Choose ye now a leader, whomsoever ye think best fitted; for some one man must needs be chief over the quarrel."

Then Kettle of the Mark answered—

"If the choice is to be left with us brothers, then we will soon choose that this duty should fall on thee; there are many things which lead to this. Thou art a man of great birth, and a mighty chief, stout of heart, and strong of body, and wise withal, and so we think it best that thou shouldst see to all that is needful in the quarrel."

"It is most fitting," said Flosi, "that I should agree to undertake this as your prayer asks; and now I will lay down the course which we shall follow, and my counsel is, that each man ride home from the Thing and look after his household during the summer, so long as men's haymaking lasts. I, too, will ride home, and be at home this summer; but when that Lord's day comes on which winter is eight weeks off, then I will let them sing me a mass at home, and afterwards ride west across Loomnips Sand; each of our men shall have two horses. I will not swell our company beyond those which have now taken the oath, for we have enough and to spare if all keep true tryst. I will ride all the Lord's day and the night as well, but at even on the second day of the week, I shall ride up to Threecorner ridge about mid-even. There shall ye then be all come who have sworn an oath in this matter. But if there be any one who has not come, and who has joined us in this quarrel, then that man shall lose nothing save his life, if we may have our way."

"How does that hang together," said Kettle, "that thou canst ride from home on the Lord's day, and come the second day of the week to Threecorner ridge?"

"I will ride," said Flosi, "up from Skaptartongue, and north of the Eyjafell Jokul, and so down into Godaland, and it may be done if I ride fast. And now I will tell you my whole purpose, that when we meet there all together, we shall ride to Bergthorsknoll with all our band, and fall on Njal's sons with fire and sword, and not turn away before they are all dead. Ye shall hide this plan, for our lives lie on it. And now we will take to our horses and ride home."

Then they all went to their booths.

After that Flosi made them saddle his horses, and they waited for no man, and rode home.

Flosi would not stay to meet Hall his father-in-law, for he knew of a surety that Hall would set his face against all strong deeds.

Njal rode home from the Thing and his sons. They were at home that summer. Njal asked Kari his son-in-law whether he thought at all of riding east to Dyrholms to his own house.

"I will not ride east," answered Kari, "for one fate shall befall me and thy sons."

Njal thanked him, and said that was only what was likely from him. There were nearly thirty fighting men in Njal's house, reckoning the house-carles.

One day it happened that Rodny Hauskuld's daughter, the mother of Hauskuld Njal's son, came to the Springs. Her brother Ingialld greeted her well, but she would not take his greeting, but yet bade him go out with her. Ingialld did so, and went out with her; and so they walked away from the farmyard both together. Then she clutched hold of him and they both sat down, and Rodny said—

"Is it true that thou hast sworn an oath to fall on Njal, and slay him and his sons?"

"True it is," said he.

"A very great dastard art thou," she says, "thou, whom Njal hath thrice saved from outlawry."

"Still it hath come to this," says Ingialld, "that my life lies on it if I do not this."

"Not so," says she, "thou shalt live all the same, and be called a better man, if thou betrayest not him to whom thou oughtest to behave best."

Then she took a linen hood out of her bag, it was clotted with blood all over, and torn and tattered, and said, "This hood, Hauskuld Njal's son, and thy sister's son, had on his head when they slew him; methinks, then, it is ill owing to stand by those from whom this mischief sprang".

"Well!" answers Ingialld, "so it shall be that I will not be against Njal whatever follows after, but still I know that they will turn and throw trouble on me."

"Now mightest thou," said Rodny, "yield Njal and his sons great help, if thou tellest him all these plans."

"That I will not do," says Ingialld, "for then I am every man's dastard, if I tell what was trusted to me in good faith; but it is a manly deed to sunder myself from this quarrel when I know that there is a sure looking for of vengeance; but tell Njal and his sons to beware of themselves all this summer, for that will be good counsel, and to keep many men about them."

Then she fared to Bergthorsknoll, and told Njal all this talk; and Njal thanked her, and said she had done well, "for there would be more wickedness in his falling on me than of all men else".

She fared home, but he told this to his sons.

There was a carline at Bergthorsknoll, whose name was Saevuna. She was wise in many things, and foresighted; but she was then very old, and Njal's sons called her an old dotard, when she talked so much, but still some things which she said came to pass. It fell one day that she took a cudgel in her hand, and went up above the house to a stack of vetches. She beat the stack of vetches with her cudgel, and wished it might never thrive, "wretch that it was!"

Skarphedinn laughed at her, and asked why she was so angry with the vetch stack.

"This stack of vetches," said the carline, "will be taken and lighted with fire when Njal my master is burnt, house and all, and Bergthora my foster-child. Take it away to the water, or burn it up as quick as you can."

"We will not do that," says Skarphedinn, "for something else will be got to light a fire with, if that were foredoomed, though this stack were not here."

The carline babbled the whole summer about the vetch-stack that it should be got indoors, but something always hindered it.

CHAPTER CXXIV.

OF PORTENTS.

At Reykium on Skeid dwelt one Runolf Thorstein's son. His son's name was Hildiglum. He went out on the night of the Lord's day, when nine weeks were still to winter; he heard a great crash, so that he thought both heaven and earth shook. Then he looked into the west "airt," and he thought he saw thereabouts a ring of fiery hue, and within the ring a man on a gray horse. He passed quickly by him, and rode hard. He had a flaming firebrand in his hand, and he rode so close to him that he could see him plainly. He was as black as pitch, and he sung this song with a mighty voice—

Here I ride swift steed,
His flank flecked with rime,
Rain from his mane drips,
Horse mighty for harm;
Flames flare at each end,
Gall glows in the midst,
So fares it with Flosi's redes
As this flaming brand flies;
And so fares it with Flosi's redes
As this flaming brand flies.

Then he thought he hurled the firebrand east towards the fells before him, and such a blaze of fire leapt up to meet it that he could not see the fells for the blaze. It seemed as though that man rode east among the flames and vanished there.

After that he went to his bed, and was senseless a long time, but at last he came to himself. He bore in mind all that had happened, and told his father, but he bade him tell it to Hjallti Skeggi's son. So he went and told Hjallti, but he said he had seen "'the Wolfs ride,' and that comes ever before great tidings".

CHAPTER CXXV.

FLOSI'S JOURNEY FROM HOME.

Flosi busked him from the east when two months were still to winter, and summoned to him all his men who had promised him help and company. Each of them had two horses and good weapons, and they all came to Swinefell, and were there that night.

Flosi made them say prayers betimes on the Lord's day, and afterwards they sate down to meat. He spoke to his household, and told them what work each was to do while he was away. After that he went to his horses.

Flosi and his men rode first west on the Sand.[69] Flosi bade them not to ride too hard at first; but said they would do well enough at that pace, and he bade all to wait for the others if any of them had need to stop. They rode west to Woodcombe, and came to Kirkby. Flosi there bade all men to come into the church, and pray to God, and men did so.

After that they mounted their horses, and rode on the fell, and so to Fishwaters, and rode a little to the west of the lakes, and so struck down west on to the Sand.[70] Then they left Eyjafell Jokul on their left hand, and so came down into Godaland, and so on to Markfleet, and came about nones[71] on the second day of the week to Threecorner ridge, and waited till mid-even. Then all had came thither save Ingialld of the Springs.

The sons of Sigfus spoke much ill of him, but Flosi bade them not blame Ingialld when he was not by, "but we will pay him for this hereafter".

CHAPTER CXXVI.

OF PORTENTS AT BERGTHORSKNOLL.

Now we must take up the story, and turn to Bergthorsknoll, and say that Grim and Helgi go to Holar. They had children out at foster there, and they told their mother that they should not come home that evening. They were in Holar all the day, and there came some poor women and said they had come from far. Those brothers asked them for tidings, and they said they had no tidings to tell, "but still we might tell you one bit of news".

They asked what that might be, and bade them not hide it. They said so it should be.

"We came down out of Fleetlithe, and we saw all the sons of Sigfus riding fully armed—they made for Threecorner ridge, and were fifteen in company. We saw, too, Grani Gunnar's son and Gunnar Lambi's son, and they were five in all. They took the same road, and one may say now that the whole country-side is faring and flitting about."

"Then," said Helgi Njal's son, "Flosi must have come from the east, and they must have all gone to meet him, and we two, Grim, should be where Skarphedinn is."

Grim said so it ought to be, and they fared home.

That same evening Bergthora spoke to her household, and said, "Now shall ye choose your meat to-night, so that each may have what he likes best; for this evening is the last that I shall set meat before my household".

"That shall not be," they said.

"It will be though," she says, "and I could tell you much more if I would, but this shall be a token, that Grim and Helgi will be home ere men have eaten their full to-night; and if this turns out so, then the rest that I say will happen too."

After that she set meat on the board, and Njal said, "Wondrously now it seems to me. Methinks I see all round the room, and it seems as though the gable wall were thrown down, but the whole board and the meat on it is one gore of blood."

All thought this strange but Skarphedinn, he bade men not be downcast, nor to utter other unseemly sounds, so that men might make a story out of them.

"For it befits us surely more than other men to bear us well, and it is only what is looked for from us."

Grim and Helgi came home ere the board was cleared, and men were much struck at that. Njal asked why they had returned so quickly, but they told what they had heard.

Njal bade no man go to sleep, but to beware of themselves.

CHAPTER CXXVII.

THE ONSLAUGHT ON BERGTHORSKNOLL.

Now Flosi speaks to his men—

"Now we will ride to Bergthorsknoll, and come thither before supper-time."

They do so. There was a dell in the knoll, and they rode thither, and tethered their horses there, and stayed there till the evening was far spent.

Then Flosi said, "Now we will go straight up to the house, and keep close, and walk slow, and see what counsel they will take".

Njal stood out of doors, and his sons, and Kari and all the serving-men, and they stood in array to meet them in the yard, and they were near thirty of them.

Flosi halted and said—"Now we shall see what counsel they take, for it seems to me, if they stand out of doors to meet us, as though we should never get the mastery over them".

"Then is our journey bad," says Grani Gunnar's son, "if we are not to dare to fall on them."

"Nor shall that be," says Flosi; "for we will fall on them though they stand out of doors; but we shall pay that penalty, that many will not go away to tell which side won the day."

Njal said to his men, "See ye now what a great band of men they have".

"They have both a great and well-knit band," says Skarphedinn; "but this is why they make a halt now, because they think it will be a hard struggle to master us."

"That cannot be why they halt," says Njal; "and my will is that our men go indoors, for they had hard work to master Gunnar of Lithend, though he was alone to meet them; but here is a strong house as there was there, and they will be slow to come to close quarters."

"This is not to be settled in that wise," says Skarphedinn, "for those chiefs fell on Gunnar's house, who were so noble-minded, that they would rather turn back than burn him, house and all; but these will fall on us at once with fire, if they cannot get at us in any other way, for they will leave no stone unturned to get the better of us; and no doubt they think, as is not unlikely, that it will be their deaths if we escape out of their hands. Besides, I am unwilling to let myself be stifled indoors like a fox in his earth."

"Now," said Njal, "as often it happens, my sons, ye set my counsel at naught, and show me no honour, but when ye were younger ye did not so, and then your plans were better furthered."

"Let us do," said Helgi, "as our father wills; that will be best for us."

"I am not so sure of that," says Skarphedinn, "for now he is 'fey'; but still I may well humour my father in this, by being burnt indoors along with him, for I am not afraid of my death."

Then he said to Kari, "Let us stand by one another well, brother-in-law, so that neither parts from the other".

"That I have made up my mind to do," says Kari; "but if it should be otherwise doomed,—well! then it must be as it must be, and I shall not be able to fight against it."

"Avenge us, and we will avenge thee," says Skarphedinn, "if we live after thee."

Kari said so it should be.

Then they all went in, and stood in array at the door.

"Now are they all 'fey,'" said Flosi, "since they have gone indoors, and we will go right up to them as quickly as we can, and throng as close as we can before the door, and give heed that none of them, neither Kari nor Njal's sons, get away; for that were our bane."

So Flosi and his men came up to the house, and set men to watch round the house, if there were any secret doors in it. But Flosi went up to the front of the house with his men.

Then Hroald Auzur's son ran up to where Skarphedinn stood, and thrust at him. Skarphedinn hewed the spearhead off the shaft as he held it, and made another stroke at him, and the axe fell on the top of the shield, and dashed back the whole shield on Hroald's body, but the upper horn of the axe caught him on the brow, and he fell at full length on his back, and was dead at once.

"Little chance had that one with thee, Skarphedinn," said Kari, "and thou art our boldest."

"I'm not so sure of that," says Skarphedinn, and he drew up his lips and smiled.

Kari, and Grim, and Helgi, threw out many spears, and wounded many men; but Flosi and his men could do nothing.

At last Flosi said, "We have already gotten great manscathe in our men; many are wounded, and he slain whom we would choose last of all. It is now clear that we shall never master them with weapons; many now there be who are not so forward in fight as they boasted, and yet they were those who goaded us on most. I say this most to Grani Gunnar's son, and Gunnar Lambi's son, who were the least willing to spare their foes. But still we shall have to take to some other plan for ourselves, and now there are but two choices left, and neither of them good. One is to turn away, and that is our death; the other, to set fire to the house, and burn them inside it; and that is a deed which we shall have to answer for heavily before God, since we are Christian men ourselves; but still we must take to that counsel."

CHAPTER CXXVIII.

NJAL'S BURNING.

Now they took fire, and made a great pile before the doors. Then Skarphedinn said.

"What, lads! are ye lighting a fire, or are ye taking to cooking?"

"So it shall be," answered Grani Gunnar's son; "and thou shalt not need to be better done."

"Thou repayest me," said Skarphedinn, "as one may look for from the man that thou art. I avenged thy father, and thou settest most store by that duty which is farthest from thee."

Then the women threw whey on the fire, and quenched it as fast as they lit it. Some, too, brought water, or slops.

Then Kol Thorstein's son said to Flosi—

"A plan comes into my mind; I have seen a loft over the hall among the crosstrees, and we will put the fire in there, and light it with the vetch-stack that stands just above the house."

Then they took the vetch-stack and set fire to it, and they who were inside were not aware of it till the whole hall was ablaze over their heads.

Then Flosi and his men made a great pile before each of the doors, and then the women folk who were inside began to weep and to wail.

Njal spoke to them and said, "Keep up your hearts, nor utter shrieks, for this is but a passing storm, and it will be long before ye have another such; and put your faith in God, and believe that He is so merciful that He will not let us burn both in this world and the next."

Such words of comfort had he for them all, and others still more strong.

Now the whole house began to blaze. Then Njal went to the door and said—

"Is Flosi so near that he can hear my voice?"

Flosi said that he could hear it.

"Wilt thou," said Njal, "take an atonement from my sons, or allow any men to go out?"

"I will not," answers Flosi, "take any atonement from thy sons, and now our dealings shall come to an end once for all, and I will not stir from this spot till they are all dead; but I will allow the women and children and house-carles to go out."

Then Njal went into the house, and said to the folk—

"Now all those must go out to whom leave is given, and so go thou out Thorhalla Asgrim's daughter, and all the people also with thee who may."

Then Thorhalla said—

"This is another parting between me and Helgi than I thought of a while ago; but still I will egg on my father and brothers to avenge this manscathe which is wrought here."

"Go, and good go with thee," said Njal, "for thou art a brave woman."

After that she went out and much folk with her.

Then Astrid of Deepback said to Helgi Njal's son—

"Come thou out with me, and I will throw a woman's cloak over thee, and tire thy head with a kerchief."

He spoke against it at first, but at last he did so at the prayer of others.

So Astrid wrapped the kerchief round Helgi's head, but Thorhilda, Skarphedinn's wife, threw the cloak over him, and he went out between them, and then Thorgerda Njal's daughter, and Helga her sister, and many other folk went out too.

But when Helgi came out Flosi said—

"That is a tall woman and broad across the shoulders that went yonder, take her and hold her."

But when Helgi heard that, he cast away the cloak. He had got his sword under his arm, and hewed at a man, and the blow fell on his shield and cut off the point of it, and the man's leg as well. Then Flosi came up and hewed at Helgi's neck, and took off his head at a stroke.

Then Flosi went to the door and called out to Njal, and said he would speak with him and Bergthora.

Now Njal does so, and Flosi said—

"I will offer thee, master Njal, leave to go out, for it is unworthy that thou shouldst burn indoors."

"I will not go out," said Njal, "for I am an old man, and little fitted to avenge my sons, but I will not live in shame."

Then Flosi said to Bergthora—

"Come thou out, housewife, for I will for no sake burn thee indoors."

"I was given away to Njal young," said Bergthora, "and I have promised him this, that we would both share the same fate."

After that they both went back into the house.

"What counsel shall we now take?" said Bergthora.

"We will go to our bed," says Njal, "and lay us down; I have long been eager for rest."

Then she said to the boy Thord, Kari's son—

"Thee will I take out, and thou shalt not burn in here."

"Thou hast promised me this, grandmother," says the boy, "that we should never part so long as I wished to be with thee; but methinks it is much better to die with thee and Njal than to live after you."

Then she bore the boy to her bed, and Njal spoke to his steward and said—

"Now shalt thou see where we lay us down, and how I lay us out, for I mean not to stir an inch hence, whether reek or burning smart me, and so thou wilt be able to guess where to look for our bones."

He said he would do so.

There had been an ox slaughtered and the hide lay there. Njal told the steward to spread the hide over them, and he did so.

So there they lay down both of them in their bed, and put the boy between them. Then they signed themselves and the boy with the cross, and gave over their souls into God's hand, and that was the last word that men heard them utter.

Then the steward took the hide and spread it over them, and went out afterwards. Kettle of the Mark caught hold of him, and dragged him out, he asked carefully after his father-in-law Njal, but the steward told him the whole truth. Then Kettle said—

"Great grief hath been sent on us, when we have had to share such ill-luck together."

Skarphedinn saw how his father laid him down, and how he laid himself out, and then he said—

"Our father goes early to bed, and that is what was to be looked for, for he is an old man."

Then Skarphedinn, and Kari, and Grim, caught the brands as fast as they dropped down, and hurled them out at them, and so it went on a while. Then they hurled spears in at them, but they caught them all as they flew, and sent them back again.

Then Flosi bade them cease shooting, "for all feats of arms will go hard with us when we deal with them; ye may well wait till the fire overcomes them".

So they do that, and shoot no more.

Then the great beams out of the roof began to fall, and Skarphedinn said—

"Now must my father be dead, and I have neither heard groan nor cough from him."

Then they went to the end of the hall, and there had fallen down a cross-beam inside which was much burnt in the middle.

Kari spoke to Skarphedinn, and said—"Leap thou out here, and I will help thee to do so, and I will leap out after thee, and then we shall both get away if we set about it so, for hitherward blows all the smoke."

"Thou shalt leap first," said Skarphedinn; "but I will leap straightway on thy heels."

"That is not wise," says Kari, "for I can get out well enough elsewhere, though it does not come about here."

"I will not do that," says Skarphedinn; "leap thou out first, but I will leap after thee at once."

"It is bidden to every man," says Kari, "to seek to save his life while he has a choice, and I will do so now; but still this parting of ours will be in such wise that we shall never see one another more; for if I leap out of the fire, I shall have no mind to leap back into the fire to thee, and then each of us will have to fare his own way."

"It joys me, brother-in-law," says Skarphedinn, "to think that if thou gettest away thou wilt avenge me."

Then Kari took up a blazing bench in his hand, and runs up along the cross-beam, then he hurls the bench out at the roof, and it fell among those who were outside.

Then they ran away, and by that time all Kari's upper-clothing and his hair were ablaze, then he threw himself down from the roof, and so crept along with the smoke.

Then one man said who was nearest—

"Was that a man that leapt out at the roof?"

"Far from it," says another; "more likely it was Skarphedinn who hurled a firebrand at us."

After that they had no more mistrust.

Kari ran till he came to a stream, and then, he threw himself down into it, and so quenched the fire on him.

After that he ran along under shelter of the smoke into a hollow, and rested him there, and that has since been called Kari's Hollow.

CHAPTER CXXIX.

SKARPHEDINN'S DEATH.

Now it is to be told of Skarphedinn that he runs out on the cross-beam straight after Kari, but when he came to where the beam was most burnt, then it broke down under him. Skarphedinn came down on his feet, and tried again the second time, and climbs up the wall with a run, then down on him came the wall-plate, and he toppled down again inside.

Then Skarphedinn said—"Now one can see what will come;" and then he went along the side wall. Gunnar Lambi's son leapt up on the wall and sees Skarphedinn; he spoke thus—

"Weepest thou now, Skarphedinn?"

"Not so," says Skarphedinn, "but true it is that the smoke makes one's eyes smart, but is it as it seems to me, dost thou laugh?"

"So it is surely," says Gunnar, "and I have never laughed since thou slewest Thrain on Markfleet."

Then Skarphedinn said—"He now is a keepsake for thee," and with that he took out of his purse the jaw-tooth which he had hewn out of Thrain, and threw it at Gunnar, and struck him in the eye, so that it started out and lay on his cheek.

Then Gunnar fell down from the roof.

Skarphedinn then went to his brother Grim, and they held one another by the hand and trode the fire; but when they came to the middle of the hall Grim fell down dead.

Then Skarphedinn went to the end of the house, and then there was a great crash, and down fell the roof. Skarphedinn was then shut in between it and the gable, and so he could not stir a step thence.

Flosi and his band stayed by the fire until it was broad daylight; then came a man riding up to them. Flosi asked him for his name, but he said his name was Geirmund, and that he was a kinsman of the sons of Sigfus.

"Ye have done a mighty deed," he says.

"Men," says Flosi, "will call it both a mighty deed and an ill deed, but that can't be helped now."

"How many men have lost their lives here?" asks Geirmund.

"Here have died," says Flosi, "Njal and Bergthora and all their sons, Thord Kari's son, Kari Solmund's son, but besides these we cannot say for a surety, because we know not their names."

"Thou tellest him now dead," said Geirmund, "with whom we have gossipped this morning."

"Who is that?" says Flosi.

"We two," says Geirmund, "I and my neighbour Bard, met Kari Solmund's son, and Bard gave him his horse, and his hair and his upper clothes were burned off him."

"Had he any weapons?" asks Flosi.

"He had the sword 'Life-luller,'" says Geirmund, "and one edge of it was blue with fire, and Bard and I said that it must have become soft, but he answered thus, that he would harden it in the blood of the sons of Sigfus or the other Burners."

"What said he of Skarphedinn?" said Flosi.

"He said both he and Grim were alive," answers Geirmund, "when they parted; but he said that now they must be dead."

"Thou hast told us a tale," said Flosi, "which bodes us no idle peace, for that man hath now got away who comes next to Gunnar of Lithend in all things; and now, ye sons of Sigfus, and ye other Burners, know this, that such a great blood feud, and hue and cry will be made about this burning, that it will make many a man headless, but some will lose all their goods. Now I doubt much whether any man of you, ye sons of Sigfus, will dare to stay in his house; and that is not to be wondered at; and so I will bid you all to come and stay with me in the east, and let us all share one fate."

They thanked him for his offer, and said they would be glad to take it.

Then Modolf Kettle's son sang a song.

But one prop of Njal's house liveth,
All the rest inside are burnt,
All but one,—those bounteous spenders,
Sigfus' stalwart sons wrought this;
Son of Gollnir[72] now is glutted
Vengeance for brave Hauskuld's death,
Brisk flew fire through thy dwelling,
Bright flames blazed above thy roof.

"We shall have to boast of something else than that Njal has been burnt in his house," says Flosi, "for there is no glory in that."

Then he went up on the gable, and Glum Hilldir's son, and some other men. Then Glum said, "Is Skarphedinn dead, indeed?" But the others said he must have been dead long ago.

The fire sometimes blazed up fitfully and sometimes burned low, and then they heard down in the fire beneath them that this song was sung—

Deep, I ween, ye Ogre offspring!
Devilish brood of giant birth,
Would ye groan with gloomy visage
Had the fight gone to my mind;
But my very soul it gladdens
That my friends[73] who now boast high,
Wrought not this foul deed, their glory,
Save with footsteps filled with gore.

"Can Skarphedinn, think ye, have sung this song dead or alive?" said Grani Gunnar's son.

"I will go into no guesses about that," says Flosi.

"We will look for Skarphedinn," says Grani, "and the other men who have been here burnt inside the house."

"That shall not be," says Flosi, "it is just like such foolish men as thou art, now that men will be gathering force all over the country; and when they do come, I trow the very same man who now lingers will be so scared that he will not know which way to run; and now my counsel is that we all ride away as quickly as ever we can."

Then Flosi went hastily to his horse and all his men.

Then Flosi said to Geirmund—

"Is Ingialld, thinkest thou, at home, at the Springs?"

Geirmund said he thought he must be at home.

"There now is a man," says Flosi, "who has broken his oath with us and all good faith."

Then Flosi said to the sons of Sigfus—"What course will ye now take with Ingialld; will ye forgive him, or shall we now fall on him and slay him?"

They all answered that they would rather fall on him and slay him.

Then Flosi jumped on his horse, and all the others, and they rode away. Flosi rode first, and shaped his course for Rangriver, and up along the river bank.

Then he saw a man riding down on the other bank of the river, and he knew that there was Ingialld of the Springs. Flosi calls out to him. Ingialld halted and turned down to the river bank; and Flosi said to him—

"Thou hast broken faith with us, and hast forfeited life and goods. Here now are the sons of Sigfus, who are eager to slay thee; but methinks thou hast fallen into a strait, and I will give thee thy life if thou will hand over to me the right to make my own award."

"I will sooner ride to meet Kari," said Ingialld, "than grant thee the right to utter thine own award, and my answer to the sons of Sigfus is this, that I shall be no whit more afraid of them than they are of me."

"Bide thou there," says Flosi, "if thou art not a coward, for I will send thee a gift."

"I will bide of a surety," says Ingialld.

Thorstein Kolbein's son, Flosi's brother's son, rode up by his side and had a spear in his hand, he was one of the bravest of men, and the most worthy of those who were with Flosi.

Flosi snatched the spear from him, and launched it at Ingialld, and it fell on his left side, and passed through the shield just below the handle, and clove it all asunder, but the spear passed on into his thigh just above the knee-pan, and so on into the saddle-tree, and there stood fast.

Then Flosi said to Ingialld—

"Did it touch thee?"

"It touched me sure enough," says Ingialld, "but I call this a scratch and not a wound."

Then Ingialld plucked the spear out of the wound, and said to Flosi—

"Now bide thou, if thou art not a milksop."

Then he launched the spear back over the river. Flosi sees that the spear is coming straight for his middle, and then he backs his horse out of the way, but the spear flew in front of Flosi's horse, and missed him, but it struck Thorstein's middle, and down he fell at once dead off his horse.

Now Ingialld tuns for the wood, and they could not get at him.

Then Flosi said to his men—

"Now have we gotten manscathe, and now we may know, when such things befall us, into what a luckless state we have got. Now it is my counsel that we ride up to Threecorner ridge; thence we shall be able to see where men ride all over the country, for by this time they will have gathered together a great band, and they will think that we have ridden east to Fleetlithe from Threecorner ridge; and thence they will think that we are riding north up on the fell, and so east to our own country, and thither the greater part of the folk will ride after us; but some will ride the coast road east to Selialandsmull, and yet they will think there is less hope of finding us thitherward, but I will now take counsel for all of us, and my plan is to ride up into Threecorner-fell, and bide there till three suns have risen and set in heaven."

CHAPTER CXXX.

OF KARI SOLMUND'S SON.

Now it is to be told of Kari Solmund's son that he fared away from that hollow in which he had rested himself until he met Bard, and those words passed between them which Geirmund had told.

Thence Kari rode to Mord, and told him the tidings, and he was greatly grieved.

Kari said there were other things more befitting a man than to weep for them dead, and bade him rather gather folk and come to Holtford.

After that he rode into Thursodale to Hjallti Skeggi's son, and as he went along Thurso water, he sees a man riding fast behind him. Kari waited for the man, and knows that he was Ingialld of the Springs. He sees that he is very bloody about the thigh; and Kari asked Ingialld who had wounded him, and he told him.

"Where met ye two?" says Kari.

"By Rangwater side," says Ingialld, "and he threw a spear over at me."

"Didst thou aught for it?" asks Kari.

"I threw the spear back," says Ingialld, "and they said that it met a man, and he was dead at once."

"Knowest thou not," said Kari, "who the man was?"

"Methought he was like Thorstein Flosi's brother's son," says Ingialld.

"Good luck go with thy hand," says Kari.

After that they rode both together to see Hjallti Skeggi's son, and told him the tidings. He took these deeds ill, and said there was the greatest need to ride after them and slay them all.

After that he gathered men and roused the whole country; now he and Kari and Ingialld ride with this band to meet Mord Valgard's son, and they found him at Holtford, and Mord was there waiting for them with a very great company. Then they parted the hue and cry; some fared the straight road by the east coast to Selialandsmull, but some went up to Fleetlithe, and other-some the higher road thence to Threecorner ridge, and so down into Godaland. Thence they rode north to Sand. Some too rode as far as

Fishwaters, and there turned back. Some the coast road east to Holt, and told Thorgeir the tidings, and asked whether they had not ridden by there.

"This is how it is," said Thorgeir, "though I am not a mighty chief, yet Flosi would take other counsel than to ride under my eyes, when he has slain Njal, my father's brother, and my cousins; and there is nothing left for any of you but e'en to turn back again, for ye should have hunted longer nearer home; but tell this to Kari, that he must ride hither to me and be here with me if he will; but though he will not come hither east, still I will look after his farm at Dyrholms if he will, but tell him too that I will stand by him and ride with him to the Althing. And he shall also know this, that we brothers are the next of kin to follow up the feud, and we mean so to take up the suit, that outlawry shall follow and after that revenge, man for man, if we can bring it about; but I do not go with you now, because I know naught will come of it, and they will now be as wary as they can of themselves."

Now they ride back, and all met at Hof and talked there among themselves, and said that they had gotten disgrace since they had not found them. Mord said that was not so. Then many men were eager that they should fare to Fleetlithe, and pull down the homesteads of all those who had been at those deeds, but still they listened for Mord's utterance.

"That," he said, "would be the greatest folly." They asked why he said that.

"Because," he said, "if their houses stand, they will be sure to visit them to see their wives; and then, as time rolls on, we may hunt them down there; and now ye shall none of you doubt that I will be true to thee Kari, and to all of you, and in all counsel, for I have to answer for myself."

Hjallti bade him do as he said. Then Hjallti bade Kari to come and stay with him; he said he would ride thither first. They told him what Thorgeir had offered him, and he said he would make use of that offer afterwards, but said his heart told him it would be well if there were many such.

After that the whole band broke up.

Flosi and his men saw all these tidings from where they were on the fell; and Flosi said—

"Now we will take our horses and ride away, for now it will be some good."

The sons of Sigfus asked whether it would be worth while to get to their homes and tell the news.

"It must be Mord's meaning," says Flosi, "that ye will visit your wives; and my guess is, that his plan is to let your houses stand unsacked; but my plan is that not a man shall part from the other, but all ride east with me."

So every man took that counsel, and then they all rode east and north of the Jokul, and so on till they came to Swinefell.

Flosi sent at once men out to get in stores, so that nothing might fall short.

Flosi never spoke about the deed, but no fear was found in him, and he was at home the whole winter till Yule was over.

CHAPTER CXXXI.

NJAL'S AND BERGTHORA'S BONES FOUND.

Kari bade Hjallti to go and search for Njal's bones, "for all will believe in what thou sayest and thinkest about them".

Hjallti said he would be most willing to bear Njal's bones to church; so they rode thence fifteen men. They rode east over Thurso-water, and called on men there to come with them till they had one hundred men, reckoning Njal's neighbours.

They came to Bergthorsknoll at mid-day.

Hjallti asked Kari under what part of the house Njal might be lying, but Kari showed them to the spot, and there was a great heap of ashes to dig away. There they found the hide underneath, and it was as though it were shrivelled with the fire. They raised up the hide, and lo! they were unburnt under it. All praised God for that, and thought it was a great token.

Then the boy was taken up who had lain between them, and of him a finger was burnt off which he had stretched out from under the hide.

Njal was borne out, and so was Bergthora, and then all men went to see their bodies.

Then Hjallti said—"What like look to you these bodies?"

They answered, "We will wait for thy utterance".

Then Hjallti said, "I shall speak what I say with all freedom of speech. The body of Bergthora looks as it was likely she would look, and still fair; but Njal's body and visage seem to me so bright that I have never seen any dead man's body so bright as this."

They all said they thought so too.

Then they sought for Skarphedinn, and the men of the household showed them to the spot where Flosi and his men heard the song sung, and there the roof had fallen down by the gable, and there Hjallti said that they should look. Then they did so, and found Skarphedinn's body there, and he had stood up hard by the gable-wall, and his legs were burnt off him right up to the knees, but all the rest of him was unburnt. He had bitten through his under lip, his eyes were wide open and not swollen nor starting out of his head; he had driven his axe into the gable-wall so hard that it had gone in up to the middle of the blade, and that was why it was not softened.

After that the axe was broken out of the wall, and Hjallti took up the axe, and said—

"This is a rare weapon, and few would be able to wield it."

"I see a man," said Kari, "who shall bear the axe."

"Who is that?" says Hjallti.

"Thorgeir Craggeir," says Kari, "he whom I now think to be the greatest man in all their family."

Then Skarphedinn was stripped of his clothes, for they were unburnt; he had laid his hands in a cross, and the right hand uppermost. They found marks on him; one between his shoulders and the other on his chest, and both were branded in the shape of a cross, and men thought that he must have burnt them in himself.

All men said that they thought that it was better to be near Skarphedinn dead than they weened, for no man was afraid of him.

They sought for the bones of Grim, and found them in the midst of the hall. They found, too, there, right over-against him under the side wall, Thord Freedmanson; but in the weaving-room they found Saevuna the carline, and three men more. In all they found there the bones of nine souls. Now they carried the bodies to the church, and then Hjallti rode home and Kari with him. A swelling came on Ingialld's leg, and then he fared to Hjallti, and was healed there, but still he limped ever afterwards.

Kari rode to Tongue to Asgrim Ellidagrim's son. By that time Thorhalla was come home, and she had already told the tidings. Asgrim took Kari by both hands, and bade him be there all that year. Kari said so it should be.

Asgrim asked besides all the folk who had been in the house at Bergthorsknoll to stay with him. Kari said that was well offered, and said he would take it on their behalf.

Then all the folk were flitted thither.

Thorhall Asgrim's son was so startled when he was told that his foster-father Njal was dead, and that he had been burnt in his house, that he swelled all over, and a stream of blood burst out of both his ears, and could not be staunched, and he fell into a swoon, and then it was staunched.

After that he stood up, and said he had behaved like a coward, "but I would that I might be able to avenge this which has befallen me on some of those who burnt him".

But when others said that no one would think this a shame to him, he said he could not stop the mouths of the people from talking about it.

Asgrim asked Kari what trust and help he thought he might look for from those east of the rivers. Kari said that Mord Valgard's son, and Hjallti, Skeggi's son, would yield him all the help they could, and so, too, would Thorgeir Craggeir, and all those brothers.

Asgrim said that was great strength.

"What strength shall we have from thee?" says Kari.

"All that I can give," says Asgrim, "and I will lay down my life on it."

"So do," says Kari.

"I have also," says Asgrim, "brought Gizur the white into the suit, and have asked his advice how we shall set about it."

"What advice did he give?" asks Kari.

"He counselled," answers Asgrim, "'that we should hold us quite still till spring, but then ride east and set the suit on foot against Flosi for the manslaughter of Helgi, and summon the neighbours from their homes, and give due notice at the Thing of the suits for the burning, and summon the same neighbours there too on the inquest before the court. I asked Gizur who should plead the suit for manslaughter, but he said that Mord should plead it whether he liked it or not, and now,' he went on, 'it shall fall most heavily on him that up to this time all the suits he has undertaken have had the worst ending. Kari shall also be wroth whenever he meets Mord, and so, if he be made to fear on one side, and has to look to me on the other, then he will undertake the duty.'"

Then Kari said, "We will follow thy counsel as long as we can, and thou shalt lead us".

It is to be told of Kari that he could not sleep of nights. Asgrim woke up one night and heard that Kari was awake, and Asgrim said—"Is it that thou canst not sleep at night?"

Then Kari sang this song—

Bender of the bow of battle,
Sleep will not my eyelids seal,
Still my murdered messmates' bidding
Haunts my mind the livelong night;
Since the men their brands abusing
Burned last autumn guileless Njal,
Burned him house and home together,
Mindful am I of my hurt.

Kari spoke of no men so often as of Njal and Skarphedinn, and Bergthora and Helgi. He never abused his foes, and never threatened them.

CHAPTER CXXXII.

FLOSI'S DREAM.

One night it so happened that Flosi struggled much in his sleep. Glum Hilldir's son woke him up, and then Flosi said—

"Call me Kettle of the Mark."

Kettle came thither, and Flosi said, "I will tell thee my dream".

"I am ready to hear it," says Kettle.

"I dreamt," says Flosi, "that methought I stood below Loom-nip, and went out and looked up to the Nip, and all at once it opened, and a man came out of the Nip, and he was clad in goatskins, and had an iron staff in his hand. He called, as he walked, on many of my men, some sooner and some later, and named them by name. First he called Grim the Red my kinsman, and Arni Kol's son. Then methought something strange followed, methought he called Eyjolf Bolverk's son, and Ljot son of Hall of the Side, and some six men more. Then he held his peace awhile. After that he called five men of our band, and among them were the sons of Sigfus, thy brothers; then he called other six men, and among them were Lambi, and Modolf, and Glum. Then he called three men. Last of all he called Gunnar Lambi's son, and Kol Thorstein's son. After that he came up to me; I asked him 'what news'. He said he had tidings enough to tell. Then I asked him for his name, but he called himself Irongrim. I asked him whither he was going; he said he had to fare to the Althing. 'What shalt thou do there?' I said. 'First I shall challenge the inquest,' he answers, 'and then the courts, then clear the field for fighters.' After that he sang this song—

"'Soon a man death's snake-strokes dealing
High shall lift his head on earth,
Here amid the dust low rolling
Battered brainpans men shall see:
Now upon the hills in hurly
Buds the blue steel's harvest bright;
Soon the bloody dew of battle
Thigh-deep through the ranks shall rise.'

"Then he shouted with such a mighty shout that methought everything near shook, and dashed down his staff, and there was a mighty crash. Then he went back into the fell, but fear clung to me; and now I wish thee to tell me what thou thinkest this dream is."

"It is my foreboding," says Kettle, "that all those who were called must be 'fey'. It seems to me good counsel that we tell this dream to no man just now."

Flosi said so it should be. Now the winter passes away till Yule was over. Then Flosi said to his men—

"Now I mean that we should fare from home, for methinks we shall not be able to have an idle peace. Now we shall fare to pray for help, and now that will come true which I told you, that we should have to bow the knee to many ere this quarrel were ended."

CHAPTER CXXXIII.

OF FLOSI'S JOURNEY AND HIS ASKING FOR HELP.

After that they busked them from home all together. Flosi was in long-hose because he meant to go on foot, and then he knew that it would seem less hard to the others to walk.

Then they fared from home to Knappvale, but the evening after to Broadwater, and then to Calffell, thence by Bjornness to Hornfirth, thence to Staffell in Lon, and then to Thvattwater to Hall of the Side.

Flosi had to wife Steinvora, his daughter.

Hall gave them a very hearty welcome, and Flosi said to Hall—

"I will ask thee, father-in-law, that thou wouldst ride to the Thing with me with all thy Thingmen."

"Now," answered Hall, "it has turned out as the saw says, 'but a short while is hand fain of blow'; and yet it is one and the same man in thy band who now hangs his head, and who then goaded thee on to the worst of deeds when it was still undone. But my help I am bound to lend thee in all such places as I may."

"What counsel dost thou give me," said Flosi, "in the strait in which I now am?"

"Thou shalt fare," said Hall, "north, right up to Weaponfirth, and ask all the chiefs for aid, and thou wilt yet need it all before the Thing is over."

Flosi stayed there three nights, and rested him, and fared thence east to Geitahellna, and so to Berufirth; there they were the night. Thence they fared east to Broaddale in Haydale. There Hallbjorn the strong dwelt. He had to wife Oddny the sister of Saurli Broddhelgi's son, and Flosi had a hearty welcome there.

Hallbjorn asked how far north among the firths Flosi meant to go. He said he meant to go as far as Weaponfirth. Then Flosi took a purse of money from his belt, and said he would give it to Hallbjorn. He took the money, but yet said he had no claim on Flosi for gifts, but still I would be glad to know in what thou wilt that I repay thee.

"I have no need of money," says Flosi, "but I wish thou wouldst ride to the Thing with me, and stand by me in my quarrel, but still I have no ties or kinship to tell towards thee."

"I will grant thee that," said Hallbjorn, "to ride to the Thing with thee, and to stand by thee in thy quarrel as I would by my brother."

Flosi thanked him, and Hallbjorn asked much about the Burning, but they told him all about it at length.

Thence Flosi fared to Broaddale's heath, and so to Hrafnkelstede, there dwelt Hrafnkell, the son of Thorir, the son of Hrafnkell Raum. Flosi had a hearty welcome there, and sought for help and a promise to ride to the Thing from Hrafnkell, but he stood out a long while, though the end of it was that he gave his word that his son Thorir should ride with all their Thingmen, and yield him such help as the other priests of the same district.

Flosi thanked him and fared away to Bersastede. There Holmstein son of Bersi the wise dwelt, and he gave Flosi a very hearty welcome. Flosi begged him for help. Holmstein said he had been long in his debt for help.

Thence they fared to Waltheofstede—there Saurli Broddhelgi's son, Bjarni's brother, dwelt. He had to wife Thordisa, a daughter of Gudmund the powerful, of Modruvale. They had a hearty welcome there. But next morning Flosi raised the question with Saurli that he should ride to the Althing with him, and bid him money for it.

"I cannot tell about that," says Saurli, "so long as I do not know on which side my father-in-law Gudmund the powerful stands, for I mean to stand by him on whichever side he stands."

"Oh!" said Flosi, "I see by thy answer that a woman rules in this house."

Then Flosi stood up and bade his men take their upper clothing and weapons, and then they fared away, and got no help there. So they fared below Lagarfleet and over the heath to Njardwick; there two brothers dwelt, Thorkel the allwise, and Thorwalld his brother; they were sons of Kettle, the son of Thidrandi the wise, the son of Kettle rumble, son of Thorir Thidrandi. The mother of Thorkel the allwise and Thorwalld was Yngvillda, daughter of Thorkel the wise. Flosi got a hearty welcome there; he told those brothers plainly of his errand, and asked for their help; but they put him off until he gave three marks of silver to each of them for their aid; then they agreed to stand by Flosi.

Their mother Yngvillda was by when they gave their words to ride to the Althing, and wept. Thorkel asked why she wept; and she answered—

"I dreamt that thy brother Thorwalld was clad in a red kirtle, and methought it was so tight as though it were sewn on him; methought too that he wore red hose on his legs and feet, and bad shoethongs were twisted round them; methought it ill to see when I knew he was so uncomfortable, but I could do naught for him."

They laughed and told her she had lost her wits, and said her babble should not stand in the way of their ride to the Thing.

Flosi thanked them kindly, and fared thence to Weaponfirth and came to Hof. There dwelt Bjarni Broddhelgi's son. Bjarni took Flosi by both hands, and Flosi bade Bjarni money for his help.

"Never," says Bjarni, "have I sold my manhood or help for bribes, but now that thou art in need of help, I will do thee a good turn for friendship's sake, and ride to the Thing with thee, and stand by thee as I would by my brother."

"Then thou hast thrown a great load of debt on my hands," said Flosi, "but still I looked for as much from thee."

Thence Flosi and his men fared to Crosswick. Thorkel Geiti's son was a great friend of his. Flosi told him his errand, and Thorkel said it was but his duty to stand by him in every way in his power, and not to part from his quarrel. Thorkel gave Flosi good gifts at parting.

Thence they fared north to Weaponfirth and up into the Fleetdale country, and turned in as guests at Holmstein's, the son of Bersi the wise. Flosi told him that all had backed him in his need and business well, save Saurli Broddhelgi's son. Holmstein said the reason of that was that he was not a man of strife. Holmstein gave Flosi good gifts.

Flosi fared up Fleetdale, and thence south on the fell across Oxenlava and down Swinehorndale, and so out by Alftafirth to the west, and did not stop till he came to Thvattwater to his father-in-law Hall's house. There he stayed half a month, and his men with him and rested him.

Flosi asked Hall what counsel he would now give him, and what he should do next, and whether he should change his plans.

"My counsel," said Hall, "is this, that thou goest home to thy house, and the sons of Sigfus with thee, but that they send men to set their homesteads in order. But first of all fare home, and when ye ride to the Thing, ride all together, and do not scatter your band. Then let the sons of Sigfus go to see their wives on the way. I too will ride to the Thing, and Ljot my son with all our Thingmen, and stand by thee with such force as I can gather to me."

Flosi thanked him, and Hall gave him good gifts at parting.

Then Flosi went away from Thvattwater, and nothing is to be told of his journey till he comes home to Swinefell. There he stayed at home the rest of the winter, and all the summer right up to the Thing.

CHAPTER CXXXIV.

OF THORHALL AND KARI.

Thorhall Asgrim's son, and Kari Solmund's son, rode one day to Mossfell to see Gizur the white; he took them with both hands, and there they were at his house a very long while. Once it happened as they and Gizur talked of Njal's burning, that Gizur said it was very great luck that Kari had got away. Then a song came into Kari's mouth.

I who whetted helmet-hewer,[74]
I who oft have burnished brand,
From the fray went all unwilling
When Njal's rooftree crackling roared;
Out I leapt when bands of spearmen
Lighted there a blaze of flame!
Listen men unto my moaning,
Mark the telling of my grief.

Then Gizur said, "It must be forgiven thee that thou art mindful, and so we will talk no more about it just now".

Kari says that he will ride home; and Gizur said "I will now make a clean breast of my counsel to thee. Thou shalt not ride home, but still thou shalt ride away, and east under Eyjafell, to see Thorgeir Craggeir, and Thorleif crow. They shall ride from the east with thee. They are the next of kin in the suit, and with them shall ride Thorgrim the big, their brother. Ye shall ride to Mord Valgard's son's house, and tell him this message from me, that he shall take up the suit for manslaughter for Helgi Njal's son against Flosi. But if he utters any words against this, then shalt thou make thyself most wrathful, and make believe as though thou wouldst let thy axe fall on his head; and in the second place, thou shalt assure him of my wrath if he shows any ill will. Along with that shalt thou say, that I will send and fetch away my daughter Thorkatla, and make her come home to me; but that he will not abide, for he loves her as the very eyes in his head."

Kari thanked him for his counsel. Kari spoke nothing of help to him, for he thought he would show himself his good friend in this as in other things.

Thence Kari rode east over the rivers, and so to Fleetlithe, and east across Markfleet, and so on to Selialandsmull. So they ride east to Holt.

Thorgeir welcomed them with the greatest kindliness. He told them of Flosi's journey, and how great help he had got in the east firths.

Kari said it was no wonder that he, who had to answer for so much, should ask for help for himself.

Then Thorgeir said, "The better things go for them, the worse it shall be for them; we will only follow them up so much the harder".

Kari told Thorgeir of Gizur's advice. After that they ride from the east to Rangrivervale to Mord Valgard's son's house. He gave them a hearty welcome. Kari told him the message of Gizur his father-in-law. He was slow to take the duty on him, and said it was harder to go to law with Flosi than with any other ten men.

"Thou behavest now as he [Gizur] thought," said Kari; "for thou art a bad bargain in every way; thou art both a coward and heartless, but the end of this shall be as is fitting, that Thorkatla shall fare home to her father."

She busked her at once, and said she had long been "boun" to part from Mord. Then he changed his mood and his words quickly, and begged off their wrath, and took the suit upon him at once.

"Now," said Kari, "thou hast taken the suit upon thee, see that thou pleadest it without fear, for thy life lies on it."

Mord said he would lay his whole heart on it to do this well and manfully.

After that Mord summoned to him nine neighbours —they were all near neighbours to the spot where the deed was done. Then Mord took Thorgeir by the hand and named two witnesses to bear witness, "that Thorgeir Thorir's son hands me over a suit for manslaughter against Flosi Thord's son, to plead it for the slaying of Helgi Njal's son, with all those proofs which have to follow the suit. Thou handest over to me this suit to plead and to settle, and to enjoy all rights in it, as though I were the rightful next of kin. Thou handest it over to me by law, and I take it from thee by law."

A second time Mord named his witnesses, "to bear witness," said he, "that I give notice of an assault laid down by law against Flosi Thord's son, for that he dealt Helgi Njal's son a brain, or a body, or a marrow wound, which proved a death wound; and from which Helgi got his death. I give notice of this before five witnesses"—here he named them all by name—"I give this lawful notice, I give notice of a suit which Thorgeir Thorir's son has handed over to me."

Again he named witnesses to "bear witness that I give notice of a brain, of a body, or a marrow wound against Flosi Thord's son, for that wound which proved a death wound, but Helgi got his death therefrom on such and such a spot, when Flosi Thord's son first rushed on Helgi Njal's son with an assault laid down by law. I give notice of this before five neighbours "—then he named them all by name—"I give this lawful notice. I give notice of a suit which Thorgeir Thorir's son has handed over to me."

Then Mord named his witnesses again "to bear witness," said he, "that I summon these nine neighbours who dwell nearest the spot"—here he named them all by name—"to ride to the Althing, and to sit on the inquest to find whether Flosi Thord's son rushed with an assault laid down by law on Helgi Njal's son, on that spot where Flosi Thord's son dealt Helgi Njal's son a brain, or a body, or a marrow wound, which proved a death wound, and from which Helgi got his death. I call on you to utter all those words which ye are bound to find by law, and which I shall call on you to utter before the court, and which belong to this suit; I call upon you by a lawful summons—I call on you so that ye may yourselves hear—I call on you in the suit which Thorgeir Thorir's son has handed over to me."

Again Mord named his witnesses, "to bear witness, that I summon these nine neighbours who dwell nearest to the spot to ride to the Althing, and to sit on an inquest to find whether Flosi Thord's son wounded Helgi Njal's son with a brain, or body, or marrow wound, which proved a death wound, and from which Helgi got his death, on that spot where Flosi Thord's son first rushed on Helgi Njal's son with an assault laid down by law. I call on you to utter all those words which ye are bound to find by law, and which I shall call on you to utter before the court, and which belong to this suit I call upon you by a lawful summons— I call on you so that ye may yourselves hear—I call on you in the suit which Thorgeir Thorir's son has handed over to me."

Then Mord said—

"Now is the suit set on foot as ye asked, and now I will pray thee, Thorgeir Craggeir, to come to me when thou ridest to the Thing, and then let us both ride together, each with our band, and keep as close as we can together, for my band shall be ready by the very beginning of the Thing, and I will be true to you in all things."

They showed themselves well pleased at that, and this was fast bound by oaths, that no man should sunder himself from another till Kari willed it, and that each of them should lay down his life for the other's life. Now they parted with friendship, and settled to meet again at the Thing.

Now Thorgeir rides back east, but Kari rides west over the rivers till he came to Tongue, to Asgrim's house. He welcomed them wonderfully well, and Kari told Asgrim all Gizur the white's plan, and of the setting on foot of the suit.

"I looked for as much from him," says Asgrim, "that he would behave well, and now he has shown it."

Then Asgrim went on—

"What heardest thou from the east of Flosi?"

"He went east all the way to Weaponfirth," answers Kari, "and nearly all the chiefs have promised to ride with him to the Althing, and to help him. They look, too, for help from the Reykdalesmen, and the men of Lightwater, and the Axefirthers."

Then they talked much about it, and so the time passes away up to the Althing.

Thorhall Asgrim's son took such a hurt in his leg that the foot above the ankle was as big and swollen as a woman's thigh, and he could not walk save with a staff. He was a man tall in growth, and strong and powerful, dark of hue in hair and skin, measured and guarded in his speech, and yet hot and hasty tempered. He was the third greatest lawyer in all Iceland.

Now the time comes that men should ride from home to the Thing, Asgrim said to Kari—

"Thou shalt ride at the very beginning of the Thing, and fit up our booths, and my son Thorhall with thee. Thou wilt treat him best and kindest, as he is footlame, but we shall stand in the greatest need of him at this Thing. With you two, twenty men more shall ride."

After that they made ready for their journey, and then they rode to the Thing, and set up their booths, and fitted them out well.

CHAPTER CXXXV.

OF FLOSI AND THE BURNERS.

Flosi rode from the east and those hundred and twenty men who had been at the Burning with him. They rode till they came to Fleetlithe. Then the sons of Sigfus looked after their homesteads and tarried there that day, but at even they rode west over Thurso-water, and slept there that night. But next morning early they saddled their horses and rode off on their way.

Then Flosi said to his men—

"Now will we ride to Tongue to Asgrim to breakfast, and trample down his pride a little."

They said that were well done. They rode till they had a short way to Tongue. Asgrim stood out of doors, and some men with him. They see the band as soon as ever they could do so from the house. Then Asgrim's men said—

"There must be Thorgeir Craggeir."

"Not he," said Asgrim. "I think so all the more because these men fare with laughter and wantonness; but such kinsmen of Njal as Thorgeir is would not smile before some vengeance is taken for the Burning, and I will make another guess, and maybe ye will think that unlikely. My meaning is, that it must be Flosi and the Burners with him, and they must mean to humble us with insults, and we will now go indoors all of us."

Now they do so, and Asgrim made them sweep the house and put up the hangings, and set the boards and put meat on them. He made them place stools along each bench all down the room.

Flosi rode into the "town," and bade men alight from their horses and go in. They did so, and Flosi and his men went into the hall, Asgrim sate on the cross-bench on the dais. Flosi looked at the benches and saw that all was made ready that men needed to have. Asgrim gave them no greeting, but said to Flosi—

"The boards are set, so that meat may be free to those that need it."

Flosi sat down to the board, and all his men; but they laid their arms up against the wainscot. They sat on the stools who found no room on the benches; but four men stood with weapons just before where Flosi sat while they ate.

Asgrim kept his peace during the meat, but was as red to look on as blood.

But when they were full, some women cleared away the boards, while others brought in water to wash their hands. Flosi was in no greater hurry than if he had been at home. There lay a pole-axe in the corner of the dais. Asgrim caught it up with both hands, and ran up to the rail at the edge of the dais, and made a blow at Flosi's head. Glum Hilldir's son happened to see what he was about to do, and sprang up at once, and got hold of the axe above Asgrim's hands, and turned the edge at once on Asgrim; for Glum was very strong. Then many more men ran up and seized Asgrim, but Flosi said that no man was to do Asgrim any harm, "for we put him to too hard a trial, and he only did what he ought, and showed in that that he had a big heart".

Then Flosi said to Asgrim, "Here, now, we shall part safe and sound, and meet at the Thing, and there begin our quarrel over again".

"So it will be," says Asgrim; "and I would wish that, ere this Thing be over, ye should have to take in some of your sails."

Flosi answered him never a word, and then they went out, and mounted their horses, and rode away. They rode till they came to Laugarwater, and were there that night; but next morning they rode on to Baitvale, and baited their horses there, and there many bands rode to meet them. There was Hall of the Side, and all the Eastfirthers. Flosi greeted them well, and told them of his journeys and dealings with Asgrim. Many praised him for that, and said such things were bravely done.

Then Hall said, "I look on this in another way than ye do, for methinks it was a foolish prank; they were sure to bear in mind their griefs, even though they were not reminded of them anew; but those men who try others so heavily must look for all evil".

It was seen from Hall's way that he thought this deed far too strong. They rode thence all together, till they came to the Upper Field, and there they set their men in array, and rode down on the Thing.

Flosi had made them fit out Byrgir's booth ere he rode to the Thing; but the Eastfirthers rode to their own booths.

CHAPTER CXXXVI.

OF THORGEIR CRAGGEIR.

Thorgeir Craggeir rode from the east with much people. His brothers were with him, Thorleif crow and Thorgrim the big. They came to Hof, to Mord Valgard's son's house, and bided there till he was ready. Mord had gathered every man who could bear arms, and they could see nothing about him but that he was most steadfast in everything, and now they rode until they came west across the rivers. Then they waited for Hjallti Skeggi's son. He came after they had waited a short while, and they greeted him well, and rode afterwards all together till they came to Reykia in Bishop's-tongue, and bided there for Asgrim Ellidagrim's son, and he came to meet them there. Then they rode west across Bridgewater. Then Asgrim told them all that had passed between him and Flosi; and Thorgeir said—

"I would that we might try their bravery ere the Thing closes."

They rode until they came to Baitvale. There Gizur the white came to meet them with a very great company, and they fell to talking together. Then they rode to the Upper Field, and drew up all their men in array there, and so rode to the Thing.

Flosi and his men all took to their arms, and it was within an ace that they would fall to blows. But Asgrim and his friends and their followers would have no hand in it, and rode to their booths; and now all was quiet that day, so that they had naught to do with one another. Thither were come chiefs from all the Quarters of the land; there had never been such a crowded Thing before, that men could call to mind.

CHAPTER CXXXVII.

OF EYJOLF BOLVERK'S SON.

There was a man named Eyjolf. He was the son of Bolverk, the son of Eyjolf the guileful, of Otterdale. Eyjolf was a man of great rank, and best skilled in law of all men, so that some said he was the third best lawyer in Iceland. He was the fairest in face of all men, tall and strong, and there was the making of a great chief in him. He was greedy of money, like the rest of his kinsfolk.

One day Flosi went to the booth of Bjarni Broddhelgi's son. Bjarni took him by both hands, and sat Flosi down by his side. They talked about many things, and at last Flosi said to Bjarni—

"What counsel shall we now take?"

"I think," answered Bjarni, "that it is now hard to say what to do, but the wisest thing seems to me to go round and ask for help, since they are drawing strength together against you. I will also ask thee, Flosi, whether there be any very good lawyer in your band; for now there are but two courses left; one to ask if they will take an atonement, and that is not a bad choice, but the other is to defend the suit at law, if there be any defence to it, though that will seem to be a bold course; and this is why I think this last ought to be chosen, because ye have hitherto fared high and mightily, and it is unseemly now to take a lower course."

"As to thy asking about lawyers," said Flosi, "I will answer thee at once that there is no such man in our band; nor do I know where to look for one except it be Thorkel Geiti's son, thy kinsman."

"We must not reckon on him," said Bjarni, "for though he knows something of law, he is far too wary, and no man need hope to have him as his shield; but he will back thee as well as any man who backs thee best, for he has a stout heart; besides, I must tell thee that it will be that man's bane who undertakes the defence in this suit for the Burning, but I have no mind that this should befall my kinsman Thorkel, so ye must turn your eyes elsewhither."

Flosi said he knew nothing about who were the best lawyers.

"There is a man named Eyjolf," said Bjarni; "he is Bolverk's son, and he is the best lawyer in the Westfirther's Quarter; but you will need to give him much money if you are to bring him into the suit, but still we must not stop at that. We must also go with our arms to all law business, and be most wary of ourselves, but not meddle with them before we are forced to fight for our lives. And now I will go with thee, and set out at once on our begging for help, for now methinks the peace will be kept but a little while longer."

After that they go out of the booth, and to the booths of the Axefirthers. Then Bjarni talks with Lyting and Bleing, and Hroi Arnstein's son, and he got speedily whatever he asked of them. Then they fared to see Kol, the son of Killing-Skuti, and Eyvind Thorkel's son, the son of Askel the priest, and asked them for their help; but they stood out a long while, but the end of it was that they took three marks of silver for it, and so went into the suit with them.

Then they went to the booths of the men of Lightwater, and stayed there some time. Flosi begged the men of Lightwater for help, but they were stubborn and hard to win over, and then Flosi said, with much wrath, "Ye are ill-behaved! ye are grasping and wrongful at home in your own country, and ye will not help men at the Thing, though they need it. No doubt you will be held up to reproach at the Thing, and very great blame will be laid on you if ye bare not in mind that scorn and those biting words which Skarphedinn hurled at you men of Lightwater."

But on the other hand, Flosi dealt secretly with them, and bade them money for their help, and so coaxed them over with fair words, until it came about that they promised him their aid, and then became so steadfast that they said they would fight for Flosi, if need were.

Then Bjarni said to Flosi—

"Well done! well done! Thou art a mighty chief, and a bold outspoken man, and reckest little what thou sayest to men."

After that they fared away west across the river, and so to the Hladbooth. They saw many men outside before the booth. There was one man who had a scarlet cloak over his shoulders, and a gold band round his head, and an axe studded with silver in his hand.

"This is just right," said Bjarni, "here now is the man I spoke of, Eyjolf Bolverk's son, if thou wilt see him, Flosi."

Then they went to meet Eyjolf, and hailed him. Eyjolf knew Bjarni at once, and greeted him well. Bjarni took Eyjolf by the hand, and led him up into the "Great Rift". Flosi's and Bjarni's men followed after, and Eyjolf's men went also with him. They bade them stay upon the lower brink of the Rift, and look about them, but Flosi, and Bjarni, and Eyjolf went on till they came to where the path leads down from the upper brink of the Rift.

Flosi said it was a good spot to sit down there, for they could see around them far and wide. Then they sat them down there. They were four of them together, and no more.

Then Bjarni spoke to Eyjolf, and said—

"Thee, friend, have we come to see, for we much need thy help in every way."

"Now," said Eyjolf, "there is good choice of men here at the Thing, and ye will not find it hard to fall on those who will be a much greater strength to you than I can be."

"Not so," said Bjarni, "Thou hast many things which show that there is no greater man than thou at the Thing; first of all, that thou art so well-born, as all those men are who are sprung from Ragnar hairybreeks; thy forefathers, too, have always stood first in great suits, both here at the Thing, and at home in their own country, and they have always had the best of it; we think, therefore, it is likely that thou wilt be lucky in winning suits, like thy kinsfolk."

"Thou speakest well, Bjarni," said Eyjolf; "but I think that I have small share in all this that thou sayest."

Then Flosi said—

"There is no need beating about the bush as to what we have in mind. We wish to ask for thy help, Eyjolf, and that thou wilt stand by us in our suits, and go to the court with us, and undertake the defence, if there be any, and plead it for us, and stand by us in all things that may happen at this Thing."

Eyjolf jumped up in wrath, and said that no man had any right to think that he could make a catspaw of him, or drag him on if he had no mind to go himself.

"I see, too, now," he says, "what has led you to utter all those fair words with which ye began to speak to me."

Then Hallbjorn the strong caught hold of him and sate him down by his side, between him and Bjarni, and said—

"No tree falls at the first stroke, friend, but sit here awhile by us."

Then Flosi drew a gold ring off his arm.

"This ring will I give thee, Eyjolf, for thy help and friendship, and so show thee that I will not befool thee. It will be best for thee to take the ring, for there is no man here at the Thing to whom I have ever given such a gift."

The ring was such a good one, and so well made, that it was worth twelve hundred yards of russet stuff.

Hallbjorn drew the ring on Eyjolf's arm; and Eyjolf said—

"It is now most fitting that I should take the ring, since thou behavest so handsomely; and now thou mayest make up thy mind that I will undertake the defence, and do all things needful."

"Now," said Bjarni, "ye behave handsomely on both sides, and here are men well fitted to be witnesses, since I and Hallbjorn are here, that thou hast undertaken the suit."

Then Eyjolf arose, and Flosi too, and they took one another by the hand; and so Eyjolf undertook the whole defence of the suit off Flosi's hands, and so, too, if any suit arose out of the defence, for it often happens that what is a defence in one suit, is a plaintiff's plea in another. So he took upon him all the proofs and proceedings which belonged to those suits, whether they were to be pleaded before the Quarter Court or the Fifth Court. Flosi handed them over in lawful form, and Eyjolf took them in lawful form, and then he said to Flosi and Bjarni.

"Now I have undertaken this defence just as ye asked, but my wish it is that ye should still keep it secret at first; but if the matter comes into the Fifth Court, then be most careful not to say that ye have given goods for my help."

Then Flosi went home to his booth, and Bjarni with him, but Eyjolf went to the booth of Snorri the priest, and sate down by him, and they talked much together.

Snorri the priest caught hold of Eyjolf's arm, and turned up the sleeve, and sees that he had a great ring of gold on his arm. Then Snorri the priest said—

"Pray, was this ring bought or given?"

Eyjolf was put out about it, and had never a word to say. Then Snorri said—

"I see plainly that thou must have taken it as a gift, and may this ring not be thy death!"

Eyjolf jumped up and went away, and would not speak about it; and Snorri said, as Eyjolf arose—

"It is very likely that thou wilt know what kind of gift thou hast taken by the time this Thing is ended."

Then Eyjolf went to his booth.

CHAPTER CXXXVIII.

OF ASGRIM, AND GIZUR, AND KARI.

Now Asgrim Ellidagrim's son talks to Gizur the white, and Kari Solmund's son, and to Hjallti Skeggi's son, Mord Valgard's son, and Thorgeir Craggeir, and says—

"There is no need to have any secrets here, for only those men are by who know all our counsel. Now I will ask you if ye know anything of their plans, for if you do, it seems to me that we must take fresh counsel about our own plans."

"Snorri the priest," answers Gizur the white, "sent a man to me, and bade him tell me that Flosi had gotten great help from the Northlanders; but that Eyjolf Bolverk's son, his kinsman, had had a gold ring given him by some one, and made a secret of it, and Snorri said it was his meaning that Eyjolf Bolverk's son must be meant to defend the suit at law, and that the ring must have been given him for that."

They were all agreed that it must be so. Then Gizur spoke to them—

"Now has Mord Valgard's son, my son-in-law, undertaken a suit, which all must think most hard, to prosecute Flosi; and now my wish is that ye share the other suits amongst you, for now it will soon be time to give notice of the suits at the Hill of Laws. We shall need also to ask for more help."

Asgrim said so it should be, "but we will beg thee to go round with us when we ask for help". Gizur said he would be ready to do that.

After that Gizur picked out all the wisest men of their company to go with him as his backers. There was Hjallti Skeggi's son, and Asgrim, and Kari, and Thorgeir Craggeir.

Then Gizur the white said—

"Now will we first go to the booth of Skapti Thorod's son," and they do so. Gizur the white went first, then Hjallti, then Kari, then Asgrim, then Thorgeir Craggeir, and then his brothers.

They went into the booth. Skapti sat on the cross-bench on the dais, and when he saw Gizur the white he rose up to meet him, and greeted him and all of them well, and bade Gizur to sit down by him, and he does so. Then Gizur said to Asgrim—

"Now shalt thou first raise the question of help with Skapti, but I will throw in what I think good."

"We are come hither," said Asgrim, "for this sake, Skapti, to seek help and aid at thy hand."

"I was thought to be hard to win the last time," said Skapti, "when I would not take the burden of your trouble on me."

"It is quite another matter now," said Gizur. "Now the feud is for master Njal and mistress Bergthora, who were burnt in their own house without a cause, and for Njal's three sons, and many other worthy men, and thou wilt surely never be willing to yield no help to men, or to stand by thy kinsmen and connections."

"It was in my mind," answers Skapti, "when Skarphedinn told me that I had myself borne tar on my own head, and cut up a sod of turf and crept under it, and when he said that I had been so afraid that Thorolf Lopt's son of Eyrar bore me abroad in his ship among his meal-sacks, and so carried me to Iceland, that I would never share in the blood feud for his death."

"Now there is no need to bear such things in mind," said Gizur the white, "for he is dead who said that, and thou wilt surely grant me this, though thou wouldst not do it for other men's sake."

"This quarrel," says Skapti, "is no business of thine, except thou choosest to be entangled in it along with them."

Then Gizur was very wrath, and said—

"Thou art unlike thy father, though he was thought not to be quite clean-handed; yet was he ever helpful to men when they needed him most."

"We are unlike in temper," said Skapti. "Ye two, Asgrim and thou, think that ye have had the lead in mighty deeds; thou, Gizur the white, because thou overcamest Gunnar of Lithend; but Asgrim, for that he slew Gauk, his foster-brother."

"Few," said Asgrim, "bring forward the better if they know the worse, but many would say that I slew not Gauk ere I was driven to it. There is some excuse for thee for not helping us, but none for heaping reproaches on us; and I only wish before this Thing is out that thou mayest get from this suit the greatest disgrace, and that there may be none to make thy shame good."

Then Gizur and his men stood up all of them, and went out, and so on to the booth of Snorri the priest.

Snorri sat on the cross-bench in his booth; they went into the booth, and he knew the men at once, and stood up to meet them, and bade them all welcome, and made room for them to sit by him.

After that, they asked one another the news of the day.

Then Asgrim spoke to Snorri, and said—

"For that am I and my kinsman Gizur come hither, to ask thee for thy help."

"Thou speakest of what thou mayest always be forgiven for asking, for help in the blood-feud after such connections as thou hadst. We, too, got many wholesome counsels from Njal, though few now bear that in mind; but as yet I know not of what ye think ye stand most in need."

"We stand most in need," answers Asgrim, "of brisk lads and good weapons, if we fight them here at the Thing."

"True it is," said Snorri, "that much lies on that, and it is likeliest that ye will press them home with daring, and that they will defend themselves so in likewise, and neither of you will allow the other's right. Then ye will not bear with them and fall on them, and that will be the only way left; for then they will seek to pay you off with shame for manscathe, and with dishonour for loss of kin."

It was easy to see that he goaded them on in everything.

Then Gizur the white said—

"Thou speakest well, Snorri, and thou behavest ever most like a chief when most lies at stake."

"I wish to know," said Asgrim, "in what way thou wilt stand by us if things turn out as thou sayest."

"I will show thee those marks of friendship," said Snorri, "on which all your honour will hang, but I will not go with you to the court. But if ye fight here on the Thing, do not fall on them at all unless ye are all most steadfast and dauntless, for you have great champions against you. But if ye are overmatched, ye must let yourselves be driven hither towards us, for I shall then have drawn up my men in array hereabouts, and shall be ready to stand by you. But if it falls out otherwise, and they give way before you, my meaning is that they will try to run for a stronghold in the 'Great Rift'. But if they come thither, then ye will never get the better of them. Now I will take that on my hands, to draw up my men there, and guard the pass to the stronghold, but we will not follow them whether they turn north or south along the river. And when you have slain out of their band about as many as I think ye will be able to pay blood-fines for, and yet keep your priesthoods and abodes, then I will run up with all my men and part you. Then ye shall promise to do us I bid you, and stop the battle, if I on my part do what I have now promised."

Gizur thanked him kindly, and said that what he had said was just what they all needed, and then they all went out.

"Whither shall we go now?" said Gizur.

"To the Northlanders' booth," said Asgrim.

Then they fared thither.

CHAPTER CXXXIX.

OF ASGRIM AND GUDMUND.

And when they came into the booth then they saw where Gudmund the powerful sate and talked with Einer Conal's son, his foster-child; he was a wise man.

Then they come before him, and Gudmund welcomed them very heartily, and made them clear the booth for them, that they might all be able to sit down.

Then they asked what tidings, and Asgrim said—

"There is no need to mutter what I have to say. We wish, Gudmund, to ask for thy steadfast help."

"Have ye seen any other chiefs before?" said Gudmund.

They said they had been to see Skapti Thorod's son and Snorri the priest, and told him quietly how they had fared with each of them.

Then Gudmund said—

"Last time I behaved badly and meanly to you. Then I was stubborn, but now ye shall drive your bargain with me all the more quickly because I was more stubborn then, and now I will go myself with you to the court with all my Thingmen, and stand by you in all such things as I can, and fight for you though this be needed, and lay down my life for your lives. I will also pay Skapti out in this way, that Thorstein gapemouth his son shall be in the battle on our side, for he will not dare to do aught else than I will, since he has Jodisa my daughter to wife, and then Skapti will try to part us."

They thanked him, and talked with him long and low afterwards, so that no other men could hear.

Then Gudmund bade them not to go before the knees of any other chiefs, for he said that would be little-hearted.

"We will now run the risk with the force that we have. Ye must go with your weapons to all law-business, but not fight as things stand."

Then they went all of them home to their booths, and all this was at first with few men's knowledge.

So now the Thing goes on.

CHAPTER CXL.

OF THE DECLARATIONS OF THE SUITS.

It was one day that men went to the Hill of Laws, and the chiefs were so placed that Asgrim Ellidagrim's son, and Gizur the white, and Gudmund the powerful, and Snorri the priest, were on the upper hand by the Hill of Laws; but the Eastfirthers stood down below.

Mord Valgard's son stood next to Gizur his father-in-law; he was of all men the readiest-tongued.

Gizur told him that he ought to give notice of the suit for manslaughter, and bade him speak up, so that all might hear him well.

Then Mord took witness and said—"I take witness to this that I give notice of an assault laid down by law against Flosi Thord's son, for that he rushed at Helgi Njal's son and dealt him a brain, or a body, or a marrow wound, which proved a death-wound, and from which Helgi got his death. I say that in this suit he ought to be made a guilty man, an outlaw, not to be fed, not to be forwarded, not to be helped or harboured in any need. I say that all his goods are forfeited, half to me, and half to the men of the Quarter, who have a right by law to take his forfeited goods. I give notice of this suit for manslaughter in the Quarter Court into which this suit ought by law to come. I give notice of this lawful notice; I give notice in the hearing of all men on the Hill of Laws; I give notice of this suit to be pleaded this summer, and of full outlawry against Flosi Thord's son; I give notice of a suit which Thorgeir Thorir's son has handed over to me."

Then a great shout was uttered at the Hill of Laws, that Mord spoke well and boldly.

Then Mord begun to speak a second time.

"I take you to witness to this," says he, "that I give notice of a suit against Flosi Thord's son, I give notice for that he wounded Helgi Njal's son with a brain, or a body, or a marrow wound, which proved a death-wound, and from which Helgi got his death on that spot where Flosi Thord's son had first rushed on Helgi Njal's son with an assault laid down by law. I say that thou, Flosi, ought to be made in this suit a guilty man, an outlaw, not to be fed, not to be forwarded, not to he helped or harboured in any need. I say that all thy goods are forfeited, half to me and half to the men of the Quarter, who have a right by law to take the goods which have been forfeited by thee. I give notice of this suit in the Quarter Court into which it ought by law to come; I give notice of this lawful notice; I give notice of it in the hearing of all men on the Hill of Laws; I give notice of this suit to be pleaded this summer, and of full outlawry against Flosi Thord's son, I give notice of the suit which Thorgeir Thorir's son hath handed over to me."

After that Mord sat him down.

Flosi listened carefully, but said never a word the while.

Then Thorgeir Craggeir stood up and took witness, and said—"I take witness to this, that I give notice of a suit against Glum Hilldir's son, in that he took firing and lit it, and bore it to the house at Bergthorsknoll, when they were burned inside it, to wit, Njal Thorgeir's son, and Bergthora Skarphedinn's daughter, and all those other men who were burned inside it there and then. I say that in this suit he ought to be made a guilty man, an outlaw, not to be fed, not to be forwarded, not to be helped or harboured in any need. I say that all his goods are forfeited, half to me, and half to the men of the Quarter, who have a right by law to take his forfeited goods; I give notice of this suit in the Quarter Court into which it ought by law to come. I give notice in the hearing of all men on the Hill of Laws. I give notice of this suit to be pleaded this summer, and of full outlawry against Glum Hilldir's son."

Kari Solmund's son declared his suits against Kol Thorstein's son, and Gunnar Lambi's son, and Grani Gunnar's son, and it was the common talk of men that he spoke wondrous well.

Thorleif crow declared his suit against all the sons of Sigfus, but Thorgrim the big, his brother, against Modolf Kettle's son, and Lambi Sigurd's son, and Hroar Hamond's son, brother of Leidolf the strong.

Asgrim Ellidagrim's son declared his suit against Leidolf and Thorstein Geirleif's son. Arni Kol's son, and Grim the red.

And they all spoke well.

After that other men gave notice of their suits, and it was far on in the day that it went on so.

Then men fared home to their booths.

Eyjolf Bolverk's son went to his booth with Flosi; they passed east around the booth, and Flosi said to Eyjolf—

"See'st thou any defence in these suits?"

"None," says Eyjolf.

"What counsel is now to be taken?" says Flosi.

"I will give thee a piece of advice," said Eyjolf. "Now thou shalt hand over thy priesthood to thy brother Thorgeir, but declare that thou hast joined the Thing of Askel the priest the son of Thorkettle, north away in Reykiardale; but if they do not know this, then may be that this will harm them, for they will be sure to plead their suit in the Eastfirther's court, but they ought to plead it in the Northlanders' court, and they will overlook that, and it is a Fifth Court matter against them if they plead their suit in another court than that in which they ought, and then we will take that suit up, but not until we have no other choice left."

"May be," said Flosi, "that we shall get the worth of the ring."

"I don't know that," says Eyjolf; "but I will stand by thee at law, so that men shall say that there never was a better defence. Now, we must send for Askel, but Thorgeir shall come to thee at once, and a man with him."

A little while after Thorgeir came, and then he took on him Flosi's leadership and priesthood.

By that time Askel was come thither too, and then Flosi declared that he had joined his Thing, and this was with no man's knowledge save theirs.

Now all is quiet till the day when the courts were to go out to try suits.

CHAPTER CXLI.

NOW MEN GO TO THE COURTS.

Now the time passes away till the courts were to go out to try suits. Both sides then made them ready to go thither, and armed them. Each side put war-tokens on their helmets.

Then Thorhall Asgrim's son said—

"Walk hastily in nothing, father mine, and do everything as lawfully and rightly as ye can, but if ye fall into any strait let me know as quickly as ye can, and then I will give you counsel."

Asgrim and the others looked at him, and his face was as though it were all blood, but great teardrops gushed out of his eyes. He bade them bring him his spear, that had been a gift to him from Skarphedinn, and it was the greatest treasure.

Asgrim said as they went away—

"Our kinsman Thorhall was not easy in his mind as we left him behind in the booth, and I know not what he will be at."

Then Asgrim said again—

"Now we will go to Mord Valgard's son, and think of naught else but the suit, for there is more sport in Flosi than in very many other men."

Then Asgrim sent a man to Gizur the white, and Hjallti Skeggi's son, and Gudmund the powerful. Now they all came together, and went straight to the court of Eastfirthers. They went to the court from the south, but Flosi and all the Eastfirthers with him went to it from the north. There were also the men of Reykdale and the Axefirthers with Flosi. There, too, was Eyjolf Bolverk's son. Flosi looked at Eyjolf, and said—

"All now goes fairly, and may be that it will not be far off from thy guess."

"Keep thy peace about it," says Eyjolf, "and then we shall be sure to gain our point."

Now Mord took witness, and bade all those men who had suits of outlawry before the court to cast lots who should first plead or declare his suit, and who next, and who last; he bade them by a lawful bidding before the court, so that the judges heard it. Then lots were cast as to the declarations, and he, Mord, drew the lot to declare his suit first.

Now Mord Valgard's son took witness the second time, and said—

"I take witness to this, that I except all mistakes in words in my pleading, whether they be too many or wrongly spoken, and I claim the right to amend all my words until I have put them into proper lawful shape. I take witness to myself of this."

Again Mord said—

"I take witness to this, that I bid Flosi Thord's son, or any other man who has undertaken the defence made over to him by Flosi, to listen for him to my oath, and to my declaration of my suit, and to all the proofs and proceedings which I am about to bring forward against him; I bid him by a lawful bidding before the court, so that the judges may hear it across the court."

Again Mord Valgard's son said—

"I take witness to this, that I take an oath on the book, a lawful until, and I say it before God, that I will so plead this suit in the most truthful, and most just, and most lawful way, so far as I know; and that I will bring forward all my proofs in due form, and utter them faithfully so long as I am in this suit."

After that he spoke in these words—

"I have called Thorodd as my first witness, and Thorbjorn as my second; I have called them to bear witness that I gave notice of an assault laid down by law against Flosi Thord's son, on that spot where he, Flosi Thord's son, rushed with an assault laid down by law on Helgi Njal's son, when Flosi Thord's son, wounded Helgi Njal's son with a brain, or a body, or a marrow wound, which proved a death-wound, and from which Helgi got his death. I said that he ought to be made in this suit a guilty man, an outlaw, not to be fed, not to be forwarded, not to he helped or harboured in any need; I said that all his goods were forfeited, half to me and half to the men of the Quarter who have the right by law to take the goods which he has forfeited; I gave notice of the suit in the Quarter Court into which the suit ought by law to come; I gave notice of that lawful notice; I gave notice in the hearing of all men at the Hill of Laws; I gave notice of this suit to be pleaded now this summer, and of full outlawry against Flosi Thord's son. I gave notice of a suit which Thorgeir Thorir's son had handed heard it. Then lots were cast as to the declarations, and he, Mord, drew the lot to declare his suit first".

Now Mord Valgard's son took witness the second time, and said—

"I take witness to this, that I except all mistakes in words in my pleading, whether they be too many or wrongly spoken, and I claim the right to amend all my words until I have put them into proper lawful shape. I take witness to myself of this."

Again Mord said—

"I take witness to this, that I bid Flosi Thord's son, or any other man who has undertaken the defence made over to him by Flosi, to listen for him to my oath, and to my declaration of my suit, and to all the proofs and proceedings which I am about to bring forward against him; I bid him by a lawful bidding before the court, so that the judges may hear it across the court."

Again Mord Valgard's son said—

"I take witness to this, that I take an oath on the book, a lawful oath, and I say it before God, that I will so plead this suit in the most truthful, and most just, and most lawful way, so far as I know; and that I will bring forward all my proofs in due form, and utter them faithfully so long as I am in this suit."

After that he spoke in these words—

"I have called Thorodd as my first witness, and Thorbjorn as my second; I have called them to bear witness that I gave notice of an assault laid down by law against Flosi Thord's son, on that spot where he, Flosi Thord's son, rushed with an assault laid down by law on Helgi Njal's son, when Flosi Thord's son, wounded Helgi Njal's son with a brain, or a body, or a marrow wound, which proved a death-wound, and from which Helgi got his death. I said that he ought to be made in this suit a guilty man, an outlaw, not to be fed, not to be forwarded, not to be helped or harboured in any need; I said that all his goods were forfeited, half to me and half to the men of the Quarter who have the right by law to take the goods which he has forfeited; I gave notice of the suit in the Quarter Court into which the suit ought by law to come; I gave notice of that lawful notice; I gave notice in the hearing of all men at the Hill of Laws; I gave notice of this suit to be pleaded now this summer, and of full outlawry against Flosi Thord's son. I gave notice of a suit which Thorgeir Thorir's son had handed over to me; and I had all these words in my notice which I have now used in this declaration of my suit. I now declare this suit of outlawry in this shape before the court of the Eastfirthers over the head of John, as I uttered it when I gave notice of it."

Then Mord spoke again—

"I have called Thorodd as my first witness, and Thorbjorn as my second. I have called them to bear witness that I gave notice of a suit against Flosi Thord's son for that he wounded Helgi Njal's son with a brain, or a body, or a marrow wound, which proved a death-wound, and from which Helgi got his death. I said that he ought to be made in this suit a guilty man, an outlaw, not he fed, not to be forwarded, not to be helped or harboured in any need; I said that all his goods were forfeited, half to me and half to the men of the Quarter who have the right by law to take the goods which he has forfeited; I gave notice of the suit in the Quarter Court into which the suit ought by law to come; I gave notice of that lawful notice; I gave notice in the hearing of all men at the Hill of Laws; I gave notice of this suit to be pleaded now this summer, and of full outlawry against Flosi Thord's son. I gave notice of a suit which Thorgeir Thorir's son had handed over to me; and I had all these words in my notice which I have now used in this declaration of my suit. I now declare this suit of outlawry in this shape before the court of the Eastfirthers over the head of John, as I uttered it when I gave notice of it."

Then Mord's witnesses to the notice came before the court, and spake so that one uttered their witness, but both confirmed it by their common consent in this form, "I bear witness that Mord called Thorodd as his first witness, and me as his second, and my name is Thorbjorn"—then he named his father's name—"Mord called us two as his witnesses that he gave notice of an assault laid down by law against Flosi Thord's son when he rushed on Helgi Njal's son, in that spot where Flosi Thord's son dealt Helgi Njal's son a brain, or a body, or a marrow wound, that proved a death-wound, and from which Helgi got his death. He said that Flosi ought to be made in this suit a guilty man, an outlaw, not to be fed, not to be forwarded, not to be helped or harboured by any man; he said that all his goods were forfeited, half to himself and half to the men of the Quarter who have the right by law to take the goods which he had forfeited; he gave notice of the suit in the Quarter Court into which the suit ought by law to come; he gave notice of that lawful notice; he gave notice in the hearing of all men at the Hill of Laws; he gave notice of this suit to be pleaded now this summer, and of full outlawry against Flosi Thord's son. He gave notice of a suit which Thorgeir Thorir's son had handed over to him. He used all those words in his notice which he used in the declaration of his suit, and which we have used in bearing witness; we have now borne our witness rightly and lawfully, and we are agreed in bearing it; we bear this witness in this shape before the Eastfirthers' Court over the head of John,[75] as Mord uttered it when he gave his notice."

A second time they bore their witness of the notice before the court, and put the wounds first and the assault last, and used all the same words as before, and bore their witness in this shape before the Eastfirthers' Court just as Mord uttered them when he gave his notice.

Then Mord's witnesses to the handing over of the suit went before the court, and one uttered their witness, and both confirmed it by common consent, and spoke in these words—"That those two, Mord Valgard's son and Thorgeir Thorir's son, took them to witness that Thorgeir Thorir's son handed over a suit for manslaughter to Mord Valgard's son against Flosi Thord's son for the laying of Helgi Njal's son; he handed over to him then the suit, with all the proofs and proceedings which belonged to the suit, he handed it over to him to plead and to settle, and to make use of all rights as though he were the rightful next of kin; Thorgeir handed it over lawfully, and Mord took it lawfully".

They bore this witness of the handing over of the suit in this shape before the Eastfirthers' Court over the head of John, just as Mord or Thorgeir had called them as witnesses to prove.

They made all these witnesses swear an oath ere they bore witness, and the judges too.

Again Mord Valgard's son took witness.

"I take witness to this," said he, "that I bid those nine neighbours whom I summoned when I laid this suit against Flosi Thord's son, to take their seats west on the river-bank, and I call on the defendant to challenge this inquest, I call on him by a lawful bidding before the court so that the judges may hear."

Again Mord took witness.

"I take witness to this, that I bid Flosi Thord's son, or that other man who has the defence handed over to him, to challenge the inquest which I have caused to take their seats west on the river-bank. I bid thee by a lawful bidding before the court so that the judges may hear."

Again Mord took witness.

"I take witness to this, that now are all the first steps and proofs brought forward which belong to the suit. Summons to hear my oath, oath taken, suit declared, witness borne to the notice, witness borne to the handing over of the suit, the neighbours on the inquest bidden to take their seats, and the defendant bidden to challenge the inquest. I take this witness to these steps and proofs which are now brought forward, and also to this that I shall not be thought to have left the suit though I go away from the court to look up proofs, or on other business."

Now Flosi and his men went thither where the neighbours on the inquest sate.

Then Flosi said to his men—

"The sons of Sigfus must know best whether these are the rightful neighbours to the spot who are here summoned."

Kettle of the Mark answered—

"Here is that neighbour who held Mord at the font when he was baptised, but another is his second cousin by kinship."

Then they reckoned up his kinship, and proved it with an oath.

Then Eyjolf took witness that the inquest should do nothing till it was challenged.

A second time Eyjolf took witness—

"I take witness to this," said he, "that I challenge both these men out of the inquest, and set them aside"—here he named them by name, and their fathers as well—"for this sake, that one of them is Mord's second cousin by kinship, but the other for gossipry,[76] for which sake it is lawful to challenge a neighbour on the inquest; ye two are for a lawful reason incapable of uttering a finding, for now a lawful challenge has overtaken you, therefore I challenge and set you aside by the rightful custom of pleading at the Althing, and by the law of the land; I challenge you in the cause which Flosi Thord's son has handed over to me."

Now all the people spoke out, and said that Mord's suit had come to naught, and all were agreed in this that the defence was better than the prosecution.

Then Asgrim said to Mord—

"The day is not yet their own, though they think now that they have gained a great step; but now some one shall go to see Thorhall my son, and know what advice he gives us."

Then a trusty messenger was sent to Thorhall, and told him as plainly as he could how far the suit had gone, and how Flosi and his men thought they had brought the finding of the inquest to a dead lock.

"I will so make it out," says Thorhall, "that this shall not cause you to lose the suit; and tell them not to believe it, though quirks and quibbles be brought against them, for that wiseacre Eyjolf has now overlooked something. But now thou shalt go back as quickly as thou canst, and say that Mord Valgard's son must go before the court, and take witness that their challenge has come to naught," and then he told him step by step how they must proceed.

The messenger came and told them Thorhall's advice.

Then Mord Valgard's son went to the court and took witness. "I take witness to this," said he, "that I make Eyjolf's challenge void and of none effect; and my ground is, that he challenged them not for their kinship to the true plaintiff, the next of kin, but for their kinship to him who pleaded the suit; I take this witness to myself, and to all those to whom this witness will be of use."

After that he brought that witness before the court.

Now he went whither the neighbours sate on the inquest, and bade those to sit down again who had risen up, and said they were rightly called on to share in the finding of the inquest.

Then all said that Thorhall had done great things, and all thought the prosecution better than the defence.

Then Flosi said to Eyjolf—"Thinkest thou that this is good law?"

"I think so, surely," he says, "and beyond a doubt we overlooked this; but still we will have another trial of strength with them."

Then Eyjolf took witness. "I take witness to this," said he, "that I challenge these two men out of the inquest"—here he named them both—"for that sake that they are lodgers, but not householders; I do not allow you two to sit on the inquest, for now a lawful challenge has overtaken you; I challenge you both and set you aside out of the inquest, by the rightful custom of the Althing and by the law of the land."

Now Eyjolf said he was much mistaken if that could be shaken; and then all said that the defence was better than the prosecution.

Now all men praised Eyjolf, and said there was never a man who could cope with him in lawcraft.

Mord Valgard's son and Asgrim Ellidagrim's son now sent a man to Thorhall to tell him how things stood; but when Thorhall heard that, he asked what goods they owned, or if they were paupers?

The messenger said that one gained his livelihood by keeping milch-kine, and "he has both cows and ewes at his abode; but the other has a third of the land which he and the freeholder farm, and finds his own food; and they have one hearth between them, he and the man who lets the land, and one shepherd".

Then Thorhall said—

"They will fare now as before, for they must have made a mistake, and I will soon upset their challenge, and this though Eyjolf had used such big words that it was law."

Now Thorhall told the messenger plainly, step by step, how they must proceed; and the messenger came back and told Mord and Asgrim all the counsel that Thorhall bad given.

Then Mord went to the court and took witness, "I take witness to this, that I bring to naught Eyjolf Bolverk's son's challenge, for that he has challenged those men out of the inquest who have a lawful right to lie there; every man has a right to sit on an inquest of neighbours, who owns three hundreds in land or more, though he may have no dairy-stock; and he too has the same right who lives by dairy-stock worth the same sum, though he leases no land."

Then he brought this witness before the court, and then he went whither the neighbours on the inquest were, and bade them sit down, and said they were rightfully among the inquest.

Then there was a great shout and cry, and then all men said that Flosi's and Eyjolf's cause was much shaken, and now men were of one mind as to this, that the prosecution was better than the defence.

Then Flosi said to Eyjolf—

"Can this be law?"

Eyjolf said he had not wisdom enough to know that for a surety, and then they sent a man to Skapti, the Speaker of the Law, to ask whether it were good law, and he sent them back word that it was surely good law, though few knew it.

Then this was told to Flosi, and Eyjolf Bolverk's son asked the sons of Sigfus as to the other neighbours who were summoned thither.

They said there were four of them who were wrongly summoned; "for those sit now at home who were nearer neighbours to the spot".

Then Eyjolf took witness that he challenged all those four men out of the inquest, and that he did it with lawful form of challenge. After that he said to the neighbours—

"Ye are bound to render lawful justice to both sides, and now ye shall go before the court when ye are called, and take witness that ye find that bar to uttering your finding; that ye are but five summoned to utter your finding, but that ye ought to be nine; and now Thorhall may prove and carry his point in every suit, if he can cure this flaw in this suit."

And now it was plain in everything that Flosi and Eyjolf were very boastful; and there was a great cry that now the suit for the Burning was quashed, and that again the defence was better than the prosecution.

Then Asgrim spoke to Mord—

"They know not yet of what to boast ere we have seen my son Thorhall. Njal told me that he had so taught Thorhall law, that he would turn out the best lawyer in Iceland when ever it were put to the proof."

Then a man was sent to Thorhall to tell him how things stood, and of Flosi's and Eyjolf's boasting, and the cry of the people that the suit for the Burning was quashed in Mord's bands.

"It will be well for them," says Thorhall, "if they get not disgrace from this. Thou shalt go and tell Mord to take witness, and swear an oath, that the greater part of the inquest is rightly summoned, and then he shall bring that witness before the court, and then he may set the prosecution on its feet again; but he will have to pay a fine of three marks for every man that he has wrongly summoned; but he may not be prosecuted for that at this Thing; and now thou shalt go back."

He does so, and told Mord and Asgrim all, word for word, that Thorhall had said.

Then Mord went to the court, and took witness, and swore an oath that the greater part of the inquest was rightly summoned, and said then that he had set the prosecution on its feet again, and then he went on, "and so our foes shall have honour from something else than from this, that we have here taken a great false step".

Then there was a great roar that Mord handled the suit well; but it was said that Flosi and his men betook them only to quibbling and wrong.

Flosi asked Eyjolf if this could be good law, but he said he could not surely tell, but said the Lawman must settle this knotty point.

Then Thorkel Geiti's son went on their behalf to tell the Lawman how things stood, and asked whether this were good law that Mord had said.

"More men are great lawyers now," says Skapti, "than I thought I must tell thee, then, that this is such good law in all points, that there is not a word to say against it; but still I thought that I alone would know this, now that Njal was dead, for he was the only man I ever knew who knew it."

Then Thorkel went back to Flosi and Eyjolf, and said that this was good law.

Then Mord Valgard's son went to the court and took witness. "I take witness to this," he said, "that I bid those neighbours on the inquest in the suit which I set on foot against Flosi Thord's son now to utter their finding, and to find it either against him or for him; I bid them by a lawful bidding before the court, so that the judges may bear it across the court."

Then the neighbours on Mord's inquest went to the court, and one uttered their finding, but all confirmed it by their consent; and they spoke thus, word for word—

"Mord Valgard's son summoned nine of us thanes on this inquest, but here we stand five of us, but four have been challenged and set aside, and now witness has been borne as to the absence of the four who ought to have uttered this finding along with us, and now we are bound by law to utter our finding. We were summoned to bear this witness, whether Flosi Thord's son rushed with an assault laid down by law on Helgi Njal's son, on that spot where Flosi Thord's son wounded Helgi Njal's son with a brain, or a body, or a marrow wound, which proved a death wound, and from which Helgi got his death. He summoned us to utter all those words which it was lawful for us to utter, and which he should call on us to answer before the court, and which belong to this suit; he summoned us, so that we heard what he said; he summoned us in a suit which Thorgeir Thorir's son had handed over to him, and now we have all sworn an oath, and found our lawful finding, and are all agreed, and we utter our finding against Flosi, and we say that he is truly guilty in this suit. We nine men on this inquest of neighbours so shapen, utter this our finding before the Eastfirthers' Court over the head of John, as Mord summoned us to do; but this is the finding of all of us."

Again a second time they uttered their finding against Flosi, and uttered it first about the wounds, and last about the assault, but all their other words they uttered just as they had before uttered their finding against Flosi, and brought him in truly guilty in the suit.

Then Mord Valgard's son went before the court, and took witness that those neighbours whom he had summoned in the suit which he had set on foot against Flosi Thord's son had now uttered their finding, and brought him in truly guilty in the suit; he took witness to this for his own part, or for those who might wish to make use of this witness.

Again a second time Mord took witness and said—

"I take witness to this that I call on Flosi, or that man who has to undertake the lawful defence which he has handed over to him, to begin his defence to this suit which I have set on foot against him, for now all the steps and proofs have been brought forward which belong by law to this suit; all witness borne, the finding of the inquest uttered and brought in, witness taken to the finding, and to all the steps which have gone before; but if any such thing arises in their lawful defence which

I need to turn into a suit against them, then I claim the right to set that suit on foot against them. I bid this my lawful bidding before the court, so that the judges may hear."

"It gladdens me now, Eyjolf," said Flosi, "in my heart to think what a wry face they will make, and how their pates will tingle when thou bringest forward our defence."

CHAPTER CXLII.

OF EYJOLF BOLVERK'S SON.

Then Eyjolf Bolverk's son went before the court, and took witness to this—

"I take witness that this is a lawful defence in this cause, that ye have pleaded the suit in the Eastfirthers' Court, when ye ought to have pleaded it in the Northlanders' Court; for Flosi has declared himself one of the Thingmen of Askel the priest; and here now are those two witnesses who were by, and who will bear witness that Flosi handed over his priesthood to his brother Thorgeir, but afterwards declared himself one of Askel the priest's Thingmen. I take witness to this for my own part, and for those who may need to make use of it."

Again Eyjolf took witness—"I take witness," he said, "to this, that I bid Mord who pleads this suit, or the next of kin, to listen to my oath, and to my declaration of the defence which I am about to bring forward; I bid him by a lawful bidding before the court, so that the judges may hear me".

Again Eyjolf took witness—

"I take witness to this, that I swear an oath on the book, a lawful oath, and say it before God, that I will so defend this cause, in the most truthful, and most just, and most lawful way, so far as I know, and so fulfil all lawful duties which belong to me at this Thing."

Then Eyjolf said—

"These two men I take to witness that I bring forward this lawful defence that this suit was pleaded in another Quarter Court, than that in which it ought to have been pleaded; and I say that for this sake their suit has come to naught; I utter this defence in this shape before the Eastfirthers' Court."

After that he let all the witness be brought forward which belonged to the defence, and then he took witness to all the steps in the defence to prove that they had all been duly taken.

After that Eyjolf again took witness and said—

"I take witness to this, that I forbid the judges, by a lawful protest before the priest, to utter judgment in the suit of Mord and his friends, for now a lawful defence has been brought before the court. I forbid you by a protest made before a priest; by a full, fair, and binding protest; as I have a right to forbid you by the common custom of the Althing, and by the law of the land."

After that he called on the judges to pronounce for the defence.

Then Asgrim and his friends brought on the other suits for the Burning, and those suits took their course.

CHAPTER CXLIII.

THE COUNSEL OF THORHALL ASGRIM'S SON.

Now Asgrim and his friends sent a man to Thorhall, and let him be told in what a strait they had come.

"Too far off was I now," answers Thorhall, "for this cause might still not have taken this turn if I had been by. I now see their course that they must mean to summon you to the Fifth Court for contempt of the Thing. They must also mean to divide the Eastfirthers' Court in the suit for the Burning, so that no judgment may be given, for now they behave so as to show that they will stay at no ill. Now shalt thou go back to them as quickly as thou canst, and say that Mord must summon them both, both Flosi and Eyjolf, for having brought money into the Fifth Court, and make it a case of lesser outlawry. Then he shall summon them with a second summons for that they have brought forward that witness which had nothing to do with their cause, and so were guilty of contempt of the Thing; and tell them that I say this, that if two suits for lesser outlawry hang over one and the same man, that he shall be adjudged a thorough outlaw at once. And for this ye must set your suits on foot first, that then ye will first go to trial and judgment."

Now the messenger went his way back and told Mord and Asgrim.

After that they went to the Hill of Laws, and Mord Valgard's son took witness.

"I take witness to this that I summon Flosi Thord's son, for that he gave money for his help here at the Thing to Eyjolf Bolverk's son. I say that he ought on this charge to be made a guilty outlaw, for this sake alone to be forwarded or to be allowed the right of frithstow [sanctuary], if his fine and bail are brought forward at the execution levied on his house and goods, but else to become a thorough outlaw. I say all his goods are forfeited, half to me and half to the men of the Quarter who have the right by law to take his goods after he has been outlawed. I summon this cause before the Fifth Court, whither the cause ought to come by law; I summon it to be pleaded now and to full outlawry. I summon with a lawful summons. I summon in the hearing of all men at the Hill of Laws."

With a like summons he summoned Eyjolf Bolverk's son, for that he had taken and received the money, and he summoned him for that sake to the Fifth Court.

Again a second time he summoned Flosi and Eyjolf, for that sake that they had brought forward that witness at the Thing which had nothing lawfully to do with the cause of the parties, and had so been guilty of contempt of the Thing; and he laid the penalty for that at lesser outlawry.

Then they went away to the Court of Laws, there the Fifth Court was then set.

Now when Mord and Asgrim had gone away, then the judges in the Eastfirthers' Court could not agree how they should give judgment, for some of them wished to give judgment for Flosi, but some for Mord and Asgrim. Then Flosi and Eyjolf tried to divide the court, and there they stayed, and lost time over that while the summoning at the Hill of Laws was going on. A little while after Flosi and Eyjolf were told that they had been summoned at the Hill of Laws into the Fifth Court, each of them with two summons. Then Eyjolf said—

"In an evil hour have we loitered here while they have been before us in quickness of summoning. Now hath come out Thorhall's cunning, and no man is his match in wit. Now they have the first right to plead their cause before the court, and that was everything for them; but still we will go to the Hill of Laws, and set our suit on foot against them, though that will now stand us in little stead."

Then they fared to the Hill of Laws, and Eyjolf summoned them for contempt of the Thing.

After that they went to the Fifth Court.

Now we must say that when Mord and Asgrim came to the Fifth Court, Mord took witness and bade them listen to his oath and the declaration of his suit, and to all those proofs and steps which he meant to bring forward against Flosi and Eyjolf. He bade them by a lawful bidding before the court, so that the judges could hear him across the court.

In the Fifth Court vouchers had to follow the oaths of the parties, and they had to take an oath after them.

Mord took witness.

"I take witness," he said, "to this, that I take a Fifth Court oath. I pray God so to help me in this light and in the next, as I shall plead this suit as I know to be most truthful, and just, and lawful. I believe with all my heart that Flosi is truly guilty in this suit, if I may bring forward my proofs; and I have not brought money into this court in this suit, and I will not bring it. I have not taken money, and I will not take it, neither for a lawful nor for an unlawful end."

The men who were Mord's vouchers then went two of them before the court, and took witness to this—

"We take witness that we take an oath on the book, a lawful oath; we pray God so to help us two in this light and in the next, as we lay it on our honour that we believe with all our hearts that Mord will so plead this suit as he knows to be most truthful, and most just, and most lawful, and that he hath not brought money into this court in this suit to help himself, and that he will not offer it, and that he hath not taken money, nor will he take it, either for a lawful or unlawful end."

Mord had summoned nine neighbours who lived next to the Thingfield on the inquest in the suit, and then Mord took witness, and declared those four suits which he had set on foot against Flosi and Eyjolf; and Mord used all those words in his declaration that he had used in his summons. He declared his suits for outlawry in the same shape before the Fifth Court as he had uttered them when he summoned the defendants.

Mord took witness, and bade those nine neighbours on the inquest to take their seats west on the river-bank.

Mord took witness again, and bade Flosi and Eyjolf to challenge the inquest.

They went up to challenge the inquest, and looked narrowly at them, but could get none of them set aside; then they went away as things stood, and were very ill pleased with their case.

Then Mord took witness, and bade those nine neighbours whom he had before called on the inquest, to utter their finding, and to bring it in either for or against Flosi.

Then the neighbours on Mord's inquest came before the court, and one uttered the finding, but all the rest confirmed it by their consent. They had all taken the Fifth Court oath, and they brought in Flosi as truly guilty in the suit, and brought in their finding against him. They brought it in in such a shape before the Fifth Court over the head of the same man over whose head Mord had already declared his suit. After that they brought in all those findings which they were bound to bring in in all the other suits, and all was done in lawful form.

Eyjolf Bolverk's son and Flosi watched to find a flaw in the proceedings, but could get nothing done.

Then Mord Valgard's son took witness. "I take witness," said he, "to this, that these nine neighbours whom I called on these suits which I have had hanging over the heads of Flosi Thord's son, and Eyjolf Bolverk's son, have now uttered their finding, and have brought them in truly guilty in these suits."

He took this witness for his own part.

Again Mord took witness.

"I take witness," he said, "to this, that I bid Flosi Thord's son, or that other man who has taken his lawful defence in hand, now to begin their defence; for now all the steps and proofs have been brought forward in the suit, summons to listen to oaths, oaths taken, suit declared, witness taken to the summons, neighbours called on to take their seats on the inquest, defendant called on to challenge the inquest, finding uttered, witness taken to the finding."

He took this witness to all the steps that had been taken in the suit.

Then that man stood up over whose head the suit had been declared and pleaded, and summed up the case. He summed up first how Mord had bade them listen to his oath, and to his declaration of the suit, and to all the steps and proofs in it; then he summed up next how Mord took his oath and his vouchers theirs; then he summed up how Mord pleaded his suit, and used the very words in his summing up that Mord had before used in declaring and pleading his suit, and which he had used in his summons, and he said that the suit came before the Fifth Court in the same shape as it was when he uttered it at the summoning. Then he summed up that men had borne witness to the summoning, and repeated all those words that Mord had used in his summons, and which they had used in bearing their witness, "and which I now," he said, "have used in my summing up, and they bore their witness in the same shape before the Fifth Court as he uttered them at the summoning". After that he summed up that Mord bade the neighbours on the inquest to take their seats, then he told next of all how he bade Flosi to challenge the inquest, or that man who had undertaken this lawful defence for him; then he told how the neighbours went to the court, and uttered their finding, and brought in Flosi truly guilty in the suit, and how they brought in the finding of an inquest of nine men in that shape before the Fifth Court. Then he summed up how Mord took witness to all the steps in the suit, and how he had bidden the defendant to begin his defence.

After that Mord Valgard's son took witness. "I take witness," he said, "to this, that I forbid Flosi Thord's son, or that other man who has undertaken the lawful defence for him, to set up his defence; for now are all the steps taken which belong to the suit, when the case has been summed up and the proofs repeated."

After that the foreman added these words of Mord to his summing up.

Then Mord took witness, and prayed the judges to give judgment in this suit.

Then Gizur the white said, "Thou wilt have to do more yet, Mord, for four twelves can have no right to pass judgment."

Now Flosi said to Eyjolf, "What counsel is to be taken now?"

Then Eyjolf said, "Now we must make the best of a bad business; but still, we will bide our time, for now I guess that they will make a false step in their suit, for Mord prayed for judgment at once in the suit, but they ought to call and set aside six men out of the court, and after that they ought to offer us to call and set aside six other men, but we will not do that, for then they ought to call and set aside those six men, and they will perhaps overlook that; then all their case has come to naught if they do not do that, for three twelves have to judge in every cause".

"Thou art a wise man, Eyjolf," said Flosi, "so that few can come nigh thee."

Mord Valgard's son took witness.

"I take witness," he said, "to this, that I call and set aside these six men out of the court"—and named them all by name—"I do not allow you to sit in the court; I call you out and set you aside by the rightful custom of the Althing, and the law of the land."

After that he offered Eyjolf and Flosi, before witnesses, to call out by name and set aside other six men, but Flosi and Eyjolf would not call them out.

Then Mord made them pass judgment in the cause; but when the judgment was given, Eyjolf took witness, and said that all their judgment had come to naught, and also everything else that had been done, and his ground was that three twelves and one half had judged, when three only ought to have given judgment.

"And now we will follow up our suits before the Fifth Court," said Eyjolf, "and make them outlaws."

Then Gizur the white said to Mord Valgard's son—

"Thou hast made a very great mistake in taking such a false step, and this is great ill-luck; but what counsel shall we now take, kinsman Asgrim?" says Gizur.

Then Asgrim said—"Now we will send a man to my son Thorhall, and know what counsel he will give us".

CHAPTER CXLIV.

BATTLE AT THE ALTHING.

Now Snorri the priest hears how the causes stood, and then he begins to draw up his men in array below the "Great Rift," between it and Hadbooth, and laid down beforehand to his men how they were to behave.

Now the messenger comes to Thorhall Asgrim's son, and tells him how things stood, and how Mord Valgard's son and his friends would all be made outlaws, and the suits for manslaughter be brought to naught.

But when he heard that, he was so shocked at it that he could not utter a word. He jumped up then from his bed, and clutched with both hands his spear, Skarphedinn's gift, and drove it through his foot; then flesh clung to the spear, and the eye of the boil too, for he had cut it clean out of the foot, but a torrent of blood and matter poured out, so that it fell in a stream along the floor. Now he went out of the booth unhalting, and walked so hard that the messenger could not keep up with him, and so he goes until he came to the Fifth Court. There he met Grim the red, Flosi's kinsman, and as soon as ever they met, Thorhall thrust at him with the spear, and smote him on the shield and clove it in twain, but the spear passed right through him, so that the point came out between his shoulders. Thorhall cast him off his spear.

Then Kari Solmund's son caught sight of that, and said to Asgrim—

"Here, now, is come Thorhall thy son, and has straightway slain a man, and this is a great shame, if he alone shall have the heart to avenge the Burning."

"That shall not be," says Asgrim, "but let us turn on them now."

Then there was a mighty cry all over the host, and then they shouted their war-cries.

Flosi and his friends then turned against their foes, and both sides egged on their men fast.

Kari Solmund's son turned now thither where Arni Kol's son and Hallbjorn the strong were in front, and as soon as ever Hallbjorn saw Kari, he made a blow at him, and aimed at his leg, but Kari leapt up into the air, and Hallbjorn missed him. Kari turned on Arni Kol's son and cut at him, and smote him on the shoulder, and cut asunder the shoulder blade and collar bone, and the blow went right down into his breast, and Arni fell down dead at once to earth.

After that he hewed at Hallbjorn and caught him on the shield, and the blow passed through the shield, and so down and cut off his great toe. Holmstein hurled a spear at Kari, but he caught it in the air, and sent it back, and it was a man's death in Flosi's band.

Thorgeir Craggeir came up to where Hallbjorn the strong was in front, and Thorgeir made such a spear-thrust at him with his left hand that Hallbjorn fell before it, and had hard work to get on his feet again, and turned away from the fight there and then. Then Thorgeir met Thorwalld Kettle rumble's son, and hewed at him at once with the axe, "the ogress of war," which Skarphedinn had owned. Thorwalld threw his shield before him, and Thorgeir hewed the shield and cleft it from top to bottom, but the upper horn of the axe made its way into his breast, and passed into his trunk, and Thorwalld fell and was dead at once.

Now it must be told how Asgrim Ellidagrim's son, and Thorhall his son, Hjallti Skeggi's son, and Gizur the white, made an onslaught where Flosi and the sons of Sigfus, and the other Burners were; then there was a very hard fight, and the end of it was that they pressed on so hard, that Flosi and his men gave way before them. Gudmund the powerful, and Mord Valgard's son, and Thorgeir Craggeir, made their onslaught where the Axefirthers and Eastfirthers, and the men of Reykdale stood, and there too there was a very hard fight.

Kari Solmund's son came up where Bjarni Broddhelgi's son had the lead. Kari caught up a spear and thrust at him, and the blow fell on his shield. Bjarni slipped the shield on one side of him, else it had gone straight through him. Then he cut at Kari and aimed at his leg, but Kari drew back his leg and turned short round on his heel, and Bjarni missed him. Kari cut at once at him, and then a man ran forward and threw his shield before Bjarni. Kari cleft the shield in twain, and the point of the sword caught his thigh, and ripped up the whole leg down to the ankle. That man fell there and then, and was ever after a cripple so long as he lived.

Then Kari clutched his spear with both hands, and turned on Bjarni and thrust at him; he saw he had no other chance but to throw himself down side-long away from the blow, but as soon as ever Bjarni found his feet, away he fell back out of the fight.

Thorgeir Craggeir and Gizur the white fell on there where Holmstein the son of Bersi the wise, and Thorkel Geiti's son were leaders, and the end of the struggle was, that Holmstein and Thorkel gave way, and then arose a mighty hooting after them from the men of Gudmund the powerful.

Thorwalld Tjorfi's son of Lightwater got a great wound; he was shot in the forearm, and men thought that Halldor Gudmund the powerful's son had hurled the spear, but he bore that wound about with him all his life long, and got no atonement for it.

Now there was a mighty throng. But though we hear tell of some of the deeds that were done, still there are far many more of which men have handed down no stories.

Flosi had told them that they should make for the stronghold in the Great Rift if they were worsted, "for there," said he, "they will only be able to attack us on one side". But the band which Hall of the Side and his son Ljot led, had fallen away out of the fight before the onslaught of that father and son, Asgrim and Thorhall. They turned down east of Axewater, and Hall said—

"This is a sad state of things when the whole host of men at the Thing fight, and I would, kinsman Ljot, that we begged us help even though that be brought against us by some men, and that we part them. Thou shalt wait for me at the foot of the bridge, and I will go to the booths and beg for help."

"If I see," said Ljot, "that Flosi and his men need help from our men, then I will at once run up and aid them."

"Thou wilt do in that as thou pleasest," says Hall, "but I pray thee to wait for me here."

Now flight breaks out in Flosi's band, and they all fly west across Axewater; but Asgrim and Gizur the white went after them and all their host. Flosi and his men turned down between the river and the Outwork booth. Snorri the priest had drawn up his men there in array, so thick that they could not pass that way, and Snorri the priest called out then to Flosi—

"Why are ye in such haste, or who chase you?"

"Thou askest not this," answered Flosi, "because thou dost not know it already; but whose fault is it that we cannot get to the stronghold in the Great Rift?"

"It is not my fault," says Snorri, "but it is quite true that I know whose fault it is, and I will tell thee if thou wilt; it is the fault of Thorwalld cropbeard and Kol."

They were both then dead, but they had been the worst men in all Flosi's band.

Again Snorri said to his men—

"Now do both, cut at them and thrust at them, and drive them away hence, they will then hold out but a short while here, if the others attack them from below; but then ye shall not go after them, but let both sides shift for themselves."

The son of Skapti Thorod's son was Thorstein gapemouth, as was written before, he was in the battle with Gudmund the powerful, his father-in-law, and as soon as Skapti knew that, he went to the booth of Snorri the priest, and meant to beg for help to part them; but just before he had got as far as the door of Snorri's booth, there the battle was hottest of all. Asgrim and his friends and his men were just coming up thither, and then Thorhall said to his father Asgrim—

"See there now is Skapti Thorod's son, father."

"I see him, kinsman," said Asgrim, and then he shot a spear at Skapti, and struck him just below where the calf was fattest, and so through both his legs. Skapti fell at the blow, and could not get up again, and the only counsel they could take who were by, was to drag Skapti flat on his face into the booth of a turf-cutter.

Then Asgrim and his men came up so fast that Flosi and his men gave way before them south along the river to the booths of the men of Modruvale. There there was a man outside one booth whose name was Solvi; he was boiling broth in a great kettle, and had just then taken the meat out, and the broth was boiling as hotly as it could.

Solvi cast his eyes on the Eastfirthers us they fled, and they were then just over against him, and then he said—"Can all these cowards who fly here be Eastfirthers, and yet Thorkel Geiti's son, he ran by as fast as any one of them, and very great lies have been told about him when men say that he is all heart, but now no one ran faster than he".

Hallbjorn the strong was near by them, and said—

"Thou shalt not have it to say that we are all cowards."

And with that he caught hold of him, and lifted him up aloft, and thrust him head down into the broth-kettle. Solvi died at once; but then a rush was made at Hallbjorn himself, and he had to turn and fly.

Flosi threw a spear at Bruni Haflidi's son, and caught him at the waist, and that was his bane; he was one of Gudmund the powerful's band.

Thorstein Hlenni's son took the spear out of the wound, and hurled it back at Flosi, and hit him on the leg, and he got a great wound and fell; he rose up again at once.

Then they passed on to the Waterfirther's booth, and then Hall and Ljot came from the east across the river, with all their band; but just when they came to the lava, a spear was hurled out of the band of Gudmund the powerful, and it struck Ljot in the middle, and he fell down dead at once; and it was never known surely who had done that manslaughter.

Flosi and his men turned up round the Waterfirther's booth, and then Thorgeir Craggeir said to Kari Solmund's son—

"Look, yonder now is Eyjolf Bolverk's son, if thou hast a mind to pay him off for the ring."

"That I ween is not far from my mind," says Kari, and snatched a spear from a man, and hurled it at Eyjolf, and it struck him in the waist, and went through him, and Eyjolf then fell dead to earth.

Then there was a little lull in the battle, and then Snorri the priest came up with his band, and Skapti was there in his company, and they ran in between them, and so they could not get at one another to fight.

Then Hall threw in his people with theirs, and was for parting them there and then, and so a truce was set, and was to be kept throughout the Thing, and then the bodies were laid out and borne to the church, and the wounds of those men were bound up who were hurt.

The day after men went to the Hill of Laws. Then Hall of the Side stood up and asked for a hearing, and got it at once; and he spoke thus—

"Here there have been hard happenings in lawsuits and loss of life at the Thing, and now I will show again that I am little-hearted, for I will now ask Asgrim and the others who take the lead in these suits, that they grant us an atonement on even terms;" and so he goes on with many fair words.

Kari Solmund's son said—

"Though all others take an atonement in their quarrels, yet will I take no atonement in my quarrel; for ye will wish to weigh these manslayings against the Burning, and we cannot bear that."

In the same way spoke Thorgeir Craggeir.

Then Skapti Thorod's son stood up and said—

"Better had it been for thee, Kari, not to have run away from thy father-in-law and thy brothers-in-law, than now to sneak out of this atonement."

Then Kari sang these verses—

Warrior wight that weapon wieldest
Spare thy speering why we fled,

Oft for less falls hail of battle,
Forth we fled to wreak revenge;
Who was he, faint-hearted foeman,
Who, when tongues of steel sung high,
Stole beneath the booth for shelter,
While his beard blushed red for shame?

Many fetters Skapti fettered
When the men, the Gods of fight,
From the fray fared all unwilling
Where the skald scarce held his shield;
Then the suttlers dragged the lawyer
Stout in scolding to their booth,
Laid him low amongst the riffraff,
How his heart then quaked for fear.

Men who skim the main on sea stag
Well in this ye showed your sense,
Making game about the Burning,
Mocking Helgi, Grim, and Njal;
Now the moor round rocky Swinestye,[77]
As men run and shake their shields,
With another grunt shall rattle
When this Thing is past and gone.

Then there was great laughter. Snorri the priest smiled, and sang this between his teeth, but so that many heard—

Skill hath Skapti us to tell
Whether Asgrim's shaft flew well;
Holmstein hurried swift to flight,
Thorstein turned him soon to fight.

Now men burst out in great fits of laughter.

Then Hall of the Side said—

"All men know what a grief I have suffered in the loss of my son Ljot; many will think that he would be valued dearest of all those men who have fallen here; but I will do this for the sake of an atonement—I will put no price on my son, and yet will come forward and grant both pledges and peace to those who are my adversaries. I beg thee, Snorri the priest, and other of the best men, to bring this about, that there may be an atonement between us."

Now he sits him down, and a great hum in his favour followed, and all praised his gentleness and good-will.

Then Snorri the priest stood up and made a long and clever speech, and begged Asgrim and the others who took the lead in the quarrel to look towards an atonement.

Then Asgrim said—

"I made up my mind when Flosi made an inroad on my house that I would never be atoned with him; but now Snorri the priest, I will take an atonement from him for thy word's sake and other of our friends."

In the same way spoke Thorleif crow and Thorgrim the big, that they were willing to be atoned, and they urged in every way their brother Thorgeir Craggeir to take an atonement also; but he hung back, and says he would never part from Kari.

Then Gizur the white said—

"Now Flosi must see that he must make his choice, whether he will be atoned on the understanding that some will be out of the atonement."

Flosi says he will take that atonement; "and methinks it is so much the better," he says, "that I have fewer good men and true against me".

Then Gudmund the powerful said—

"I will offer to hansel peace on my behalf for the slayings that have happened here at the Thing, on the understanding that the suit for the Burning is not to fall to the ground."

In the same way spoke Gizur the white and Hjallti Skeggi's son, Asgrim Ellidagrim's son and Mord Valgard's son.

In this way the atonement came about, and then hands were shaken on it, and twelve men were to utter the award; and Snorri the priest was the chief man in the award, and others with him. Then the manslaughters were set off the one against the other, and those men who were over and above were paid for in fines. They also made an award in the suit about the Burning.

Njal was to be atoned for with a triple fine, and Bergthora with two. The slaying of Skarphedinn was to be set off against that of Hauskuld the Whiteness priest. Both Grim and Helgi were to be paid for with double fines; and one full man-fine should be paid for each of those who had been burnt in the house.

No atonement was taken for the slaying of Thord Kari's son.

It was also in the award that Flosi and all the Burners should go abroad into banishment, and none of them was to sail the same summer unless he chose; but if he did not sail abroad by the time that three winters were spent, then he and all the Burners were to become thorough outlaws. And it was also said that their outlawry might be proclaimed either at the Harvest-Thing or Spring-Thing, whichever men chose; and Flosi was to stay abroad three winters.

As for Gunnar Lambi's son, and Grani Gunnar's son. Glum Hilldir's son, and Kol Thorstein's son, they were never to be allowed to come back.

Then Flosi was asked if he would wish to have a price put upon his wound, but he said he would not take bribes for his hurt.

Eyjolf Bolverk's son had no fine awarded for him, for his unfairness and wrongfulness.

And now the settlement and atonement was handselled, and was well kept afterwards.

Asgrim and his friends gave Snorri the priest good gifts, and he had great honour from these suits.

Skapti got a fine for his hurt.

Gizur the white, and Hjallti Skeggi's son, and Asgrim Ellidagrim's son, asked Gudmund the powerful to come and see them at home. He accepted the bidding, and each of them gave him a gold ring.

Now Gudmund rides home north, and had praise from every man for the part he had taken in these quarrels.

Thorgeir Craggeir asked Kari to go along with him, but yet first of all they rode with Gudmund right up to the fells north. Kari gave Gudmund a golden brooch, but Thorgeir gave him a silver belt, and each was the greatest treasure. So they parted with the utmost friendship, and Gudmund is out of this story.

Kari and Thorgeir rode south from the fell, and down to the Rapes,[78] and so to Thurso-water.

Flosi, and the Burners along with him, rode east to Fleetlithe, and he allowed the sons of Sigfus to settle their affairs at home. Then Flosi heard that Thorgeir and Kari had ridden north with Gudmund the powerful, and so the Burners thought that Kari and his friend must mean to stay in the north country; and then the sons of Sigfus asked leave to go east under Eyjafell to get in their money, for they had money out on call at Headbrink. Flosi gave them leave to do that, but still bade them be ware of themselves, and be as short a time about it as they could.

Then Flosi rode up by Godaland, and so north of Eyjafell Jokul, and did not draw bridle before he came home east to Swinefell.

Now it must be said that Hall of the Side had suffered his son to fall without a fine, and did that for the sake of an atonement, but then the whole host of men at the Thing agreed to pay a fine for him, and the money so paid was not less than eight hundred in silver, but that was four times the price of a man; but all the others who had been with Flosi got no fines paid for their hurts, and were very ill pleased at it.

CHAPTER CXLV.

OF KARI AND THORGEIR.

Those two, Kari Solmund's and Thorgeir Craggeir, rode that day east across Markfleet, and so on east to Selialandsmull. They found there some women. The wives knew them, and said to them—

"Ye two are less wanton than the sons of Sigfus yonder, but still ye fare unwarily."

"Why do ye talk thus of the sons of Sigfus, or what do ye know about them?"

"They were last night," they said, "at Raufarfell, and meant to get to Myrdale to-night, but still we thought they must have some fear of you, for they asked when he would be likely to come home."

Then Kari and Thorgeir went on their way and spurred their horses.

"What shall we lay down for ourselves to do now," said Thorgeir, "or what is most to thy mind? Wilt thou that we ride on their track?"

"I will not hinder this," answers Kari, "nor will I say what ought to be done, for it may often be that those live Long who are slain with words alone;[79] but I well know what thou meanest to take on thyself, thou must mean to take on thy hands eight men, and after all that is less than it was when thou slewest those seven in the sea-crags,[80] and let thyself down by a rope to get at them; but it is the way with all you kinsmen, that ye always wish to be doing some famous feat, and now I can do no less than stand by thee and have my share in the story. So now we two alone will ride after them, for I see that thou hast so made up thy mind."

After that they rode east by the upper way, and did not pass by Holt, for Thorgeir would not that any blame should be laid at his brother's door for what might be done.

Then they rode east to Myrdale, and there they met a man who had turf-panniers on his horse. He began to speak thus—

"Too few men, messmate Thorgeir, hast thou now in thy company."

"How is that?" says Thorgeir.

"Why," said the other, "because the prey is now before thy hand. The sons of Sigfus rode by a while ago, and mean to sleep the whole day east in Carlinedale, for they mean to go no farther to-night than to Headbrink."

After that they rode on their way east on Arnstacks heath, and there is nothing to be told of their journey before they came to Carlinedale-water.

The stream was high, and now they rode up along the river, for they saw their horses with saddles. They rode now thitherward, and saw that there were men asleep in a dell and their spears were standing upright in the ground a little below them. They took the spears from them, and threw them into the river.

Then Thorgeir said—

"Wilt thou that we wake them?"

"Thou hast not asked this," answers Kari, "because thou hast not already made up thy mind not to fall on sleeping men, and so to slay a shameful manslaughter."

After that they shouted to them, and then they all awoke and grasped at their arms.

They did not fall on them till they were armed.

Thorgeir Craggeir runs thither where Thorkel Sigfus' son stood, and just then a man ran behind his back, but before he could do Thorgeir any hurt, Thorgeir lifted the axe, "the ogress of war," with both hands, and dashed the hammer of the axe with a back-blow into the head of him that stood behind him, so that his skull was shattered to small bits.

"Slain is this one," said Thorgeir; and down the man fell at once, and was dead.

But when he dashed the axe forward, he smote Thorkel on the shoulder, and hewed it off, arm and all.

Against Kari came Mord Sigfus' son, and Sigmund Sigfus' son, and Lambi Sigurd's son; the last ran behind Kari's back, and thrust at him with a spear; Kari caught sight of him, and leapt up as the blow fell, and stretched his legs far apart, and so the blow spent itself on the ground, but Kari jumped down on the spear-shaft, and snapped it in sunder. He had a spear in one hand, and a sword in the other, but no shield. He thrust with the right hand at Sigmund Sigfus' son, and smote him on his breast, and the spear came out between his shoulders, and down he fell and was dead at once. With his left hand he made a cut at Mord, and smote him on the hip, and cut it asunder, and his backbone too; he fell flat on his face, and was dead at once.

After that he turned sharp round on his heel like a whipping-top, and made at Lambi Sigurd's son, but he took the only way to save himself, and that was by running away as hard as he could.

Now Thorgeir turns against Leidolf the strong, and each hewed at the other at the same moment, and Leidolf's blow was so great that it shore off that part of the shield on which it fell.

Thorgeir had hewn with "the ogress of war," holding it with both hands, and the lower horn fell on the shield and clove it in twain, but the upper caught the collar bone and cut it in two, and tore on down into the breast and trunk. Kari came up just then, and cut off Leidolf's leg at mid-thigh, and then Leidolf fell and died at once.

Kettle of the Mark said—"We will now run for our horses, for we cannot hold our own here, for the overbearing strength of these men".

Then they ran for their horses, and leapt on their backs; and Thorgeir said—

"Wilt thou that we chase them? if so, we shall yet slay some of them."

"He rides last," says Kari, "whom I would not wish to slay, and that is Kettle of the Mark, for we have two sisters to wife; and besides, he has behaved best of all of them as yet in our quarrels."

Then they got on their horses, and rode till they came home to Holt. Then Thorgeir made his brothers fare away east to Skoga, for they had another farm there, and because Thorgeir would not that his brothers should be called truce-breakers.

Then Thorgeir kept many men there about him, so that there were never fewer than thirty fighting men there.

Then there was great joy there, and men thought Thorgeir had grown much greater, and pushed himself on; both he and Kari too. Men long kept in mind this hunting of theirs, how they two rode upon fifteen men and slew those five, but put those ten to flight who got away.

Now it is to be told of Kettle, that they rode as they best might till they came home to Swinefell, and told how bad their journey had been.

Flosi said it was only what was to be looked for; "and this is a warning that ye should never do the like again".

Flosi was the merriest of men, and the best of hosts, and it is so said that he had most of the chieftain in him of all the men of his time.

He was at home that summer, and the winter too.

But that winter, after Yule, Hall of the Side came from the east, and Kol his son. Flosi was glad at his coming, and they often talked about the matter of the Burning. Flosi said they had already paid a great fine, and Hall said it was pretty much what he had guessed would come of Flosi's and his friends' quarrel. Then he asked him what counsel he thought best to be taken, and Hall answers—

"The counsel I give is, that thou beest atoned with Thorgeir if there be a choice, and yet he will be hard to bring to take any atonement."

"Thinkest thou that the manslaughters will then be brought to an end?" asks Flosi.

"I do not think so," says Hall; "but you will have to do with fewer foes if Kari be left alone; but if thou art not atoned with Thorgeir, then that will be thy bane."

"What atonement shall we offer him?" asks Flosi.

"You will all think that atonement hard," says Hall, "which he will take, for he will not hear of an atonement unless he be not called on to pay any fine for what he has just done, but he will have fines for Njal and his sons, so far as his third share goes."

"That is a hard atonement," says Flosi.

"For thee at least," says Hall, "that atonement is not hard, for thou hast not the blood-feud after the sons of Sigfus; their brothers have the blood-feud, and Hamond the halt after his son; but thou shalt now get an atonement from Thorgeir, for I will now ride to his house with thee, and Thorgeir will in anywise receive me well; but no man of those who are in this quarrel will dare to sit in his house on Fleetlithe if they are out of the atonement, for that will be their bane; and, indeed, with Thorgeir's turn of mind, it is only what must be looked for."

Now the sons of Sigfus were sent for, and they brought this business before them; and the end of their speech was, on the persuasion of Hall, that they all thought what he said right, and were ready to be atoned.

Grani Gunnar's son and Gunnar Lambi's son said—

"It will be in our power, if Kari be left alone behind, to take care that he be not less afraid of us than we of him."

"Easier said than done," says Hall, "and ye will find it a dear bargain to deal with him. Ye will have to pay a heavy fine before you have done with him."

After that they ceased speaking about it.

CHAPTER CXLVI.

THE AWARD OF ATONEMENT WITH THORGEIR CRAGGEIR.

Hall of the Side and his son Kol, seven of them in all, rode west over Loomnip's Sand, and so west over Arnstacksheath, and did not draw bridle till they came into Myrdale. There they asked whether Thorgeir would be at home at Holt, and they were told that they would find him at home.

The men asked whither Hall meant to go.

"Thither to Holt," he said.

They said they were sure he went on a good errand.

He stayed there some while and baited their horses, and after that they mounted their horses and rode to Solheim about even, and they were there that night, but the day-after they rode to Holt.

Thorgeir was out of doors, and Kari too, and their men, for they had seen Hall's coming. He rode in a blue cape, and had a little axe studded with silver in his hand; but when they came into the "town," Thorgeir went to meet him, and helped him off his horse, and both he and Kari kissed him and led him in between them into the sitting-room, and sate him down in the high seat on the dais, and they asked him tidings about many things.

He was there that night. Next morning Hall raised the question of the atonement with Thorgeir, and told him what terms they offered him; and he spoke about them with many fair and kindly words.

"It may be well known to thee," answers Thorgeir, "that I said I would take no atonement from the Burners."

"That was quite another matter then," says Hall; "ye were then wroth with fight, and, besides, ye have done great deeds in the way of manslaying since."

"I daresay ye think so," says Thorgeir, "but what atonement do ye offer to Kari?"

"A fitting atonement shall be offered him," says Hall, "if he will take it."

Then Kari said—

"I pray this of thee, Thorgeir, that thou wilt be atoned, for thy lot cannot be better than good."

"Methinks," says Thorgeir, "it is ill done to take an atonement, and sunder myself from thee, unless thou takest the same atonement as I."

"I will not take any atonement," says Kari, "but yet I say that we have avenged the Burning; but my son, I say, is still unavenged, and I mean to take that on myself alone, and see what I can get done."

But Thorgeir would take no atonement before Kari said that he would take it ill if he were not atoned. Then Thorgeir handselled a truce to Flosi and his men, as a step to a meeting for atonement; but Hall did the same on behalf of Flosi and the sons of Sigfus.

But ere they parted, Thorgeir gave Hall a gold ring and a scarlet cloak, but Kari gave him a silver brooch, and there were hung to it four crosses of gold. Hall thanked them kindly for their gifts, and rode away with the greatest honour. He did not draw bridle till he came to Swinefell, and Flosi gave him a hearty welcome. Hall told Flosi all about his errand and the talk he had with Thorgeir, and also that Thorgeir would not take the atonement till Kari told him he would quarrel with him if he did not take it; but that Kari would take no atonement.

"There are few men like Kari," said Flosi, "and I would that my mind were shapen altogether like his."

Hall and Kol stayed there some while, and afterwards they rode west at the time agreed on to the meeting for atonement, and met at Headbrink, as had been settled between them.

Then Thorgeir came to meet them from the west, and then they talked over their atonement, and all went off as Hall had said.

Before the atonement, Thorgeir said that Kari should still have the right to be at his house all the same if he chose.

"And neither side shall do the others any harm at my house; and I will not have the trouble of gathering in the fines from each of the Burners; but my will is that Flosi alone shall be answerable for them to me, but he must get them in from his followers. My will also is that all that award which was made at the Thing about the Burning shall be kept and held to; and my will also is, Flosi, that thou payest me up my third share in unclipped coin."

Flosi went quickly into all these terms.

Thorgeir neither gave up the banishment nor the outlawry.

Now Flosi and Hall rode home east, and then Hall said to Flosi—

"Keep this atonement well, son-in-law, both as to going abroad and the pilgrimage to Rome,[81] and the fines, and then thou wilt be thought a brave man, though thou hast stumbled into this misdeed, if thou fulfillest handsomely all that belongs to it."

Flosi said it should be so.

Now Hall rode home east, but Flosi rode home to Swinefell, and was at home afterwards.

CHAPTER CXLVII.

KARI COMES TO BJORN'S HOUSE IN THE MARK.

Thorgeir Craggeir rode home from the peace-meeting, and Kari asked whether the atonement had come about. Thorgeir said that they now fully atoned.

Then Kari took his horse and was for riding away.

"Thou hast no need to ride away," says Thorgeir, "for it was laid down in our atonement that thou shouldst be here as before if thou chosest."

"It shall not be so, cousin, for as soon as ever I slay a man they will be sure to say that thou wert in the plot with me, and I will not have that; but I wish this, that thou wouldst let me hand over in trust to thee my goods, and the estates of me and my wife Helga Njal's daughter, and my three daughters, and then they will not be seized by those adversaries of mine."

Thorgeir agreed to what Kari wished to ask of him, and then Thorgeir had Kari's goods handed over to him in trust.

After that Kari rode away. He had two horses and his weapons and outer clothing, and some ready money in gold and silver.

Now Kari rode west by Selialandsmull and up along Markfleet, and so on up into Thorsmark. There there are three farms all called "Mark". At the midmost farm dwelt that man whose name was Bjorn, and his surname was Bjorn the white; he was the son of Kadal, the son of Bjalfi. Bjalfi had been the freedman of Asgerda, the mother of Njal and Holt-Thorir; Bjorn had to wife Valgerda, she was the daughter of Thorbrand, the son of Asbrand. Her mother's name was Gudlauga, she was a sister of Hamond, the father of Gunnar of Lithend; she was given away to Bjorn for his money's sake, and she did not love him much, but yet they had children together, and they had enough and to spare in the house.

Bjorn was a man who was always boasting and praising himself, but his housewife thought that bad. He was sharpsighted and swift of foot.

Thither Kari turned in as a guest, and they took him by both hands, and he was there that night. But the next morning Kari said to Bjorn—

"I wish thou wouldst take me in, for I should think myself well housed here with thee. I would too that thou shouldst be with me in my journeyings, as thou art a sharpsighted, swift-footed man, and besides I think thou wouldst be dauntless in an onslaught."

"I can't blame myself," says Bjorn, "for wanting either sharp sight, or dash, or any other bravery; but no doubt thou camest hither because all thy other earths are stopped. Still, at thy prayer, Kari, I will not look on thee as an everyday man; I will surely help thee in all that thou askest."

"The trolls take thy boasting and bragging," said his housewife, "and thou shouldst not utter such stuff and silliness to any one than thyself. As for me, I will willingly give Kari meat and other good things, which I know will be useful to him; but on Bjorn's hardihood, Kari, thou shalt not trust, for I am afraid that thou wilt find it quite otherwise than he says."

"Often hast thou thrown blame upon me," said Bjorn, "but for all that I put so much faith in myself that though I am put to the trial I will never give way to any man; and the best proof of it is this, that few try a tussle with me because none dare to do so."

Kari was there some while in hiding, and few men knew of it.

Now men think that Kari must have ridden to the north country to see Gudmund the powerful, for Kari made Bjorn tell his neighbours that he had met Kari on the beaten track, and that he rode thence up into Godaland, and so north to Goose-sand, and then north to Gudmund the powerful at Modruvale.

So that story was spread over all the country.

CHAPTER CXLVIII.

OF FLOSI AND THE BURNERS.

Now Flosi spoke to the Burners, his companions—

"It will no longer serve our turn to sit still, for now we shall have to think of our going abroad and of our fines, and of fulfilling our atonement as bravely as we can, and let us take a passage wherever it seems most likely to get one."

They bade him see to all that. Then Flosi said—

"We will ride east to Hornfirth; for there that ship is laid up, which is owned by Eyjolf nosy, a man from Drontheim, but he wants to take to him a wife here, and he will not get the match made unless he settles himself down here. We will buy the ship of him, for we shall have many men and little freight. The ship is big and will take us all."

Then they ceased talking of it.

But a little after they rode east, and did not stop before they came east to Bjornness in Hornfirth, and there they found Eyjolf, for he had been there as a guest that winter.

There Flosi and his men had a hearty welcome, and they were there the night. Next morning Flosi dealt with the captain for the ship, but he said he would not be hard to sell the ship if he could get what he wanted for her. Flosi asked him in what coin he wished to be paid for her; the Easterling says he wanted land for her near where he then was.

Then Eyjolf told Flosi all about his dealings with his host, and Flosi says he will pull an oar with him, so that his marriage bargain might be struck, and buy the ship of him afterwards. The Easterling was glad at that. Flosi offered him land at Borgarhaven, and now the Easterling holds on with his suit to his host when Flosi was by, and Flosi threw in a helping word, so that the bargain was brought about between them.

Flosi made over the land at Borgarhaven to the Easterling, but shook hands on the bargain for the ship. He got also from the Easterling twenty hundreds in wares, and that was also in their bargain for the land.

Now Flosi rode back home. He was so beloved by his men that their wares stood free to him to take either on loan or gift, just as he chose.

He rode home to Swinefell, and was at home a while.

Then Flosi sent Kol Thorstein's son and Gunnar Lambi's son east to Hornfirth. They were to be there by the ship, and to fit her out, and set up booths, and sack the wares, and get all things together that were needful.

Now we must tell of the sons of Sigfus how they say to Flosi that they will ride west to Fleetlithe to set their houses in order, and get wares thence, and such other things as they needed. "Kari is not there now to be guarded against," they say, "if he is in the north country as is said."

"I know not," answers Flosi, "as to such stories, whether there be any truth in what is said of Kari's journeyings; methinks, we have often been wrong in believing things which are nearer to learn than this. My counsel is that ye go many of you together, and part as little as ye can, and be as wary of yourselves as ye may. Thou, too, Kettle of the Mark, shalt bear in mind that dream which I told thee, and which thou prayedst me to hide; for many are those in thy company who were then called."

"All must come to pass as to man's life," said Kettle, "as it is foredoomed; but good go with thee for thy warning."

Now they spoke no more about it.

After that the sons of Sigfus busked them and those men with them who were meant to go with them. They were eight in all, and then they rode away, and ere they went they kissed Flosi, and he bade them farewell, and said he and some of those who rode away would not see each other more. But they would not let themselves be hindered. They rode now on their way, and Flosi said that they should take his wares in Middleland, and carry them east, and do the same in Landsbreach and Woodcombe.

After that they rode to Skaptartongue, and so on the fell, and north of Eyjafell Jokul, and down into Godaland, and so down into the woods in Thorsmark.

Bjorn of the Mark caught sight of them coming, and went at once to meet them.

Then they greeted each other well, and the sons of Sigfus asked after Kari Solmund's son.

"I met Kari," said Bjorn, "and that is now very long since; he rode hence north on Goose-sand, and meant to go to Gudmund the powerful, and methought if he were here now, he would stand in awe of you, for he seemed to be left all alone."

Grani Gunnar's son said—

"He shall stand more in awe of us yet before we have done with him, and he shall learn that as soon as ever he comes within spearthrow of us; but as for us, we do not fear him at all, now that he is all alone."

Kettle of the Mark bade them be still, and bring out no big words.

Bjorn asked when they would be coming back.

"We shall stay near a week in Fleetlithe," said they; and so they told him when they should be riding back on the fell.

With that they parted.

Now the sons of Sigfus rode to their homes, and their households were glad to see them. They were there near a week.

Now Bjorn comes home and sees Kari, and told him all about the doings of the sons of Sigfus, and their purpose.

Kari said he had shown in this great faithfulness to him, and Bjorn said—

"I should have thought there was more risk of any other man's failing in that than of me if I had pledged my help or care to any one."

"Ah," said his mistress, "but you may still be bad and yet not be so bad as to be a traitor to thy master."

Kari stayed there six nights after that.

CHAPTER CXLIX.

OF KARI AND BJORN.

Now Kari talks to Bjorn and says—

"We shall ride east across the fell and down into Skaptartongue, and fare stealthily over Flosi's country, for I have it in my mind to get myself carried abroad east in Alftafirth."

"This is a very riskful journey," said Bjorn, "and few would have the heart to take it save thou and I."

"If thou backest Kari ill," said his housewife, "know this, that thou shalt never come afterwards into my bed, and my kinsmen shall share our goods between us."

"It is likelier, mistress," said he, "that thou wilt have to look out for something else than this if thou hast a mind to part from me; for I will bear my own witness to myself what a champion and daredevil I am when weapons clash."

Now they rode that day east on the fell to the north of the Jokul, but never on the highway, and so down into Skaptartongue, and above all the homesteads to Skaptarwater, and led their horses into a dell, but they themselves were on the look-out, and had so placed themselves that they could not be seen.

Then Kari said to Bjorn—

"What shall we do now if they ride down upon us here from the fell?"

"Are there not but two things to be done," said Bjorn; "one to ride away from them north under the crags, and so let them ride by us, or to wait and see if any of them lag behind, and then to fall on them."

They talked much about this, and one while Bjorn was for flying as fast as he could in every word he spoke, and at another for staying and fighting it out with them, and Kari thought this the greatest sport.

The sons of Sigfus rode from their homes the same day that they had named to Bjorn. They came to the Mark and knocked at the door there, and wanted to see Bjorn; but his mistress went to the door and greeted them. They asked at once for Bjorn, and she said he had ridden away down under Eyjafell, and so east under Selialandsmull, and on east to Holt, "for he has some money to call in thereabouts," she said.

They believed this, for they knew that Bjorn had money out at call there.

After that they rode east on the fell, and did not stop before they came to Skaptartongue, and so rode down along Skaptarwater, and baited their horses just where Kari had thought they would. Then they split their band. Kettle of the Mark rode east into Middleland, and eight men with him, but the others laid them down to sleep, and were not ware of aught until Kari and Bjorn came up to them. A little ness ran out there into the river; into it Kari went and took his stand, and bade Bjorn stand back to back with him, and not to put himself too forward, "but give me all the help thou canst".

"Well," says Bjorn, "I never had it in my head that any man should stand before me as a shield, but still as things are thou must have thy way; but for all that, with my gift of wit and my swiftness I may be of some use to thee, and not harmless to our foes."

Now they all rose up and ran at them, and Modolf Kettle's son was quickest of them, and thrust at Kari with his spear. Kari had his shield before him, and the blow fell on it, and the spear stuck fast in the shield. Then Kari twists the shield so smartly, that the spear snapped short off, and then he drew his sword and smote at Modolf; but Modolf made a cut at him too, and Kari's sword fell on Modolf's hilt, and glanced off it on to Modolph's wrist, and took the arm off, and down it fell, and the sword too. Then Kari's sword passed on into Modolf's side, and between his ribs, and so Modolf fell down and was dead on the spot.

Grani Gunnar's son snatched up a spear and hurled it at Kari, but Kari thrust down his shield so hard that the point stood fast in the ground, but with his left hand he caught the spear in the air, and hurled it back at Grani, and caught up his shield again at once with his left hand. Grani had his shield before him, and the spear came on the shield and passed right through it, and into Grani's thigh just below the small guts, and through the limb, and so on, pinning him to the ground, and he could not get rid of the spear before his fellows drew him off it, and carried him away on their shields, and laid him down in a dell.

There was a man who ran up to Kari's side, and meant to cut off his leg, but Bjorn cut off that man's arm, and sprang back again behind Kari, and they could not do him any hurt. Kari made a sweep at that same man with his sword, and cut him asunder at the waist.

Then Lambi Sigfus' son rushed at Kari, and hewed at him with his sword. Kari caught the blow sideways on his shield, and the sword would not bite; then Kari thrust at Lambi with his sword just below the breast, so that the point came out between his shoulders, and that was his death-blow.

Then Thorstein Geirleif's son rushed at Kari, and thought to take him in flank, but Kari caught sight of him, and swept at him with his sword across the shoulders, so that the man was cleft asunder at the chine.

A little while after he gave Gunnar of Skal, a good man and true, his death-blow. As for Bjorn, he had wounded three men who had tried to give Kari wounds, and yet he was never so far forward that he was in the least danger, nor was he wounded, nor was either of those companions hurt in that fight, but all those that got away were wounded.

Then they ran for their horses, and galloped them off across Skaptarwater as hard as they could; and they were so scared that they stopped at no house, nor did they dare to stay and tell the tidings anywhere.

Kari and Bjorn hooted and shouted after them as they galloped off. So they rode east to Woodcombe, and did not draw bridle till they came to Swinefell.

Flosi was not at home when they came thither, and that was why no hue and cry was made thence after Kari.

This journey of theirs was thought most shameful by all men.

Kari rode to Skal, and gave notice of these manslayings as done by his hand; there, too, he told them of the death of their master and five others, and of Grani's wound, and said it would be better to bear him to the house if he were to live.

Bjorn said he could not bear to slay him, though he said he was worthy of death; but those who answered him said they were sure few had bitten the dust before him. But Bjorn told them he had it now in his power to make as many of the Sidemen as he chose bite the dust; to which they said it was a bad look out.

Then Kari and Bjorn ride away from the house.

CHAPTER CL.

MORE OF KARI AND BJORN.

Then Kari asked Bjorn—

"What counsel shall we take now? Now I will try what thy wit is worth."

"Dost thou think now," answered Bjorn, "that much lies on our being as wise as ever we can?"

"Ay," said Kari, "I think so surely."

"Then our counsel is soon taken," says Bjorn. "We will cheat them all as though they were giants; and now we will make as though we were riding north on the fell, but as soon as ever we are out of sight behind the brae, we will turn down along Skaptarwater, and hide us there where we think handiest, so long as the hue and cry is hottest, if they ride after us."

"So will we do," said Kari; "and this I had meant to do all along."

"And so you may put it to the proof," said Bjorn, "that I am no more of an everyday body in wit than I am in bravery."

Now Kari and his companion rode as they had purposed down along Skaptarwater, till they came where a branch of the stream ran away to the south-east; then they turned down along the middle branch, and did not draw bridle till they came into Middleland, and on that moor which is called Kringlemire; it has a stream of lava all around it.

Then Kari said to Bjorn that he must watch their horses, and keep a good look-out; "but as for me," he says, "I am heavy with sleep".

So Bjorn watched the horses, but Kari lay him down, and slept but a very short while ere Bjorn waked him up again, and he had already led their horses together, and they were by their side. Then Bjorn said to Kari—

"Thou standest in much need of me, though! A man might easily have run away from thee if he had not been as brave-hearted as I am; for now thy foes are riding upon thee, and so thou must up and be doing."

Then Kari went away under a jutting crag, and Bjorn said—

"Where shall I stand now?"

"Well!" answers Kari, "now there are two choices before thee; one is, that thou standest at my back and have my shield to cover thyself with, if it can be of any use to thee; and the other is, to get on thy horse and ride away as fast as thou canst."

"Nay," says Bjorn, "I will not do that, and there are many things against it; first of all, may be, if I ride away, some spiteful tongues might begin to say that I ran away from thee for faintheartedness; and another thing is, that I well know what game they will think there is in me, and so they will ride after me, two or three of them, and then I should be of no use or help to thee after all. No! I will rather stand by thee and keep them off so long as it is fated."

Then they had not long to wait ere horses with pack-saddles were driven by them over the moor, and with them went three men.

Then Kari said—

"These men see us not."

"Then let us suffer them to ride on," said Bjorn.

So those three rode on past them; but the six others then came riding right up to them, and they all leapt off their horses straightway in a body, and turned on Kari and his companion.

First, Glum Hilldir's son rushed at them, and thrust at Kari with a spear; Kari turned short round on his heel, and Glum missed him, and the blow fell against the rock. Bjorn sees that, and hewed at once the head off Glum's spear. Kari leant on one side and smote at Glum with his sword, and the blow fell on his thigh, and took off the limb high up in the thigh, and Glum died at once.

Then Vebrand and Asbrand the sons of Thorbrand ran up to Kari, but Kari flew at Vebrand and thrust his sword through him, but afterwards he hewed off both of Asbrand's feet from under him.

In this bout both Kari and Bjorn were wounded.

Then Kettle of the Mark rushed at Kari, and thrust at him with his spear. Kari threw up his leg, and the spear stuck in the ground, and Kari leapt on the spear-shaft, and snapped it in sunder.

Then Kari grasped Kettle in his arms, and Bjorn ran up just then, and wanted to slay him, but Kari said—

"Be still now. I will give Kettle peace; for though it may be that Kettle's life is in my power, still I will never slay him."

Kettle answers never a word, but rode away after his companions, and told those the tidings who did not know them already.

They told also these tidings to the men of the Hundred, and they gathered together at once a great force of armed men, and went straightway up all the water-courses, and so far up on the fell that they were three days in the chase; but after that they turned back to their own homes, but Kettle and his companions rode east to Swinefell, and told the tidings there.

Flosi was little stirred at what had befallen them, but said no one could tell whether things would stop there, "for there is no man like Kari of all that are now left in Iceland".

CHAPTER CLI.

OF KARI AND BJORN AND THORGEIR.

Now we must tell of Bjorn and Kari that they ride down on the Sand, and lead their horses under the banks where the wild oats grew, and cut the oats for them, that they might not die of hunger. Kari made such a near guess, that he rode away thence at the very time that they gave over seeking for him. He rode by night up through the Hundred, and after that he took to the fell; and so on all the same way as they had followed when they rode east, and did not stop till they came to Midmark.

Then Bjorn said to Kari—

"Now shalt thou be my great friend before my mistress, for she will never believe one word of what I say; but everything lies on what you do, so now repay me for the good following which I have yielded to thee."

"So it shall be; never fear," says Kari.

After that they ride up to the homestead, and then the mistress asked them what tidings, and greeted them well.

"Our troubles have rather grown greater, old lass!"

She answered little, and laughed; and then the mistress went on to ask—

"How did Bjorn behave to thee, Kari?"

"Bare is back," he answers, "without brother behind it, and Bjorn behaved well to me. He wounded three men, and, besides, he is wounded himself, and he stuck as close to me as he could in everything."

They were three nights there, and after that they rode to Holt to Thorgeir, and told him alone these tidings, for those tidings had not yet been heard there.

Thorgeir thanked him, and it was quite plain that he was glad at what he heard. He asked Kari what now was undone which he meant to do.

"I mean," answers Kari, "to kill Gunnar Lambi's son and Kol Thorstein's son, if I can get a chance. Then we have slain fifteen men, reckoning those five whom we two slew together. But one boon I will now ask of thee."

Thorgeir said he would grant him whatever he asked.

"I wish, then, that thou wilt take under thy safeguard this man whose name is Bjorn, and who has been in these slayings with me, and that thou wilt change farms with him, and give him a farm ready stocked here close by thee, and so hold thy hand over him that no vengeance may befall him; but all this will be an easy matter for thee who art such a chief."

"So it shall be," says Thorgeir.

Then he gave Bjorn a ready-stocked farm at Asolfskal, but he took the farm in the Mark into his own hands. Thorgeir flitted all Bjorn's household stuff and goods to Asolfskal, and all his live stock; and Thorgeir settled all Bjorn's quarrels for him, and he was reconciled to them with a full atonement. So Bjorn was thought to be much more of a man than he had been before.

Then Kari rode away, and did not draw rein till he came west to Tongue to Asgrim Ellidagrim's son. He gave Kari a most hearty welcome, and Kari told him of all the tidings that had happened in these slayings.

Asgrim was well pleased at them, and asked what Kari meant to do next.

"I mean," said Kari, "to fare abroad after them, and so dog their footsteps and slay them, if I can get at them."

Asgrim said there was no man like him for bravery and hardihood.

He was there some nights, and after that he rode to Gizur the white, and he took him by both hands. Kari stayed there some while, and then he told Gizur that he wished to ride down to Eyrar.

Gizur gave Kari a good sword at parting.

Now he rode down to Eyrar, and took him a passage with Kolbein the black; he was an Orkneyman and an old friend of Kari, and he was the most forward and brisk of men.

He took Kari by both hands, and said that one fate should befall both of them.

CHAPTER CLII.

FLOSI GOES ABROAD.

Now Flosi rides east to Hornfirth, and most of the men in his Thing followed him, and bore his wares east, as well as all his stores and baggage which he had to take with him.

After that they busked them for their voyage, and fitted out their ship.

Now Flosi stayed by the ship until they were "boun". But as soon as ever they got a fair wind they put out to sea. They had a long passage and hard weather.

Then they quite lost their reckoning, and sailed on and on, and all at once three great waves broke over their ship, one after the other. Then Flosi said they must be near some land, and that this was a ground-swell. A great mist was on them, but the wind rose so that a great gale overtook them, and they scarce knew where they were before they were dashed on shore at dead of night, and the men were saved, but the ship was dashed all to pieces, and they could not save their goods.

Then they had to look for shelter and warmth for themselves, and the day after they went up on a height. The weather was then good.

Flosi asked if any man knew this land, and there were two men of their crew who had fared thither before, and said they were quite sure they knew it, and, say they—

"We are come to Hrossey in the Orkneys."

"Then we might have made a better landing," said Flosi, "for Grim and Helgi, Njal's sons, whom I slew, were both of them of Earl Sigurd Hlodver's son's bodyguard."

Then they sought for a hiding-place, and spread moss over themselves, and so lay for a while, but not for long, ere Flosi spoke and said—

"We will not lie here any longer until the landsmen are ware of us."

Then they arose, and took counsel, and then Flosi said to his men—

"We will go all of us and give ourselves up to the Earl; for there is naught else to do, and the Earl has our lives at his pleasure if he chooses to seek for them."

Then they all went away thence, and Flosi said that they must tell no man any tidings of their voyage, or what manner of men they were, before he told them to the Earl.

Then they walked on until they met men who showed them to the town, and then they went in before the Earl, and Flosi and all the others hailed him.

The Earl asked what men they might be, and Flosi told his name, and said out of what part of Iceland he was.

The Earl had already heard of the Burning, and so he knew the men at once, and then the Earl asked Flosi—"What hast thou to tell me about Helgi Njal's son, my henchman?"

"This," said Flosi, "that I hewed off his head."

"Take them all," said the Earl.

Then that was done, and just then in came Thorstein, son of Hall of the Side. Flosi had to wife Steinvora, Thorstein's sister. Thorstein was one of Earl Sigurd's bodyguard, but when he saw Flosi seized and held, he went in before the Earl, and offered for Flosi all the goods he had.

The Earl was very wroth a long time, but at last the end of it was, by the prayer of good men and true, joined to those of Thorstein, for he was well backed by friends, and many threw in their word with his, that the Earl took an atonement from them, and gave Flosi and all the rest of them peace. The Earl held to that custom of mighty men that Flosi took that place in his service which Helgi Njal's son had filled.

So Flosi was made Earl Sigurd's henchman, and he soon won his way to great love with the Earl.

CHAPTER CLIII.

KARI GOES ABROAD.

Those messmates Kari and Kolbein the black put out to sea from Eyrar half a month later than Flosi and his companions from Hornfirth.

They got a fine fair wind, and were but a short time out. The first land they made was the Fair Isle; it lies between Shetland and the Orkneys. There that man whose name was David the white took Kari into his house, and he told him all that he had heard for certain about the doings of the Burners. He was one of Kari's greatest friends, and Kari stayed with him for the winter.

There they heard tidings from the west out of the Orkneys of all that was done there.

Earl Sigurd bade to his feast at Yule Earl Gilli, his brother-in-law, out of the Southern Isles; he had to wife Swanlauga, Earl Sigurd's sister; and then too came to see Earl Sigurd that king from Ireland whose name was Sigtrygg. He was a son of Olaf rattle, but his mother's name was Kormlada; she was the fairest of all women, and best gifted in everything that was not in her own power, but it was the talk of men that she did all things ill over which she had any power.

Brian was the name of the king who first had her to wife, but they were then parted. He was the best-natured of all kings. He had his seat in Connaught, in Ireland; his brother's name was Wolf the quarrelsome, the greatest champion and warrior; Brian's foster-child's name was Kerthialfad. He was the son of King Kylfi, who had many wars with King Brian, and fled away out of the land before him, and became a hermit; but when King Brian went south on a pilgrimage, then he met King Kylfi, and then they were atoned, and King Brian took his son Kerthialfad to him, and loved him more than his own sons. He was then full grown when these things happened, and was the boldest of all men.

Duncan was the name of the first of King Brian's sons; the second was Margad; the third, Takt, whom we call Tann, he was the youngest of them; but the elder sons of King Brian were full grown, and the briskest of men.

Kormlada was not the mother of King Brian's children, and so grim was she against King Brian after their parting, that she would gladly have him dead.

King Brian thrice forgave all his outlaws the same fault, but if they misbehaved themselves oftener, then he let them be judged by the law; and from this one may mark what a king he must have been.

Kormlada egged on her son Sigtrygg very much to kill King Brian, and she now sent him to Earl Sigurd to beg for help.

King Sigtrygg came before Yule to the Orkneys, and there, too, came Earl Gilli, as was written before.

The men were so placed that King Sigtrygg sat in a high seat in the middle, but on either side of the king sat one of the earls. The men of King Sigtrygg and Earl Gilli sate on the inner side away from him, but on the outer side away from Earl Sigurd, sate Flosi and Thorstein, son of Hall of the Side, and the whole hall was full.

Now King Sigtrygg and Earl Gilli wished to hear of these tidings which had happened at the Burning, and so, also, what had befallen since.

Then Gunnar Lambi's son was got to tell the tale, and a stool was set for him to sit upon.

CHAPTER CLIV.

GUNNAR LAMBI'S SON'S SLAYING.

Just at that very time Kari and Kolbein and David the white came to Hrossey unawares to all men. They went straightway up on land, but a few men watched their ship.

Kari and his fellows went straight to the Earl's homestead, and came to the hall about drinking time.

It so happened that just then Gunnar was telling the story of the Burning, but they were listening to him meanwhile outside. This was on Yule-day itself.

Now King Sigtrygg asked—

"How did Skarphedinn bear the Burning?"

"Well at first for a long time," said Gunnar, "but still the end of it was that he wept." And so he went on giving an unfair leaning in his story, but every now and then he laughed out loud.

Kari could not stand this, and then he ran in with his sword drawn, and sang this song—

Men of might, in battle eager,
Boast of burning Njal's abode,
Have the Princes heard how sturdy
Seahorse racers sought revenge?
Hath not since, on foemen holding
High the shield's broad orb aloft,
All that wrong been fully wroken?
Raw flesh ravens got to tear.

So he ran in up the hall, and smote Gunnar Lambi's son on the neck with such a sharp blow, that his head spun off on to the board before the king and the earls, and the board was all one gore of blood, and the Earl's clothing too.

Earl Sigurd knew the man that had done the deed, and called out—

"Seize Kari and kill him."

Kari had been one of Earl Sigurd's bodyguard, and he was of all men most beloved by his friends; and no man stood up a whit more for the Earl's speech.

"Many would say, Lord," said Kari, "that I have done this deed on your behalf, to avenge your henchman."

Then Flosi said—"Kari hath not done this without a cause; he is in no atonement with us, and he only did what he had a right to do".

So Kari walked away, and there was no hue and cry after him. Kari fared to his ship, and his fellows with him. The weather was then good, and they sailed off at once south to Caithness, and went on shore at Thraswick to the house of a worthy man whose name was Skeggi, and with him they stayed a very long while.

Those behind in the Orkneys cleansed the board, and bore out the dead man.

The Earl was told that they had set sail south for Scotland, and King Sigtrygg said—

"This was a mighty bold fellow, who dealt his stroke so stoutly, and never thought twice about it!"

Then Earl Sigurd answered—

"There is no man like Kari for dash and daring."

Now Flosi undertook to tell the story of the Burning, and he was fair to all; and therefore what he said was believed.

Then King Sigtrygg stirred in his business with Earl Sigurd, and bade him go to the war with him against King Brian.

The Earl was long steadfast, but the end of it was that he let the king have his way, but said he must have his mother's hand for his help, and be king in Ireland, if they slew Brian. But all his men besought Earl Sigurd not to go into the war, but it was all no good.

So they parted on the understanding that Earl Sigurd gave his word to go; but King Sigtrygg promised him his mother and the kingdom.

It was so settled that Earl Sigurd was to come with all his host to Dublin by Palm Sunday.

Then King Sigtrygg fared south to Ireland, and told his mother Kormlada that the Earl had undertaken to come, and also what he had pledged himself to grant him.

She showed herself well pleased at that, but said they must gather greater force still.

Sigtrygg asked whence this was to be looked for?

She said there were two vikings lying off the west of Man; and that they had thirty ships, and, she went on, "they are men of such hardihood that nothing can withstand them. The one's name is Ospak, and the other's Brodir. Thou shalt fare to find them, and spare nothing to get them into thy quarrel, whatever price they ask."

Now King Sigtrygg fares and seeks the vikings, and found them lying outside off Man; King Sigtrygg brings forward his errand at once, but Brodir shrank from helping him until he, King Sigtrygg, promised him the kingdom and his mother, and they were to keep this such a secret that Earl Sigurd should know nothing about it; Brodir too was to come to Dublin on Palm Sunday.

So King Sigtrygg fared home to his mother, and told her how things stood.

After that those brothers, Ospak and Brodir, talked together, and then Brodir told Ospak all that he and Sigtrygg had spoken of, and bade him fare to battle with him against King Brian, and said he set much store on his going.

But Ospak said he would not fight against so good a king.

Then they were both wroth, and sundered their band at once. Ospak had ten ships and Brodir twenty.

Ospak was a heathen, and the wisest of all men. He laid his ships inside in a sound, but Brodir lay outside him.

Brodir had been a Christian man and a mass-deacon by consecration, but he had thrown off his faith and become God's dastard, and now worshipped heathen fiends, and he was of all men most skilled in sorcery. He had that coat of mail on which no steel would bite. He was both tall and strong, and had such long locks that he tucked them under his belt. His hair was black.

CHAPTER CLV.

OF SIGNS AND WONDERS.

It so happened one night that a great din passed over Brodir and his men, so that they all woke, and sprang up and put on their clothes.

Along with that came a shower of boiling blood.

Then they covered themselves with their shields, but for all that many were scalded.

This wonder lasted all till day, and a man had died on board every ship.

Then they slept during the day, but the second night there was again a din, and again they all sprang up. Then swords leapt out of their sheaths, and axes and spears flew about in the air and fought.

The weapons pressed them so hard that they had to shield themselves, but still many were wounded, and again a man died out of every ship.

This wonder lasted all till day.

Then they slept again the day after.

But the third night there was a din of the same kind, and then ravens flew at them, and it seemed to them as though their beaks and claws were of iron.

The ravens pressed them so hard that they had to keep them off with their swords, and covered themselves with their shields, and so this went on again till day, and then another man had died in every ship.

Then they went to sleep first of all, but when Brodir woke up, he drew his breath painfully, and bade them put off the boat. "For," he said, "I will go to see Ospak."

Then he got into the boat and some men with him, but when he found Ospak he told him of the wonders which had befallen them, and bade him say what he thought they boded.

Ospak would not tell him before he pledged him peace, and Brodir promised him peace, but Ospak still shrank from telling him till night fell.

Then Ospak spoke and said—"When blood rained on you, therefore shall ye shed many men's blood, both of your own and others. But when ye heard a great din, then ye must have been shown the crack of doom, and ye shall all die speedily. But when weapons fought against you, that must forbode a battle; but when ravens pressed you, that marks the devils which ye put faith in, and who will drag you all down to the pains of hell."

Then Brodir was so wroth that he could answer never a word, but he went at once to his men, and made them lay his ships in a line across the sound, and moor them by bearing their cables on shore at either end of the line, and meant to slay them all next morning.

Ospak saw all their plan, and then he vowed to take the true faith, and to go to King Brian, and follow him till his death-day.

Then he took that counsel to lay his ships in a line, and punt them along the shore with poles, and cut the cables of Brodir's ships. Then the ships of Brodir's men began to fall aboard of one another when they were all fast asleep; and so Ospak and his men got out of the firth, and so west to Ireland, and came to Connaught.

Then Ospak told King Brian all that he had learnt, and took baptism, and gave himself over into the king's hand.

After that King Brian made them gather force over all his realm, and the whole host was to come to Dublin in the week before Palm Sunday.

CHAPTER CLVI.

BRIAN'S BATTLE.

Earl Sigurd Hlodver's son busked him from the Orkneys, and Flosi offered to go with him.

The Earl would not have that, since he had his pilgrimage to fulfil.

Flosi offered fifteen men of his band to go on the voyage, and the Earl accepted them, but Flosi fared with Earl Gilli to the Southern Isles.

Thorstein, the Son of Hall of the Side, went along with Earl Sigurd, and Hrafn the red, and Erling of Straumey.

He would not that Hareck should go, but said he would be sure to be the first to tell him the tidings of his voyage.

The Earl came with all his host on Palm Sunday to Dublin, and there too was come Brodir with all his host.

Brodir tried by sorcery how the fight would go, but the answer ran thus, that if the fight were on Good Friday King Brian would fall but win the day; but if they fought before, they would all fall who were against him.

Then Brodir said that they must not fight before the Friday.

On the fifth day of the week a man rode up to Kormlada and her company on an apple-grey horse, and in his hand he held a halberd; he talked long with them.

King Brian came with all his host to the Burg, and on the Friday the host fared out of the Burg, and both armies were drawn up in array.

Brodir was on one wing of the battle, but King Sigtrygg on the other.

Earl Sigurd was in the mid battle.

Now it must be told of King Brian that he would not fight on the fast-day, and so a shieldburg[82] was thrown round him, and his host was drawn up in array in front of it.

Wolf the quarrelsome was on that wing of the battle against which Brodir stood; but on the other wing, where Sigtrygg stood against them, were Ospak and his sons.

But in mid battle was Kerthialfad, and before him the banners were borne.

Now the wings fall on one another, and there was a very hard fight, Brodir went through the host of the foe, and felled all the foremost that stood there, but no steel would bite on his mail.

Wolf the quarrelsome turned then to meet him, and thrust at him thrice so hard that Brodir fell before him at each thrust, and was well-nigh not getting on his feet again; but as soon as ever he found his feet, he fled away into the wood at once.

Earl Sigurd had a hard battle against Kerthialfad, and Kerthialfad came on so fast that he laid low all who were in the front rank, and he broke the array of Earl Sigurd right up to his banner, and slew the banner-bearer.

Then he got another man to bear the banner, and there was again a hard fight.

Kerthialfad smote this man too his death blow at once, and so on one after the other all who stood near him.

Then Earl Sigurd called on Thorstein the son of Hall of the Side, to bear the banner, and Thorstein was just about to lift the banner, but then Asmund the white said—

"Don't bear the banner! for all they who bear it get their death."

"Hrafn the red!" called out Earl Sigurd, "bear thou the banner."

"Bear thine own devil thyself," answered Hrafn.

Then the Earl said—

"'Tis fittest that the beggar should bear the bag;" and with that he took the banner from the staff and put it under his cloak.

A little after Asmund the white was slain, and then the Earl was pierced through with a spear.

Ospak had gone through all the battle on his wing, he had been sore wounded, and lost both his sons ere King Sigtrygg fled before him.

Then flight broke out throughout all the host.

Thorstein Hall of the Side's son stood still while all the others fled, and tied his shoe-string. Then Kerthialfad asked why he ran not as the others.

"Because," said Thorstein, "I can't get home to-night, since I am at home out in Iceland."

Kerthialfad gave him peace.

Hrafn the red was chased out into a certain river; he thought he saw there the pains of hell down below him, and he thought the devils wanted to drag him to them.

Then Hrafn said—

"Thy dog,[83] Apostle Peter! hath run twice to Rome, and he would run the third time if thou gavest him leave."

Then the devils let him loose, and Hrafn got across the river.

Now Brodir saw that King Brian's men were chasing the fleers, and that there were few men by the shieldburg.

Then he rushed out of the wood, and broke through the shieldburg, and hewed at the king.

The lad Takt threw his arm in the way, and the stroke took it off and the king's head too, but the king's blood came on the lad's stump, and the stump was healed by it on the spot.

Then Brodir called out with a loud voice—

"Now let man tell man that Brodir felled Brian."

Then men ran after those who were chasing the fleers, and they were told that King Brian had fallen, and then they turned back straightway, both Wolf the quarrelsome and Kerthialfad.

Then they threw a ring round Brodir and his men, and threw branches of trees upon them, and so Brodir was taken alive.

Wolf the quarrelsome cut open his belly, and led him round and round the trunk of a tree, and so wound all his entrails out of him, and he did not die before they were all drawn out of him.

Brodir's men were slain to a man.

After that they took King Brian's body and laid it out. The king's head had grown fast to the trunk.

Fifteen men of the Burners fell in Brian's battle, and there, too, fell Halldor the son of Gudmund the powerful, and Erling of Straumey.

On Good Friday that event happened in Caithness that a man whose name was Daurrud went out. He saw folk riding twelve together to a bower, and there they were all lost to his sight. He went to that bower and looked in through a window slit that was in it, and saw that there were women inside, and they had set up a loom. Men's heads were the weights, but men's entrails were the warp and weft, a sword was the shuttle, and the reels were arrows.

They sang these songs, and he learnt them by heart--

THE WOOF OF WAR.

See! warp is stretched
For warriors' fall,
Lo! weft in loom
'Tis wet with blood;
Now fight foreboding,
'Neath friends' swift fingers,
Our gray woof waxeth
With war's alarms,
Our warp bloodred,
Our weft corseblue.

This woof is y-woven
With entrails of men,
This warp is hardweighted
With heads of the slain,
Spears blood-besprinkled
For spindles we use,
Our loom ironbound,
And arrows our reels;
With swords for our shuttles
This war-woof we work;
So weave we, weird sisters,
Our warwinning woof.

Now War-winner walketh
To weave in her turn.
Now Swordswinger steppeth,
Now Swiftstroke, now Storm;
When they speed the shuttle
How spear-heads shall flash!
Shields crash, and helmgnawer[84]
On harness bite hard!

Wind we, wind swiftly
Our warwinning woof.
Woof erst for king youthful
Foredoomed as his own,
Forth now we will ride,
Then through the ranks rushing
Be busy where friends

Blows blithe give and take.

Wind we, wind swiftly
Our warwinning woof,
After that let us steadfastly
Stand by the brave king;
Then men shall mark mournful
Their shields red with gore,
How Swordstroke and Spearthrust
Stood stout by the prince.

Wind we, wind swiftly
Our warwinning woof;
When sword-bearing rovers
To banners rush on,
Mind, maidens, we spare not
One life in the fray!
We corse-choosing sisters
Have charge of the slain.

Now new-coming nations
That island shall rule.
Who on outlying headlands
Abode ere the fight;
I say that King mighty
To death now is done,
Now low before spearpoint
That Earl bows his head.

Soon over all Ersemen
Sharp sorrow shall fall,
That woe to those warriors
Shall wane nevermore;
Our woof now is woven.
Now battle-field waste,
O'er land and o'er water
War tidings shall leap.

Now surely 'tis gruesome
To gaze all around,
When bloodred through heaven
Drives cloudrack o'er head;
Air soon shall be deep hued

With dying men's blood
When this our spaedom
Comes speedy to pass.

So cheerily chant we
Charms for the young king,
Come maidens lift loudly
His warwinning lay;
Let him who now listens
Learn well with his ears,
And gladden brave swordsmen
With bursts of war's song.

Now mount we our horses,
Now bare we our brands,
Now haste we hard, maidens,
Hence far, far away.

Then they plucked down the woof and tore it asunder, and each kept what she had hold of.

Now Daurrud goes away from the slit, and home; but they got on their steeds and rode six to the south, and the other six to the north.

A like event befell Brand Gneisti's son in the Faroe Isles.

At Swinefell, in Iceland, blood came on the priest's stole on Good Friday, so that he had to put it off.

At Thvattwater the priest thought he saw on Good Friday a long deep of the sea hard by the altar, and there he saw many awful sights, and it was long ere he could sing the prayers.

This event happened in the Orkneys, that Hareck thought he saw Earl Sigurd, and some men with him. Then Hareck took his horse and rode to meet the Earl. Men saw that they met and rode under a brae, but they were never seen again, and not a scrap was ever found of Hareck.

Earl Gilli in the Southern Isles dreamed that a man came to him and said his name was Hostfinn, and told him he was come from Ireland.

The Earl thought he asked him for tidings thence, and then he sang this song—

I have been where warriors wrestled,
High in Erin sang the sword,
Boss to boss met many bucklers.
Steel rung sharp on rattling helm;

I can tell of all their struggle;
Sigurd fell in flight of spears;
Brian fell, but kept his kingdom
Ere he lost one drop of blood.

Those two, Flosi and the Earl, talked much of this dream. A week after, Hrafn the red came thither, and told them all the tidings of Brian's battle, the fall of the king, and of Earl Sigurd, and Brodir, and all the Vikings.

"What," said Flosi, "hast thou to tell me of my men?"

"They all fell there," says Hrafn, "but thy brother-in-law Thorstein took peace from Kerthialfad, and is now with him."

Flosi told the Earl that he would now go away, "for we have our pilgrimage south to fulfil".

The Earl bade him go as he wished, and gave him a ship and all else that he needed, and much silver.

Then they sailed to Wales, and stayed there a while.

CHAPTER CLVII.

THE SLAYING OF KOL THORSTEIN'S SON.

Kari Solmund's son told master Skeggi that he wished he would get him a ship. So master Skeggi gave Kari a long-ship, fully trimmed and manned, and on board it went Kari, and David the white, and Kolbein the black.

Now Kari and his fellows sailed south through Scotland's Firths, and there they found men from the Southern Isles. They told Kari the tidings from Ireland, and also that Flosi was gone to Wales, and his men with him.

But when Kari heard that, he told his messmates that he would hold on south to Wales, to fall in with Flosi and his band. So he bade them then to part from his company, if they liked it better, and said that he would not wish to beguile any man into mischief, because he thought he had not yet had revenge enough on Flosi and his band.

All chose to go with him; and then he sails south to Wales, and there they lay in hiding in a creek out of the way.

That morning Kol Thorstein's son went into the town to buy silver. He of all the Burners had used the bitterest words. Kol had talked much with a mighty dame, and he had so knocked the nail on the head, that it was all but fixed that he was to have her, and settle down there.

That same morning Kari went also into the town. He came where Kol was telling the silver.

Kari knew him at once, and ran at him with his drawn sword and smote him on the neck; but he still went on telling the silver, and his head counted "ten" just as it spun off the body.

Then Kari said—

"Go and tell this to Flosi, that Kari Solmund's son hath slain Kol Thorstein's son. I give notice of this slaying as done by my hand."

Then Kari went to his ship, and told his shipmates of the manslaughter.

Then they sailed north to Beruwick, and laid up their ship, and fared up into Whitherne in Scotland, and were with Earl Malcolm that year.

But when Flosi heard of Kol's slaying, he laid out his body, and bestowed much money on his burial.

Flosi never uttered any wrathful words against Kari.

Thence Flosi fared south across the sea and began his pilgrimage, and went on south, and did not stop till he came to Rome. There he got so great honour that he took absolution from the Pope himself, and for that he gave a great sum of money.

Then he fared back again by the east road, and stayed long in towns, and went in before mighty men, and had from them great honour.

He was in Norway the winter after, and was with Earl Eric till he was ready to sail, and the Earl gave him much meal, and many other men behaved handsomely to him.

Now he sailed out to Iceland, and ran into Hornfirth, and thence fared home to Swinefell. He had then fulfilled all the terms of his atonement, both in fines and foreign travel.

CHAPTER CLVIII.

OF FLOSI AND KARI.

Now it is to be told of Kari that the summer after he went down to his ship and sailed south across the sea, and began his pilgrimage in Normandy, and so went south and got absolution and fared back by the western way, and took his ship again in Normandy, and sailed in her north across the sea to Dover in England.

Thence he sailed west, round Wales, and so north, through Scotland's Firths, and did not stay his course till he came to Thraswick in Caithness, to master Skeggi's house.

There he gave over the ship of burden to Kolbein and David, and Kolbein sailed in that ship to Norway, but David stayed behind in the Fair Isle.

Kari was that winter in Caithness. In this winter his housewife died out in Iceland.

The next summer Kari busked him for Iceland. Skeggi gave him a ship of burden, and there were eighteen of them on board her.

They were rather late "boun," but still they put to sea, and had a long passage, but at last they made Ingolf's Head. There their ship was dashed all to pieces, but the men's lives were saved. Then, too, a gale of wind came on them.

Now they ask Kari what counsel was to be taken; but he said their best plan was to go to Swinefell and put Flosi's manhood to the proof.

So they went right up to Swinefell in the storm. Flosi was in the hall. He knew Kari as soon as ever he came into the hall, and sprang up to meet him, and kissed him, and sate him down in the high-seat by his side.

Flosi asked Kari to be there that winter, and Kari took his offer. Then they were atoned with a full atonement.

Then Flosi gave away his brother's daughter Hildigunna, whom Hauskuld the priest of Whiteness had had to wife, to Kari, and they dwelt first of all at Broadwater.

Men say that the end of Flosi's life was, that he fared abroad, when he had grown old, to seek for timber to build him a hall; and he was in Norway that winter, but the next summer he was late "boun"; and men told him that his ship was not seaworthy.

Flosi said she was quite good enough for an old and death-doomed man, and bore his goods on shipboard and put out to sea. But of that ship no tidings were ever heard.

These were the children of Kari Solmund's son and Helga Njal's daughter—Thorgerda and Ragneida, Valgerda, and Thord who was burnt in Njal's house. But the children of Hildigunna and Kari were these, Starkad, and Thord, and Flosi.

The son of Burning-Flosi was Kolbein, who has been the most famous man of any of that stock.

And here we end the STORY of BURNT NJAL.

FOOTNOTES:

[1] Guðbrandr Vigfússon.

[2] This word is invented like Laxdæla, Gretla, and others, to escape the repetition or the word Saga, after that of the person or place to which the story belongs. It combines the idea of the subject and the telling in one word.

[3] Many particulars mentioned in the Saga as wonderful are no wonders to us. Thus in the case of Gunnar's bill, when we are told that it gave out a strange sound before great events, this probably only means that the shaft on which it was mounted was of some hard ringing wood unknown in the north. It was a foreign weapon, and if the shaft were of lance wood, the sounds it gave out when brandished or shaken would be accounted for at once without a miracle.

[4] There can be no doubt that it was considered a grave offence to public morality to tell a Saga untruthfully. Respect to friends and enemies alike, when they were dead and gone, demanded that the histories of their lives, and especially of their last moments, should be told as the events had actually happened. Our own Saga affords a good illustration of this, and shows at the same time how a Saga naturally arose out of great events. When King Sigtrygg was Earl Sigurd's guest at Yule, and Flosi and the other Burners were about the Earl's court, the Irish king wished to hear the story of the Burning, and Gunnar Lambi's son was put forward to tell it at the feast on Christmas day. It only added to Kari's grudge against him to hear Gunnar tell the story with such a false leaning, when he gave it out that Skarphedinn had wept for fear of the fire, and the vengeance which so speedily overtook the false teller was looked upon as just retribution. But when Flosi took up the story, he told it fairly and justly for both sides, "and therefore," says the Saga, "what he said was believed".

[5] Öresound, the gut between Denmark and Sweden, at the entrance of the Baltic, commonly called in English, The Sound.

[6] That is, he came from what we call the Western Isles or Hebrides. The old appellation still lingers in "Sodor (*i.e.* the South isles) and Man".

[7] This means that Njal was one of those gifted beings who, according to the firm belief of that age, had a more than human insight into things about to happen. It answers very nearly to the Scottish "second sight".

[8] Lord of rings, a periphrasis for a chief, that is, Mord.

[9] Earth's offspring, a periphrasis for woman, that is, Unna.

[10] "Oyce," a north country word for the mouth of a river, from the Icelandic *ós*

[11] "The Bay," the name given to the great bay in the east of Norway, the entrance of which from the North Sea is the Cattegat, and at the end of which is the Christiania Firth. The name also applies to the land round the Bay, which thus formed a district, the boundary of which, on the one side, was the promontory called Lindesnæs, or the Naze, and on the other, the Göta-Elf, the river on which the Swedish town of Gottenburg stands, and off the mouth of which lies the island of Hisingen, mentioned shortly after.

[12] Permia, the country one comes to after doubling the North Cape.

[13] A town at the mouth of the Christiania Firth. It was a great place for traffic in early times, and was long the only mart in the south-east of Norway.

[14] Rill of wolf—stream of blood.

[15] A province of Sweden.

[16] An island in the Baltic, off the coast of Esthonia.

[17] Endil's courser—periphrasis for a ship.

[18] Sigar's storm—periphrasis for a sea-fight.

[19] Grieve, *i.e.*, bailiff, head workman.

[20] Swanbath's beams, periphrasis for gold.

[21] "Thou, that heapest hoards," etc.—merely a periphrasis for man, and scarcely fitting, except in irony, to a splitter of firewood.

[22] That is, slew him in a duel.

[23] This shows that the shields were oblong, running down to a point.

[24] "Ocean's fire," a periphrasis for "gold". The whole line is a periphrasis for "bountiful chief".

[25] "Rhine's fire," a periphrasis for gold.

[26] "Water-skates," a periphrasis for ships.

[27] "Great Rift," Almannagjá—The great volcanic rift, or "geo," as it would be called in Orkney and Shetland, which bounds the plain of the Althing on one side.

[28] Thorgrim Easterling and Thorbrand.

[29] "Frodi's flour," a periphrasis for gold.

[30] "Sea's bright sunbeams," a periphrasis for gold.

[31] Constantinople.

[32] Hlada or Lada, and sometimes in the plural Ladir, was the old capital of Drontheim, before Nidaios—the present Drontheim—was founded. Drontheim was originally the name of the country round the firth of the same name, and is not used in the old Sagas for a town.

[33] The country round the Christiania Firth, at the top of the "Bay".

[34] A town in Sweden on the Göta-Elf.

[35] The mainland of Orkney, now Pomona.

[36] Now Stroma, in the Pentland Firth.

[37] By so doing Hrapp would have cleared himself of his own outlawry.

[38] "Prop of sea-waves' fire," a periphrasis for a woman that bears gold on her arm.

[39] "Skates that skim," etc., a periphrasis for ships.

[40] "Odin's mocking cup," mocking songs.

[41] An allusion to the Beast Epic, where the cunning fox laughs at the flayed condition of his stupid foes, the wolf and bear. We should say, "Don't stop to speak with him, but rather beat him black and blue".

[42] "Sea-stag," periphrasis for ship.

[43] "Sea-fire bearers," the bearers of gold, men, that is, Helgi and Grim.

[44] "Byrnie-breacher," piercer of coats of mail.

[45] "Noisy ogre's namesake," an allusion to the name of Skarphedinn's axe, "the ogress of war".

[46] Rood-cross, a crucifix.

[47] His son was Glum who fared to the burning with Flosi.

[48] "Forge which foams with song," the poet's head, in which songs are forged, and gush forth like foaming mead.

[49] "Hero's helm-prop," the hero's, man's, head which supports his helm.

[50] It is needless to say that this Hall was not Hall of the Side.

[51] "Wolf of Gods," the "*caput lupinum*," the outlaw of heaven, the outcast from Valhalla, Thangbrand.

[52] "The other wolf," Gudleif.

[53] "Swarthy skarf," the skarf, or *pelecanus cardo*, the cormorant. He compares the message of Thorwald to the cormorant shimming over the waves, and says he will never take it. "Snap at flies," a very common Icelandic metaphor from fish rising to a fly.

[54] Maurer thinks the allusion is here to some mythological legend on Odin's adventures which has not come dawn to us.

[55] "He that giant's," etc., Thor.

[56] "Mew-field's bison," the sea-going ship, which sails over he plain of the sea-mew.

[57] "Bell's warder," the Christian priest whose bell-ringing formed part of the rites of the new faith.

[58] "Falcon of the strand," ship.

[59] "Courser of the causeway," ship.

[60] "Gylfi's hart," ship.

[61] "Viking's snow-shoe," sea-king's ship.

[62] "Boiling Kettle," This was a hver, or hot spring.

[63] This was the "Raven's Rift," opposite to the "Great Rift" on the other side of the Thingfield.

[64] "Warrior's temper," the temper of Hauskuld of Whiteness.

[65] "Snake-land's stem," a periphrasis for woman, Rodny.

[66] "He that hoardeth ocean's fire," a periphrasis for man, Hauskuld of Whiteness.

[67] "Baltic side." This probably means a part of the Finnish coast in the Gulf of Bothnia.

[68] "Wild man of the woods." In the original Finngálkn, a fabulous monster, half man and half beast.

[69] "Sand," Skeidará sand.

[70] "Sand," Mælifell's sand.

[71] "Nones," the well-known canonical hour of the day, the ninth hour from six A.M., that is, about three o'clock P.M., when one of the church services took place.

[72] "Son of Gollnir," Njal, who was the son of Thorgeir Gelling or Gollnir.

[73] "My friends," ironically of course.

[74] "Helmet-hewer," sword.

[75] John for a man, and Gudruna for a woman, were standing names in the Formularies of the Icelandic code, answering to the "M or N" in our Liturgy, or to those famous fictions of English Law. "John Doe and Richard Roe".

[76] "Gossipry," that is, because they were gossips, *God's sib*, relations by baptism.

[77] "Swinestye," ironically for Swinefell, where Flosi lived.

[78] This is the English equivalent for the Icelandic Hrepp, a district. It still lingers in "the Rape of Bramber," and other districts in Sussex and the south-east.

[79] "With words alone," The English proverb, "Threatened men live long".

[80] "Sea crags." Hence Thorgeir got his surname "Craggeir".

[81] "Pilgrimage to Rome." This condition had not been mentioned before.

[82] "Shieldburg" that is, a ring of men holding their shields locked together.

[83] "Thy dog," etc. Meaning that he would go a third time on a pilgrimage to Rome If St. Peter helped him out of this strait.

[84] "Helmgnawer," the sword that bites helmets.